Communications in Computer and Information Science **866**

Commenced Publication in 2007
Founding and Former Series Editors:
Alfredo Cuzzocrea, Xiaoyong Du, Orhun Kara, Ting Liu, Dominik Ślęzak,
and Xiaokang Yang

Editorial Board

More information about this series at http://www.springer.com/series/7899

Ernesto Damiani · George Spanoudakis
Leszek Maciaszek (Eds.)

Evaluation of Novel Approaches to Software Engineering

12th International Conference, ENASE 2017
Porto, Portugal, April 28–29, 2017
Revised Selected Papers

 Springer

Editors
Ernesto Damiani
Khalifa University
Abu Dhabi
United Arab Emirates

George Spanoudakis
City University London
London
UK

Leszek Maciaszek
Macquarie University, Sydney
Wroclaw University of Economics
Wroclaw
Poland

ISSN 1865-0929   ISSN 1865-0937 (electronic)
Communications in Computer and Information Science
ISBN 978-3-319-94134-9   ISBN 978-3-319-94135-6 (eBook)
https://doi.org/10.1007/978-3-319-94135-6

Library of Congress Control Number: 2018947449

Printed on acid-free paper

This Springer imprint is published by the registered company Springer International Publishing AG
part of Springer Nature
The registered company address is: Gewerbestrasse 11, 6330 Cham, Switzerland

Preface

The present book includes extended and revised versions of a set of selected papers from the 12th International Conference on Evaluation of Novel Approaches to Software Engineering (ENASE 2017), held in Porto, Portugal, during April 28–29, 2017.

ENASE 2017 received 102 paper submissions from 30 countries, of which 14% are included in this book. The papers were selected by the event chairs and their selection is based on a number of criteria that include the classifications and comments provided by the Program Committee members, the session chairs' assessment, and also the program chairs' global view of all papers included in the technical program. The authors of selected papers were then invited to submit a revised and extended version of their paper having at least 30% innovative material.

The mission of ENASE (Evaluation of Novel Approaches to Software Engineering) is to be a prime international forum for discussing and publishing research findings and IT industry experiences related to novel approaches to software engineering. The conference acknowledges an evolution in systems and software thinking due to contemporary shifts of the computing paradigm to e-services, cloud computing, mobile connectivity, business processes, and societal participation. By publishing the latest research on novel approaches to software engineering and by evaluating them against systems and software quality criteria, ENASE conferences advance knowledge and research in software engineering, including and emphasizing service-oriented, business-process-driven, and ubiquitous mobile computing. ENASE aims at identifying the most hopeful trends and proposing new directions for consideration by researchers and practitioners involved in large-scale systems and software development, integration, deployment, delivery, maintenance, and evolution.

The papers selected to be included in this book contribute to the understanding of relevant trends of current research on the evaluation of novel approaches to software engineering, including: meta-modelling and model-driven development (p. 111, p. 174, p. 212), cloud computing and SOA (p. 22, p. 134), business process management (p. 46, p. 67, p. 174), requirements engineering (p. 89, p. 174), user interface design (p. 3), formal methods (p. 150, p. 197), software product lines (p. 111), and embedded systems (p. 230).

We would like to thank all the authors for their contributions and the reviewers for ensuring the quality of this publication.

April 2017

Ernesto Damiani
George Spanoudakis
Leszek Maciaszek

Organization

Conference Chair

Leszek Maciaszek — Wroclaw University of Economics, Poland and Macquarie University, Sydney, Australia

Program Co-chairs

Ernesto Damiani — EBTIC-KUSTAR, UAE
George Spanoudakis — City University London, UK

Program Committee

Frederic Andres — Research Organization of Information and Systems, Japan
Guglielmo De Angelis — CNR - IASI, Italy
Claudio Ardagna — Universitá degli Studi di Milano, Italy
Ayse Basar Bener — Ryerson University, Canada
Jan Olaf Blech — RMIT University, Australia
Markus Borg — SICS Swedish ICT AB, Lund, Sweden
Glauco Carneiro — Salvador University (UNIFACS), Brazil
Tomas Cerny — Baylor University, USA
Rebeca Cortazar — University of Deusto, Spain
Bernard Coulette — Université Toulouse Jean Jaurès, France
Ernesto Damiani — EBTIC-KUSTAR, UAE
Mariangiola Dezani — Universitá di Torino, Italy
Angelina Espinoza — Universidad Autónoma Metropolitana, Iztapalapa (UAM-I), Spain
Vladimir Estivill-Castro — Griffith University, Australia
Anna Rita Fasolino — Università degli Studi di Napoli Federico II, Italy
Maria João Ferreira — Universidade Portucalense, Portugal
Stéphane Galland — Université de Technologie de Belfort Montbéliard, France
Juan Garbajosa — Technical University of Madrid, UPM, Spain
Frédéric Gervais — Université Paris-Est, LACL, France
Atef Gharbi — INSAT, Tunisia
Vaidas Giedrimas — Siauliai University, Lithuania
Claude Godart — Henri Poincare University, Nancy 1, France

Lukasz Radlinski	West Pomeranian University of Technology, Poland
Stefano Russo	Universitá di Napoli Federico II, Italy
Krzysztof Sacha	Warsaw University of Technology, Poland
Markus Schatten	University of Zagreb, Croatia
Stefan Schönig	University of Bayreuth, Germany
Keng L. Siau	Missouri University of Science and Technology, USA
Marcin Sikorski	Gdansk University of Technology, Poland
Josep Silva	Universitat Politècnica de València, Spain
Michal Smialek	Warsaw University of Technology, Poland
Ioana Sora	Politehnica University of Timisoara, Romania
Andreas Speck	Christian Albrechts University Kiel, Germany
Maria Spichkova	RMIT University, Australia
Witold Staniszkis	Rodan Development, Poland
Armando Stellato	University of Rome, Tor Vergata, Italy
Chang-ai Sun	University of Science and Technology Beijing, China
Jakub Swacha	University of Szczecin, Poland
Stephanie Teufel	University of Fribourg, Switzerland
Feng-Jian Wang	National Chiao Tung University, Taiwan
Krzysztof Wecel	Poznan University of Economics, Poland
Bernhard Westfechtel	University of Bayreuth, Germany
Martin Wirsing	Ludwig-Maximilians-Universität München, Germany
Igor Wojnicki	AGH University of Science and Technology, Poland
Alfred Zimmermann	Reutlingen University, Germany

Additional Reviewers

Ahmed Alharthi	RMIT University, Australia
Nicola Amatucci	University of Naples Federico II, Italy
Abhijeet Banerjee	NUS, Singapore
Thomas Buchmann	University of Bayreuth, Germany
Michael Emmi	Nokia Bell Labs, USA
Carlos Fernandez-Sanchez	Universidad Politécnica de Madrid, Spain
Tarik Fissaa	SIME/IMS, Morocco
Walid Gaaloul	Institut TELECOM, France
Filippo Gaudenzi	Università degli Studi di Milano, Italy
Franco Mazzanti	Istituto di Scienza e Tecnologie dell'Informazione A. Faedo, Italy
Anas Motii	IRIT, France
Laura Nenzi	IMT Alti Studi di Lucca, Italy
Antonio Pecchia	Università degli Studi di Napoli Federico II, Italy
Abdelfetah Saadi	Houari Boumediene University of Science and Technology, Algeria
Felix Schwägerl	University of Bayreuth, Germany

Jeremy Sproston   Università degli Studi di Torino, Italy
Chengnian Sun   UC Davis, USA
Jiannan Zhai   FAU, USA
Zhiqiang Zuo   University of California, Irvine, USA

Invited Speakers

Paris Avgeriou   University of Groningen, The Netherlands
Hermann Kaindl   TU Wien, Austria
Marco Brambilla   Politecnico di Milano, Italy

Contents

Service Science and Business Information Systems

Guidelines for Designing User Interfaces to Analyze Genetic Data.
Case of Study: GenDomus 3
    Carlos Iñiguez-Jarrín, Alberto García S., José F. Reyes Román,
    and Óscar Pastor López

Biologically Inspired Anomaly Detection Framework 23
    Tashreen Shaikh Jamaluddin, Hoda Hassan,
    and Haitham Hamza

Genomic Tools*: Web-Applications Based on Conceptual Models
for the Genomic Diagnosis 48
    José F. Reyes Román, Carlos Iñiguez-Jarrín, and Óscar Pastor

Technological Platform for the Prevention and Management
of Healthcare Associated Infections and Outbreaks 70
    Maria Iuliana Bocicor, Maria Dascălu, Agnieszka Gaczowska,
    Sorin Hostiuc, Alin Moldoveanu, Antonio Molina,
    Arthur-Jozsef Molnar, Ionuț Negoi, and Vlad Racoviță

Software Engineering

Exploiting Requirements Engineering to Resolve Conflicts
in Pervasive Computing Systems 93
    Osama M. Khaled, Hoda M. Hosny, and Mohamed Shalan

Assisting Configurations-Based Feature Model Composition:
Union, Intersection and Approximate Intersection 116
    Jessie Carbonnel, Marianne Huchard, André Miralles,
    and Clémentine Nebut

A Cloud-Based Service for the Visualization and Monitoring
of Factories 141
    Guillaume Prévost, Jan Olaf Blech, Keith Foster,
    and Heinrich W. Schmidt

An Operational Semantics of UML2.X Sequence Diagrams
for Distributed Systems 158
    Fatma Dhaou, Ines Mouakher, J. Christian Attiogbé,
    and Khaled Bsaies

Fast Prototyping of Web-Based Information Systems Using
a Restricted Natural Language Specification   183
    Jean Pierre Alfonso Hoyos and Felipe Restrepo-Calle

Model-Based Analysis of Temporal Properties   208
    Maria Spichkova

Towards a Java Library to Support Runtime Metaprogramming   224
    Ignacio Lagartos, Jose Manuel Redondo, and Francisco Ortin

Design Approaches for Critical Embedded Systems: A Systematic
Mapping Study   243
    Daniel Feitosa, Apostolos Ampatzoglou, Paris Avgeriou,
    Frank J. Affonso, Hugo Andrade, Katia R. Felizardo,
    and Elisa Y. Nakagawa

Author Index   275

Service Science and Business Information Systems

Guidelines for Designing User Interfaces to Analyze Genetic Data. Case of Study: GenDomus

Carlos Iñiguez-Jarrín[1,2](✉), Alberto García S.[1],
José F. Reyes Román[1,3], and Óscar Pastor López[1]

[1] Research Center on Software Production Methods (PROS),
Universitat Politècnica de València, Camino Vera s/n., 46022 Valencia, Spain
{ciniguez,algarsi3,jreyes,opastor}@pros.upv.es
[2] Departamento de Informática y Ciencias de la Computación,
Escuela Politécnica Nacional, Ladrón de Guevara E11-253, Quito, Ecuador
[3] Department of Engineering Sciences, Universidad Central del Este (UCE),
Ave. Francisco Alberto Caamaño Deñó., 21000 San Pedro de Macorís,
Dominican Republic

Abstract. New Generation Technologies (NGS) have opened new opportunities in the genetic field. Analyzing data from large quantities of DNA sequenced to transform it into knowledge has become a challenge. Several tools have been developed to support the genetic analysis, however, most of them have user interfaces that make it difficult to obtain knowledge from genetic data. The lack of design guidelines in this domain leads to the development of user interfaces that are far from satisfying the interaction needs of the domain. From the experience of designing GenDomus, a web-based application to support geneticists in the analysis of genetic data, several interaction-related considerations emerged. Based on such considerations, we present guidelines for designing user interfaces that support geneticists in the analysis of genetic data. Such guidelines become important recommendations to be considered in the design of user interfaces in the genetic field.

Keywords: User interface design · Design guidelines · GenDomus
Genomic information

1 Introduction

The Next-Generation Sequence (NGS) technologies [1] have promoted the proliferation of software applications to allow practitioners to manage huge considerable DNA genetic information. The analysis of genetic data is a domain that requires collaborative coordination between clinicians of several fields to identify and analyze patterns to justify or discard genetic anomalies. In this domain, several supporting tools have been developed, especially for analyzing variant[1] genomic files (e.g., VCF [2]). These tools

---

[1] Variation (or variants): naturally occurring genetic differences among organisms in the same species [citable by Nature Edu.].

© Springer International Publishing AG, part of Springer Nature 2018
E. Damiani et al. (Eds.): ENASE 2017, CCIS 866, pp. 3–22, 2018.
https://doi.org/10.1007/978-3-319-94135-6_1

include powerful data operations (*filtering*, *unions*, *comparing*, etc.), capable to operate at a low level over file data. However, to operate these tools, geneticists must have high computational skills, since the user interfaces (UI) provided by the tools lack the interaction mechanisms to facilitate the data analysis.

The UI's goal is, among other things, to maximize learning speed, minimize cognitive load, provide visual clues, promote visual quality, minimize error rate, maximize the speed of use, and provide adequate aesthetics. To achieve this goal, UI designers rely on *design guidelines* defined from the observation of problems and needs in UI design. Constantly refining the guidelines is important to maintain their validity. As needs and problems arise, new guidelines must appear to address them. The design guidelines are recommendations rather than standards and serve to guide a designer to get UI's adapted to the real needs of the domain and guarantee the use of them. From a more global perspective, UI design guidelines become key guides for better human-machine interaction.

In a previous work [3], we focused on (a) defining *general design guidelines* to address aspects related to interaction and collaboration which are indispensable for the design of genetic data analysis applications and (b) reporting the progress in the implementation of *GenDomus*, a web application designed under the general design guidelines to facilitate the genetic analysis for diagnosing genetic diseases. This work extends the previous work by refining the general guidelines, specifically, these that address the interaction issues in the analysis of genetic variants. From the general design guidelines and interviews with domain specialists, we derive fine-grained design guidelines focused on dealing with interaction issues. The derived guidelines become the starting point for a new iteration in the GenDomus implementation. The advances over our previous work [3] are:

(a) To describe a motivating scenario to illustrate how GenDomus works in the genetic analysis.
(b) To extend high-level interaction guidelines by defining low-level guidelines based on lessons learned from the implementation of GenDomus.
(c) To define design guidelines related to the platform that supports the application.

To achieve these advances following this research line, we firstly overview and analyze the current tools for analyzing genomic data and outline the common functionalities and characteristics between them. In Sect. 3, we make an overview of the workflow to guide the genetic data analysis. Section 4 describes the GenDomus application by mainly focusing on the UI's. In Sect. 5, we present the motivating scenario upon which GenDomus application has been demonstrated to the stakeholders. Section 6 extends the general design guidelines from the lessons learned of designing the GenDomus application. Finally, we close the paper presenting the conclusions and outlining future work.

2   Related Works

Some tools have been developed to process the sequenced DNA data. A literature review about tools to manipulate genetic data from VCF files was presented in a previous work [3]. It serves as source of information to define new guidelines to address interaction issues.

In that literature review, eight tools such as VCF-Miner [4], DECIPHER [5], BIERapp [6], ISAAC [7], PolyTB [8], DraGnET [9], Variant Tool Chest (VTC) [10] and VCF Tools [2] were selected considering following criteria: *relevance* (tools reporting the highest number of citations by articles or experiments in the genomic domain), *modernity* (tools that have emerged in the last 6 years), *collaboration* (tools that incorporate collaborative aspects), *cognitive support* (tools supporting the cognitive process of users).

The analysis of these tools allows identifying a set of characteristics that become a generic profile of a genetic analysis application. Table 1 shows the characteristics categorized into usability, collaboration, data operations, cognitive aspects and UI and their correspondence with each tool.

Table 1. Comparative tool analysis.

| Characteristic | Description | Tools | | | | | | | |
		VCF-Miner	DECIPHER	BiERapp	ISAAC	PolyTB	DraGnET	VTC	VCFTools
Interface type	Application platform	WEB	WEB	WEB	WEB	WEB	WEB	CLI	CLI
Usability									
Easy-to-use	Non-technical users are able to use the tool	✓	✓	✓	✓	✓	✓		
Collaborative aspects									
Collaborative synchronous analysis	Real-time and co-located analysis								
Share data	Share data between members of team			✓		✓			
Cognitive aspects									
Interpret	Explain the meaning of data behaviour		✓		✓	✓			
Perceive	Acquire knowledge through data graphs		✓		✓	✓			
Operations over the data									
Operation	Description	VCF-Miner	DECIPHER	BiERapp	ISAAC	PolyTB	DraGnET	VTC	VCFTools
Query	Find data on a specific topic	✓	✓	✓	✓	✓	✓		
Filter	Exclude the data which are not wanted	✓	✓	✓	✓	✓	✓		✓
Annotate	Add notes to data	✓					✓		✓
Static visualization	Read only data graph		✓		✓	✓			
Interactive visualization	Data filtering enabled by graphs								

(continued)

Table 1. (*continued*)

Operations over the data

Operation	Description	VCF-Miner	DECIPHER	BiERapp	ISAAC	PolyTB	DraGnET	VTC	VCFTools
Prediction	Recommend data or related actions								
Store reusable actions	Store actions to be reused	✓		✓				✓	
Merge	Link data from different data sets							✓	✓
Intersection	Obtain the common data between two data sets							✓	✓
Compaction	Estimate the similarities or differences between two or more data sets	✓	✓		✓		✓	✓	✓
Complement	Obtain the data set that does not belong to the selected data set							✓	✓

As is shown in the Table 1, the predominating architectures in the applications of genetic analysis are *standalone* and *client-server*. Applications such as VTC and VCF Tools have been built under a standalone architecture where the deployment of the application is done on the same machine where the application is developed and executed. On the other hand, web-based applications such as VCF Miner, DECIPHER, BierApp, ISAAC, PolyTB and DraGNET have been obviously designed under a client-server architecture, a distributed approach where clients make requests and servers respond to such requests.

The UI styles that predominate in genetic analysis tools are the *Command Line Interface* (CLI) and *graphical user interface* (GUI). Tools based on CLI interact with the user through commands that execute specific actions. This kind of interaction implies a high cognitive load for the user, which is why these kinds of interfaces are probably more complicated to use. By contrast, GUIs allow direct manipulation (i.e., the user interacts directly with the interface elements) and are available as desktop UI's or as web user interfaces (WUI) that are accessible from web browsers. The authors of WUI-based tools argue that using the web as a platform makes possible to create easy-to-use tools and reduce the cognitive load of the end-user. In fact, using web forms to search for variants with just one mouse click is easier than remembering the sequence of commands and symbols to search for variants via CLI.

Collaboration mechanisms encourage the synergy of the geneticists. ISAAC and DraGnET are web-based applications that incorporate collaboration mechanisms to allow users to share data between them and publish information available to external users. Such collaboration mechanisms rely on the communication capabilities provided by the platform architecture. In contrast to standalone architecture, web architecture support a distributed communication between several points, therefore, the tools based on web platform can implement collaborative mechanisms.

The data graphical visualization is a feature to help users perceive the shape of data and it is present in some tools. Although the tabular format is commonly used by the tools to represent the data, tools such as DECIPHER, ISAAC, and PolyTB take advantage of data graphical visualization to support the cognitive human capabilities to data analysis (i.e., *perceiving* and *interpreting*).

Operations on data are functionalities closely related to the platform on which the tool is implemented. Powerful data operations such as *merge, intersect, compare* and *complement* are more common on the CLI-based tools such as VCF Tools and VTC. In contrast, data operations to retrieve data (e.g., *querying* and *filtering*) are more common on web-based tools.

Although there are several tools aimed to support the diagnosis of genetic diseases, there is not a standard guide containing all the functionalities and features required to design a genetic analysis application. GenDomus is a web-based application designed to support the genetic analysis by incorporating interaction and collaborative mechanisms. However, the real contribution of the GenDomus design is to gather the functionalities present on the domain tools and define a set of guidelines that serves as useful recommendations to design genetic applications. We have already made a first endeavor by defining general guidelines where the interaction and collaborative aspects are treated. In the next sections, we will overview the set of defined guidelines and refine them by incorporating more detailed guidelines.

3   Genetic Diagnosis Scenario

Human diseases can be determined through the genes that cause them [11], a deterministic approach that turns a disease into a genetic condition. The genetic diagnosis aims to identify the genetic elements that cause a certain disease. The genetic diagnosis starts from a tissue sample and includes the analysis of mutations within genes and the interpretation of the effects that cause such mutations from information.

A genetic diagnosis project requires the active participation of several specialists (i.e., *biologists, geneticists, bioinformatics*, etc.), working on a collaboratively way to analyze the genetic samples and identify relevant patterns in the data. The resulting findings are documented in a final report as evidence of the analysis. For example, in the case of genetic analysis for diagnosing diseases described by Villanueva et al. [12], the geneticists analyze the genetic variants contained in a DNA samples which have been obtained from a VCF format file. The geneticists search for genetic variants related to one pathology, identify relevant patterns in the data and define whether or not the patient is at risk of developing a certain disease.

For such scenario, a workflow for diagnosing genetic diseases was defined in [3]. The workflow is made up of three stages: *Data Selection, Variant Analysis* and *Curation*.

- *Data Selection:* The geneticists select the suitable data sources (i.e., genetic data sources) to compare with the samples containing genetic variants. The next stages related to the data analysis rely on the data selected in this stage since selecting data sources that are not suitable for analysis will produce inaccurate results or incorrect diagnostics.
- *Variant Analysis:* The geneticists work collaboratively exploring the genetic variants in the sample, filtering the data to focus on the relevant genetic variants. To interpret the effects produced for each genetic variation, the geneticists gather information about diseases which are related to the genetic variation. The aim of this stage is to select the relevant genetic variants that can lead to relevant findings.
- *Curation:* In this stage, specialists consolidate all findings and proceed to draw conclusions that support the diagnostic report.

4   GenDomus

GenDomus is a web-based solution that incorporates advanced interaction and collaborative mechanisms to help geneticists when diagnosing genetic diseases. The project was carried out by the PROS Research Center's Genome Group[2] and participated in an applied science European project that encourages the use of FIWARE Future Internet platform as a cloud platform of public use and free of royalties. In fact, the GenDomus architecture was designed considering the FIWARE[3] Generic Enablers (GEs) to support the interactive and collaborative features inherent to the diagnosis of genetic diseases.

The GEs are the key components in the development of future internet applications (i.e., FIWARE applications). Each GE provides a set of application programming interfaces APIs and its open reference for components development, which are accessible from FIWARE catalogue together with its description and documentation [13]. To design and implement the web UI, considering the need of visual data representation, collaboration and interaction, we have considered two GEs: *WireCloud* [14] and *2D-UI* [15].

WireCloud, a web application for mashups, offers powerful functionalities (e.g., *heterogeneous data integration, business logic* and *web UI components*) that allows users to create their own dashboards with RIA functionalities [16]. In fact, WireCloud follows the philosophy of turning users into the developers of their own applications. Consequently, the users are provided by a *Composition Editor*, called "*dashboard*", to *edit, name, place* and *resize* visual components. Dashboards are used to *set up* the connections and interactions between the visual components (i.e., *widgets, operators* and *back-end services*) in a customized way. Instead, the server side provides services and functionalities like cross-domain proxy to *access to external sources*, store the data and persistence state of mashups and the capability to *connect to other FIWARE GEs*. The widgets are the UI components developed under web technologies (HTML, CSS

---

[2] http://www.pros.webs.upv.es.

[3] https://www.fiware.org/.

and JavaScript) capable to send and receive state change events from the remainder widgets placed on the dashboard by an event based *wiring engine*. For instance, a component containing Google maps to represent a position by a coordinate. On the other hand, the operators are useful components to provide data or back-end services to widgets. Developers can create both widgets and operators and make them available to the end user through FIWARE catalogue[4]. On the one hand, the developers create widgets and operators, packed in zipped file format (*wgt*) and upload them to the FIWARE catalogue. While on the other hand, the users create their own dashboards using the available operators and widgets from the catalogue [13]. WireCloud's dashboards provide dynamism and interaction between the visible components through the "*wiring*" and "*piping*" mechanisms. These mechanisms are useful for orchestrating the widget-to-widget interaction and widget-to-back services respectively [17].

The generic enabler 2D-UI is a JavaScript library for generating advanced and dynamic Web UI's based on HTML5. Its implementation supports the use of W3C standards, the ability to define reusable web components that support 2D and 3D interactions and the reduction of fragmentation issues produced in the presentation of graphical UI's across devices. The main idea is to enclose in a single web component, both the graphical UI and the mechanism for recording and reporting of events produced by input devices. The web components implementation is achieved by Polymer[5] JavaScript library, whereas the register and notification of events is achieved by Input API, an application programming interface to deal with the events produced by input devices (e.g., *mouse, keyboard, game pad*) on the web browser. Polymer allows creating fully functional interoperable components, which work as DOM standard elements, which means a web component package HTML code, a functionality expressed on JavaScript and customized CSS styles for the proper functioning of the component.

WireCloud widgets can be reused within the dashboard to show different information in form and content, according to the needs of the user. For example, in Fig. 2A, the same widget has been used to create three graphical components, the first one displaying the number of variants per chromosome through a Pie chart (Fig. 2Ab), the second one displaying the number of genetic variants by phenotype through a Bar chart (Fig. 2Ac) and the last one (Fig. 2Ad) displaying the number of genetic variants by clinical significance.

The statistical graphs support trigger events caused by sector selection and chart resizing due to the nvd3[6] JavaScript library used for this purpose. The nvd3 library provides a set of suitable statistical charts to represent a huge amount of data. For this prototype, we have used the *Pie Chart* and the *Discrete Bar Chart*. In this way, these charts incorporate filter mechanisms by selecting chart sectors which makes it possible to create dynamic queries in an ease way.

GenDomus is built upon a suitable *Conceptual Model of the Human Genome* (CMHG) [18] that gather the domain concepts (e.g., chromosome, gen, variation, VCF,

---

[4] https://catalogue.fiware.org/.

[5] https://www.polymer-project.org/1.0/.

[6] http://nvd3.org/.

etc.) and its relationships as is described in [3]. Through the CMHG, *GenDomus* can integrate the data sources required to the diagnosis of genetic diseases and create valuable links to the genetic variants form the samples.

At the front-end level, GenDomus consists of three UI's (data loading, genetic variant analysis and curation) that address each of the phases of the workflow for diagnosing genetic diseases discussed in the previous section.

In this section, we detail the UI's of the application highlighting the technological components provided by the FIWARE platform and how they have been orchestrated to address the aspects of interaction and collaboration.

4.1   Graphical User Interface

The front end is composed of three (3) complementary web interfaces: *data loading*, *genetic variant analysis* and *curation*, which are implemented under web standards such as HTML5, JavaScript (Bootstrap[7], jQuery[8]) and CSS. The three UI's are aimed at covering the three stages of genetic diagnosis described in the Sect. 3 of this paper.

Through the "Data loading" web page (Fig. 1), the geneticists select the genetic samples to be analyzed along with the genetic databases with which the geneticists want to compare. This UI is composed of three web components that retrieve information from the underlying genome CM. The web component "*project-info*" (Fig. 1a) presents the information of the genetic analysis project created to identify the analysis in process together with the number of samples and data sources for the analysis. The "Samples" panel (Fig. 1b) lists the genetic samples grouped by analysis study, while the "Data Sources" panel (Fig. 1c) lists the available public genetic databases.

The "Genetic Variant Analysis" web page (Fig. 2A) incorporates a dashboard where the user can place and set up widgets that incorporate bi-dimensional (2D) statistical charts to represent how the data is distributed. The charts bring dynamism to the data exploration, since every data chart placed on the dashboard is sensitive to interactions and changes in the others. In fact, each effect caused by selecting a chart sector is propagated and visualized in the rest of charts; thereby we provide an easy use aesthetic system to build dynamic queries.

The genetic samples selected in the Data loading web page (Fig. 1b) are showed in the Analysis web page through the Data List component (Fig. 2Aa) with the option to select or deselect the samples participants in the data exploration. Interlinked charts provide visualization of filter propagation effect and it serves as a helpful feedback resource for users. The filters generated are showed in a filter stack panel (Fig. 2Ae) enabling user to remember the actions executed, modify the query options or infer information about the data showed in the graph. Ordering functionality is provided to user to customize the view. The widgets have been developed based on the WireCloud documentation, compressed in a file with "*wgt*" extension and uploaded on FIWARE catalogue to be used by the final user.

---

[7] http://getbootstrap.com/.

[8] https://jquery.com/.

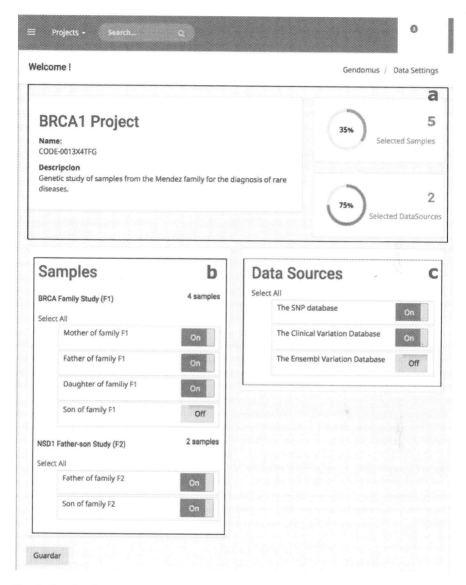

Fig. 1. Data loading web page allows to select the available samples and data sources to perform the genetic data analysis (Source: [3]).

In addition, interaction with data can be performed through any web-based device (e.g. tablets, laptops). The main idea is to filter the information graphically to identify relevant information related to genetic diseases.

Because of the filtering and data exploration in the *genetic variant analysis* web page, the resulting genetic variants that accomplish with the filter constraints are showed in the table of results contained in the "Curation" web page (Fig. 2B).

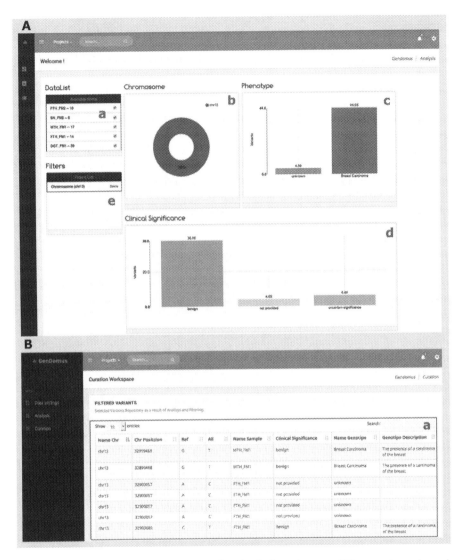

Fig. 2. GenDomus web user interfaces. The Analysis web page (A) presents a dynamic dashboard containing interlinked widgets: The Sample widget lists the set of samples selected in the data loading web page, three statistical 2D charts to explore the data and a filter list to store each selected chart sector. The curation web page (B) lists the filtered variants by user to be considered in the diagnosis disease report. (Source: [3]).

The "Curation" web page allow the project leader together to analysts to filter and compare the data to draw up conclusions to support the making decision. Formulating a diagnosis report implies gather the findings all together. The main idea is to analyze the filtered information, generate data value and appropriate information for supporting the decision-making that will be documented in the final report. This UI is built by the web component *"curation-table"* (Fig. 2Ba) which shows in tabular format the detail of selected genetic variants because of the interaction in the dashboard mentioned in the variant analysis stage.

Additionally, the design of web UI's has been adapted to wide range of display devices because of Accessibility guideline implementation.

Based on the workflow for the diagnosis of genetic diseases, the following section describes a motivating scenario that illustrates how the interaction and collaboration mechanisms provided by GenDomus become a useful tool for genetic analysis.

5   Motivating Scenario: The Collaborative Room

GenDomus is a prototype in continuous evolution. In fact, a first demonstration of the application based on a motivating scenario, has already been made to project's stakeholders. The motivating scenario describes how the mechanisms of interaction and collaboration incorporated in *GenDomus* are useful for the genetic analysis, specifically the genetic analysis for diagnosing genetic diseases. In this section, we describe the motivating scenario and highlight the functionalities provided by *GenDomus* that intent to make the genetic analysis an easy activity.

5.1   Motivating Scenario

James, Francis and Johan (assumed names), a team of geneticists, plan a diagnosis session to study the samples of a family of 4 members and determine if the presence of cancer in one of them (the daughter specifically) has genetic reasons and, if applicable, identify which members of the family are carriers of the same disease.

To this end, the geneticists meets in the "cognitive room" (Fig. 3), a physical room specially designed to facilitate the collaborative work of geneticists. This room is equipped with several display devices (i.e., laptop, smart TV, tablet) that access to the GenDomus application through the internet.

As a first step, James (the team leader) uses one of the smart TV's located on the left wall of the room (Fig. 3a), to select the genetic samples and the data sources for the analysis, as shown in Fig. 1. He selects the samples from each member of the family as well as ClinVar and dbSNP (SNP database), the data sources that will provide information about diseases. Then, *GenDomus* processes the data by matching each genetic variation in the samples with the information from data sources. After the process, the resulting genetic variants together with its related disease information are displayed in the curation screen, as shown in Fig. 2B, by using a second smart TV located on the right wall of the room (Fig. 3b).

Now, the geneticists have a huge set of data to be analyzed. Therefore, the geneticists need to visualize how the data is distributed, from different perspectives, as well as to apply filter conditions to focus on the relevant genetic variants. Each team member adds a data chart to the analysis screen displayed through the smart TV located in the center of the room (Fig. 3c). James, the team leader, uses his laptop to create, drag and drop a pie chart that shows how the variants are distributed with respect to the "chromosomes", (as shown in Fig. 2Ab). At the same time, Francis uses his tablet

Fig. 3. Collaborative room for diagnosing genetic diseases.

(Fig. 3d) to create a bar chart that shows how the variants are distributed with respect to "clinical significance" (as shown in Fig. 2Ad) whereas Johan, using his laptop, creates a bar chart that shows how the variants are distributed with respect to "phenotypes" (or diseases), as shown in Fig. 2Ac.

Since the data charts have interactive capabilities, James and his colleagues interact directly with them to filter the genetic variants. In fact, Francis uses his tablet (Fig. 3d) to filter the variants related with the chromosome 13 (the chromosome where the cancer-related BRCA1 and BRCA2 genes are located) by selecting the corresponding sector in the Pie Chart (Fig. 2Ab). Because of this interaction, every device in the collaborative room automatically synchronizes its state, so the geneticists can follow the data analysis in progress from either their mobile devices or the smart TVs, without losing any of the actions performed in the analysis.

During the diagnostic session, Johan observes in the curation screen (Fig. 3b) that according to ClinVar, most of the variants are "benign" (the variation has not effect on the breast cancer disease); however, there are other variants that have been categorized differently.

Johan wants to analyze these variants without interrupting or affecting the analysis carried out by the whole team; therefore, He uses his tablet to access his individual work space and filters the variants. He realizes that the variants are "intronic variants" (i.e., a variation located within a region of the gene that does not change the amino acid code), and informs it to their colleagues. Thanks to Johan's individual analysis, the team decides to discard the benign and intronic variants from the variants causing the disease.

From the remaining set of variants, the team use the curation screen (Fig. 3b) to filter the variants whose "clinical significance" is "uncertain" but they realize that such variants are not present in the sample of the daughter (the one with cancer) and therefore these must also be discarded.

Consequently, the geneticists team concludes that the cancer of the daughter of the family is not genetically related.

This motivating scenario has illustrated how the interactive and collaborative capabilities of GenDomus are useful for the diagnosis of genetic diseases. From a more abstract perspective, these tangible capabilities are the result of applying general design guidelines that specifically address both the interaction and collaboration aspects. In the next section, we describe the design guidelines that have been considered in the GenDomus design and that we think, these can be considered, in a broader sense, as general guidelines for the design and implementation of genetic analysis applications.

6   Design Guidelines

In a previous work [3], we present the design guidelines upon which the GenDomus application was designed. These guidelines address the *interaction*, *collaboration*, and *platform* issues that are central to GenDomus design. We call these guidelines as **high-level guidelines** (HLG's) as they address the above issues from a rather general point of view.

Figure 4 summarize the HLG's by showing the guidelines grouped by issues. While the **interaction issues** group the *visualization* and *prediction* guidelines, the **collaboration issues** group the *communication*, *accessibility* and *workspaces* guidelines. Supporting the issues of interaction and collaboration, we can find the **platform issues** grouping the guidelines to deal, among others, with infrastructure, performance, storage issues.

Although these HLG's become useful recommendations for designing genetic analysis applications, they are very general and lose sight of the detail of problems in the domain. Therefore, **low-level design guidelines** (LLG's) are needed to refine and specify the HLG's.

In this work, our goal is to define LLG's to refine the HLG's related to the issues of *interaction* and *platform* since such issues are closely related to our main target: The UI design.

To achieve this goal, we take advantage of the lessons learned from the design and implementation of GenDomus, since such lessons are useful for (a) enriching each HLG by providing a set of LLG's that refine it, and (b) adding new guidelines to deal with technological platform aspects.

The set of guidelines (i.e., HLG's and LLG's) is described following a top-down perspective. First, we describe the HLG's by highlighting how it was applied to *GenDomus*, and then we describe the LLG's to refine each HLG.

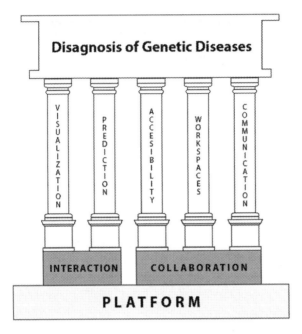

Fig. 4. Fundamental design guidelines for genetic diseases' diagnosis applications.

6.1   Design Guidelines for User Interfaces

From the HLG's (i.e., *visualization* and *prediction*) that address the interaction issues, we derive LLG's. In other words, we refine each HLG by incorporating the observations obtained from interviews with geneticists.

Interviews with geneticists from TellmeGen[9], a recognized genetic laboratory from Valencia, Spain, yielded important and more detailed observations. TellmeGen offers personal genetic services. Through its on-line platform, it is possible to perform personal genetic tests in an easy, comfortable and fast way. The interviews conducted in this laboratory arose some recommendations related to the interaction of how to search for information and how to document the findings.

The guidelines presented here aim to improve the usability of the system, thus providing a better user experience.

HLG: Visualization

Provide appropriate interactive visualization mechanisms for data discovery and knowledge extraction.

When analyzing genetic data, analysts are challenged to gain knowledge from high and heterogeneous volume of data. The human capacity to figure out the data relationships hidden into extensive sequence of data, is limited; therefore, visualization mechanisms are needed to shape the data and explore it. As the well-known saying

---

[9] http://www.tellmegen.com/.

goes: "*A picture is worth a thousand words*", information graphs (*maps, flowcharts, bar plots, pie charts, etc.*) become a powerful mechanism for understanding and expressing knowledge that is often difficult through other forms of expression (e.g. verbal, written). Tidwell [19] mentions that good interactive information graphics allows users to answer questions such as: *How is the data organized? What is related to what? How can these data be exploited?* The interactive graphics provide significant advantages over static graphics. Through interactive graphics, users move from being passive observers to being the main and active actors in the discovery of knowledge, deciding how they want to visualize, explore and analyze the data and their relationships.

GenDomus incorporates information graphics as a powerful and suitable mechanism to (a) *concretize the form of data*, (b) *understand data easily*, (c) *explore data from a visual and interactive perspective*, (d) *draw conclusions and transmit knowledge from what the user sees and thinks*. For example, the available GenDomus data charts (i.e., pie chart and bar chart) are used to show the data distribution from the different point of views as well as data filtering mechanisms. In this way, a Pie Chart is not only useful to show the data distribution across multiple sectors, but also to filter the data by "*clicking*" on a certain chart sector. Consequently, the entire data set is segregated under the given filter condition and the new data distribution, from each perspective, is visualized instantaneously through the different graphic components (e.g., charts, data table) involved into the same analysis space. In this way, information graphics make the data filtering an easier direct data manipulation task allowing the user to be aware of the data behavior change.

LLG 1: Interactive Data Charts. – *Provide interactive data charts that allow both visualizing how the data is distributed and filtering the data across multiple criteria.*

Unlike command-line-based applications that require the user to enter certain commands to filter data, web-based applications have more visual interfaces (web forms) to facilitate data filtering. The trend is to enable users without advanced computer skills to perform data operations in an easy, intuitive and efficient way. In this respect, interactive charts support such a trend and become powerful mechanisms for visualizing and filtering data.

The study of *biological pathways* [20] is a clear scenario where the LLG 1 can be applied. The study of biological pathways is relevant to know the roots of a human disease. Therefore, knowing the genetic variants involved in different biological pathways becomes a necessity. By using interactive data charts, such as a *Column chart*, geneticists can visualize the behavior of genetic variants with respect to biological pathways and filter the genetic variants to find which of them are related to a certain disease. Concretely, each column in the chart represents a *pathway* from the data set and the variable height of the column depends on the number of genetic variants contained in the pathway. Once the columns have been displayed, the geneticist can select one or another column to filter the variants or show, through another UI control such as the *data table*, the list of genetic variants related to the selected pathway.

LLG 2: Parallel Visualization. – *Provide parallel visualization mechanisms that allow visual comparisons on the data.*

A scenario where LLG 2 can be applied, for example, is the comparison of biological pathways. The user needs to compare biological pathways (one healthy with one sick) to determine the problems caused by the mutations. Parallel visualization of pathways allows the user to easily and intuitively identify genetic differences and draw conclusions about them.

LLG 3: Operations between Samples. – *Provide set operations (i.e., join, intersection, difference, complement) to produce new datasets or compare two or more similar datasets.*

One scenario where this guideline is applied is the comparison of genetic samples. Genetic samples contain numerous amounts of genetic variation. Analyzing two genetic samples involves, among other things, identifying and visualizing, at the level of genetic variation, the differences between the samples (for example, listing the genetic variants that are in one sample and are not in the other). In this scenario, set operations play a key role. The intersection operation, for example, will allow to quickly identify the coincident variants between the two samples. The execution of each set operation produces new sets of genetic variants that can be used in later operations.

HLG: Prediction
Use the user-data interactions as a source of information to predict the next steps in the knowledge discovery.

LLG 4: Literature Search Methods. – *Improve the literature search process through recommendations based on a history of user interactions.*

To interpret the effects produced by certain genetic variation, geneticists review the clinical literature (e.g., clinical studies, research articles, clinical reports) in search of evidence to support the such interpretation.

The search and review process of literature is not trivial. Geneticists use extensive lists of terms like query strings to retrieve, through web browsers, documents or content related to the search string. In some cases, the results are not as expected, because some terms have not been included in the search string.

This process can be facilitated by using user interactions as a natural means to generate precise search strings and to recommend literature associated with the topic of interest. The application can recommend the revision of some literature related to the subject of interest, based on analysis of user interactions in the literature search process (e.g., search terms, applied data filters, search criteria defined, etc.) and interactions stored in a database of previously defined knowledge.

LLG 5: Documentation of Findings. –*Provide the user with ways to record their findings during genetic data analysis.*

Throughout the analysis of data, geneticists observe certain behaviors in the data or information that are relevant when making decisions and generate conclusions. For example, to interpret what a genetic variation represents, geneticists read literature (e.g., blogs, medical articles) with information on diseases related to such genetic variation. During review and reading of literature, the geneticist needs to record genes, mutations or diseases strongly related to genetic variation. In addition, as if a reference manager were (e.g., *Mendeley*[10] or *Zotero*[11]), the annotations should include the information of the resource to which they refer. This information will serve for further review.

LLG 6: Interfaces with Assisted Interaction. *– Use the end user interaction to guide the user in the data analysis.*

The amount of data involved in genetic analysis is so large and scattered. Consequently, the user gets lost when browsing or exploring the data. From the set of interactions performed on previous data analysis, the UI should be able to assist the user on performing the data analysis. Previous interactions, performed by geneticists in past analysis, can be the source of knowledge for current and future analysis.

Each interaction performed contains information about WHAT and WHY a certain analysis action (e.g., select, filter, navigate) was performed, therefore, the user can be guided in the data exploration by using the experience of other experts. When looking for disease-causing variants, for example, the interactions from previous diagnostics are useful for answering questions such as *What other navigable options do I have from here? Which data relationships were explored by other analysts in similar searches? Why were they explored? What other information was searched in previous and similar diagnostics?*

6.2 Platform Design Guidelines

From the previous experience that has been generated from the development of Gen-Domus, six guidelines have been extracted and defined with the aim of laying the foundations of the platform that supports the execution of GenDomus. This platform will inherit and enhance existing GenDomus capabilities. These guidelines are defined for the sole purpose of accelerating genetic analysis, facilitating work, and automating existing repetitive tasks as much as possible. Thus, we describe the guidelines:

LLG 7: Scalability Support. *– The system must support scalability in both computing and storage capacity.*

The initial amount of data used on the platform will be high; nonetheless, this amount will not be static and will, over the time, be increased with new genetic information thanks to the work of geneticists identifying and isolating this information.

Likewise, the number of users and professionals who carry out analysis through our tool will grow, meaning that the load of the system will increase too. The tool must handle this increase of data and concurrent users satisfactorily, it must have the elasticity to allow dynamic growing of stored knowledge base and compute capacity to manage possible peaks of use of the application.

LLG 8: Availability. *– Complete availability of the system must be guaranteed.*

With a growing user base, to important scalable dimensions are identified: on the one hand, the greater the application is used, the more information will be stored in the system and therefore more frequently will be accessed. On the other hand, the more the

---

[10] https://mendeley.com/.

[11] https://www.zotero.org/.

application is accessed, the more dependent of the application the users will be. This implies that the platform must offer high availability.

Application architecture will have the necessary mechanisms to guarantee its availability in most situations.

LLG 9: Transparent Processing. – *Data loading and data modification must be transparent to the user.*

The goal of the users of the application should be to focus on the analysis and extraction of new information from data, hiding the obtaining of the data. This guideline worked well in GenDomus but was limited: data sources could only be managed before starting the analysis. Our purpose is to improve the guideline even more in the new application. For this reason, data sources will be handled in a way that will permit the user to dynamically change the working data set: adding and deleting different data sources while an analysis is being done.

LLG 10: Query Execution Time. – *To reduce the queries processing time.*

The goal of the platform is to speed up genetic analysis. Therefore, the minimum processing time of a query execution must be determined, analyzed and reduced considering the existing hardware capabilities.

Unlike the current GenDomus architecture, the next one will guarantee a maximum execution time until an executed query returns the information; moreover, when possible, the information will be delivered and shown to the user "on the fly", no need to wait until the full set of data is created or processed.

The usability needs of end users are changing; however, the set or defined guidelines becomes a starting point to improve the usability of GenDomus. Future requirements will be added to meet the needs of end-users. The goal is to design the necessary interaction in the domain and generate usable UI's that address the challenge of consuming genetic data.

7   Conclusions and Future Work

In this work, we presented refined guidelines for designing UI's aimed to the genetic analysis. These guidelines have been derived from general guidelines proposed in an earlier work, the experience learned from the design of a web based prototype application (called GenDomus) for the genetic analysis as well as from the observations obtained from interviews with geneticists.

In this work, we presented a motivating scenario that illustrate how the GenDomus application can facilitate the genetic analysis.

To understand how the GenDomus application facilitates the activities of genetic analysis, we provided a narrated motivating scenario called "Collaborative Room". This scenario, from which a demonstration of GenDomus for the stakeholders was made, allowed us to identify in more detail the guidelines necessary to design UI's suitable for the genetic analysis.

We present a set of 10 low-level design guidelines that address interaction and platform issues in the design of genetic analysis UI's. These low-level guidelines refine the high-level guidelines defined in an earlier work. The set of design guidelines becomes a powerful tool that allows designers to design UI's suitable for the genetic analysis domain. It is important to note that, just as the data consumption needs in the genetic analysis domain are constantly evolving, the guidelines presented in this paper are susceptible to refinements as the domain needs are updated.

For the future, we will implement the low-level guidelines into the GenDomus application and will plan to validate the application in real scenarios.

Acknowledgements. The author thanks the members of the PROS Center's Genome group for fruitful discussions. In addition, it is also important to highlight that Secretaría Nacional de Educación, Ciencia y Tecnología (*SENESCYT*) and Escuela Politécnica Nacional from Ecuador and the Ministry of Higher Education, Science and Technology (*MESCyT*) from Santo Domingo, Dominican Republic, have supported this work. This project also has the support of Generalitat Valenciana through project IDEO (PROMETEOII/2014/039) and Spanish Ministry of Science and Innovation through project DataME (ref: TIN2016-80811-P).

The author thanks Francisco Valverde Giromé and María José Villanueva Del Pozo for their collaboration with this project.

References

1. Mardis, E.R.: The impact of next-generation sequencing technology on genetics. Trends Genet. **24**(3), 133–141 (2008)
2. Danecek, P., et al.: The variant call format and VCF tools. Bioinformatics **27**(15), 2156–2158 (2011). https://doi.org/10.1093/bioinformatics/btr330
3. Iñiguez-Jarrin, C., García, A., Reyes, J.F., Pastor, O.: GenDomus: interactive and collaboration mechanisms for diagnosing genetic diseases. In: ENASE 2017 - Proceedings of the 12th International Conference on Evaluation of Novel Approaches to Software Engineering, Porto, Portugal, 28–29 April 2017, pp. 91–102 (2017). https://doi.org/10.5220/0006324000910102
4. Hart, S.N., Duffy, P., Quest, D.J., Hossain, A., Meiners, M.A., Kocher, J.-P.: VCF-Miner: GUI-based application for mining variants and annotations stored in VCF files. Brief. Bioinform. **17**(2), 346 (2016). https://doi.org/10.1093/bib/bbv051
5. Chatzimichali, E.A., et al.: Facilitating collaboration in rare genetic disorders through effective matchmaking in DECIPHER. Hum. Mutat. **36**(10), 941–949 (2015). https://doi.org/10.1002/humu.22842
6. Alemán, A., Garcia-Garcia, F., Salavert, F., Medina, I., Dopazo, J.: A web-based interactive framework to assist in the prioritization of disease candidate genes in whole-exome sequencing studies. Nucleic Acids Res. **42**(W1), 1–6 (2014). https://doi.org/10.1093/nar/gku407
7. Baier, H., Schultz, J.: ISAAC - InterSpecies Analysing Application using Containers. BMC Bioinform. **15**(1), 18 (2014). https://doi.org/10.1186/1471-2105-15-18
8. Coll, F., et al.: PolyTB: a genomic variation map for Mycobacterium tuberculosis. Tuberculosis (Edinb) **94**(3), 346–354 (2014). https://doi.org/10.1016/j.tube.2014.02.005
9. Duncan, S., Sirkanungo, R., Miller, L., Phillips, G.J.: DraGnET: software for storing, managing and analyzing annotated draft genome sequence data. BMC Bioinform. **11**, 100 (2010). https://doi.org/10.1186/1471-2105-11-100
10. Ebbert, M.T.W., et al.: Variant Tool Chest: an improved tool to analyze and manipulate variant call format (VCF) files. BMC Bioinform. **15**(Suppl 7), S12 (2014). https://doi.org/10.1186/1471-2105-15-S7-S12

11. Genetic Alliance, District of Columbia Department of Health: Understanding Genetics. Genetic Alliance (2010). https://www.ncbi.nlm.nih.gov/books/NBK132149/

12. Villanueva, M.J., Valverde, F., Pastor, O.: Involving end-users in domain-specific languages development experiences from a bioinformatics SME. In: ENASE 2013 - Proceedings of the 8th International Conference on Evaluation of Novel Approaches to Software Engineering, pp. 97–108 (2013). https://doi.org/10.5220/0004450000970108

13. Fiware.org: Welcome to the FIWARE Wiki (2016)

14. Introduction to WireCloud. https://wirecloud.conwet.etsiinf.upm.es/slides/1.1_Introduction.html#slide1

15. Fiware Catalogue - 2D-UI. http://catalogue.fiware.org/enablers/2d-ui

16. Fiware.org: FIWARE Catalogue - Application Mashup - Wirecloud (2015). https://catalogue.fiware.org/enablers/application-mashup-wirecloud

17. FIWARE Academy: Application Mashup Generic Enabler (WireCloud). http://edu.fiware.org/course/view.php?id=53. Accessed 24 Apr 2016

18. Reyes Román, J.F., Pastor, Ó., Casamayor, J.C., Valverde, F.: Applying conceptual modeling to better understand the human genome. In: Comyn-Wattiau, I., Tanaka, K., Song, I.-Y., Yamamoto, S., Saeki, M. (eds.) ER 2016. LNCS, vol. 9974, pp. 404–412. Springer, Cham (2016). https://doi.org/10.1007/978-3-319-46397-1_31

19. Tidwell, J.: Designing Interfaces, vol. XXXIII, no. 2. O'Reilly, Sebastopol (2012)

20. National Human Genome Research Institute: Biological Pathways Fact Sheet - National Human Genome Research Institute (NHGRI) (2015). https://www.genome.gov/27530687/biological-pathways-fact-sheet/. Accessed 15 Aug 2017

Biologically Inspired Anomaly Detection Framework

Tashreen Shaikh Jamaluddin[1], Hoda Hassan[2(✉)],
and Haitham Hamza[3]

[1] Computer Science Department, AASTMT Academy,
Qism El-Nozha, Cairo, Egypt
shaikh.tashreen@hotmail.com
[2] Electrical Engineering Department, British University in Egypt,
ElShrouk, Cairo, Egypt
hoda.hassan@bue.edu.eg
[3] Computer Science Department, Cairo University,
Ahmed Zewail st., Cairo, Egypt
hshamza@acm.org

Abstract. Service-Oriented Computing is largely accepted as a well-founded reference paradigm for Service-Oriented Architecture that integrates Service-Oriented Middleware and the Web Service interaction patterns. In most SOA applications, SOAP as a communication protocol is adopted to develop Web services. SOAP is highly extensible and ensures confidentiality and integrity as specified within the WS-Security standards. Securing this protocol is obviously a vital issue for securing Web services and SOA applications.

One of the functionalities of SOM is to provide strong security solutions for SOC based applications. As distinct models of SOM started to develop to suit particular requirements, a complete security solution for SOA applications emerged as a new challenge. Moreover, with the wide adoption of SOC, web service applications are no longer contained within tightly controlled environments, and thus could be subjected to malicious attacks, such as Denial of Service attacks. To present, one of the most critical issues for SOM is the absence of a complete security solution. This is a state that threatens the successfulness of the Web services and SOA applications.

Our proposed Biologically Inspired Anomaly Detection Framework presents a generic security service that protects web services against denial of service attacks at the service-oriented middleware layer. It employs three processes, namely: (i) the Initiation Process, (ii) the Recognition Process and (iii) the Co-stimulation Process. These processes constitute the detection mechanism of DoS attacks usually infused in the SOAP message in the service interaction of SOA.

To evaluate our work, we have developed a prototype that showed that our proposed security service was able to detect SOAP-based DoS attacks targeting a web service. The results show that the proposed prototype was capable to detect most attacks administered to the system. The average percentage of attack detection for our prototype was 73.41% as compared to an external commercial parser which was 44.09%.

© Springer International Publishing AG, part of Springer Nature 2018
E. Damiani et al. (Eds.): ENASE 2017, CCIS 866, pp. 23–47, 2018.
https://doi.org/10.1007/978-3-319-94135-6_2

Keywords: Service-Oriented Computing (SOC)
Service-Oriented Architecture (SOA) · Web service
Service-Oriented Middleware (SOM) · SOAP message
Denial of Service (DoS) attacks

1   Introduction

Service-Oriented Architecture (SOA) serves as a flexible architectural approach to create and integrate software systems built from autonomous services [1, 2]. With SOA, integration becomes protocol-independent, distributed, and loosely coupled, i.e. clean separation of service interfaces from internal implementations, as end solution that is likely to be composed of services. In SOA, software resources are packaged as "services", which are self-contained modules that provide standard business functionality. These modules are independent of the state or context of other services. The concept of developing applications from standalone services further advanced to incorporate web services. A web service is a specific kind of service that exposes its feature over the Web using standard protocols and Internet languages through an identifying URI [3]. Web service protocols and technologies include: XML, XML Schema, Web Services Description Language (WSDL), Universal Discovery Description and Integration (UDDI) and Simple Object Access Protocol (SOAP). Web-service-based applications can be developed from services that can be accessed and integrated over the Internet using open Internet standards [3, 4]. Web Services has published interface where it communicates with other requesting execution of their operations in order to collectively support a common business task [5]. In most web-service based-applications, SOAP is adopted as the underlying communication protocol. SOAP is a highly extensible protocol and ensures confidentiality and integrity as specified within the WS-Security standards [4].

Service-Oriented Computing (SOC) is now largely accepted as a well-founded reference paradigm for SOA that integrates SOM and the web service interaction pattern. SOC paradigm refers to the set of concepts, principles, and methods that represent computing in SOA, in which software applications are constructed based on independent component services with standard interfaces. The main advantage of this approach is interoperability and loose coupling among software components that allow users to use commonly required services to develop their applications [6]. In SOC Service-Oriented Middleware (SOM) is an essential software layer that provides abstraction, interoperability and other services like the distribution of functionality, scalability, load balancing and fault tolerance [7]. With the emerge of software as a service (SaaS) and SOM, the concept of a more sophisticated framework under SOC came into existence. Thus, SOM was developed as a vehicle to ease the use of the SOC by offering solutions and approaches that made SOC more usable and feature-rich.

SOM operates as a management layer to provide efficient communication functionalities between interacting web services. Accordingly, as mentioned in [7] middleware is challenged by the security problems generated though web services. Some of security challenges faced by SOM include insufficient communication security, identity management and authentication, access control, and trust management [6].

Moreover, as there are no standard security guidelines for designing SOM [6], for application developers, it became difficult to provide secure access to services and message protection to the accessing party in a distributed environment. Ultimately, it affects the operation of SOM, which is supposed to improve security features of SOC [6]. To fully utilize security features of SOM within the business environment, vendors started to develop SOM functionalities that were suited to their particular business requirements. Several SOM security models that were studied in [6, 7] operate in an SOA environment, yet they do not apply full security solutions. This situation arises the problem to secure applications (exposed as services) mainly because:

No standard security guidelines for security design in SOM,
Highly distributed applications, networks, heterogenous environment, and communication load for hardware,
Loosely coupled functionalities (for service integration) for software.

Designing independent SOM models only incorporate the set of functionalities required within the application domain, but generate the risk of malicious attacks [8]. Usually in XML Denial of Service (DoS) attacks, the operational parameters of messages coming from legitimate users are changed in real-time by adding additional elements or replacing existing elements within the message. As a result, messages between hosts can be easily intercepted and altered, resulting in untraceable intrusion attacks. Therefore, it is paramount to resolve SOM deficiencies in handling unauthorized access. Especially that SOM is required to deal with large volumes of data and high communication loads over a highly heterogeneous network. To summarize, in order to achieve a secure Web service communication by SOAP messages over distributed environments, well-defined SOM security approaches are needed to provide complete security solutions [9]. A preliminary work proposed by Al-Jaroodi et al. [10] to develop a general set of security requirements through independent "security as a service" components. These security services can offer a variety of security functionalities that could be adapted to SOM.

Bio-inspired security approaches have been proposed in literature as an alternative to traditional security systems where the attack or the attack behavior is not previously known. In Bio-inspired security systems attacks and anomalies are detected as changes in the environment or deviations from the normal system behavior in complex problem domains. These domains include both the application and the network-level systems to analyze the intrusion or anomaly detection problems. In Bio-inspired approaches, the role of the "human immune system" is detection and protection from infections according to two behaviors as follows [11]:

a. Self-optimization process: Leucocytes launches a detection response to invading pathogens leading to unspecific response.
   Self-learning process: Immune response remembers past encounters, which represents immunological memory. B-cells and T-cells allow a faster response the second time around showing a very specific response.

Both of these behaviors have been extensively used in many applications for anomaly detection, data mining, machine learning, pattern recognition, agent based systems, control, and robotics [11]. The application based techniques utilize the self-optimization and self-learning processes for gearing application behavior at a time of intrusion detection. These approaches include detecting deviations from normal behavior of users browsing web pages, to monitor characteristics of HTTP sessions, and to monitor a number of client's requests. In many of these approaches, self-optimization or self-organization serve as a primary defense mechanism.

For intrusion detection self-optimization and self-learning are robust and efficient defense mechanism to protect web servers against application layer DoS attacks [11]. Moreover, as these techniques have been popular in solving intrusion detection problems in network and application domain [12], we surmise that it would help us to develop a robust security mechanism to combat DoS attacks.

The main contributions of this extended paper which is based on work in [20] are (i) to present an application-level Bio-inspired Anomaly Detection Framework (BADF) that draws on the ideology of the Danger Theory (DT) previously proposed in [12] for heterogeneous networks. The presented framework is designed as a generic framework that improves the security features of the SOM by applying the DT principles to protect web-service based-applications from Denial of Service (DoS) attacks. (ii) Based on BADF, we derive an architecture for a generic "security as a service" (SECaaS) web service. Our derived security service is identified as a message-protection service as mentioned in [10]. It aims to protect incoming SOAP messages against XML Denial of Service (DoS) attacks. BADF is evaluated by developing a prototype for the "security as a service" (SECaaS) architecture, and showing the ability of the SECaaS web-service to detect different types of DoS attacks induced within SOAP requests.

The rest of this paper is organized as follows; Sect. 2 overviews related work with respect to SOAP message attacks and possible mitigation methods. Section 3 presents our Bio-inspired Anomaly Detection Framework (BADF) and the SECaaS architecture. In Sect. 4 we describe our evaluation environment and results. Finally, in Sect. 5 we conclude the paper and mention our future work.

2   Related Work

To secure Web services, WS-Security standard define an XML Schema which is a precise description of the content of any XML document. Though being a very powerful language for restricting the actual appearance of an XML document, i.e. SOAP message, the active use of XML Schema validation is often omitted in XML-processing applications due to performance reasons [1]. However, recent works in [13] have shown that missing XML Schema validation in Web Service server systems enables various XML-SOAP based attack vulnerabilities. The SOAP based attacks exploit XML based messages and parsers, and pave the way to introduce DoS attacks to restrict system's availability. Several papers addressed the topic of DoS attacks on SOAP messages as it became crucial to understand the DoS impact on the operation of Web Services.

The XML-SOAP based attacks on Web services is being widely studied and classified as Coercive parsing and Oversize payload [15], SOAPAction spoofing [1, 2], XML injection and Parameter tampering [17]. All aforementioned SOAP based attacks exploit XML parser to prevent legitimate users from accessing the attacked web services resulting in DoS. Gruschka et al. [15] studied the Coercive parsing and Oversize payload attacks were excessive amount of XML data are infused in the Clients SOAP messages to retaliate the server firewall. To detect excessive payload on firewall Gruschka et al. [15] have proposed a Web service Firewall namely Check Way Gateway, that validates the incoming SOAP requests against the strict XML Schema generated from the WSDL file associated with the Web Service. The firewall performs schema validation through event-based parsing using a SAX (Simple API for XML) interface to detect attacks in the SOAP request. The performance time for this firewall is faster than compared to other attacks detection techniques. The authors in [1, 2] classified the SOAPAction spoofing and Oversize payload as DoS attacks were attackers gain access to the servers by exploiting application vulnerabilities though flooding malformed web service requests. They pointed that the advancement in new technologies and standards have generated loopholes that supported the widespread of DoS attacks. In this series, the authors in [29] surveyed the several SOAP based attacks out of which XML injection and Parameter tampering were reported that contaminate SOAP messages to facilitate DoS attacks. XML injection attacks insert and modifies indefinite XML tags within a SOAP message, were as Parameter tampering bypass the input validation in order to access the unauthorized information to achieve DoS attack. Both attacks, compromise the web service availability by exhausting server resources, that requires comprehensive and collaborative defense approach for SOA services.

In recent years, the necessity of using the SOM in SOA environment ensures that security risks are minimized through well-defined security policies and access control countermeasures as noted in [1, 2]. Moreover, the most important countermeasures presently used to mitigate DoS attacks are XML Schema Validation [13], XML Schema Hardening [13] and Self-adaptive Schema Hardening [18]. XML Schema validation ensures that the SOAP messages should abide the same set of valid XML Schema as described from the WSDL file. The XML Schema describes strict specifications themselves, but additionally needs to be hardened to strictly prohibit any malicious content that is not specified in the XML Schema. It is important for a schema to adapt for better validation rules learned from the new strains of SOAP message attacks. Several papers [2, 13, 18] surveyed and proposed Schema Validation, Strict WS-Security Policy Enforcement, Schema Hardening, and Event-based SOAP message processing as a countermeasure for web service attacks. Both XML Schema Validation and Hardening techniques have been used to fend XML Signature Wrapping and DoS attacks. Jenson et al. [19] have studied the WS-* Specification and proposed improvised XML Schema definitions to strengthen XML Schema validation to detect Signature Wrapping attacks. The evaluation showed the performance degradation due to increased processing time through applying hardening definitions. Vipul et al. proposed a new self-adaptive schema-hardening algorithm in [13] and its enhanced version in [18]. From the accumulated malicious SOAP messages, the algorithm obtains strict fine-tuned schema to be used to validate SOAP messages. The algorithm was capable to detect most SOAP based attacks contrived on the Web services. Even though the algorithm detected most SOAP based attacks compared to other mitigation techniques, but lacks performance evaluation. In [18] the authors automates schema-hardening process to increase the efficiency of the validation process to detect attacks. However, no evaluation results were presented for the proposed self-adaptive schema-hardening algorithm.

In networks, Hashim et al. [12] adopted the ideology of the Danger Theory (DT) from the field of biology to defend DoS/DDoS attacks in a heterogeneous environment. An Anomaly Detection Framework is proposed to detect DoS attacks that constitute three main processes, namely Initiation Process (IP), Recognition Process (RP), and Co-stimulation Process (CP). The framework analyzes the network traffic pattern to determine the abnormal behavior or real presence of intrusion attacks. This pattern triggers the IP that studies the abnormal network traffic deviation and signals the presence of malicious bandwidth attacks (such as DoS, DDoS or Worms) to RP. The RP is responsible detects malicious anomalies in the network deviated traffic and informs nearby nodes about the possible presence of an attack. The CP confirm an attack by cross-examining the information gained from IP and RP and alerts the nearby nodes in the network about the presence of DoS attacks. The framework's attack detection time and the Quality of Service (QoS) performance showed that it is robust and adaptive in different network domains to detect DoS, DDoS or Worms attacks.

3 Proposed Work

To protect against SOAP based DoS attacks, it is crucial to design and implement a flexible and secure SOAP message security validation scheme. In this paper, we present an application-level Bio-inspired Anomaly Detection Framework (BADF) that acts as a generic security service to protect web-service based-applications as well as the SOM itself from DoS attacks. We describe in more detail the functions and the operation of the BADF framework, the most important information about system processes, and the distribution of the components in SOM, together with the required infrastructure. Moreover, the interaction patterns of the BADF framework within the SOAs environment, concerning the SOM services operations are detailed out. Based on BADF, we derive a "SECurity as a Service" (SECaaS) architecture to be implemented as a web service in the SOM. Our architecture will use a reformed version of the self-adaptive schema-hardening algorithm proposed by Vipul et al. [18] to mitigate SOAP based DoS attacks. In order to capture all these topics in a clear and consistent manner, the proposed framework will be described as a generic message protection security service to realize the vision set by Al-Jaroodi et al. [10] for SOM security services. To protect Web Service from DoS attacks, the BADF is designed as a SOAP message protection security service that uses the countermeasures employed for web services.

Our proposed system would be based on SOA architecture, where Web services communicate with three elements (i) the Service Client, (ii) the UDDI Registry, and (iii) the Service Provider. Our architecture will use a reformed version of the self-adaptive schema-hardening algorithm proposed by [18] to mitigate SOAP based DoS attacks. Our choice to focus on SOAP as the communication protocol stems from the fact that most Web services are offered over HTTP using SOAP within SOA [21]. In order to use a web service, Clients send SOAP-requests (XML document) to request a Web service, which has been previously published to the UDDI registry by the Service provider. When receiving the SOAP-request message, Service providers respond with a SOAP-response message to fulfil the Client's request. To guard against SOAP DoS attacks, the SOAP-request message need to be handled carefully before it is parsed for in-memory representation in case attacks are infused within the request. Our security service is designed to handle SOAP-request message attack and provide mitigation against XML SOAP-based attacks. In Sect. 3.1, we illustrate BADF inter-action in the SOA and preliminary penetration testing phase required for BADF online operation. In Sect. 3.2 we present our proposed framework and then in Sect. 3.3 we derive its complexity. Moreover, in Sect. 3.4 we outline the components of our derived architecture.

3.1 BADF Interaction in the SOA

The proposed BADF is a framework for a generic security service that interacts with SOAP messages similar to any other web service in the SOA environment. SOA platform is composed of three main components, which are (i) the Service Client, (ii) the UDDI Registry, and (iii) the Service Provider. The communication among these three components is executed through SOAP messages, i.e. SOAP is used as the communication protocol. The BADF is designed as a generic security service to operate at the SOM layer. Initially, the BADF is activated in response to the SOAP request messages received at the registry as part of the message exchange occurring within SOA. The BADF interaction within the SOA is illustrated in the Fig. 1 and described below.

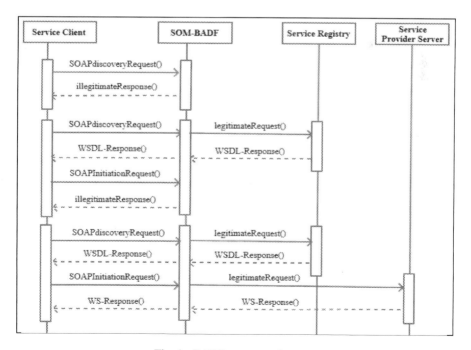

Fig. 1. BADF sequence diagram.

1. The Service registry (UDDI) uses the information included within the service description (WSDL) to catalogue each web service, thus the Service Client queries a service by sending a SOAP discovery request to the registry. The SOAP request will pass through BADF. Here, BADF as a security service is activated to filter the SOAP request, and passes it to the registry if it is legitimate. If it is an illegitimate request, the BADF drops the request and sends SOAP response with attack vectors. In case the request is legitimate, the Service registry searches for the requested service and replies with a SOAP-response with the service description, indicating where to locate the service and how to invoke it. Now, the Service Client sends SOAP initiation request to the server of the Service Provider.

2. SOM as a gateway: When a Service Client makes a SOAP initiation request call it passes through the SOM layer. Within the SOM the BADF would serve as a Web service. Here, BADF as a security service is activated to protect requested Web service from incoming SOAP request. If the SOAP request is legitimate, it is passed to the Service Provider.

3. Service Provider Response: Initially the Server provider publishes the web service description (WSDL) to the Service Registry for the Service Client to discover/find it. Upon receiving a SOAP initiation request, the Service Client gets access to the server of the Web Service. With the SOAP-response the Service Provider binds the Service Client to access the requested task of the service.

Initially, the BADF processes would operate offline periodically for penetration testing. This is an essential learning phase, where each SOAP request and its relative schemas are collected in the repository. This training set of schemata would help to learn the improvements required in the Service Provider Reference Schema (SPRS). It would also enable our system to learn new trend of SOAP-DoS attacks that have not been previously studied by our system. In the learning phase, the training set of schemata are generated as follows:

1. IP would perform the validation and if an attack situation is detected it drop the request but activates the RP for analyzing the schema based on the detected attack.

2. The RP performs the schema hardening on the requested schema, and store a copy of hardened schema with the SPRS. This schema would be used at IP for the next incoming SOAP request.

3. After a corpus of hardened schemata gets accumulated by the RP, the CP develops a single hardened schema by merging SPRS with all hardened schemata. This merged schema will be used at IP for attack detection for the next round of incoming SOAP request. And the learning process continues periodically until a larger attack detection ratio is achieved compared to already addressed attacks in the system.

In our evaluation, as the CP algorithm is not completely implemented, the training set is generated only with the RP consecutively. For BADF use case, we applied the hardening on a copy of SPRS in the first iteration of RP. Each time the RP is activated, the hardening would be performed on the same generated copy and would be used by IP for next SOAP request. This would strengthen the validation at IP, as the schema is tuned not only from the attacked sections, but also for the lenient structure of the schema, as attackers contriving malformed incoming SOAP message could use this lenient schema structure. As a result, validation and hardening provides self-learning and self-optimization to combat future attacks. Similar to CP learning, the process continues periodically until a larger attack ratio is achieved compared to already addressed attacks. This penetration-testing phase would strengthen the validation process of BADF, as the reference schema is developed from administered range of DoS attacks techniques.

3.2   Biologically Inspired Anomaly Detection Framework (BADF)

Our proposed Biologically Inspired Anomaly Detection Framework (BADF) draws on the biologically inspired Anomaly Detection Framework presented in networks by Hashim et al. [12]. Our framework employs the three processes defined in [12] namely: (i) the Initiation Process (IP), (ii) the Recognition Process (RP) and (iii) the Co-stimulation Process (CP). Figure 2 shows the interaction of the three processes within BADF and the details of their operation are presented below.

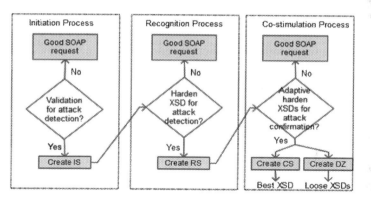

Fig. 2. Biologically inspired anomaly detection framework (BADF) (Source [20]).

i. Initiation Process

Receiving a SOAP request at the UDDI registry activates the Initiation Process (IP). The IP is responsible for validating the XML schema of the incoming SOAP-request messages. The XML schema validation is an important measure for checking the syntactical correctness of incoming messages. Schema validation checks for the presence of broken attributes or additional unusual elements within the message body. Detection of malfunctioned elements is considered as traces of attacks. These attack traces are marked within the XML schema and will be referred to here on as "attack vectors". In order to perform SOAP validation, the IP checks the received message structure against the XML Schema Document (XSD) associated with the corresponding Web Service. Usually, the XSD is a modified XML Schema derived from the WSDL, which is a Web Service interface description document. Initially, the XSD provided by the Service Provider (SP) will be used as the reference schema (RS) for the validation step at IP. However, this Service Provider Reference Schema (SPRS) will be later replaced by the XSD updated at the RP and CP. Thus, the main task of the IP is to ensure the correctness of SOAP input parameters and operations, as specified in the web service description and as required by the Service provider. During validation, if the message does not abide by the schema structure of the XSD, the message is identified as an attack. The SOAP message is dropped, but the attacks vectors are identified to be used in the RP. Accordingly, the IP would send a SOAP-response message to the Client indicating the presence of an attack. Since an attack can also be due to the weak strictness of the service schema document (XSD), it is important to further investigate the schema itself. The schema used for validation should be as strict as possible to hamper modification inside the message body.

It is possible that false positive situation arises, when Clients send SOAP request with unintentional wrong queries. This always happen when schema grammar rules are not strictly defined. For example, to register a new client "createUser" action is performed with clients details as shown in Fig. 3(a). But in Fig. 3(b) the schemata declares the definition "deleteAllUsers" element within "createUsers" element, this would delete all users data if client accidently select "deleteAllUsers" Hence, it is important to separate both "createUser" and "deleteAllUsers" actions in schema for the same element <createUser>.

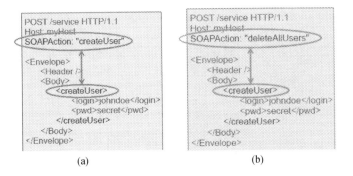

(a)   (b)

Fig. 3. False positive example of SOAP message.

To combat false positive situations due to schema inefficiencies, any detected attack by the IP is sent to the RP and the CP for further investigation. Thus, in case the validation of a SOAP message fails, the IP generates a danger signal, namely the Initiation Signal (IS), for any malformed SOAP message to initiate the Recognition Process (RP). In addition, IP marks the attack vectors identified in the defective XSD in the XSD repositories to be further investigated by the RP.

ii. Recognition Process

The Recognition Process (RP) is initiated when receiving the IS signal. The RP is responsible for XML schema hardening of any defective XSDs. Thus, the RP reads the attack vectors of the message that was previously identified as an attack, as well as the corresponding XSD for further investigation. To develop a hardened XSD, the RP would first read the Web Service description document of the attacked web service. Basically, this description describes the grammar that XSD should follow. This description is parsed to develop a stricter grammar structure that would enhance the XSD operation. The structure contents, elements, rules, and definitions of the updated schema should all abide by the set of Web service description specifications as defined by the service provider and written in the WSDL. As not all grammar description is possible here, we present a subset of grammar rules as examples in what follows for the concrete part of the schema:

a. Replacing maxOccurs = "unbounded" in complex data types with an adequate number, e.g. maxOccurs = "2000". This limitation it is no longer possible to flood a Web Service with endless series of elements.

Replacing simple types without length restriction with a corresponding data type containing a length restriction. This can be implemented by adding an XML Schema facette to the simple type definition inside the types section of the Web Service description. Restricting simple types is easier and more natural than limiting the message's total length.

Removing all operations, which are not intended to be called from the Internet.

Abiding by the WSDL specifications, the RP generates the schema structure that represents the hardened XSD and stores the updated XSD into the Schema repository to be subsequently used by the IP in the validation step. However, the RP would not update the reference schema (SPRS) initially given by the service provider. Typically, from now on the newly hardened schema (XSD) would be used as the reference schema instead of the SPRS. After performing the hardening step, the RP decides whether the IS was issued as a result of an attack, or as a result of a lenient schema. The RP identifies an attack situation, when the structure of the SOAP message to interact with services is altered, as compared to concrete part of XSD. On the contrary, a lenient schema is an XSD that usually has loose grammar definitions for both abstract and concrete part. For example, a SOAP message in Fig. 3 has a lenient schema which is shown in Fig. 4. In Fig. 4(a) is a lenient schema as it has a "deleteAllUser" action specified within "createUser" element. Even though the schema structure is logical to a delete user with the input username/password, but there is a possibility of unhandled input operations. Hence, in Fig. 4(b) the element "deleteAllUser" is separated from element "createUser" by the RP.

In case of an attack, the RP immediately issues the Recognition Signal (RS) for investigating the attack further at the Co-stimulation Process (CP). In case of a lenient schema, the RP issues the Recognition Signal (RS) only after the number of logged XSDs for a specific web service has exceeded a preset threshold indicating recurring incidences of false positive alerts.

i. Co-stimulation Process

The Co-stimulation Process (CP) is initiated as a result of the RS signal issued by the RP. The CP is responsible for self-adaptive schema hardening for all defective XSDs that have been accumulated for all SOAP messages requesting a specific Web service. The purpose of the CP is to develop improvised solutions learned from the detection of

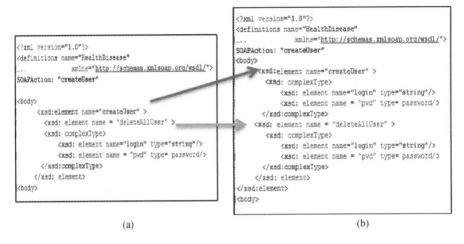

Fig. 4. Example of (a) lenient schema and (b) hardened schema.

an attack at the IP and its consequent mitigation at RP. The CP is a crucial step as the validation and hardening of XML schemata that were previously detected, and recognized as attacks, could possess some inaccuracies while issuing the danger signals; IS and RS. This inaccuracy could be due to the flexible and permissive nature of the schemata, where security issues might arise, yet are not evident at first sight. Hence, a complete refinement is necessary to generate a strict XML Schema that would be learned from multiple logged-in hardened-XSD attacks for a particular Web service. Upon receiving the RS, the CP would be activated to perform self-adaptive schema hardening to develop a strict XML schema (XSD) to be later used at the IP for validation.

The self-adaptive algorithm that is used by the CP in our proposed framework draws on the self-adaptive algorithm presented by [18], with some modifications, which will be pointed out later. The algorithm presented herein considers only the malformed XSDs that were logged by the RP. The algorithm initially measures the similarity between each malformed XSDs with respect to the SPRS. Based on this similarity measure the algorithm generates a reduced set of self-hardened schemata. These 'self-hardened' schemata are then merged together to obtain one single XML Schema (XSD). Basically, this new XSD would not update the SPRS rather it would update the hardened-XSD produced at the RP to be used in the validation step at the IP thereafter. We anticipate that our algorithm will achieve time efficiency by confining its operation to the malformed XSDs thus minimizing the time required to attain progressive results (shown in Sect. 3.3). The stages of our algorithm are shown in Fig. 5. As shown in the figure, our algorithm is similar to Vipul in the first and second stage only. Furthermore, our algorithm takes as input the XSDs hardened by the RP in contrast to Vipul et al. [18] algorithm that works on XSDs generated from SOAP-requests. The stages of CP algorithm are detailed below.

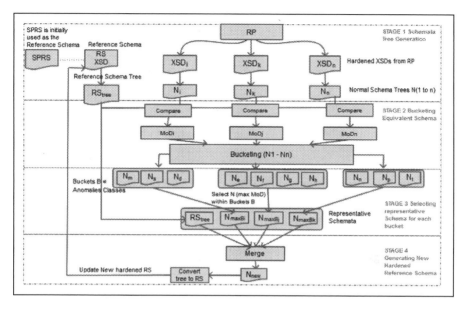

Fig. 5. CP Schema hardening algorithm (Source [20]).

Stage 1 Schema Tree Generation. As pointed out by [18], it is inconvenient to directly compare XSDs. Therefore, all hardened XSDs generated at the RP, as well as the reference XSD, will be first transformed to normalized tree representations. To generate the normalized schema tree representations we use the same methodology adopted in [18], where each XSD is traversed and for each XSD tag encountered a node will be introduced. Each node in the generated schema tree will have the following four attributes:

- Node Name: this represents the name given to an Element and/or an Attribute. However, for nodes that do not have a name, such as nodes that represent meta-data as complexType, simpleType, sequence, etc...., Node Name will be the name for the meta-data that the node represents,
- Node Type: this represents the type of the node such as an element, an attribute, an extension, a restriction, a sequence, a complexType or a simpleType, etc....,
- Data Type: data type of a node, and
- Cardinality: this refers to the minimum and maximum number of occurrences of an element.

For each of the generated trees, a tree signature is devised using a key generation function that uniquely identifies each schema tree.

Stage 2 Bucketing Equivalent Schemas. The main aim of this stage is to determine the equivalence among the generated trees in an attempt to cluster equivalent schemata together. We opine that XSDs generated due to similar attack attempts, or similar malformed SOAP-requests will have high equivalence, thus will fall into the same bucket. As in [18], equivalence among two schema trees is determined through the measure of difference (MoD), which is two dimensional scalar quantity that represents an extent to which two schemas differ. The similarity between normalized schema tree (Ni) and reference schema tree (RS) is derived through the *Graftcost* and *Prunecost*, from Compute Cost algorithm in Fig. 6 and detailed in [18]. The total insertion cost for all nodes calculated at the root node for RS is called graftcost. Similarly, the total deletion cost for all nodes calculated at the root node for Ni is called prunecost. The graftcost of tree RS and prunecost of tree Ni are used to derive MoD. For calculating the MoD among all schemata we adopt the algorithm presented in [18, 22] shown in Fig. 7, which reduces the number of comparisons by determining the equivalence among schemata by calculating the MoD between each of the normalized schema trees (N_i) and the reference schema tree (RS). Schema trees that have similar MoD with respect to the reference schema tree will be considered equivalent and will be grouped together in the same Bucket. In this work, similar MoD means that the two dimensional

```
     Input: root r for tree T
     Output: Cost for creating T

1    sum₀ = GetNodeCost(r)
2    for each child in r do      //Get Cost for a node at a time from leaf to root
3        ComputeCost (child)
4        sum₀ += Cost (child)
5    end for
6    sum₁ = infinity
7    if rContainedIn is not empty then   //Get subtree traversal cost, if similar
8        sum₁ = GetTreeCost(r);
9    end if
10   Cost(r) = Min(sum₀, sum₁)
11   return Cost
```

Fig. 6. Compute cost algorithm.

```
     Input: tree RS, tree N, GraftCost, PruneCost
     Output: measure of difference (MoD)

1    M = Degree(treeRS)
2    N = Degree(treeN)
3
4    //Edit distance measure between a source tree N and a destination tree RS
5    Distance = new int[M][N]
6    //Comparing trees attributes Name and Type are equal setup insertion/ deletion
7    if ((treeRS→Name == treeN→Name) && (treeRS→Type == treeN →Type))
8        Distance[0][0] = 1
9    else
10       Distance[0][0] = 0
11
12   for (int j = 1; j ≤ N; j++)
13       Distance [0][j] = Distance [0][j-1] + Graftcost(treeNⱼ)  //Add Insertion Cost
14   for (int i = 1; i ≤ M; i++)
15       Distance [i][0] = Distance [i-1][0] + PruneCost(treeRSᵢ)  //Add Deletion Cost
16   for (int i = 1; i ≤ M; i++)
17       for (int j = 1; j ≤ N; j++)
18           dist[i][j] = min{          //Choose min of subtrees cost
19               Distance [i-1][j-1] + GetMeasureOfDifference(treeRS[i], treeN[j])
20               Distance [i][j-1] + Graftcost(treeN[j])
21               Distance [i-1][j] + Prunecost(treeRS[i])
22           }
23   return Distance[M][N]   // MoD measure for tree N and tree RS
```

Fig. 7. Measure of Difference (MoD).

scalar quantity calculated for the MoD is within a given range. For our purpose, we create a list for each bucket that stores the schema tree signature and its equivalent MoD value with respect to the reference schema.

Stage 3 Selecting Representative Schema Tree for Each Bucket. We speculate that the schema trees grouped into the same bucket are those that represent the XSDs that have been generated in response to similar anomaly situations. Accordingly, the schema trees grouped within the same bucket represent the XSDs that incorporate the refinements/updates that detect one class of anomalies. Furthermore, we reason that within each bucket, the schema tree with the maximum MoD with respect to the reference schema tree can be considered the representative schema tree for the rest of the trees within the same bucket as a larger MoD implies a greater degree of hardening has been applied to the schema. Thus to get a representative schema tree for each bucket, we sort the list created for each bucket in the previous step in descending order based on the value of the MoD, and pick the schema tree with the highest MoD.

Stage 4 Generating a New Hardened Reference Schema. A new hardened reference schema tree will be created by merging the reference schema tree with all representative schema trees identified in the previous step. This merging step ensures that the newly generated reference schema tree will incorporate all hardening refinements/updates required to detect the different anomaly classes that have been encountered so far. The newly generated reference schema tree will be converted back to an XSD representation and passed back to the IP to be used in the validation step. To do so, the CP activates the Co-stimulation signal (CS) to update the reference schema to the newly generated XSD. In addition, the CP activates the Danger Zone (DZ) signal that maps the left out schema trees within each bucket to associated SOAP-requests, to be used at the network level to identify sources of anomalies.

3.3   Complexity Analysis of BADF

The validation and hardening steps used in IP and RP are based on selection operations therefore, the time complexity is constant. The CP-algorithm is based on Edit Distance [18, 22] and XSDs Edit Distance [23], where the complexity for Stage 1 and 2 have already been proven within each of the cited references. In addition, for Stage 4 the algorithms for constructing the deltas from XS-Diff [24] and XSD_merge [25] algorithms have been proven as optimal algorithms for both time and space. In what follows we will be discussing the complexity analysis from the respective papers for CP stages. The following notations will be used in our analysis.

  i. RS is the reference schema tree
 ii. N_i is the normalized tree i for N number of trees
iii. $|N_i|$ is number of nodes in tree i
 iv. $N_{max} = max(|N_1|, |N_2|, ...|N_n|)$ where i = 1 to n
  v. N_1 and N_2 are two representative schema trees
 vi. $V_b > V_1$ and $V_b -> V_2$ are delta documents
vii. M is a path in tree N_i

viii. $|M|$ is number of nodes on the path or sequence in tree N_i

ix. C is the number of components in tree N_i, where C are group of similar nodes

Stage 1. The XSD documents are parsed to construct XSD trees (RS inclusive). For an XSD_i, a normalized tree (N_i) would be constructed in $O(|N_i|)$.

Stage 2. The graftcost and prunecost in Fig. 6 can be calculated by post-order traversals of both trees; RS and N_i, which costs $O(|RS||N_{max}|)$ as shown in [38]. The algorithm in Fig. 7 is a dynamic programming procedure that computes the MoD from the pre-computed graft and prune cost of RS and N_i trees. Complexity of MoD computation depends on the nodes of the input trees RS and N_i, as it is called once for each pair of nodes at the same depth in the input trees. This results in a complexity of O $(|RS||N_{max}|)$ for Stage 1 and 2 as proved in [22, 23].

Stage 3. Selection of representative tree and bucketing is a selective operation with a constant cost.

Stage 4: To develop a hardened reference schema, the complexity of the three-way merging algorithm presented in [25] is derive into two steps (i) derive deltas cost and (ii) merging cost.

Delta Cost. To derive delta, we adopted XSDiff algorithm in [24]. First, for every node in both trees RS and N_i, a call is made that finds the matching component. The general definition of this function would be to enumerate all components and choose the best one defined as the one component with the closest ancestor. It works by enumerating components and testing the ancestor up to a given depth in the trees. The time complexity of matching is O (C log $(|M|)$), where C is the number of components, M is the maximum path and log $(|M|)$ is the maximum path length allowed for ancestor's lookup or a match.

Second, the delta construction depends on the matches obtained previously. These matches are important for the two major operations: (i) insert/delete, and (ii) migrate/update operations. Finding components that have been deleted or inserted only requires testing components in both trees RS and N_1 which have been matched. The insert and delete operations works in linear time with cost $O(|M|)$ as stated in [24].

Finding components that requires update or migrate operations, the Longest Common Subsequence (LCS) algorithm is applied on the sequential components. The LCS have a time and space cost of $O(C^2/log(C))$ [26], where C^2 is the space cost and C is the number of components. In practical applications, when applying LCS on a fixed length of input nodes for merging, the algorithm obtains subsequences that has time and space cost in O(C) [26]. As given in [24] the number of components (C) is always less than the input tree (N_1) nodes. Using LCS merging heuristic for the number of components gives cost in O(C). To derive optimal delta as stated in [24], the matching takes (C log $(|M|)$), where log($|M|$) is constant for migrate/update operation. So, the overall worst-case time and space complexity to derive delta is O(C).

Merging Cost. The merging complexity evaluation depends on the delta operation cost. To derive a hardened merge tree N_{Merge}, the algorithm in [25] takes as a input an edited tree version N_1 and the deltas of the $V_b \rightarrow V_1$ and $V_b \rightarrow V_2$. Algorithm in [25] loops over the components of input tree N_1 and tries to detect duplicates components in given deltas ($V_b \rightarrow V_1$ and $V_b \rightarrow V_2$) using the update, move, and delete procedures. This costs $O(C)$ for input tree N_1. Finally, we note that the number of delta operation for component lookup in delta $V_b \rightarrow V_1$ will affect the running time. As stated in [25], the initial size of components C for the input tree N_i, increases with delta operation. Therefore, the number of components is maximally $O(C)$ since $C < N_1$ then the overall complexity will be bounded by $O(C)$. The delta operation cost is $O(C)$ which dominated the cost of maximum number of components. Hence, the overall complexity of optimal merging as mentioned in [25] is $O(C)$.

The overall complexity of CP is approximated as the complexity of the two major stages which are Stage 2 and 4. Stage 2 has an asymptotic time complexity of $O(|RS\| N_{max}|)$, while stage 4 has an optimal $O(C)$ time complexity. If we consider the costs of these two steps further, we find that by using dynamic programming in MoD the cost to edit the distance between pairs of trees of various sizes grows in an almost perfect linear fashion with tree size [22]. Similarly, the delta operations performed on the size of components will also grow linearly. Therefore we can conclude that the overall asymptotic time complexity of the CP algorithm in the worst case scenario will be bounded by the maximum of these two operations, i.e., the complexity of $O(CP) = \max (O(|RS\|N_{max}|), O(C))$.

3.4 Security as a Service Based on BADF

Based on our previously presented framework we derive an architecture that illustrates the execution of the BADF processes to detect and mitigate SOAP-based DoS attacks. The derived Security as a Service (SECaaS) architecture is labelled as the "SECaaS Architecture" in Fig. 8. The components of the Security Service are (i) the SOAP message validator to validate SOAP messages, (ii) the Schema repository to stored XSDs, (iii) the SOAP-request repository to store malicious requests, (iv) the Schema hardening mitigation parser to develop hardened schema, and (v) the Reference Schema. The proposed Security Service is published within the UDDI registry as a stand-alone web service and acts as a generic Web service that secures other web services running in the UDDI registry at the application layer. Each of the SECaaS processes operates independently and their execution is loop-free and sequential. In addition, each process depends on the different instances of the XSDs that is stored progressively in the schema repository for the correct overall operation of the security service.

Our Security Service is activated when a client sends a SOAP-request to the registry requesting a particular web service. For example, in Fig. 8, a SOAP-request is sent to the registry requesting one of the published web services, namely "WS-Response". The SOAP-request for "Web service 1" is handed to our Security Service. Accordingly the IP loads the XSD that is associated with "WS-Response". Initially, this XSD is provided by the service provider and represents the reference schema that will be used

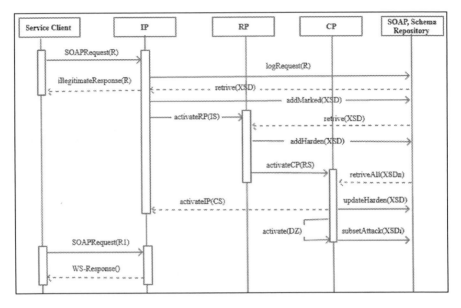

Fig. 8. SECaaS architecture sequence diagram.

by the message validator to validate the SOAP-request message. If the validation of the message fails, the following steps are executed:

(i)   The IP logs the SOAP message as a malicious message in the SOAP-request repository;
(ii) The IP replies to the client with a SOAP-response message identifying the attack vectors
(iii) The IP marks attack traces within the XSD
(iv) The IP triggers the Initiation Signal (IS) to activate the RP.

Upon receiving the IS, the RP retrieves the XSD that has been previously accessed and marked by IP from the schema repository. The RP generates a hardened XSD by applying the hardening rules to the accessed XSD. The refined XSD is stored in the schema repository to replace the older XSD that was previously associated with the message of web service at IP. Typically, as mentioned earlier, the RP generates the Recognition Signal (RS) based on the threshold value for false positive or in response to a detected attack, to initiate the CP.

On receiving the RS, the CP is activated, which means that the dubious SOAP-requests for a particular Web service has either exceeded a given threshold value or has been identified with high confidence as an attack. The CP retrieves all accumulated XSDs for all logged SOAP-requests for a given web service from the repository, and initiates the self-adaptive schema-hardening algorithm over all XSDs for the same Web service request. The hardened XSD would update the last logged XSD by RP that was used as reference schema in the previous processes.

4   Evaluation

The BADF evaluation will be performed by evaluating the SECaaS architecture that we
have derived in the previous section. We have developed a prototype for the SCEaaS
architecture on a localhost and tested its behaviour against DoS SOAP-attacks. The
SECaaS prototype, as shown in Fig. 9, is composed of the main components of the
SOA, namely the SOAP Service Client, the Service Registry UDDI, and the SOAP
Server. The prototype components implement the IP and RP only, whereas the CP is
not implemented completely, we present some rudimentary work.

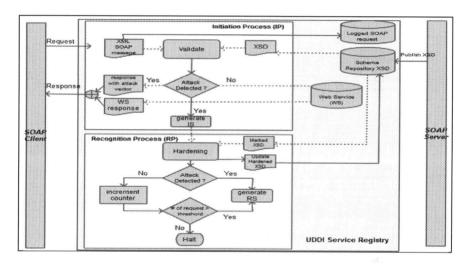

Fig. 9. Flowchart for SECaaS architecture (Source [20]).

4.1   The Development Environment

In our implementation, we have used Eclipse JAX-WS as the SOAP engine and
Apache Tomcat juddi-tomcat-3.3.2 on Microsoft Windows 7 as the SOAP server. For
the Service Registry UDDI, we used jUDDI version juddi-distro-3.3.2. All the user and
service information about the published schema were stored in the MySQL Community
Server 5.5.14 database for jUDDI. All the Web services were developed using Java
(Java SE) version jdk1. 6.0_21. For testing our security service against incoming SOAP
messages we used SoapUI, which is a GUI for unit and load testing of SOAP web
services. To evaluate SECaaS performance, its responses were compared to the
responses generated by an external validation/parser tool [27] that is used in our base
case scenario. We reverted to this evaluation methodology since the comparative
evaluation with the literature mitigation techniques was not possible. This can be
attributed to the fact that to the extent of our knowledge the concept of SECaaS specific
to DoS attacks has not been presented before. Most of the reported work falls short of
evaluation results and address general web service attacks. The techniques discussed in
[15, 19] focused on performance evaluation and used large data sets for testing a

number of web service elements. However, in our case, we care to evaluate the efficacy of SECaaS to detect SOAP based DoS attacks within the SOA. Therefore, we reverted to a local host implementation since an online implementation was not feasible.

To validate the efficacy of our security service on localhost, we built Disease Information Web services, which has multiple APIs. The service operates on 1000 different health trace dataset gathered into a disease database.

4.2   The Types of Attacks

Our evaluation scenarios use four different DoS SOAP-attacks, namely Parameter Tampering, XDoS, XML Injection, and Oversize/Recursive payload. The Parameter Tampering attack infuses malicious content with node/tags within message query to deceive the validator. The XDoS attack tries to exhaust the system resources on the server by iteratively declaring strings. The XML Injection injects additional nodes or modifies existing nodes so as to change the operation parameters of the message. Finally, the Recursive payload adds additional nodes repeatedly, which are excessively large, to deplete CPU cycles. All these attacks (listed in Table 1) were performed using a malicious insider or man-in-the-middle techniques of DoS. Hence, to generate a good set of inputs to be used in testing, we looked at the WSDL document of Disease Web Service to find loopholes. These attacks traces were included in the SOAP request to measure the efficiency of SECaaS Architecture.

Table 1. DoS SOAP-based attacks detected comparison (Source [20]).

# Attack type	Attack code	Attack details	SOAP REQ & Parameters	Attack results	
				SECaaS on	SECaaS off
Parameter tampering	PT-1	Buffer Overflow of String Types	\<name> 'Cornary temperedtext-CAD' \</name>	detected	detected
	PT-2	Buffer Overflow of Integer Types	\<ldl> −1 \</ldl>	detected	undetected
	PT-3	Field Manipulation causes URL manipulation	\<heart_diseases RegistrationNumber = "1295857444"> ...... \</heart_diseases>	detected	undetected
XDoS	XD-1	XML Extra Long Names	\<name> Ischemic Heart Diseases \</name> *repeated 50 times*	detected	detected
	XD-2	XML Namespace Prefix Attack	\<xs:heart_diseases description = "Common type" *—repeated 100 times—*>	detected	undetected

(continued)

Table 1. (*continued*)

# Attack type	Attack code	Attack details	SOAP REQ & Parameters	Attack results	
				SECaaS on	SECaaS off
XML injection	XIJ-1	Reference Entity Attack	\<name> &xxe; \</name>	detected	undetected
	XIJ-2	Internal Entity Attack 1	\<name> > \</name>	detected	undetected
	XIJ-3	Internal Entity Attack 2	\<name> < \</name>	detected	undetected
	XIJ-4	Invalid XML meta-characters (quotes)	\<xs:attribute heart_diseases = ''> 345675453' \</xs: attribute>	detected	detected
	XIJ-5	Invalid XML meta-characters (comment tag)	\<xs:attribute treatment_cost = ''> 465 < !– \</xs:attribute>	detected	undetected
Recursive payload	RP-1	Tag recursive calls	\<level> \<level> — Beginner— \</level> \</level> > *called 100 times*	detected	detected
	RP-2	XML Recursive Entity Expansion	\<!ENTITY x8 "&x7; &x7;"> *called as* \<attack> &x8; \</attack>	detected	undetected

4.3   Evaluating the SECaaS Architecture

Our evaluation is composed of two scenarios; a base scenario and a SECaaS scenario. In the base scenario, the security service was turned off and an external parser was used to validate the SOAP requests. In the SECaaS scenario, the security service was turned on and the SOAP requests were validated at IP. In each scenario, we send one malformed SOAP-request followed by several legitimate SOAP requests. Each malformed SOAP-request comprises an attack and invokes a specific web service with some tampered input parameter. Table 1 details the different attacks that were administered to the system in each scenario and the response in each case.

As shown in Table 1, SECaaS prototype was capable of detecting all contrived attacks in contrast to the base case, which missed several attacks. The summary of the results of our evaluation can be seen in Fig. 10. As can be seen, the SECaaS prototype is more capable of attacks detection compared to the base case. We note that our evaluation has covered only a subset of the possible SOAP attacks mentioned in literature, since the exhaustive enumeration of all possible SOAP attacks is not possible. However, we claim that the results obtained provide a proof of concept and show the efficacy of our SECaaS architecture to defend web services against SOAP based attacks.

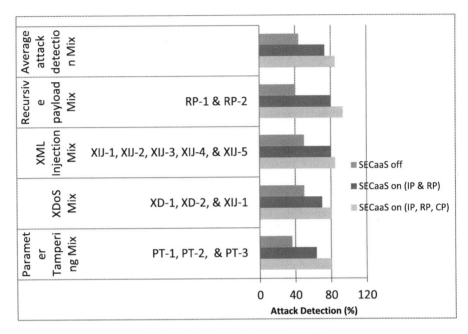

Fig. 10. Attack detection results (%).

4.4 Preliminary Work on CP

Due to the time limitation and un-availability of tools we did not design the tree transformation API. Instead, we designed a corpus of schema trees individually as normalized tree representations. The XSDs stored in the Schema repository at the RP are converted into tree structures to be fed into Stage 2 of the CP algorithm. The number of schema trees generated for this test, their type and notations are listed in Table 2 below.

Table 2. Number of schema tree generation.

Schema Tree Generated	Schema Tree Attack Type	Notation
Reference Schema Tree		**RS**
Normalized Schema Tree	Un-attacked	NS_i
Normalized Schema Tree	Un-attacked	NS_j
Normalized Schema Trees for Parameter Tampering	PT-1	N_{P1}
	PT-2	N_{P2}
Normalized Schema Trees for XDoS	XD-1	N_{d1}
	XD-2	N_{d2}
Normalized Schema Trees for XML Injection	XIJ-1	N_{X1}
	XIJ-2	N_{X2}

In Stage 2 in the CP, each of the schema trees Ni, are compared with the RS tree to compute the MoD between the two trees. Based on the MoD, all trees are clustered into buckets. From our analysis and experimentation, two or three buckets are generated

Table 3. Bucketing trees in each trial.

# of Trials	Set of Input Trees	Bucket(B₁)	Bucket(B₂)	Bucket(B₃)
First Trial	NS$_i$, NS$_j$ N$_{P1}$,N$_{P2}$, N$_{d1}$, N$_{d2}$, N$_{X1}$,N$_{X2}$	NS$_i$, N$_{P1}$,N$_{P2}$ N$_{d1}$	N$_{d2}$	NS$_j$ N$_{X1}$, N$_{X2}$
Second Trial	NS$_i$, NS$_j$ N$_{P1}$,N$_{P2}$, N$_{d1}$, N$_{d2}$,	NS$_i$, N$_{P1}$,N$_{P2}$ N$_{d1}$	N$_{d2}$	NS$_j$
Third Trial	N$_{P1}$,N$_{P2}$, N$_{d1}$, N$_{d2}$, N$_{X1}$, N$_{X2}$	N$_{P1}$,N$_{P2}$	N$_{d1}$, N$_{d2}$	N$_{X1}$,N$_{X2}$

each time as we repeated Stage 2. Therefore, we tried to initiate Stage 2 testing process by sending some combination of normalized schema trees with the reference schema tree. The input schema trees combination set and the resulted buckets clustered schema trees are shown in Table 3.

Therefore, the aim of performing different sets of trials (e.g. 3 trials in Table 3) on Stage 2 was to test the correctness of the CP-algorithm. From the bucketing results in Table 3, we came to conclude that the algorithm used for bucketing in CP was able to distinguish classes of anomalies as seen from the separation of schemas into different buckets. For example, Bucket B$_1$ had trees for parameter tampering, B$_2$ had trees for XDoS, and B$_3$ had trees for XML Injection. It is worthy to note that the third trial perfectly identified each class of anomalies into separate buckets. Therefore, we selected the representative schema trees with the maximum MoD from the third trial as follows; B$_1$ = {N$_{P1}$}, B$_2$ = {N$_{d2}$}, and B$_3$ = {N$_{X2}$}. All these schema trees get to be merged with the RS tree to develop a hardened N$_{new}$ schema tree. The evaluation results for N$_{new}$ as a new reference schema is indicated in Fig. 10. AS expected the attack detection improved when adding CP to IP and RP.

5   Conclusion

In this paper the topic of security in the context of Web services and SOM was addressed. Especially the focus was to address the SOAP based DoS attacks on the Web service and to strengthen the SOM security. To secure web service based applications the Bio-inspired Anomaly Detection Framework (BADF) is presented. Based on BADF we derive "Security as a Service" (SECaaS) architecture and its prototype for evaluation. The evaluation shows that our prototype was able to detect most SOAP based DoS attacks compared to commercial external parser. We also presented some rudimentary work of CP algorithm and tested its behavior with IP and RP, which showed good results. Therefore, our future work would be to fully integrate and evaluate CP in the BADF. Moreover, to focus on performance evaluation of the presented works in comparison to other techniques.

References

1. Jensen, M., Gruschka, N., Herkenhoner, R., Luttenberger, N.: SOA and web services: new technologies, new standards - new attacks. In: ECOWS 2007 Fifth European Conference on Web Services, pp. 35–44 (2007). https://doi.org/10.1109/ecows.2007.9
2. Jensen, M., Gruschka, N., Herkenhoner, R.: A survey of attacks on web services. J. Comput. Sci. Res. Dev. **24**, 185–197 (2009). https://doi.org/10.1007/s00450-009-0092-6
3. Bichler, M., Lin, K.J.: Service-oriented computing. IEEE Comput. **39**(3), 99–101 (2006). https://doi.org/10.1109/MC.2006.102
4. Gudgin, M., Hadley, M., Mendelsohn, N., Moreau, J.J., Nielsen, H.F., Karmarkar, A., Lafon, Y.: SOAP Version 1.2. In: W3C Recommendation specification—SOAP Version 1.2, vol. 24 (2007). http://www.w3.org/TR/soap12
5. Web Services Security: SOAP Messages Security 1.1. In OASIS Standard. http://www.oasis-open.org/
6. Al-Jaroodi, J., Mohamed, N.: Service-oriented middleware: a survey. J. Netw. Comput. Appl. **35**, 211–220 (2010). https://doi.org/10.1016/j.jnca.2011.07.013
7. Al-Jaroodi, J., Mohamed, N., Aziz, J.: Service oriented middleware: trends and challenges. In: Proceedings of the 2010 Seventh International Conference on Information Technology: New Generations (ITNG). IEEE CPS, Las Vegas, USA (2010). https://doi.org/10.1109/itng.2010.55
8. Lazarevic, A., Kumar, V., Srivastava, J.: Intrusion detection: survey. In: Kumar, V., Srivastava, J., Lazarevic, A. (eds.) Managing Cyber Threats: Issues, Approaches, and Challenges, vol. 5, pp. 19–78. Springer, New York (2005). https://doi.org/10.1007/0-387-24230-9_2
9. Al-Jaroodi, J., Jawhar, I., Al-Dhaheri, A., Al-Abdouli, F., Mohamed, N.: Security middleware approaches and issues for ubiquitous applications. Comput. Math. Appl. **60**, 187–197 (2010). https://doi.org/10.1016/j.camwa.2010.01.009. Science Direct
10. Al-Jaroodi, J., Al-Dhaheri, A.: Security issues of service-oriented middleware. Int. J. Comput. Sci. Netw. Secur. **11**(1) (2011)
11. Dressler, F.: Benefits of bio-inspired technologies for networked embedded systems: an overview. In: Dagstuhl Seminar Proceedings. Schloss Dagstuhl, Wadern, Germany (2006)
12. Hashim, F., Munasinghe, K.S., Jamalipour, A.: Biologically inspired anomaly detection and security control frameworks for complex heterogeneous networks. Proc. IEEE Trans. Netw. Serv. Manage. **7**(4), 268–281 (2010). https://doi.org/10.1109/TNSM.2010.1012.0360
13. Vipul, P., Mohandas, R., Alwyn. R.P.: Attacks on web services and mitigation schemes. In: Proceedings of the 2010 International Conference, Security and Cryptography (SECRYPT) (2010)
14. Schäfer, G., Sisalem, D., Kuthan, J.: Denial of Service Attacks and Sip Infrastructure Attack Scenarios and Prevention Mechanisms (2017). https://www.researchgate.net/publication/237572832_DENIAL_OF_SERVICE_ATTACKS_AND_SIP_INFRASTRUCTURE_Attack_Scenarios_and_Prevention_Mechanisms
15. Gruschka, N., Luttenberger, N.: Protecting web services from DoS attacks by SOAP message validation. In: IFIP TC-11 21st International Information Security Conference, SEC, vol. 201, pp. 22–24 (2006)
16. Gruschka, N., Iacono, L.: Vulnerable cloud: SOAP message security validation revisited. In: IEEE International Conference on Web Services ICWS (2009). https://doi.org/10.1109/icws.2009.70
17. Gupta, A.N., Thilagam, P.S.: Attacks on web services need to secure XML on web. Comput. Sci. Eng. Int. J. (CSEIJ) **3**(5) (2013). https://doi.org/10.5121/cseij.2013.3501

18. Patel, V., Mohandas, R., Pais, A.: Safeguarding web services using self-adaptive schema hardening algorithm. In: Wyld, David C., Wozniak, M., Chaki, N., Meghanathan, N., Nagamalai, D. (eds.) CNSA 2011. CCIS, vol. 196, pp. 383–392. Springer, Heidelberg (2011). https://doi.org/10.1007/978-3-642-22540-6_37

19. Jensen, M., Meyer, C., Somorovsky, J., Schwenk, J.: On the effectiveness of XML schema validation for countering XML signature wrapping attacks. IEEE (2011). https://doi.org/10.1109/iwsscloud.2011.6049019

20. Shaikh, J.T., Hassan, H., Hamza, H.: Biologically inspired security as a service for service-oriented middleware. In: Proceedings of the 12th International Conference on Evaluation of Novel Approaches to Software Engineering (ENASE), vol. 1, pp. 121–132. ISBN: 978–989-758-250-9 (2017). https://doi.org/10.5220/0006337801210132

21. OASIS UDDI Specification TC. https://www.oasis-open.org/committees/uddi-spec/faq.php

22. Nierman, A., Jagadish, H.: Evaluating structural similarity in XML documents. In: Proceedings of the Fifth International Workshop on the Web and Databases WebDB, Citeseer, Wisconsin, USA, pp. 61–66 (2002)

23. Mlýnková, I.: Equivalence of XSD constructs and its exploitation in similarity evaluation. In: Meersman, R., Tari, Z. (eds.) OTM 2008. LNCS, vol. 5332, pp. 1253–1270. Springer, Heidelberg (2008). https://doi.org/10.1007/978-3-540-88873-4_24

24. Baqasah, A., Pardede, E., Rahayu, W., Holubova, I.: XS-Diff: XML schema change detection algorithm. Int. J. Web Grid Serv. **11**(2), 160–192 (2015). https://doi.org/10.1504/ijwgs.2015.068897

25. Baqasah, A., Pardede, E., Rahayu, W.: A new approach for meaningful XML schema merging. In: Proceedings of the 16th International Conference on Information Integration and Web-based Applications & Services, pp. 430–439 (2014). https://doi.org/10.1145/2684200.2684302

26. Marian, A., Abiteboul, S., Cobena, G., Mignet. L.: Change-centric management of versions in an XML warehouse. In: Proceedings of the 27th International Conference on Very Large Data Bases, pp. 581–590 (2001)

27. Using XML Schema. http://www.mantidproject.org/Using_XML_Schema

Genomic Tools*: Web-Applications Based on Conceptual Models for the Genomic Diagnosis

José F. Reyes Román[1,2(✉)], Carlos Iñiguez-Jarrín[1,3], and Óscar Pastor[1]

[1] PROS Research Center, Universitat Politècnica de València,
Camino Vera s/n. 46022, Valencia, Spain
{jreyes, ciniguez, opastor}@pros.upv.es
[2] Department of Engineering Sciences, Universidad Central del Este (UCE),
Ave. Francisco Alberto Caamaño Deñó, 21000 San Pedro de Macorís,
Dominican Republic
[3] Departamento de Informática y Ciencias de la Computación,
Escuela Politécnica Nacional, Ladrón de Guevara E11-253, Quito, Ecuador

Abstract. Although experts in the genomics field now work with bioinformatics tools (*software*) to generate genomic diagnoses, the fact is that these solutions do not fully meet their needs. From the perspective of *Information Systems* (IS), the real problems lie in the lack of an approach (i.e., Software Engineering techniques) that can generate correct structures for data management. Due to the problems of *dispersion*, *heterogeneity* and the *inconsistency* of the data, understanding the genomic domain is a huge challenge. To demonstrate the advantages of *Conceptual Modeling* (CM) in complex domains -such as *genomics*- we propose two web-based tools for genomic diagnosis that incorporates: (i) a *Conceptual Model for the direct-to-consumer genetic tests* (DCGT), and (ii) our *Conceptual Model of the Human Genome* (CMHG), both with the aim of taking advantage of *Next-Generation Sequencing* (NGS) for ensuring genomic diagnostics that help to maximize the *Precision Medicine* (PM).

Keywords: Geneslove.me · DCGT · VarSearch · BPMN · CMHG
Conceptual modeling · Precision medicine

1 Introduction

The study and understanding of the human genome (how life works on our planet) could probably be considered one of the great challenges of our century. Thanks to the advances in NGS (*Next-Generation Sequencing*) [1], there has been considerable growth in the generation of genomic and molecular information. In addition, the interactions that are available with this genomic knowledge have a direct impact on the medical environment and *Precision Medicine* (PM) [2].

The application of *Conceptual Modeling* (CM) [3] techniques to the genomic domain now provides solutions and optimizes some of the processes carried out by experts (i.e., in *genetic laboratories* and *hospitals*), and helps to solve the problems that

© Springer International Publishing AG, part of Springer Nature 2018
E. Damiani et al. (Eds.): ENASE 2017, CCIS 866, pp. 48–69, 2018.
https://doi.org/10.1007/978-3-319-94135-6_3

arise in handling the large amounts of information from different sequencing methods. The use of advanced *Information System* (IS) engineering approaches can be useful in this domain due to the huge amount of biological information to be *captured*, *understood* and effectively *managed*. A considerable part of modern Bioinformatics is devoted to the management of genomic data. The existence of a large set of diverse data sources containing large amounts of data in continuous evolution makes it difficult to find convincing solutions [4]. When we addressed this problem from the IS perspective, we understood that precise CMs were required to understand the relevant information in the domain and to clearly fix and represent it to obtain an effective data management strategy.

Research and genetic diagnoses are typical examples of the work done by experts - *biologists*, *researchers* or *geneticists*- every day. However, some information is required to perform these tasks. *Where are these data?* Currently, this information is dispersed in genomic repositories including *web sites*, *databanks*, *public files*, etc., which are completely heterogeneous, redundant, and inconsistent (containing partial information) [5]. In addition, most of these just focus on storing specific information in order to solve a specific problem (e.g., *UniProt*: a catalog of information on proteins).

Due to these characteristics, we are able to estimate the difficulty of experts in finding and manipulating certain genomic information, making this goal almost impossible to achieve. Another relevant factor in the domain is the constant growth and updating of the data (i.e., *biological concepts*). The use of standard definitions of concepts is not mandatory, so that sometimes the same term can have different definitions, in which case the meaning of the concept depends on the interpretation given to it by the expert. After studying this situation, we decided to develop a *Genomic Information System* (GeIS) for facilitating the elaboration of end-user's genetic tests. Two strategies have been followed for accomplishing an adequate data treatment and management policy:

1. To provide *"GenesLove.Me"* (GLM) as a web application designed to generate *direct-to-consumer genetic tests* (DCGT) supported by BPMN [6] and CM [3] techniques to study and analyze the essential elements of the processes involved in the genomic diagnosis process and improve the development of GeIS.

   The current availability of DCGT has a great number of advantages for the genomic domain, making it easier for end-users to access early genetic-origin diseases diagnosis services. Romeo-Malanda [7] defines *"direct-to-consumer genetic analysis[1]"* as a term which is used to describe analytic services offered to detect *'polymorphism'* and *'health-related genetic variations'*.

2. To develop a prototype tool ("VarSearch") for helping the treatment and management of genomic data. This application contrasts a set of genomic variations with the information contained in a database that follows the Conceptual Model of the Human Genome (CMHG). This model is much more general and "ambitious" with respect to the behavior of the human genome, and it consists of the following

---

[1] This type of analysis is available through direct sales systems in *pharmacies* or other *health care bodies*, but the *Internet* has become the main selling channel for *direct-to-consumer genetic analyses* [7].

"views": Structural, Transcription, Variation, Phenotypic, Pathways, and Bibliographic references [4, 8].

Applying GeIS to the bioinformatics domain is a fundamental requirement, since it allows us to structure our *Human Genome Database* (HGDB) with curated and validated data (to treat the data that will be used in the proposed application, we implemented the *SILE methodology* [9]).

The initial research on applying CM approaches to the human genome was reported in the works of Paton [10] and Ram [11]. The main goal in Ram's work was to show the advantages and benefits of using CM to compare and search for the protein in 3D (see other related works in [12]). Reyes et al. describes a CMHG [4] which proposes a domain definition at the conceptual level. From this CMHG, we generated a GeIS to support *VarSearch*. The application of CM helps us to better understand and manage the knowledge of the human genome.

The efficient use of advances in genomic research allows the patient to be treated in a more direct way, which is reflected in results such as: *"better health"* and *"quality of life"*. The genomic domain requires methodologies and modeling techniques capable of integrating innovative ideas into: (a) data management; (b) process improvement; and (c) the inclusion of quality standards.

In this context, the goal of the present study, which is based on our previous work [13], is to explain the functionality of the prototype called *"VarSearch"*, which starts and ends its interaction in the BPMN described above in processes **T10** and **T11**. This tool has been developed with the objective of generating the genetic diagnosis that will be provided to the end-user through the *GenesLove.Me* platform. The advances over our previous work [13] are:

- The description of genetic tools based on conceptual models for the generation of genomic diagnoses, which contribute greatly to the management of the data participating in PM, and
- The explanation of the *VarSearch* prototype, which is used to generate the genomic diagnosis from the HGDB. In addition, preliminary steps will be described to work with the prototype, such as loading the database, selecting different data repositories, and others.

The paper is divided into the following sections: Sect. 2 reviews the present state of the art. Section 3 describes BPMN applied to the genomic diagnosis process. Section 4 contains the two genetic tools (*"GenesLove.Me"* and *"VarSearch"*) based on conceptual models. Section 5 describes a case study with the *VarSearch* tool, and Sect. 6 summarizes the conclusions and outlines future work.

2 Related Work

Bioinformatics now play an important role in contributing advances to the medical and technological sector. Genetic testing reveals existing knowledge about *"genes"* and *"variations"* in the genomic domain, which is used to diagnose diseases of genetic origin in order to *prevent* or *treat* them. This brings PM closer to end-users (i.e., *clients* or *patients*).

The study of genomics (i.e., *data repositories, genetic variations, diseases, treatments*, etc.) is constantly growing and is increasingly seeking to ensure the application of PM. DNA sequencing began in 1977 and since then software tools have been developed for its analysis. Thanks to NGS Technologies [14], it is now possible to manipulate files (e.g., VCF: *Variant Call Format*) in order to generate genetic diagnoses in a more agile and efficient way [15].

2.1 Precision Medicine (PM) and Genetic Tests

PM is a way of treating patients that allows doctors to identify an illness and select the treatment most likely to help the patient according to a genetic concept of the disease in question (therefore it has also been called *Personalized Medicine*) [16]. The advantages of genetic tests are innumerable and allow us to identify mutations or alterations in the genes and are of great use and interest in clinical (*personalized medicine*) and the early diagnosis of diseases. By 2008 there were around 1,200 genetic tests available around the world [17], but they had some limitations (e.g., *data management, genome sequencing*, etc.) and their cost was quite high.

For this reason, companies were interested in reducing costs and providing services to end-users in the comfort of their own homes. Technological advances played a fundamental role in the genomic environment, since the introduction of the NGS for sequencing samples made it possible to obtain sequences more quickly and cheaply [18, 19].

23andMe is an American company that offers a wide range of services [20], and the type of information obtained from genetic samples is oriented to (i) *genetic history* (ancestors) and (ii) *personal health* (risk of diseases), and is presented mostly in probabilistic terms [21].

In the same way, in Spain companies of this type have emerged (e.g., TellMeGen[2] or IMEGEN[3]), all with the aim of providing genetic tests to end-users, simply and in the form of providing a diagnosis that allows end-users to take reactive or corrective actions (e.g., *prevention* and *treatment*) to improve their quality of life.

The genomic tools presented in this work goes one step beyond from an *Information Systems* and *Conceptual Modeling* points of view, providing a working platform strictly dependent on a precise *Conceptual Model of the Human Genome* (CMHG), that semantically characterizes the genomic data to be managed and interpreted.

2.2 Genetic Tools for Annotating Variations

In genomic practical settings, the annotation of variation is the most common strategy used for trying to determine which are the correct data to be considered. In this work, we consider *SnpEff, Annovar*, and *VEP*, which are three of the major tools that attempt to classify variants.

---

[2] www.tellmegen.com/.

[3] https://www.imegen.es/.

SnpEff [22] annotates and predicts the effects of genetic variants building a local database by downloading information from trusted resources. After the database is loaded, SnpEff can analyze thousands of variants per second. However, loading a database is a very expensive task from the point of view of resources, and it is even recommended to increase the default Java memory parameters.

On the other hand, although SnpEff can be run in a distributed fashion (using *Amazon Cloud Services*), and offers limited web interfaces, it is command-line oriented. SnpEff can also be integrated with other tools such as GATK[4] or Galaxy[5].

The Annovar software tool annotates variants [23]. The first step when using Annovar scripts is to populate its local database tables using an extensive set of external sources. It is then possible to annotate variants from a VCF file to get a separate custom tab file. wAnnovar (*Web Annovar*) provides an easy and intuitive web-based access to the most popular Annovar functionalities and allows users to submit their own files and wait for the results of the analysis report. Like SnpEff, Annovar is command-line oriented and does not provide a well-documented API for framework integration.

VEP (*Variant Effect Predictor*) [24] determines the effect of the variants by querying external databases directly, with no need to load the local database (although it is recommended for performance reasons). Like SnpEff and Annovar, it is command-line oriented and web-access is functionally limited. In order to achieve integration, basic VEP functionalities can be extended using VEP plugins. Table 1 compares *VarSearch* with these three tools:

Table 1. Annotation tools comparison.

Feature	SnpEff	Annovar	VEP	VarSearch
Distributed architecture	√	√	√	√
Type of application	Desktop	Desktop	Desktop	Web
Multiple database sources	√	√	√	√
Standard input formats	√	√	√	√
Standard output formats	√	X	√	√
Design paradigm	Data-oriented	Data-oriented	Data-oriented	Model-driven
Integration facilities	√	X	√	√

As shown, *VarSearch* overcomes limitations by:

- Being based on a Java EE multitier applications architecture, which is a solid approach to high-level applications in complex and heterogeneous environments. This allows *VarSearch* to be easily integrated with other web applications; the software is fully localized, etc.
- Using a service oriented framework [25], which improves interoperability and integration.

---

[4] https://software.broadinstitute.org/gatk/.

[5] https://usegalaxy.org/.

- Relying on a model-driven instead of a data-oriented paradigm. *VarSearch* uses a projection of the CMHG.
- Providing a functionally complete web interface with the ability to download results in standard output file formats, which can then be post-processed by third-party tools.

As *VarSearch* follows a "*client/server*" architecture, data loading has no impact on client performance, thus improving user experience. Data loading can be done off-line on the server so that researchers can query data on the fly with a short response time.

3   BPMN: Genomic Diagnosis Process

The *GemBiosoft* company is a spin-off of the Universitat Politècnica de València (UPV), founded in 2010. The main objective of this company is to define the CMHG to obtain a precise schema to *manage*, *integrate* and *consolidate* the large amount of genomic data in continuous growth within the genomic domain.

GemBiosoft has a web application called "*GenesLove.Me*" which offers DCGT to the consumer. The information provided by the genetic tests is accessible online to all users without prior registration (anonymous users). For example, non-registered users of the web application are able to consult all information related to the diagnosis of rare diseases of genetic origin, their characteristics, treatment, tutorials and videos of the way in which the process is performed.

The access security in *GenesLove.Me* is controlled by profiles. Users can access GLM under three profiles: (1) clients (patients), (2) provider and (3) administrator. An authenticated user with a certain access profile is authorized to carry out the operations corresponding to the access profile.

(1) *Clients (patients)*: Users with this profile are able to contract the services offered by selecting the services (DCGT) they are interested in and then paying the fee. The user is able to monitor the notifications and messages related to the diagnoses, besides consulting the histories of all the studies and treatments carried out and updating the information associated with his profile.
(2) *Supplier*: Users with this profile are able to generate notifications about the change of status in the treatment of samples. After receiving the genetic sample, the user activates the sample by entering its code number. They can then track the sample until the sequence file is generated. They can also update their profiles and consult all the activated samples (in progress and finalized).
(3) *Administrator*: A user with administration privileges performs administration and maintenance tasks of the web application, such as:
  (a) *publishing online results* (the administrator uploads the resulting diagnoses from the analysis performed on samples sequenced by the *VarSearch* tool. *The* application automatically notifies the user when his/her results have been published);
  (b) *publishing advertisements*;

(c) *publishing new diagnostic services to diagnose new diseases*; and
(d) *consulting payment reports and the application usage report* (custom time period).

Genetic tests are currently offered with the aim of detecting a person's predisposition to contracting a disease of hereditary origin [26]. The bioinformatics domain seeks to provide the necessary mechanisms and means to generate genetic diagnoses that allow the end-users (*patients*) to obtain these results to facilitate a personalized prevention treatment.

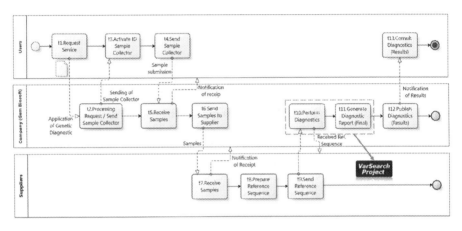

Fig. 1. Genetic diagnosis process [13].

In order to improve the understanding of the whole process using a different CM technique (*business process-oriented*), Fig. 1 shows a BPMN diagram describing the genetic diagnosis process (from the end-user's service request until he/she receives his/her genetic test report).

Our goal is to reinforce the CM perspective of this work, in order to make CM an essential working procedure to design and implement effective and efficient genomic tools. In this process, the three actors/users specified are involved: (1) The *client* (patient) who requests the service to determine whether or not he/she has a disease of genetic origin; (2) The *company*, in this case *GemBiosoft*, which is in charge of managing and performing the genomic diagnosis; and (3) the *Suppliers*, who in this case prepare the file containing the reference of the patient involved in the genetic test.

The general process begins when the end-user (*patient*) enters the web application and requests the genetic analysis (t1: task 1). The company (*GemBiosoft*) processes this request and proceeds to send the sample container to the client (t2). When the client receives the container, he must activate it by registering its identifier in the web application (t3), then place the sample in the container and send it back to the company (t4). Upon receipt of the sample, the company confirms that it meets the necessary requirements for the study and notifies the customer of its receipt (t5). The next step is to determine the supplier who will be responsible for sequencing the samples and send him the sample (t6). The selected supplier receives the sample and notifies its reception to the company (t7). Sequence preparation is initiated through the sequencing technology used by the supplier (t8). The supplier sends the resulting sequence of the sample (file) to the company (t9). *The company confirms its reception to the supplier and proceeds to analyze the sequenced sample as part of the genetic diagnosis* (**t10**). *The definitive diagnosis report* (**t11**) *is then generated.* The company (in this case the administrator/user) proceeds to publish the genetic diagnosis (result) in the web application and the end-users are automatically notified of the results (t12). To end the process, the end-user accesses the web application to obtain the diagnosis and make any queries (results) (t13). In this work, we want to go deeper into tasks 't10' and 't11', to better understand the genomic diagnosis generation process.

The BPMN gives companies the ability to understand their internal business procedures in graphical notation and the ability to communicate these procedures in a standard way [27].

Through the model shown in Fig. 1, it facilitates the understanding of commercial collaboration and transactions between organizations. In this figure, we can see the interactions between end-users, company and suppliers [15]. The company is interested in providing a web application that allows end-users to obtain a quality genetic test in a simple way that aids the treatment and prevention of diseases of genetic origin.

3.1   Exploitation Tasks 10 and 11 (T10–T11)

In this work, we want to enhance the use of *VarSearch* to generate the genomic diagnostics offered through GLM[6]. For this, it is important to note that GLM includes interaction with *VarSearch* (see tasks 10 and 11 of Fig. 1), an application developed by PROS Research Center[7] to automatically identify the relevant information contained in the genomic databases and directly related to the genetic variations of the sequenced sample.

VarSearch relies heavily on a CMHG, which makes integration of external genomic databases feasible. However, due to the large amount of information available, the data loaded in *VarSearch* are the result of a selective loading process [9] where the selected data correspond to the relevant information on the disease to be analyzed.

4   Genetic Tools Based on Conceptual Models

It is widely accepted that applying conceptual models facilitates the understanding of complex domains (*like genetics*). In our case we used this approach to define two models representing:

(a)   the characteristics and the processes of DCGT [13], and
(b)   the behavior of the human genome (CMHG) [28]. One of the leading benefits of CM is that it accurately represents the relevant concepts of the analyzed domain.

---

[6] http://geneslove.me/index.php.

[7] http://www.pros.webs.upv.es/.

After performing an initial analysis of the problem domain, the next step is to design a domain representation in the form of a conceptual model.

Our conceptual models can evolved with the new discoveries made in the field of genomics in order to improve data processing to ensure effective PM. We can thus see how CM gives positive support to the knowledge in which precision medicine plays a key role [28]. It is important to highlight that the advantage of CM for representing this domain is that it eases the integration of new knowledge into the model [5].

4.1   GenesLove.Me (GLM)

After an analysis of the requirements required for this work, important decisions were taken to arrive at an adequate representation of the basic and essential concepts in the understanding of the domain under study.

Figure 2 presents the conceptual model proposed, which can be classified into three main parts: (a) *Stakeholders*: represents all the participants involved in the web application; (b) *Genetic diagnostics*: represents everything related to diseases offered, diagnoses and samples of patients; and (c) *Sales management*: represents the management of services offered, purchases and payments.

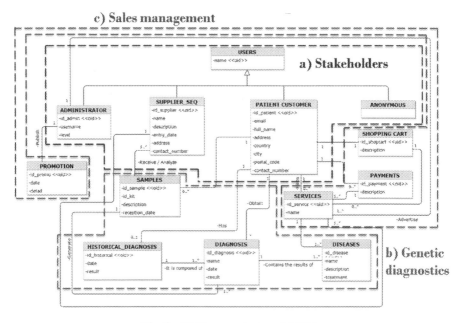

Fig. 2. GLM conceptual model [13].

The complete description of the CM can be found in the previous work [13]. Through our CM we incorporate genetic data currently used in the PM, achieving a conceptual representation that meets the needs of the bioinformatics domain. As we mentioned above, this model aims to improve the conceptual definition of the treatment related to genomic diagnosis, and thus leave a conceptual framework for further improvements.

4.2   VarSearch (*Prototype*)

A GeIS can be defined as a system that *collects*, *stores*, *manages* and *distributes* information related to the behavior of the human genome. As mentioned above, the GeIS described here is based on the CMHG [4, 8, 28]. This section deals with the preliminary steps and the design and implementation of the prototype.

4.2.1   First Steps

VarSearch is based upon the *E-Genomic Framework* (EGF), described in depth in different research papers such as [25, 29]. For the implementation of the tool, a series of steps were carried out to ensure its good performance, as explained below:

(a) *Human Genome Database (HGDB).* The transformation of our model defined for the database schema (*logical model*) was almost automatic, using the Moskitt tool (https://www.prodevelop.es/es/products/moskitt). The MOSKitt project aims to provide a set of open source tools and a technological platform for supporting the execution of software development methods which are based in model driven approaches, including *graphical modeling tools*, *model transformations*, *code generation* and *collaboration support* [30]. In this task, we found two different levels of abstraction in the model. The conceptual model represents the domain from the point of view of scientific knowledge, while the database schema (Fig. 3) focuses on the efficient storage and retrieval of data.

For this reason, the details of the physical representation must be considered to improve the final implementation. It is important to emphasize the integration of the two tables "*Validation*" and "*Curator*" in the DB schema. These tables are not actually part of the knowledge representation of the domain, but are necessary for the development and implementation of the tool (*Explained in detail in* Sect. 4.2.2).

To load the HGDB the SILE methodology [9] was used, which was developed to improve the loading processes and guarantee the treatment of "*curated data*". SILE was used to perform the "*search*" and "*identification*" of variations associated with a specific disease (a task validated by experts in the genetic domain, for example, *biologists, geneticists, biomedical engineers*).

When the identified and curated data have been obtained the "*selective loading*" is performed (through the loading module) in the HGDB. The data loaded are then "*exploited*" by *VarSearch*. Some of the diseases -*of genetic origin*- studied and loaded were *Alcohol Sensitivity* [15], *Neuroblastoma* (Table 2 shows a set of variations detected for Neuroblastoma) [31], and others.

(b) *Selection of the different data sources.* For the choice of data sources, we addressed the requirements raised in this first phase of the project. After conducting studies and analysis of various genomic repositories, we selected the following databases: NCBI, dbSNP, UMD and BIC.

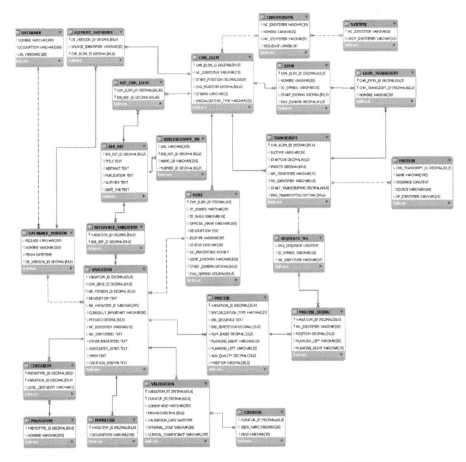

Fig. 3. Database schema (*Human Genome Database*, HGDB).

Table 2. Selection of partially annotated variations stored in *Varsearch* database. For each variation, gene symbol, chromosome, HGVS name using the gene as reference, reference and alternative allele, variation type, clinical significance and RS identifier are shown.

Id_Symbol	HG_identifier	NC_identifier	Position	REF	ALT	Specialization_type	Clinically_importan	DB_Variatin_id
KIF1B	1	NG_008069.1: g.91501A > T	10297206	A	T	SNV	Risk Factor	rs121908161
KIF1B	1	NG_008069. 1:g. 69713 69716delCCTT	10275418 −10275421	CCTT	−	Deletion	Uncertain Significance	rs886044975
ALK	2	NG_009445.1: g.705736T > G	29220831	T	G	SNV	Pathogenic	rs281864719
ALK	2	NG_009445.1: g.716694T > C	29209873	T	C	SNV	Pathologic	rs113994092
KIF1B	1	NG_008069.1:g. 26608_26609dupTA	10232313 −10232314	−	TA	Duplication	Likely Benign	rs112765394

NCBI [32] (https://www.ncbi.nlm.nih.gov/) is a data source with curated data on structural concepts of DNA sequencing. From this repository, we extracted information related to *chromosomes, genes, transcripts, exons…* and everything related to the *"Structural view"* of our conceptual model. dbSNP [33], BIC [34] and UMD [35] are databases of variations that store curated information on genetic differences between individuals. The main reason for using dbSNP is because it not only focuses on variations of a specific gene or region, but also contains variations related to all chromosomes and updates the information immediately. BIC and UMD were selected because of the requirements of a research group that was collaborating with us in a project (*Future Clinic*) focused on *"breast cancer"*. This group helped us to test the performance of our GeIS and its associated tool. Currently, we are studying and analyzing other genomic repositories like: *ClinVar, dbGaP, 1000 Genomes, ALFRED*, and others [5].

(c) *Genetic loading module.* For the loading process of the HGDB, a load module was designed to store the data from the previously measured data sources. This load module was developed using an ETL strategy [36] with three different levels: *extraction, transformation*, and *load* (see Fig. 4). Each level is completely independent of the others, facilitating and clarifying the design of the system and improving its *flexibility* and *scalability*. As can be seen in Fig. 4, all the necessary information is extracted from the source databases in the first layer (1). All this raw unstructured data goes to the second layer (2) where several transformations are made in order to format the data according to the structure of our database schema. These transformed data are sent to the third layer (3), which communicates directly with the database (following the above-mentioned SILE methodology in Task "*a*", Sect. 4.2.1).

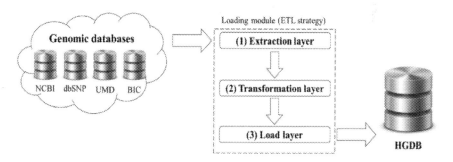

Fig. 4. Load module.

4.2.2   Design and Implementation of VarSearch

VarSearch is a web application that allows the analysis of variations obtained from the DNA sequenciation of biological samples and which is stored in FASTA or VCF file formats [37]. Different users can access the application in private spaces in the HGDB and each user can address his own variations. The validation of variations that they consider relevant can be included. It also offers storage for the users' variations to find similarities in the file analysis process. Another advantage is the inclusion of the information obtained from the data sources, together with the user validations in the database, which is an improvement in performance related to the search for variations. *VarSearch* can find variations in our database from a provided file (see Fig. 5).

The variations found are displayed to the user, and any additional information that the file lacks can be calculated and validated. Any variations of the file that have not been found in our database can also be stored. After inserting one or more variations not found in a file -*because they are considered relevant to the user*- and reanalyzing this file, these inserted variations will be found in our database and displayed to the user. Figure 6 shows how the functionality has been grouped into three main packages: (1) *User management*: a user can act as administrator and control other users, or can create new users and modify or eliminate their Information. (2) *Data load management*: the system allows the user to load the files to be analyzed in both VCF and FASTA format, compare the variations in these files to the variations in the HGDB used by *VarSearch*. (3) *Data analysis*: After analyzing and verifying the variations in the input files, the user can list the variations and classify them by multiple criteria (*position, chromosome*, etc.). There is also a series of functionalities related to the login and modification of account information that has not been grouped in any functionality package.

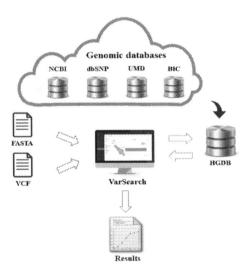

Fig. 5. VarSearch application.

- *Confidentiality of the information.* As this information is a company's primary resource, *VarSearch* restricts access to it. When a user validates a variation, he can choose a privacy category:

    (a) *Public content*, if he is willing to share the knowledge with other users, or
    (b) *Private content*, allowing access only to the owner-user and hidden from other users. All the variations can only be accessed by the user who created them.

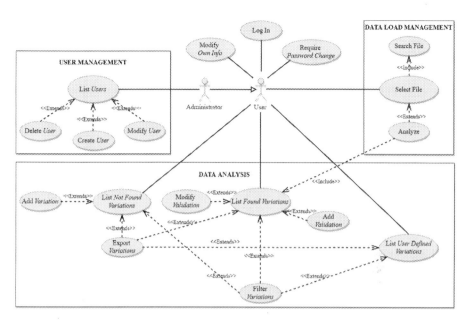

Fig. 6. *VarSearch's* general use case diagram (domain).

- *VarSearch Architecture.* In order to make it accessible to all users, *VarSearch* was designed as a web application with HTML5 technology in a language common to all current browsers. The information is managed by the MySQL database. The *VarSearch* architecture consists of the following elements:

  (a) A distributable database based on MySQL (using software tools like: Navicat *Enterprise* and *MySQL Workbench*). For the initial validation of this database, we only loaded the information related to chromosomes 13 and 22.
  (b) A set of REST services [38] developed in Java using Hibernate and Jersey, which are deployed on a Tomcat server 7.
  (c) A web application, which uses the Bootstrap framework for general organization of the interface and files, together with jQuery to define advanced interface components and invoke REST services.
  (d) It also includes a *"mini"* REST service to manage users and roles, which is based on the same architecture and technologies as the other REST services. The data layer is based solely on MySQL (you can see the VarSearch architecture represented in Fig. 7).

The application entry point is a file with variations detected by a sequencing machine in VCF or FASTA format. With this input the database is searched to detect any variations, additional information on the diseases they may cause and the associated bibliography. *VarSearch* users follow this process when working with the tool:

(1) A VCF file is uploaded from the web.
(2) The file is then processed and parsed. The entries are shown on an HTML table and the variants of each VCF entry can be seen.

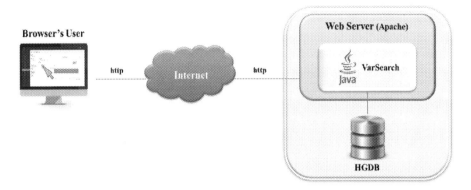

Fig. 7. VarSearch architecture.

(3) The variations present in the input file can be annotated against the database and the annotated file is downloaded in *.xls, *.csv and *.pdf format or its contents viewed in another HTML table.

To parse the VCF file and annotate the variants, *VarSearch* relies on *snpEff* and *snpSift* [39] tools, and so well tested libraries are used instead of reinventing the wheel. This also ensures VCF standard support, using ANN files for variant annotation.

If another type of information is considered useful for annotation and not covered by the procedure described, *VarSearch* uses the "*INFO*" field to introduce the desired values. As *VarSearch* is based on EGF, new genome annotation files can be quickly integrated by developing the proper parser module, either by a custom development or integrating a third-party tool or library.

All the information associated with the variations found in our HGDB can be obtained. For variations in the lists, user validations can be integrated for future searches with the "*Add Validation*" option. Another advantage of *VarSearch* is the user management (new users can be created and edited using the "*User Management*" option).

One of the objectives of *VarSearch* is to continue the extension and implementation of all the knowledge defined in our CMHG, such as the treatment of pathways and metabolic routes [28]. This tool facilitates the analysis and search for variations, improving the generation of genomic diagnoses associated with diseases of genetic origin. End-users will find the web application easy to use and they are guaranteed security for their data [40].

5 Case Studies

In the previous work [13], the case study applied to *GenesLove.Me* was defined, explaining all the processes involved in the management of DTCG (Sect. 3). In summary, the test cases were performed with the implemented solution.

The validation scenario consisted of a group of five (5) users, who made requests for genetic testing for "*lactose intolerance*". To begin the process, each user involved in the case study authorized the procedure through an "*informed consent*" [15, 41], which becomes a legal support that establishes the rights and obligations of the service offered and its expected scope.

Next, the following case studies performed with the prototype *VarSearch* are presented.

5.1 Using the VarSearch Prototype

To verify *VarSearch* performance, two case studies were carried out. In the first, VarSearch was used to analyze a VCF file. The second compared the time spent on searching for variations manually and using the application; it is important to highlight that this prototype has as end-users the geneticists and experts responsible for the generation of the genomic diagnostics. To access the application *VarSearch* users must have an account provided by Gembiosoft SME (http://gembiosoft.com/). After logging in, a file is selected for analysis. *VarSearch* reads all records and transforms them into variations.

These transformations depend on the file information: for example, the FASTA files contain a *genetic sequence* (NG), and so require the reference on which the variation is based to be to the "NG" sequence. In contrast, VCF files use positions relative to *chromosomes* (NC). Once the file records have been converted into variations, the next step is to search for these variations in our HGDB. After the analysis, the "*variations found*" and "*variations not found*" can be differentiated.

- **Found Variations Management.** Found variations are those extracted from the file in which information has been found in the HGDB, which means that this variation has been found in at least one genomic repository. A found variation has much more information than the variation obtained from the file and allows us to calculate and submit·detailed information to the user.

Having analyzed the VCF file, all the variations found are displayed to the user, in each case calculating the *HGVS notation*[8], its *data source identifier*, *clinical significance*, and the *number of validations* and *databases found* together with their *bibliographic references*. This information is calculated for VCF and FASTA; however, VCF variations are sorted by samples. Figure 8 shows the results obtained by analyzing a VCF file with a single sample. For this sample (5323-BRCAyA), a number of variations were found with the corresponding information. A variation can have validations made by users. The validation column corresponds to the number of validations that each variation has and if a validation is private, only the owner will see it. Another *VarSearch* feature is its support for multiple bibliographical references. A variation can be found in different databases and may contain different bibliographic references.

---

[8] http://www.hgvs.org/mutnomen/.

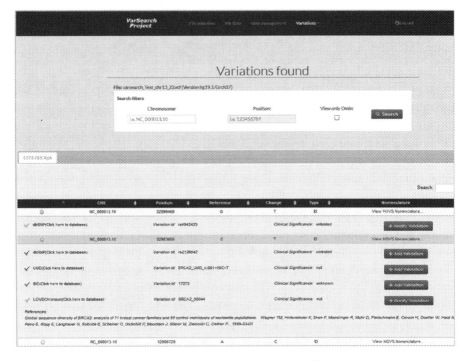

Fig. 8. Analysis of VCF file using VarSearch.

- **Not found Variations (*insertion and treatment*).** The user who is analyzing variations may find a variation in the file, which was not found in the database (see Fig. 9). Using his experience and knowledge he may consider some variations as relevant despite not being found.

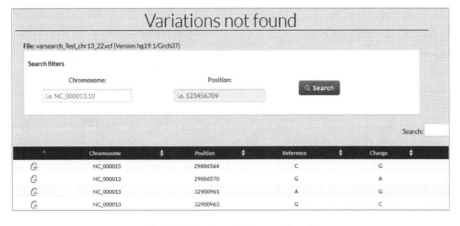

Fig. 9. List of variations not found.

With *VarSearch* the user can insert the not found variations or any variation considered key to the study. If the user has inserted certain variations that had not been found, on reanalyzing the file these inserted variations are compared with the variations in the file, showing the similarities.

In order to differentiate the variations of the different repositories from user variations, the results obtained from the user's experience and the results from years of study of different biomedical databases are differentiated.

5.2   Improved Efficiency and Time in Finding Variations with VarSearch

To validate the effectiveness and performance of the proposed software, some experiments were performed to measure efficiency and time. A study was conducted to compare the time spent searching for variations manually with an automatic search of all the repositories mentioned above using *VarSearch*.

A manual search of one variation involves detecting the variation in the VCF or FASTA file, a search for the variation in the different repositories, and the identification and verification of the variation. *VarSearch* was tested for the time it needed to search for several variations, calculating the time evolution according to the number of variations involved (2, 5 and 7). The results can be seen in Fig. 10.

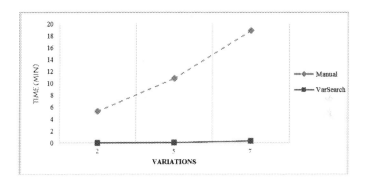

Fig. 10. Time optimization.

As can be seen in Fig. 10, the cost of performing a manual search rises to 5'32 min for 2 variations, 10'83 min for 5 variations and 18'89 min for 7 variations.

However, with *VarSearch* the time remains constant at between 2 and 3 s for different variations, which confirms its efficient performance. Using this prototype thus significantly reduces the time spent on the search for variations. Also, it must be remembered that the manual search process does not calculate additional information for variations. If this information were necessary, the search time would increase significantly, however, with *VarSearch* this time remains constant because this information has already been calculated in the search for variations.

6 Conclusions and Future Research

This paper describes a study and analysis of the implementation of two web application to facilitate DCGT, the first offer the services (*genomic diagnosis*) to the final user using an interface easy to use -*GenesLove.Me*-, and the second is a prototype for the generation of the diagnosis using our HGDB -*VarSearch*-. Through these applications, we can inform end-users about their predisposition to suffer certain genetically based illnesses.

Through the development of our web applications we seek to provide end-users with a genomic diagnosis in a secure and reliable way. The use of BPMN and Conceptual Modeling based approaches for this type of service aids the understanding of the participants in the processes in the genomic domain and improves the processes involved.

Bioinformatics is a domain that is constantly evolving, and with the application of conceptual models, we can extend our genomic knowledge and conceptual representation accurately and simply.

In this work, we have focused mainly on the description of the prototype "*VarSearch*", which plays a fundamental role in processes 10 and 11 of the BPMN previously described, because with this prototype we generated the genomic diagnosis facilitated through *GenesLove.Me*.

VarSearch is a flexible new analysis framework or web application that provides a powerful resource for exploring both "*coding*" and "*non-coding*" genetic variations. To do this, *VarSearch* integrates VCF format input/output with an expanding set of genome information. *VarSearch* (and other tools built on EGF) will therefore facilitate research into the genetic basis of human diseases. EGF can also be expected to allow the development of new tools in diverse *e-genomics* contexts. As genetic laboratories are now oriented to facilitating *genetic procedures*, *web access*, *usability* and *feasibility*, the definition of different *profiles* are therefore important goals. All this allows the user to configure the tool according to his specific needs. These necessities include inserting genetic variations and validating its own variations, thus increasing its "*know-how*".

Future research work will also be aimed at:

- The application of *Data Quality* (DQ) metrics to enhance our HGDB.
- The study and treatment of new diseases of genetic origin (continue expanding the list of illnesses available in the web application).
- Implementation of data management mechanisms to enhance the quality of personalized medicine.
- Improving/develop the next version of *VarSearch* (version 2.0) for genetic diagnosis (including -*haplotypes and statistical factors-*).
- We also intend to extend the model with studies on the treatment of "*haplogroups*", including subjects with a similar genetic profile who share a common ancestor.

Acknowledgements. This work was supported by the *MESCyT* of the Dominican Republic and also by the Generalitat Valenciana through project IDEO (PROMETEOII/2014/039), the Spanish Ministry of Science and Innovation through Project DataME (ref: TIN2016-80811-P).

The authors are grateful to Jorge Guerola M., David Roldán Martínez, Alberto García S., Ana León Palacio, Francisco Valverde Girome, Ainoha Martín, Verónica Burriel Coll, Mercedes Fernández A., Carlos Iñiguez-Jarrín, Lenin Javier Serrano and Ma. José Villanueva for their valuable assistance.

References

1. Buermans, H.P.J., den Dunnen, J.T.: Next generation sequencing technology: advances and applications. Biochimica et Biophysica Acta (BBA) – Mol. Basis Dis. **1842**(10), 1932–1941 (2014). https://doi.org/10.1016/j.bbadis.2014.06.015
2. Grosso, L.A.: Precision medicine and cardiovascular diseases. Rev. Colomb. Cardiol. **23**(2), 73–76 (2016). https://doi.org/10.1007/978-3-540-39390-0
3. Olivé, A.: Conceptual Modeling of Information Systems, pp. 1–445. Springer, Heidelberg (2007). https://doi.org/10.1007/978-3-540-39390-0
4. Reyes Román, J.F., Pastor, Ó., Casamayor, J.C., Valverde, F.: Applying conceptual modeling to better understand the human genome. In: Comyn-Wattiau, I., Tanaka, K., Song, I.-Y., Yamamoto, S., Saeki, M. (eds.) ER 2016. LNCS, vol. 9974, pp. 404–412. Springer, Cham (2016). https://doi.org/10.1007/978-3-319-46397-1_31
5. Reyes Román, J.F., Pastor, Ó., Valverde, F., Roldán, D.: How to deal with Haplotype data: an extension to the conceptual schema of the human genome. CLEI Electron. J. **19**(3) (2016). http://dx.doi.org/10.19153/cleiej.19.3.2
6. Object Management Group: Business Process Model and Notation (2016). http://www.bpmn.org/
7. Romeo-Malanda, S.: Análisis genéticos directos al consumidor: cuestiones éticas y jurídicas (2009). http://www.institutoroche.es/legalactualidad/85/analisis
8. Pastor López, O., Reyes Román, J.F., Valverde Giromé, F.: Conceptual Schema of the Human Genome (CSHG). Technical report (2016). http://hdl.handle.net/10251/67297
9. Reyes Román, J.F., Pastor, O.: Use of GeIS for early diagnosis of alcohol sensitivity. In: Proceedings of the 9th International Joint Conference on Biomedical Engineering Systems and Technologies, vol. 3, pp. 284–289 (2016). https://doi.org/10.5220/0005822902840289
10. Bornberg-Bauer, E., Paton, N.W.: Conceptual data modelling for bioinformatics. Briefings Bioinform. **3**(2), 166–180 (2002). https://doi.org/10.1093/bib/3.2.166
11. Ram, S., Wei, W.: Modeling the semantics of 3D protein structures. In: Conceptual Modeling–ER 2004, Proceedings, pp. 696–708 (2004). https://doi.org/10.1007/978-3-540-30464-7_52
12. Pastor, M.A., Burriel, V., Pastor, O.: Conceptual modeling of human genome mutations: a dichotomy between what we have and what we should have. In: BIOSTEC Bioinformatics 2010, pp. 160–166 (2010). ISBN 978-989-674-019-1
13. Reyes Román, J.F., Iñiguez-Jarrín, C., Pastor, O.: GenesLove.Me: a model-based web-application for direct-to-consumer genetic tests. In: Proceedings of the 12th International Conference on Evaluation of Novel Approaches to Software Engineering, pp. 133–143, Porto, Portugal, 28–29 April (2017). ISBN 978-989-758-250-9, https://doi.org/10.5220/0006340201330143
14. Mardis, E.R.: The $1,000 genome, the $100,000 analysis? Genome Med. **2**(11), 84 (2010)
15. Reyes Román, J.F.: Integración de haplotipos al modelo conceptual del genoma humano utilizando la metodología SILE. Universitat Politècnica de València (2014). http://hdl.handle.net/10251/43776

16. Aguilar Cartagena, A.: Medicina Personalizada, Medicina De Precisión, ¿Cuán Lejos Estamos De La Perfección? Carcinos **5**, 1–2 (2015)
17. Grupo RETO Hermosillo, A.: El cáncer de mama (2016). http://gruporetohermosilloac.com/index.php
18. Metzker, M.L.: Sequencing technologies - the next generation. Nat. Rev. Genet. **11**(1), 31–46 (2010)
19. Voelkerding, K.V., Dames, S.A., Durtschi, J.D.: Next-generation sequencing: from basic research to diagnostics. Clin. Chem. **55**(4), 641–658 (2009)
20. 23andMe: 23andMe (2016). https://www.23andme.com/
21. 23andMe: How it works? (2016). https://www.23andme.com/howitworks/
22. Cingolani, P.: snpEff: variant effect prediction (2012)
23. Wang, K., Li, M., Hakonarson, H.: ANNOVAR: functional annotation of genetic variants from high-throughput sequencing data. Nucleic Acids Res. **38**(16), e164–e164 (2010)
24. McLaren, W., Gil, L., Hunt, S.E., Riat, H.S., Ritchie, G.R., Thormann, A., Cunningham, F.: The ensembl variant effect predictor. Genome Biol. **17**(1), 122 (2016)
25. Roldán, D., Pastor, O., Fernández, M.: An integration architecture framework for e-genomics services. In: IEEE RCIS (2014). https://doi.org/10.1109/rcis.2014.6861063
26. U. S. National Library of Medicine: What is genetic testing? Genetics Home Reference (2017)
27. Chinosi, M., Trombetta, A.: BPMN: an introduction to the standard. Comput. Stand. Interfaces **34**(1), 124–134 (2012)
28. Reyes Román, J.F., León, A., Pastor, Ó.: Software engineering and genomics: the two sides of the same coin? In: Proceedings of the International Conference on Evaluation of Novel Approaches to Software Engineering (ENASE 2017), pp. 1–6 (2017). https://doi.org/10.5220/0006368203010307
29. Roldán M.D., Pastor López, Ó., Reyes Román, J.F.: E-genomic framework for delivering genomic services. An application to JABAWS. In: 9th RCIS (IEEE), pp. 516–517 (2015). https://doi.org/10.1109/RCIS.2015.7128915
30. Muñoz, J., Llacer, M., Bonet, B.: Configuring ATL transformations in MOSKitt. In: Proceedings of the 2nd. International Workshop on Model Transformation with ATL (MtATL 2010), CEUR Workshop Proceedings (2010)
31. Burriel, V., Reyes Román, J.F., Heredia C.A., Iñiguez-Jarrín, C., León, A.: GeIS based on conceptual models for the risk assessment of neuroblastoma. In: 11th RCIS (IEEE), pp. 1–2 (2017). https://doi.org/10.1109/RCIS.2017.7956581
32. National Center for Biotechnology Information (2017). https://www.ncbi.nlm.nih.gov/
33. Sherry, S.T., Ward, M.H., Kholodov, M., Baker, J., Phan, L., Smigielski, E.M., Sirotkin, K.: dbSNP: the NCBI database of genetic variation. Nucleic Acids Res. **29**(1), 308–311 (2001)
34. Szabo, C., Masiello, A., Reyes Román, J.F., Brody, L.C.: The breast cancer information core: database design, structure, and scope. Hum. Mutat. **16**(2), 123 (2000)
35. Béroud, C., Collod-Béroud, G., Boileau, C., Soussi, T., Junien, C.: UMD (Universal mutation database): a generic software to build and analyze locus-specific databases. Hum. Mutat. **15**(1), 86 (2000)
36. Zhou, H., Yang, D., Xu, Y.: An ETL strategy for real-time data warehouse. In: Wang, Y., Li, T. (eds.) Practical Applications of Intelligent Systems. Advances in Intelligent and Soft Computing, vol. 124, pp. 329–336. Springer, Heidelberg (2011). https://doi.org/10.1007/978-3-642-25658-5_41
37. Claverie, J.M., Notredame, C.: Bioinformatics for Dummies. Wiley, Hoboken (2011)
38. Haupt, F., Karastoyanova, D., Leymann, F., Schroth, B.: A model-driven approach for REST compliant services. In: IEEE International Conference on Web Services (ICWS), pp. 129–136 (2014)

39. Tolhuis, B., Wesselink, J.J.: NA12878 Platinum Genome GENALICE MAP analysis report (2015)
40. León, A., Reyes, J., Burriel, V., Valverde, F.: Data quality problems when integrating genomic information. In: Link, S., Trujillo, J.C. (eds.) ER 2016. LNCS, vol. 9975, pp. 173–182. Springer, Cham (2016). https://doi.org/10.1007/978-3-319-47717-6_15
41. de Galicia, C.A.: Ley 3/2001, reguladora del consentimiento informado y de la historia clínica de los pacientes (2001)

Technological Platform for the Prevention and Management of Healthcare Associated Infections and Outbreaks

Maria Iuliana Bocicor[1(✉)], Maria Dascălu[2], Agnieszka Gaczowska[3],
Sorin Hostiuc[4], Alin Moldoveanu[2], Antonio Molina[5],
Arthur-Jozsef Molnar[1], Ionuț Negoi[4], and Vlad Racoviță[1]

[1] SC Info World SRL, Bucharest, Romania
{iuliana.bocicor,arthur.molnar,vlad.racovita}@infoworld.ro
[2] Polytechnic University of Bucharest, Bucharest, Romania
maria.dascalu@upb.ro, alin.moldoveanu@cs.pub.ro
[3] NZOZ Eskulap, Skierniewice, Poland
agaczkowska@gmail.com
[4] Carol Davila University of Medicine and Pharmacy, Bucharest, Romania
soraer@gmail.com, negoiionut@gmail.com
[5] Innovatec Sensing & Communication, Alcoi, Spain
amolina@innovatecsc.com

Abstract. Hospital acquired infections are infections that occur in patients during hospitalization, which were not present at the time of admission. They are among the most common adverse events in healthcare around the world, leading to increased mortality and morbidity rates, prolonged hospitalization periods and considerable financial burden on both hospitals and patients. Preventive guidelines and regulations have been devised, however compliance to these is frequently poor and there is much room for improvement. This paper presents the prototype of an extensible, configurable cyber-physical system, developed under European Union funding, that will assist in the prevention of hospital infections and outbreaks. Integrating a wireless sensor network for the surveillance of clinical processes with configurable monitoring software built around a workflow engine as key component, our solution detects deviations from established hygiene practices and provides real-time information and alerts whenever an infection risk is discovered. The platform is described from both hardware and software perspective, with emphasis on the wireless network's elements as well as the most important software components. Furthermore, two clinical workflows of different complexity, which are included in the system prototype are detailed. The finalized system is expected to facilitate the creation and automated monitoring of clinical workflows that are associated with over 90% of hospital infections.

© Springer International Publishing AG, part of Springer Nature 2018
E. Damiani et al. (Eds.): ENASE 2017, CCIS 866, pp. 70–90, 2018.
https://doi.org/10.1007/978-3-319-94135-6_4

1   Introduction

Hospital acquired infections (HAI), also known as healthcare associated infections or nosocomial infections are among the most common adverse events in healthcare around the world, affecting between 8% and 12% of patients admitted to hospitals in the European Union [13,22], and 5% to 10% of hospitalized patients in the United States every year [10]. Hospital infections refer to those infections that occur in patients during hospitalization, which were not present or incubating at the time of admission, including *"infections acquired in the hospital but appearing after discharge, and also occupational infections among staff of the facility"* [57].

HAI are prevalent across the globe, regardless of geographical, social or economic factors [12,21,51,59,60]. In addition to their most critical consequences, which are an increased rate of mortality and morbidity (an annual number of 37 000 deaths in Europe, 99 000 attributable deaths in the USA [60], 8 000 in Canada [9] and between 7% and 46% attributed mortality rates in Southeast Asia [34]), HAI also translate in prolonged hospitalization periods (5 to 29.5 days worldwide [61]) and further administered treatments. This leads to a considerable financial burden, estimated between $28 and 45 billion in the United States [48], $129 million in extra costs incurred in Canada [9,27], and €7 billion in Europe, in 2008 [20]. Furthermore, the problem of HAI is closely connected with antimicrobial resistance, another fundamental difficulty for modern healthcare and a significant threat to public health. Many bacterial species, such as Pseudomonas, Acinetobacter, Staphylococcus aureus or Clostridium difficile have developed to be resistant to a wide range of antibiotics. In many cases, they also represent major causes of HAI [32].

Having been recognized as a significant issue for 30 years now [51], surveillance has been in place and measures and precautions have been taken [11,62] especially during the past decade, in order to reduce nosocomial infection rates. When specific steps are taken by medical personnel, infection rates have been shown to decrease by more than 70% [11]. Preventive efforts have proven to be successful, as a report from the Agency of Healthcare Research and Quality [1] estimates a 17% decline in the rate of HAI from 2010 to 2013 in the United States. However, the issue is still a delicate one and there is much room for improvement.

This paper presents an extensible, configurable cyber-physical system that will assist in the prevention of HAI and outbreaks [7]. Integrating a wireless sensor network (WSN) for the surveillance of clinical workflows with configurable monitoring software, our solution detects deviations from established hygiene practices and provides real-time information and alerts, whenever nonconformity is discovered. The hardware network of wireless sensors that can be deployed within variable-sized clinical locations collect real-time information from the clinical setting, such as substance or material availability (soap, antimicrobial agents, sterile gloves) and environmental conditions affecting the spread of pathogens (oxygen levels, airflow, temperature), thereby providing a complete image of the hospital environment in real time. Monitoring of complex processes such as management of indwelling urinary catheters, postoperative care, intubation or endoscopy is possible by describing them using software workflows that are interpreted and executed by a workflow engine. When the sequence of transitions inferred by the system from sensor data presents deviations from the expected flow, the system alerts responsible personnel. The system will also provide advanced analytics, which are extremely important for pinpointing difficult infection sources that elude existing workflows and for the identification of existing activities targeted towards outbreak prevention and control.

The system is researched and built within a European Union-funded project and its current stage of development represents a proof of concept, including multifunctional smart sensors for monitoring the use of soap, antimicrobial gel and water sink together with two clinical workflows that describe the required hygiene procedures in the case of the general practitioner's office and for minor surgeries that are performed within the clinic where the system will be first deployed. This paper details the smart devices employed, the hardware-software integration as well as the software components that ensure the cyber-physical system achieves its objective of lowering the number and severity of hospital infections.

2   State of the Art

In recent years several concrete measures have been taken to reduce the risk of infections in hospitals. As such, guidelines and rules of prevention have been devised for healthcare personnel and patients' safety [33]. As a response of the necessities within the hospital environment, various software or hybrid hardware and software systems have been developed to ensure strict compliance with and enforcement of these instructions.

2.1   Monitoring Hand Hygiene

Proper hand hygiene is considered the single most valuable tool in preventing the spread of healthcare-associated infections [33]. Despite existing information, hand hygiene measures are still not widely adopted, being applied in only 40% of cases when it is required [43]. Thus, the underlying idea used by quite a large number of systems is continuous monitoring of healthcare workers' hand hygiene and real-time alert generation in case of non-compliance with established guidelines.

Numerous existing Information and Communication Technology (ICT) solutions use this idea of continuous surveillance and immediate notification in case of hygiene rule violation. IntelligentM [41] and Hyginex [30] are two systems that combine sensors attached to soap, disinfectant dispensers or faucets with Radio Frequency Identification (RFID) enabled bracelets designed to be worn by medical personnel. Whenever hygiene events are omitted, the systems detect the violation and the bracelet alerts the clinician using vibrations or luminous signals. Biovigil Technology [4] and MedSense [26] are similar systems which use wearable badges attached to healthcare workers' uniforms. While Biovigil uses chemical sensors placed at hospital ward entrances to detect whether hand hygiene is undertaken, MedSense employs beacons placed above patient beds or in other points of care, with the aim to establish a wireless patient zone. This allows the badge to identify hand hygiene opportunities by detecting when the badge enters or exits a patient zone. SwipeSense [50] is composed of a series of small, recyclable alcohol-based gel dispensers, which can be worn by medical personnel together with proximity sensors mounted on hospital walls and a monitoring web platform. Due to this design, the system allows clinicians to perform hand hygiene without interrupting their activities to walk to a sink or a disinfectant dispenser [45]. UltraClenz's Patient Safeguard System [53] is somewhat similar to MedSense, in that it employs a patient based approach, as opposed to the room based approach of previously presented technologies. The system prompts workers to sanitize before and after every patient contact. Unlike other systems presented so far, DebMed [16] does not use RFID technology, nor any devices for medical personnel. It integrates a wireless network of dispensers that send data to a server via hubs and modems installed on each floor. The server application uses a customizable algorithm [18] to estimate the number of hand hygiene opportunities per patient-day and compares this number with the actual hand hygiene events that were performed.

2.2 Disinfection Robots

The systems mentioned in the previous section prevent the spread of HAI by ensuring that transmission is not induced by medical personnel via contaminated hands. But transmission can also occur via air or contaminated surfaces. Preventing this using chemicals or ultraviolet light has proven successful.

Short-wavelength ultraviolet (UV-C) light provides a strong germicidal effect, by inducing cellular damage and cell death in pathogens. Water, air and surfaces can be purified using UV-C. However, humans must avoid direct UV-C irradiation due to its harmful effects.

Several types of solutions using UV-C or chemical substances have been developed for air and surface disinfection, in the form of disinfection robots. Tru-D Smart UVC [52] scans the room to be disinfected and computes the optimal UV-C light dose required for disinfection according to the particularities of the room. These include its size, geometry, surface reflectivity and the amount and location of equipment present. The robot performs disinfection of the entire room, from top to bottom in one cycle and from one location, ensuring that the ultraviolet light reaches even shadowed areas. The Xenex "Germ-Zapping Robot" [63] called "Little Moe" can disinfect a room using pulses of high-intensity, high-energy ultraviolet light. The deactivation of pathogens takes place in less than five minutes and the disinfected room remains at a low microbial load until it is re-contaminated by a person or the ventilation system. The UV-Disinfection Robot developed by Blue Ocean Robotics [5] has the same purpose as Little Moe and Tru-D. The robot can drive autonomously when called upon by medical personnel and the approximate time it needs for fully disinfecting a room is between 10 to 15 min.

In addition to UV-C light, certain chemical substances or chemical reactions can be used to eliminate harmful bacteria. The Bioquell Q-10 robot [3] emits hydrogen peroxide vapours, which are safe for hospital and equipment surfaces, as well as for other technological machinery and computers, but are deadly to pathogens. This antibacterial bleaching agent is also toxic to humans and therefore another solution must be distributed across the room after disinfection, to make it safe for humans to enter. A different approach is taken by Sterisafe Decontamination technology [47]: the Sterisafe robot does not employ any chemicals, but disinfects rooms, including corners and shadowed areas, and removes gases and harmful particles using activated oxygen, also known as ozone. Compared to UV-C light robots, Sterisafe's main advantages are that it disinfects hard to reach surfaces (under beds, behind equipment), while as opposed to the Bioquell Q-10 robots, it completely removes the ozone and other by-products at the end of the disinfection cycle, leaving the room safe for people. A comparison study effectuated by Andersen et al. [2] concluded that disinfection with UV-C light is very effective, but it's best used in conjunction with chemical disinfection, to ensure good cleaning of shadowed areas.

2.3   Infections and Outbreak Management

The fight against infections is reinforced through other types of systems that were designed for infection management, such as clinical decision support systems or identification of models that shape the spread of disease. Protocol Watch [39] is a decision support system used to improve compliance with the "Surviving Sepsis Campaign" international guidelines [49], simplifying the implementation of sepsis prevention protocols by regularly checking certain medical parameters of patients. Other relevant software systems developed to enhance treatment policy in case of an infection outbreak are RL6:Infection [40] and Accreditrack [23]. Through proactive monitoring and integration of data obtained from several hospital systems, RL6:Infection helps responsible persons to optimize their initiatives and to make the right decisions concerning infection prevention, based on data collected and presented by the system. Accreditrack was designed to ensure compliance with hand hygiene guidelines, to verify nosocomial infection management processes as well as to provide visibility and transparency for these processes.

Another beneficial endeavour for modelling the spread of disease, for identification of control policies and for ensuring the adoption of correct medical practices is building contact networks [15]. A number of studies have modelled interactions in clinical settings using data collected by wireless sensor networks and electronic medical records, and illustrated that contact network knowledge can be used in preventing and handling hospital infections [25,29,31,46,54,55].

The systems presented in this section are effective, but they all address the issue of hospital infections from a singular direction. Systems for monitoring hand hygiene specifically target processes involving disinfection of hands, disinfection robots are useful for disinfecting rooms and equipment, while systems for managing outbreaks are particularly targeted towards that definite goal. The problem of hospital infections and outbreaks however, is a complex one, and we believe a more comprehensive approach will provide a better solution. The platform we propose intends to tackle HAI from several directions, using a two-pronged approach. First, a basic line of defence able to monitor clinical workflows most prone to infection transmission in real time will handle both pathogen-agnostic and pathogen-specific scenarios. Second, an advanced line of defence will be created, that will employ risk maps and will build contact networks using the data gathered as part of the basic line of defence. To the best of our knowledge, our proposed system is the first of its kind to combine a sensor network and software in a cyber-physical platform of the intended versatility. The following sections of the paper describe our proposed system in more detail.

3   HAI-OPS - Platform Overview

The platform we propose is developed within the Hospital Acquired Infection and Outbreak Prevention System (HAI-OPS) research project [28], which aims to build a pragmatic, automated solution to significantly decrease overall mortality and morbidity associated with HAI by specifically targeting their most common sources and pathways of transmission. To achieve this, the system will leverage advances in computing power and availability of custom-developed, affordable hardware that will be combined with a configurable, workflow-based software system [8].

HAI-OPS will address several clinical and maintenance processes and procedures, such as hand hygiene, catheter management, invasive procedures and surgical care. The system will employ an approach that allows the definition and execution of custom Business Process Model and Notation (BPMN) [37] encoded workflows, which model various clinical and maintenance processes. The cyber-physical platform will be configurable so that it covers differences between clinical unit location and layout, differences in types and specifics of undertaken procedures, as well as variation between existing hygiene guidelines. Furthermore, it will offer interoperability with hospital information systems (HIS) and will allow patient and infection data analysis using risk maps and contact networks. As such, the system will also be geared to help hospital epidemiologists in the fight against infection and outbreaks.

The cornerstone of the proposed system is the detection of events happening within the monitored location which are deemed relevant to infection prevention. For the purposes of the pilot deployment, the system will detect the following event types:

- *Presence of persons within the clinical unit.* The system will monitor employees working in clinical or auxiliary positions as well as patients. Person monitoring will be achieved using passive RFID tags embedded in badges. Employees will be provided with permanent customized badges linked to their user profile. Patients will receive a temporary tag when checking into the clinic reception, a mandatory step before any appointment. The use of passive technology allows keeping tags light and inexpensive, while powered elements are embedded in the environment.

- *Person enters or leaves a room.* The passive tags issued to personnel as well as patients, as described above, will be detected by active RFID antennas mounted within the door frames of monitored rooms. This will allow identification of the person as well as determine their direction of movement.
- *Person undertakes hand hygiene.* According to the regulations within the partner clinic, hand hygiene can be undertaken using either soap and water, or antimicrobial gel. Both are at the disposal of medical personnel and are placed near the sink within all rooms where clinical activities require it. The system will employ sensor-equipped soap and gel dispensers that transmit an event whenever they are used. Furthermore, the system will employ active RFID installed near the sink to also identify the person who is undertaking hand hygiene. As such, hand hygiene is a high-level event that the software identifies based on several low-level events: proximity to sink area and use of soap dispenser or antimicrobial gel.
- *Person equips gloves.* Dispensers for single-use gloves are installed throughout the clinic, near the sink in all rooms where their use might be required. Dispensers will be equipped with sensors that emit an event whenever they are used.
- *Patient examination start.* For most workflows, this is the first contact between patient and medical personnel. Patient examinations always take place within a designated area of the room, which usually has a patient bed installed. The system will detect the patient examination event using several low-level events, namely practitioner and patient proximity to the consultation bed as well as thermal imaging data based on an array-type sensor.
- *Equipment is used.* Certain procedures require the use of single-use or sterilized equipment. Dispensers are monitored for the single use items. Equipment that can be reused must be sterilized in the autoclave, and witness strips must be employed to prove that the sterilization process was complete. In this case, barcode strips will be printed and affixed to sterilized packages, which will be scanned using a wall-mounted reader when first opened. This will ensure the traceability of the sterilization process for equipment.
- *Surface disinfection.* This is undertaken using spray-type disinfectant in recipients. Like in the case of other dispensers, sensors will detect and emit an event when used.

4   Modelling Clinical Processes

The HAI-OPS platform will monitor various clinical processes defined and encoded as workflows. A workflow engine will create and execute instances of workflows and emit real-time alerts when infection risks are detected, based on the expected succession of actions encoded. Any clinical process can be seen as a sequence of events, conditions and activities and thus modelled using BPMN notation. In this section we describe and model two workflows that are proposed for implementation within the clinical partner of the project, the NZOZ Eskulap [36] outpatient clinic in Skierniwice, Poland.

4.1 General Practitioner

The consultation workflow taking place in the general practitioner (GP) office
is the first one considered, given the number of daily consultations and the high
degree of event overlap that exists with other workflows taking place within the
partner clinic. The simplified BPMN-like model of this workflow, as it takes place
within the partner clinic is illustrated in Fig. 1.

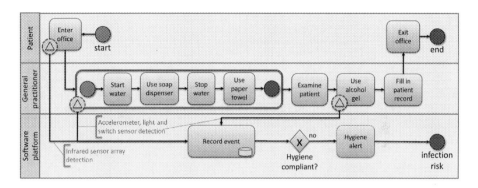

Fig. 1. General practitioner workflow (from [7]).

An instance of this workflow is created every time a patient enters the GP's
office. This is detected using an RFID active system mounted at the door frame,
as well as the RFID passive tag the patient receives at the clinic reception when
checking in for the appointment. All sensor types employed, along with their
positioning inside the GP's office are detailed in Sect. 5.

After a short conversation, during which the GP might write down various
details about the patient's medical issues, patient examination starts. This is
detected by a combination of sensors: the RFID tags of the doctor and the
patient, a proximity sensor mounted at the side of the bed and additionally an
infrared sensor mounted over the bed, used for checking presence. Given the flow
modelled in Fig. 1, the system detects that patient examination starts, at which
point it checks that hand hygiene was undertaken by the general practitioner.
Existing regulations precisely detail how to undertake hand hygiene correctly.
Thus, hands must be sanitized according to 10 steps for effective hygiene [58].

Assuming that all medical personnel are aware of the detailed actions and
correct procedure for proper hand washing, the system will only check that the
sink, disinfectants and paper towel dispenser were operated. A collection of sensors mounted on the tap, soap, disinfectant and paper towel dispensers detects
the sequence of actions performed. If the sequence is detected in accordance
with the provided workflow, the system acknowledges that compliance has been
achieved. Otherwise, an alert is generated, sent to the GP and persisted within
the system. In such a situation, if the workflow is violated, its instance is stopped
and the hygiene breach is recorded. After receiving notification, the GP will have

to perform hand hygiene before examining the patient, or else the system will continue recording and sending alerts. If the workflow continues without interruption, its last step requires the GP to disinfect their hands using antimicrobial gel after the last contact with the patient. This event is again recorded by the system using the same sensors situated in the disinfectant dispenser area. When the examination is finished, the GP updates the patient's record and the patient leaves the office. The workflow is thus completed. All actions detected during workflow execution are persisted by the system to allow statistics and advanced analyses.

The presented workflow accounts for an ordinary GP consultation. However, some examinations, such as those involving the head, eyes, ears, nose and throat or those concerning patients with skin infections require additional precautions which should be included in the associated workflow. More precisely, new actions must be added, referring to the doctor employing disposable gloves which must be put on before examination and disposed of immediately after the procedure is completed.

4.2   Minor Surgery

Minor surgeries represent the most complex clinical workflow currently undertaken within the NZOZ Eskulap clinic [36]. Given the documented risk of infection following surgical procedures, as well as the complexity of invasive procedures that involve both medical personnel and equipment, we believe these workflows are suitable for assessing the impact and performance of the proposed system. Furthermore, ascertaining that our system does not impose additional overhead for existing processes is equally important to consider.

Minor surgeries are undertaken by a team that consists of a surgeon and a nurse, who must follow a well established hygiene protocol. The equipment used during the procedure is either single use or must be sterilized. A traceability

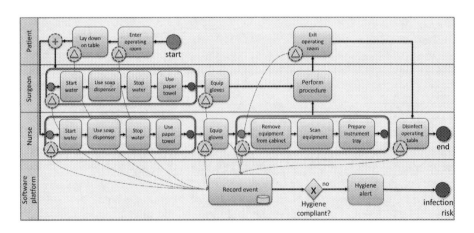

Fig. 2. Minor surgery workflow.

system must be employed to allow proving that equipment underwent proper sterilization. The minor surgery suite consists of a consultation room, which is the first room entered by the patient, and continues with the operating room itself, which can be accessed only from the consultation room. In most cases, minor surgery involves several patient appointments. These include the initial consultation, the intervention itself and one or more follow-up appointments for examination or dressing change.

Given the purpose of our system, we do not examine the medical procedures that take place in detail, but focus our attention on those steps that experts deem to present high infection risk. In the following we detail the types of surgical appointments that take place at the Eskulap clinic:

- *Patient examination.* This is undertaken within the consultation room, in the presence of the surgeon, and with the possible participation of the nurse. Hygiene requirements are similar to those in the general practitioner's office: both the surgeon and nurse must undertake hand hygiene before and after patient examination.
- *Dressing change.* This takes place in the operating room, in the presence of at least one medical practitioner. The hygiene requirements are similar to those during patient examination.
- *Minor surgery.* Interventions can take place with or without an immediately preceding patient examination. Surgeries are undertaken only within the operating room, and consist in a series of well defined steps:
  1. Appointment starts when the patient enters the operating room
  2. Patient lays down on the operating table.
  3. The nurse undertakes hand hygiene and equips single use gloves.
  4. The nurse prepares the equipment to be used. Sterilized equipment is taken out of the cabinet, the autoclave sterilization strip is checked and the pouch is opened on the instrument tray.
  5. The surgeon undertakes hand hygiene and equips single use gloves.
  6. After the procedure is complete, the patient leaves the surgery suite.
  7. Nurse disinfects the surgery table.
  8. The appointment is complete.

Given that procedures for patient examination and dressing change are similar to those in the general practitioner's office, Fig. 2 illustrates only the expected event flow taking place within the operating room. As shown in the figure, there exists a degree of overlap between the described workflows. This is both expected, as events such as person movement, hand hygiene and equipment use and sterilization are the cornerstones of preventing infection transmission. Furthermore, a high degree of overlap will allow for the reuse of custom developed devices and will lower the cost of deploying and maintaining the system.

4.3   Known Challenges

We identified some challenges regarding the interaction of the system with the clinical processes mentioned in the previous subsections, which might emerge particularly due to the various possible constraints. We present these challenges below, including solutions that have already been identified, or potential solutions that are still being investigated within the project.

Firstly, the natural course of clinical processes must not be disrupted by the HAI-OPS platform. The system should not interfere with normal clinical activities, should achieve minimal overhead on clinical processes, as well as high usability and maximal automation so that manual intervention is required only when a risk is detected. Clinical staff must not experience any other modifications from their usual activities; hygiene activities must be performed identically with alerts sent to practitioners through their smartphones.

The placement of sensors within offices, surgery theaters, or generally, in any hospital room, is a challenge within itself. Different types of sensors will be used to detect proximity, position and movement. This requires setting up an appropriate topology for positioning them that will ensure the accurate detection of monitored workflows. Furthermore, the system must take into consideration various restrictions that exist in medical units, such as radio frequency shielding, influence of electromagnetic radiation or Bluetooth interference with medical devices [17,42,56]. To overcome all these, our system will use communication protocols such as healthcare-targeted Bluetooth Low Energy profiles [38], or even wired communication when necessary together with custom designed intelligent devices.

Finally, the most complex challenge regards the possibility of other persons entering the consultation or surgery rooms during examination or minor surgery. If the new person touches one of the practitioners or the patient, they must perform hand disinfection once again. While identification persons can be made as soon as they enter the room, detecting contact between physician, patient and another person is a very difficult task from a technological standpoint. Our project aims to address this challenge by limiting detection to the area of the consultation bed or surgery table using a proximity sensor array placed over the area, as detailed within Sect. 5. A definitive solution to this challenge is to trigger the execution of a new workflow once an external person enters the examination/surgery room during consultation or minor surgery. We are still investigating possible solutions which involve the clear detection of contact, to avoid having to trigger a new workflow instance in cases when this is not absolutely necessary.

5   The Wireless Sensor Network

The hardware platform consists of a Wireless Sensor Network (WSN) addressed to measure and communicate to the software system information about the workflow related actions that are taking place inside the clinical location. All these events are generated by various types of sensors which have different computational, communication and power requirements. For this reason, we designed two different types of hardware nodes: dummy and smart nodes.

Dummy nodes are small, cheap and plain. They are only able to detect simple, low-level actions and send corresponding events to one of the smart nodes.

A dummy node usually integrates a proximity sensor and an accelerometer. The proximity sensor features an interrupt function for range detection up to 200 mm. The node sends the triggered events to smart nodes using BLE communication, which is further explained in Sect. 5.1. Both the sensors and the communication module stand for low current consumption, thus it is possible to power supply the device for several years using a small, coin-type battery.

Dummy nodes are able to detect *what* action is taking place, but the smart nodes are the ones that complete this information by adding *who* is triggering it, *where* and *when* it took place. In the general practitioner's office, the smart node has to find out which person is involved in every action triggered by the dummy nodes (e.g. washing hands, dispensing soap, and so on). To achieve that goal, it communicates with an RFID reader and a thermal array sensor. The location of the smart node inside the GP's office is delimited by the passive infrared array sensor. In this case, it is placed over the consultation bed. This sensor is able to trigger the event when the patient lies down for consultation and when the doctor gets close to them, which is the trigger for starting the patient examination.

The smart node placed within each room will receive RFID information using two antennas. One of them is placed at the door frame and the other at the water sink. Both antennas have different size and gain, which leads to different distance detection ranges. The antenna placed at the door frame aims to detect all badges worn inside the room by patients, practitioners or other identifiable persons. This antenna must be placed opposite to the corridor in order to avoid false positives. On the other hand, the antenna placed near the sink will have a detection range up to 80 cm. This is because this antenna must detect only the badge associated to the person using the sink.

In addition to the smart node, the sensor network in the GP office includes four dummy nodes in charge of triggering low-level events denoting that equipment is being used. These include the soap dispenser, disinfectant gel, disposable gloves and the trash can. All these devices have been modified to electronically detect use and transmit the event to the smart node. Figure 3 shows the sensor node with BLE connectivity and its location within the trash can and glove dispenser.

Installation of the sensor network in the minor surgery room is similar to the GP office, except that the minor surgery ward involves two rooms, the consultation room and the operating room. As both include an area for hand hygiene and consultation bed, we find that most devices must be duplicated. RFID readers must be installed at both door rooms and both water sinks. It's also necessary to detect the same triggered events as in the GP office: use of soap dispenser or antimicrobial gel, use of the glove dispenser and trash can. However, there are also some important differences between the surgery room and the GP office. First, there must be a way to ensure that the doctor is going to use disinfected equipment before surgery. After the autoclave sterilization procedure is completed, a barcode sticker is attached to every bag where items are packaged. When the nurse is preparing the equipment, all the items to be used are iden-

Fig. 3. Dummy nodes located in trash can and gloves dispenser.

tified through a barcode reader placed on the wall near the equipment cabinet. Second, surgery lamps prevent thermal array sensors in the ceiling from detecting when the patient is laying down on the operating table. This event is triggered using a combination of infrared sensors and RFID signal quality levels. Finally, the system must detect when the operating table is cleaned after each procedure. For this, a smart holder for the disinfectant spray has been built to detect, using a simple electronic switch, when the spray is used.

5.1   Communication Infrastructure

In June 2010, the Bluetooth Special Interest Group (SIG) published the 4.0 version, which introduced a new specification, known as Bluetooth Low Energy (BLE) [6]. This allows devices that do not require transmitting large volumes of data to connect to each other and communicate while consuming a minimum amount of energy.

This HAI-OPS platform is developed around this technology. Dummy nodes include a BLE112 Smart Module from Bluegiga [44], which integrates features required for BLE applications including radio, software stack and GATT-based profiles. Moreover, it has flexible hardware interfaces to connect different peripherals and sensors and it is powered directly from a standard 3 V coin cell battery.

The network architecture used in the HAI-OPS platform is a star topology, which in its simplest form consists of a central device that can connect to multiple peripherals. The Generic Attribute Profile (GATT) establishes how to exchange data over BLE. It makes use of the Attribute protocol (ATT) which is used to store services, characteristics and related data in a table. Most of the ATT protocol is pure client-server: the client takes the initiative, while the server responds. But it also has notifications and indication capabilities, in which the server takes the initiative of notifying a client that an attribute value has changed. The lowest concept in GATT communications is the characteristic, which encapsulates single data, such as sensor measurements.

All data generated by dummy nodes is collected by a smart node and sent to a database server. Smart nodes generate more data than dummy nodes and therefore require a more powerful communication interface. First of all, the smart node must have full time connectivity to the central server and must always be available for receiving events from dummy nodes. Second, data sent by smart nodes has to reach a web server which may be located inside or outside the local area network. In both cases, smart devices have to reach a router or an access point which is most likely located in another room, separated by several walls. Finally, data generated by some sensors like the RFID or the passive-infrared array require a transmission rate of several Mbits/s.

The smart node integrates an Ethernet connector which allows it to connect to the local network deployed in the building. In situations when cable installation is not possible in certain locations, the smart device may use its 802.11n wireless module.

Data exchanged between smart nodes and the database server is formatted in JavaScript Object Notation (JSON) format [19]. JSON is text, so it is easy to work with the data as objects, with no complicated paring and translations. Moreover, when storing data, the data has to be a certain format, and text is always one of the legal formats.

6   Software Components

The HAI-OPS cyber-physical platform's software architecture employs a client-server model, with a server installed for each clinical unit, to which multiple heterogeneous clients can connect. Considering this aspect, the present section discusses the essential components of the platform's server side, followed by the expected components that make up the client.

Being a cyber-physical platform, the hardware devices required to measure and record activities and their associated software are of major importance. Each such device contains the required networking hardware and software controller that allow it to connect to the HAI-OPS server in order to transmit live data. We refer the reader to Sect. 5 for more details about the hardware side of these devices. The software applications that manage the hardware equipment vary, according to device type: for dummy nodes, we used the "BLE SW Update Tool" [44], while smart nodes' software was created using the Python programming language, including support from specialized libraries for operations such as access to system Bluetooth and BLE resources, reading and writing of digital pins, communication with the RFID sensor, Inter-Integrated Circuit communication [35] or analog to digital conversion.

6.1   Server Modules

Providing real-time alerts in case of detected infection risk is the leading feature of the server software. However, to achieve this, the system first needs to be able to receive data from connected devices and hospital information systems (when available), to process and analyze the data and to monitor the infection risk using workflow technology. In addition, the server-side software will also perform analyses on collected data, which must thus be persisted. As a consequence of all these, the server main components, which are detailed below, are grouped into four major categories: data acquisition, workflow engine, data store and client facing subsystems.

Data Acquisition. This component's main goal is to send the data recorded by the platform's connected devices to the system's data store persistent repository. A REST architecture [24] is implemented by the server to receive sensor data and the incoming readings are JSON formatted [19]. All measurements transmitted to the server by the sensors have at least the following essential fields: a Uniform Resource Locator (URL) and a sensor unique identifier for identification of the reading, its source node and the time stamp. In addition to these, each measurement might contain further attributes according to its type: presence sensors might send boolean values, RFID readers will send the identification tag detected and so on.

As a secondary purpose, the data acquisition component can interact with hospital information systems. Such systems contain a wealth of information that can be used for prevention of infections and outbreaks, such as patient susceptibility data, arrangement and location of patients and patient beds, information about patients that are immunosuppressed or otherwise at a greater risk for contracting infections. Data received from these external systems is stored in the data repository, from where it is expected to be reused for further analyses.

Workflow Engine. A modelling component allows creating, deleting and updating workflows monitored by the system. These workflows can be executed by any commercial off the shelf workflow engine implementation that understands BPMN notation. The workflow engine interprets events, such as inputs from deployed sensors and acts upon them according to a predefined process, represented by the modelled workflow. The workflow engine component also integrates a generic adapter interface that can be developed to have various implementations, to abstract the particularities of the specific workflow engine employed. As such, HAI-OPS can be used with any major workflow engine implementation, as long as a suitable workflow adapter component is implemented. Monitored workflows can be managed via a user interface, as detailed within Sect. 6.2 by the system's administrator and they are persisted in the data store.

Data Store. This component is the system's data repository, being responsible with data persistence for registered users and devices, workflow instances and workflow metadata, as well as raw data recorded from the network of connected devices or any input transmitted by deployed hospital information systems. All stored data will be used for complex analyses part of the system's advanced line of defence geared towards pin-pointing elusive reasons of infection and for monitoring outbreaks. The data store is implemented using Couchbase Server [14].

Client Facing Subsystems. This component includes those subsystems which are connected to client components detailed in Sect. 6.2, offering server-side functionality for real-time alerting, data analysis and user and device management.

Real-Time Alerting. This is a key component of the system, as it is directly responsible with creating and transmitting the alerts. Whenever an instantiated workflow reaches a point where an infection risk is detected, the workflow engine adapter component will send the required data to this subsystem, which will create an alert and send it to responsible end-users. All alerts contain at least the following information: the workflow, device and person responsible as well as date and time information together with a textual description. The alert data is sent to the user through the alerter client component installed on the users' smartphone. In case of alert, the involved person will have to take corrective measures. All generated alerts are persisted in the data store.

Data Analysis. This component provides the advanced data analysis capabilities of the platform. Using data received from the connected devices and existing hospital information systems, its purpose is to aggregate context information and sensor readings and provide information regarding outbreak and infection risk, as well as to facilitate the identification of infection sources and means of transmission in the case of outbreak. It is directly connected to the client epidemiology user interface detailed in Sect. 6.2, which allows epidemiologists to visualize analyses results.

User and Device Management. All information regarding users and devices is deposited within the data store repository, thus being made available to other system components. Both entity types need to be uniquely identifiable, as workflow execution and alert transmission is tightly linked with involved users and connected devices registered within the system. System users can have one of the administrator, epidemiologist or clinical personnel roles with a role-based access permission system put into place.

6.2   Client Components

Two client applications are included in the HAI-OPS platform: the *Alerter Client* mobile application used to transmit alerts to clinical personnel using their smartphones or other smart wearables, and the *Administration Client* web application that provides the required features to enable management of connected devices, users and workflows.

Alerter Client. Users registered within the system will have the Alerter Client application installed on their smartphone. The application will provide two features: (1) Receive push notification when an alert is generated for the involved person; (2) View history of past alerts for the involved person. The received message will contain detailed information regarding why the alert was generated as well as a meaningful description. As further development, we will also analyze the possibility of using alternate means of notification, such as using short text messages (SMS) that will be received by the registered user's mobile device, which would allow personnel to receive alerts without installing additional software. While the current platform of choice is the smartphone, the system can work with any programmable device, such as smart wearables or a custom design active badge based on RFID technology.

Administration Client. User, workflow and smart device administration will be achieved using a web application locally installed at each medical unit where the HAI-OPS platform is deployed. The administration client will provide user interfaces for:

- Visualizing the complete history and details for the alerts that were generated for a specific user. Users having administrator privileges will be able to view the entire alert history for any registered user.
- Managing HAI related data. This interface is targeted towards epidemiologists and will allow them to visualize the results of various statistical analyses applied on collected data (e.g. statistics based on historical alert data, aggregated by user, workflow or by sensor). This information will allow identification of infection and outbreak hotspots, as well as of locations where additional disinfection procedures or staff are needed. This interface will also have access to more complex reports, including risk maps and contact networks which, in conjunction with historical alert data, are important instruments for the identification of transmission pathways.
- Administration of connected devices, registered users and monitored workflows. The associated user interface will only be available to users registered as administrators. They are responsible with managing system users and employed smart devices. When the system is deployed in a clinical unit, the administrator will manage the monitored workflows, and will modify them as required, maintaining a continuous communication with the clinical personnel.

7   Conclusions

Seven to ten people out of every 100 hospitalized patients worldwide acquire at least one hospital infection [60]. The risk of contacting or transmitting a hospital acquired infection can be greatly reduced, provided that medical units are equipped with efficient tools that ensure compliance to sanitation regulations and that medical personnel pay particular attention to hygiene.

Through our research within the HAI-OPS project [28] and through the platform under development, we are aiming to bring a contribution towards decreasing infection-related morbidity and mortality, to help prevent outbreaks and also have an indirect positive impact regarding other connected issues, such as the war against antimicrobial resistant pathogens.

The HAI-OPS platform is still under development and the present paper depicts this system in its current stage, emphasizing both hardware and software components. Using a wireless network of smart devices and sensors to monitor clinical processes that might be involved in infection transmission, the system detects potential risks in real-time and immediately alerts involved persons. Two clinical processes of different complexity, which were included in the system's prototype, as they were selected for implementation during the first pilot deployment, are detailed in this paper for exemplification: general practitioner examination and minor surgery. Similarly to all clinical processes that will be included in the system, according to medical activities that take place at various deployment locations, these processes are BPMN encoded and are executed by a workflow engine. In case of a process violation, which is detected via the wireless sensor network, the engine communicates this to the real-time alerting subsystem, which promptly sends notifications to responsible medical personnel. Thus, any clinical process can only be completely and successfully executed when preventive guidelines are followed.

Current achievements constitute the basic line of defense which our system offers for protection against infections. As further development, we intend to add an advanced line of defence, which will bring the platform to its maturity. This will include advanced analysis tools and algorithms to process data collected by sensors during large periods of time. Together with information extracted from hospital systems, risk maps will be constructed to depict the degree of infectious risk at room level. Contact networks will be used to analyze the source and spread of infection. These will be presented in an easy to understand, visual form and will assist epidemiologists in pinpointing elusive reasons of infection, in monitoring outbreaks and, most importantly, in planning infection prevention and control.

Acknowledgments. This work was supported by a grant of the Romanian National Authority for Scientific Research and Innovation, CCCDI UEFISCDI, project number 47E/2015, *HAI-OPS - Hospital Acquired Infection and Outbreak Prevention System.*

References

1. Agency for Healthcare Research and Quality: Interim Update on 2013 Annual Hospital-Acquired Condition Rate and Estimates of Cost Savings and Deaths Averted From 2010 to 2013 (2013). https://www.ahrq.gov/sites/default/files/wysiwyg/professionals/quality-patient-safety/pfp/interimhacrate2013.pdf
2. Andersen, B., Banrud, H., Boe, E., Bjordal, O., Drangsholt, F.: Comparison of UV C light and chemicals for disinfection of surfaces in hospital isolation units. Infect. Control Hosp. Epidemiol. **27**, 729–734 (2006)
3. Bioquell: Bioquell Q-10 (2016). http://www.bioquell.com/en-uk/products/life-science-products/archive-hc-products/bioquell-q10/
4. BIOVIGIL Healthcare Systems Inc.: Biovigil and our team (2015). http://www.biovigilsystems.com/about/
5. Blue Ocean Robotics: Uv-disinfection robot (2017). https://blue-ocean-robotics.com/uv-disinfection/
6. Bluetooth SIG Inc.: Bluetooth low energy (2017). https://www.bluetooth.com/what-is-bluetooth-technology/how-it-works/low-energy

7. Bocicor, I., Dascalu, M., Gaczowska, A., Hostiuc, S., Moldoveanu, A., Molina, A., Molnar, A.J., Negoi, I., Racovita, V.: Wireless sensor network based system for the prevention of hospital acquired infections. In: 13th International Conference on Evaluation of Novel Approaches to Software Engineering (2017)

8. Bocicor, M.I., Molnar, A.J., Taslitchi, C.: Preventing hospital acquired infections through a workflow-based cyber-physical system. In: Proceedings of the 11th International Conference on Evaluation of Novel Software Approaches to Software Engineering, pp. 63–68 (2016)

9. Canadian Union of Public Employees: Health care associated infections: backgrounder and fact sheet (2014). http://cupe.ca/health-care-associated-infections-backgrounder-and-fact-sheet

10. Centers for Disease Control and Prevention: Preventing Healthcare-Associated Infections. https://www.cdc.gov/washington/~cdcatWork/pdf/infections.pdf

11. Centers for Disease Control and Prevention: HAI Data and Statistics (2016). https://www.cdc.gov/hai/surveillance/

12. Coello, R., Glenister, H., Fereres, J., Bartlett, C., Leigh, D., Sedgwick, J., Cooke, E.: The cost of infection in surgical patients: a case-control study. J. Hosp. Infect. **25**, 239–250 (1993)

13. Collins, A.: Preventing health care-associated infections. In: Fagerberg, J., Mowery, D.C., Nelson, R.R. (eds.) Patient Safety and Quality: An Evidence-Based Handbook for Nurses, Chap. 41, pp. 547–570. Agency for Healthcare Research and Quality (US) (2008)

14. Couchbase: Couchbase Server (2017). https://www.couchbase.com/

15. Curtis, D., Hlady, C., Kanade, G., Pemmaraju, S., Polgreen, P., Segre, A.: Healthcare worker contact networks and the prevention of hospital-acquired infections. Plos One (2013). https://doi.org/10.1371/journal.pone.0079906

16. DebMed - The Hand Hygiene Compliance and Skin Care Experts: A different approach to hand hygiene compliance (2016). http://debmed.com/products/electronic-hand-hygiene-compliance-monitoring/a-different-approach/

17. Department of Veterans Affairs: MRI Design Guide (2008). https://www.wbdg.org/ccb/VA/VADEGUID/mri.pdf

18. Diller, T., Kelly, J., Blackhurst, D., Steed, C., Boeker, S., McElveen, D.: Estimation of hand hygiene opportunities on an adult medical ward using 24-hour camera surveillance: validation of the HOW2 Benchmark Study. Am. J. Infect. Control **42**, 602–607 (2014)

19. Ecma International: The JSON Data Interchange Format (2013). http://www.ecma-international.org/publications/files/ECMA-ST/ECMA-404.pdf

20. European Academies Science Advisory Council: Healthcare-associated infections: the view from EASAC. The Royal Society, London (2013). http://www.easac.eu/fileadmin/PDF_s/reports_statements/Healthcare-associated.pdf

21. European Centre for Disease Prevention and Control: Annual epidemiological report. antimicrobial resistance and healthcare-associated infections 2014 (2015). http://ecdc.europa.eu/en/publications/Publications/antimicrobial-resistance-annual-epidemiological-report.pdf

22. European Commission: Questions and Answers on patient safety, including the prevention and control of healthcare associated infections (2008). http://europa.eu/rapid/press-release_MEMO-08-788_en.htm

23. Excelion Technology Inc.: Accreditrack (2013). http://www.exceliontech.com/accreditrack.html

24. Fielding, R.T.: Architectural styles and the design of network-based software architectures, Doctoral dissertation, University of California (2000)

25. Friggeri, A., Chelius, G., Fleury, E., Fraboulet, A., Mentre, A., Lucet, J.C.: Reconstructing social interactions using an unreliable wireless sensor network. Comput. Commun. **34**, 609–618 (2011)
26. General Sensing: Medsense clear. hand hygiene compliance monitoring (2014). http://www.generalsensing.com/medsenseclear/
27. Government of Newfoundland and Labrador. Department of Health and Community Services: HAI Report 2009–2012 (2013). http://www.health.gov.nl.ca/health/publichealth/cdc/hai/hai_2012.pdf
28. HAI-OPS (2017). http://haiops.eu
29. Hornbeck, T., Naylor, D., Segre, A.M., Thomas, G., Herman, T., Polgreen, P.M.: Using sensor networks to study the effect of peripatetic healthcare workers on the spread of hospital associated infections. J. Infect. Dis. **206**, 1549–1557 (2012)
30. Hyginex: Introducing hyginex generation 3 (2015). http://www.hyginex.com/
31. Mastrandrea, R., Soto-Aladro, A., Brouqui, P., Barrat, A.: Enhancing the evaluation of pathogen transmission risk in a hospital by merging hand-hygiene compliance and contact data: a proof-of-concept study. BMC Res. Notes **8**, 426 (2015)
32. Mehrad, B., Clark, N., Zhanel, G., Lynch, J.: Antimicrobial resistance in hospital-acquired gram-negative bacterial infections. Chest **147**, 1413–1421 (2015)
33. Mehta, Y., Gupta, A., Todi, S., Myatra, S., Samaddar, D., Bhattacharya, P.V.P., Ramasubban, S.: Guidelines for prevention of hospital acquired infections. Indian J. Crit. Care Med. **18**, 149–163 (2014)
34. Ling, M.L., Apisarnthanarak, A., Madriaga, G.: The burden of healthcare-associated infections in Southeast Asia: a systematic literature review and meta-analysis. Clin. Infect. Dis. **60**, 1690–1699 (2015)
35. NXP Semiconductors: I2C-bus specification and user manual (2014). http://www.nxp.com/docs/en/user-guide/UM10204.pdf
36. NZOZ Eskulap: NZOZ Eskulap (2016). www.eskulapskierniewice.pl/
37. Object Management Group: Business process model and notation (2015). http://www.bpmn.org/
38. Omre, A.: Bluetooth low energy: wireless connectivity for medical monitoring. J. Diab. Sci. Technol. **4**, 457–463 (2010)
39. Philips: Protocolwatch - SSC Sepsis (2015). http://www.healthcare.philips.com/main/products/patient_monitoring/products/protocol_watch/
40. RL Solutions: The RL6 Suite/Infection Surveillance (2015). http://www.rlsolutions.com/rl-products/infection-surveillance
41. Ryan, J.: Medtech profiles: Intelligentm - a simple yet powerful app to dramatically reduce hospital-acquired infections (2013). https://medtechboston.medstro.com/profiles-intelligentm/
42. Saraf, S.: Use of mobile phone in operating room. J. Med. Phys. **34**, 101–1002 (2009)
43. SHEA/IDSA Practice Recommendation: Strategies to prevent surgical site infections in acute care. Infection Control and Hospital Epidemiology, vol. 29 (2008)
44. Silicon Labs: Bluegiga Bluetooth Smart Software Stack (2017). https://www.silabs.com/products/development-tools/software/bluegiga-bluetooth-smart-software-stack
45. Simonette, M.: Tech solutions to hospital acquired infections (2013). http://www.healthbizdecoded.com/2013/06/tech-solutions-to-hospital-acquired-infections/
46. Stehle, J., Voirin, N., Barrat, A., Cattuto, C., Colizza, V., Isella, L., Regis, C., Pinton, J.F., Khanafer, N., Van den Broeck, N., Vanhems, P.: Simulation of an SEIR infectious disease model on the dynamic contact network of conference attendees. BMC Med. **9**, 87 (2011)

47. SteriSafe ApS: Decontamination and disinfection robot for hospitals (2017). http://sterisafe.eu/about-sterisafe/
48. Stone, P.: Economic burden of healthcare-associated infections: an american perspective. Expert Rev. Pharmacoecon Outcomes Res. **9**, 417–422 (2009)
49. Surviving Sepsis Campaign: International Guidelines for Management of Severe Sepsis and Septic Shock: 2012 (2012). http://www.sccm.org/Documents/SSC-Guidelines.pdf
50. Swipe Sense: Hand hygiene. Redefined (2015). https://www.swipesense.com/
51. Tikhomirov, E.: WHO programme for the control of hospital infections. Chemioterapia **6**, 148–151 (1987)
52. Tru-D Smart UVC: About tru-d (2016). http://tru-d.com/why-uvc-disinfection/
53. UltraClenz: Patient safeguard system (2016). http://www.ultraclenz.com/patient-safeguard-system/
54. Vanhems, P., Barrat, A., Cattuto, C., Pinton, J.F., Khanafer, N., Regis, C., Kim, B., Comte, B., Voirin, N.: Estimating potential infection transmission routes in hospital wards using wearable proximity sensors. PloS One **8**, e73970 (2013)
55. Voirin, N., Payet, C., Barrat, A., Cattuto, C., Khanafer, N., Regis, C., Kim, B., Comte, B., Casalegno, J.S., Lina, B., Vanhems, P.: Combining high-resolution contact data with virological data to investigate influenza transmission in a tertiary care hospital. Infect. Control Hosp. Epidemiol. **36**, 254–260 (2015)
56. Wallin, M., Wajntraub, S.: Evaluation of bluetooth as a replacement for cables in intensive care and surgery. Critical Care and Trauma, pp. 763–767 (2003)
57. World Health Organization: Prevention of hospital-acquired infections - a practical guide (2002). http://www.who.int/csr/resources/publications/whocdscsreph200212.pdf
58. World Health Organization: How to handwash? (2009). http://www.who.int/gpsc/5may/How_To_HandWash_Poster.pdf
59. World Health Organization: The burden of health care-associated infection worldwide (2010). http://www.who.int/gpsc/country_work/summary_20100430_en.pdf
60. World Health Organization: Health care-associated infections - fact sheet (2011). http://www.who.int/gpsc/country_work/gpsc_ccisc_fact_sheet_en.pdf
61. World Health Organization: Report on the burden of endemic health care-associated infection worldwide (2011). http://apps.who.int/iris/bitstream/10665/80135/1/9789241501507_eng.pdf
62. World Health Organization: Clean Care is Safer Care - Five moments for hand hygiene (2015). http://www.who.int/gpsc/tools/Five_moments/en/
63. Xenex: Xenex germ-zapping robots (2015). http://www.xenex.com/

Software Engineering

Exploiting Requirements Engineering to Resolve Conflicts in Pervasive Computing Systems

Osama M. Khaled[(✉)], Hoda M. Hosny[(✉)], and Mohamed Shalan[(✉)]

Department of Computer Science and Engineering,
The American University in Cairo, Cairo, Egypt
{okhaled, hhosny, mshalan}@aucegypt.edu

Abstract. Pervasive computing systems are complex and challenging. In this research, a novice statistical approach is introduced to resolve conflicts among the pervasive system requirements. It is based on a basic requirements model used in our reference architecture for pervasive computing (PervCompRA-SE). The approach uses the normal distribution rules to validate the solutions for the conflicts. It can save time and effort for the business analyst and the software architect especially when the system scope is too large, the access to the stakeholders is limited, or when there are constraints on the project's timelines.

Keywords: Pervasive computing · Ubiquitous computing
Requirements engineering · Software engineering
Requirements conflict resolution

1 Introduction

Requirements Engineering (RE) is an engineering approach to breakdown the complexity of the requirements in an abstract way which explains the needs of the users and at the same time offers a framework that governs the scope of the software system to guarantee the success of the software project [1]. A business analyst, who gathers and elicits requirements, also works on building the functional and quality requirements and on explaining the use cases which are anticipated by the users. The use cases are also used to generate the test cases which will, at a later stage, be used to validate the software implementation [2, 3].

It is a challenging activity which requires a high level of understanding to make sure that the users' requirements are captured correctly especially if there are many stakeholders with contradicting needs. One of the main responsibilities of the business analyst is to resolve the conflicts between the requirements in order to have a consistent requirements' model. The resolution of the conflicts between the functional requirements may sometimes be quite clear. In its simplest forms, the conflict could be resolved by removing one of the contradicting requirements upon agreement with the stakeholders. But in other times it may be a complex situation.

Accordingly, another important task for the business analyst is to speculate the priorities and the precedence of the requirements based on how they impact each other.

E. Damiani et al. (Eds.): ENASE 2017, CCIS 866, pp. 93–115, 2018.
https://doi.org/10.1007/978-3-319-94135-6_5

This will drive the implementation by highlighting the requirements which should be ideally implemented first so that the next ones will be more easily implemented. Even if there is no sequential implementation of the requirements, it gives hints about the grouping of the requirements and hence about the candidate technical modules that may be designed in the high level architecture.

The quality requirements of the system could be treated the same way, especially that quality requirements could have conflicts by nature. For example, the requirements to tighten the security of the system will most likely conflict with the requirements to boost the response time. The tasks of the business analyst, or possibly the software architect in this case, is more important as it may not be clear, especially for the users, on how to resolve the conflicts of the quality needs. Users are usually akin to tell their functional needs more than state their quality requirements [4].

In this research work, the requirements of the quality features pertaining to the pervasive system are endeavored in order to generate statistical knowledge about the quality features so that the generation of the architectural model is moderated as well as the optimization parameters which are refined at runtime. This can also help the business analyst arrive at the best decisions with the minimal engagement of the stakeholders.

The paper presents this research study as follows: Sect. 2 presents the related work, Sect. 3 describes the proposed methodology, Sect. 4 gives details about the tradeoff analysis of the essential requirements of the studied quality features, Sect. 5 lists the identified conflicts between the requirements, Sect. 6 presents the resolutions of the conflicts, and Sect. 7 describes the adopted evaluation techniques. In Sect. 8 the applicability of the research outcomes is discussed, and Sect. 9 concludes the paper.

2   Related Work

The art of requirements engineering in the field of pervasive computing has recently received a considerable amount of attention from researchers. The Authors in [5–8] introduced some interesting elicitation techniques which they presented as peculiar to pervasive computing Additional contributions could be reviewed from [9].

Some relevant contributions which resolve conflicting requirements are surveyed through subjective opinions or preset preferences by the users. They simply eliminate a requirement in favor of another requirement. For example, Salado and Nilchiani [10] worked on identifying conflicts using a "tension matrix" mechanism using a set of heuristics. They remove the conflicting requirement according to specific criteria.

Sadana and Liu [11] adopted a similar approach which depicts a hierarchy of conflicting requirements and potential conflicts among the quality attributes. The Authors make a link between the quality attributes and the conflicts similar to that presented in this research work and that will be explained later.

Oster et al. [12] organize stakeholder requirements as preferences. They use a conditional importance network (CI-Nets) to identify and resolve conflicts between the stakeholder requirements. If conditions are met then the preferences are kept, else if there are conflicts among them, then the least preferred ones are removed.

Conflict resolution requires the analyst to first assign a priority for every requirement in one way or another. A priority of the requirement is made mostly via subjective methods. Galaster and Eberlein [13] provide such an approach which requires subjective opinion from business and technical stakeholders about every requirement. They associate different generic attributes with every requirement and ask the stakeholders to define their values in order to get an overall ranking for the requirement.

Mendizabal and Spier [4] provided a prioritization approach for the performance optimization requirements based on actual performance statistics. They collected performance data about some pages in a web application and assigned a performance rank using a ranking formula and then decided with the stakeholders on which pages to include in the performance enhancement exercise. The authors recognized the disadvantage of their empirical choices for the weights of the parameters used in the ranking formula as they found some least demanded pages still included. This could have been avoided if the stakeholders, including domain experts, were asked to assign the weights for these parameters as well.

The surveyed research efforts about conflict resolution usually take simple approaches by eliminating the least important requirement. To our knowledge, this work represents the first attempt to introduce balanced solutions for conflicting requirements through a statistical approach that depends on the strength of these solutions. It offers a practical guidance to the architects who need to satisfy most of the conflicting requirements.

3 Methodology

A pervasive system is highly volatile as its users are in continuous movement along with their devices. Context sensitivity characterizes a pervasive system in order to detect the surrounding changes, and the pervasive system must *adapt* to these changes in order to make a rational response. It is an environment-interactive system [14] given that visitor devices appear and disappear spontaneously.

Accordingly, an approach was adopted in this research work that is inspired from the process re-engineering concept [15, 16]. A normal process is practiced after it is designed whether it is for industrial or business activities. Since changes happen all the time, it is usually required at some point in time to improve the process. Hence, a process re-engineering project could be initiated to improve the efficiency of the process.

The main objectives of process re-engineering are to maximize the value of the tasks which add value to the customer, minimize the tasks which are essential (but do not add value to the customer), and eliminate the tasks which are a complete waste to the whole process [17].

Inspired by the process re-engineering concept, the requirements are stated as a set of maximize, minimize, and eliminate needs for desirable and non-desirable values [18]. The relationships among the requirements are modeled, if they exist, in a similar way. Hence, a requirement A could *minimize* the need of requirement B if requirement A helps requirement B to minimize the non-desired value. The same is said about requirement A maximizing requirement B. However, if two requirements have conflicting needs, then they are modeled as (*requirement A conflicts with requirement*

B). This approach is different from the classical approach [19] of having "positive correlation", "negative correlation", or conflict between two requirements in the sense that both *minimize* and *maximize* relationships are "positive correlation" relationships and their analysis becomes simpler from the process re-engineering perspective.

A trade-off analysis exercise is included in the form of an intensive statistical study of the requirements. A subjective study was conducted as well to validate the statistically-driven priorities with the priorities of the users [20]. The trade-off analysis is extended to introduce balanced solutions for the identified conflicts between the requirements [18, 21].

4   Requirements Trade-off Analysis

The most challenging activity in this research work was to identify the basic requirements, as listed in the Appendix, which should suffice for a software engineer to draft a new concrete architecture for a pervasive system. A solid basic list of 55 requirements was identified as listed in our research work [18, 20]. These requirements were driven based on the most prevalent and critical quality features in pervasive computing [22, 23] as shown in Table 1.

Table 1. Pervasive system quality features.

Feature	Description
Adaptable Behavior	The system must respond dynamically to changes in the environment as needed [20]
Context Sensitivity	The system must have the ability to sense and retrieve data from its environment [22]
Experience Capture	The system must capture and register experiences for later use [22]
Fault Tolerance	The system must detect errors and take the appropriate recovery actions [22]
Heterogeneity of Devices	The system must use different device technologies seamlessly [22]
Invisibility	The system must integrate computing resources and guarantee that the user has the minimum awareness of them [22]
Privacy and Trust	The system must ensure that personal operations confidentiality is protected and accessed only by trusted entities [22]
Quality of Service	The system must set expectation for its services by setting constraints on the provided services. For example, system response may be considered invalid if it is received after a certain period of time [22]
Safety	The system must provide immunity for its users and interacting devices from harm and damage
Security	It is concerned with protecting data from being leaked to unauthorized individuals, protecting data from corruption and alternation, and ensuring accessibility to data whenever requested
Service Omnipresence	The system should give its users the feeling that they carry computer services wherever they move [22]

The requirements were written in a generic way to suit a business reference architecture. For example, in order to achieve the *Service Omnipresence* quality feature, it is essential to distribute computing power, enrich the experience of the highly-used scenarios, provide Informative messages, use a unique user identifier and utilize the user's cell phone. The *Heterogeneity of Devices* requires another set of requirements. Its basic requirements are to maximize the number of device technologies, provide a unique identifier for every object, and render content on a maximum number of devices.

It was clear from the initial survey that some requirements do conflict (negative impact) with each other, and other requirements positively impact each other. Hence, a relationship matrix was built between all the requirements to emphasize on the kind of impact, if it exists. For example, it is required to *maximize the number of device technologies* in order to provide *Heterogeneity of Devices* and at the same time, it is required to *minimize conflicting usage of the shared resources* in order to guarantee an overall *Safety* for the pervasive system. As manufacturers usually do not provide compatible technologies with each other's products [18], and even between different products from the same manufacturer, the probability of conflicts among shared resources increases. An empirical decision was taken, based on knowledge, to resolve the conflict for that requirement in the *Safety* quality feature if a conflict exists. The results of these decisions were validated as will be explained below.

All the requirements were reviewed and checked against each other to identify whether they *minimize, maximize,* or *conflict* with each other. The weights of the quality features are calculated according to a simple formula, as shown in Eq. (1), which calculates the complexity of the quality feature

$$QF_s = \sum_{rq=1}^{n} QF_{rq} * \sum_{rl=0}^{z} QF_{rl} * \sum_{ft=1}^{y} QF_{ft} \tag{1}$$

The requirements for every quality feature were counted ($\sum_{rq=1}^{n} QF_{rq}$), multiplied it by the sum of the number of relations for the requirements in the quality feature ($\sum_{rl=0}^{z} QF_{rl}$) and then multiplied the result by the number of covered quality features ($\sum_{ft=1}^{y} QF_{ft}$). The score was normalized by dividing it by the sum of all the scores to get the *Weight* as computed by Eq. (1). The results, shown in Table 2, are sorted by weight from highest to lowest. It is important to note that the *relations* and the *features* cover self-reference. Hence, if there is a maximize relationship, for example, between two requirements in one quality feature, it gets counted.

The complexity equation can be explained as follows:

1. The requirements in a feature represent its *size*.
2. The number of covered features represents the *feature coupling*.
3. The relationships of the requirements in a feature represent the *density of the feature coupling*.

Table 2. Quality features requirements complexity weights.

Feature	# Requirements $\sum\limits_{rq=1}^{n} QF_{rq}$	# Relations $\sum\limits_{rl=0}^{z} QF_{rl}$	# Features $\sum\limits_{ft=1}^{y} QF_{ft}$	Score QF_s	Weight QF_s/total score
Safety	10	11	4	440	0.209524
Security	8	11	5	440	0.209524
Service Omnipresence	5	11	6	330	0.157143
Fault Tolerance	6	7	5	210	0.1
Heterogeneity of Devices	3	11	4	132	0.062857
Privacy and Trust	4	8	4	128	0.060952
Context Sensitivity	5	6	4	120	0.057143
Quality of Service	4	6	4	96	0.045714
Adaptable behavior	4	7	3	84	0.04
Experience Capture	3	7	4	84	0.04
Invisibility	4	3	3	36	0.017143
Grand Total	**56**	**88**	**46**	**2100**	**1**

5   Requirements Conflict Identification

From the requirements relationship matrix, 12 pairs of conflicts were identified, which were given IDs as shown in Table 3 where Req A and Req B columns contain the IDs of the conflicting requirements.

Table 3. Conflicting requirements [21].

Conf ID	Req A	Req B	Conf ID	Req A	Req B
1	54	19	7	18	44
2	10	27	8	45	30
3	53	27	9	5	27
4	18	38	10	44	30
5	18	35	11	49	30
6	18	14	12	21	3

The adopted process to identify the conflicts is as follows:

1. Iterate over every requirement and check if its value contradicts with another requirement's value
2. Mark a found pair of requirements as a conflict and give it an ID.

3. Justify the conflict in details.
4. Study the conflict deeply to identify the superseding requirement
5. Justify the superseding decision.

The conflicts were reviewed critically to provide a rationale for each conflict as follows:

1. *Conflict #1:* The system must be decisive about the identity of the user especially if there are more than one device joining the system which belong to the same user.
2. *Conflict #2:* The system should capture personal knowledge about the user if he/she agrees about that in order to have a better control on private information.
3. *Conflict #3:* Informative messages must be filtered for confidential information in order not to cause leakage of private information.
4. *Conflict #4:* The normal incompatibilities among the manufacturers may generate conflicts among the shared resources.
5. *Conflict #5:* Unexpected side effects may increase as the system acquires more device technologies.
6. *Conflict #6:* As the number of device joins to the system increases, the probability of faults increases especially if the device technology is new or has not been tested before.
7. *Conflict #7:* Different manufacturers may have different operating systems which may be vulnerable to attacks, which increases the security threat to the whole system.
8. *Conflict #8:* The performance of the system degrades as the security rules over the data transmission increases which may impact the availability of the system at some point of time
9. *Conflict #9:* The system must carefully collect private data about the users from its sensors in order to minimize the risk of revealing data to unauthorized entities.
10. *Conflict #10:* The average processing power of the smart devices increases if the system forces additional security rules over them.
11. *Conflict #11:* Counter-measure actions add burden on the average processing power of the system which degrades the performance of the services.
12. *Conflict #12:* The system should issue wise notifications to the users in a way that does not lead to unnecessary interactions.

The above analysis shows that there are 16 requirements that have possible conflicts which represent around 30% of the discovered requirements. They are scattered across all the quality features as shown in Table 4.

The 12 conflicts are shown among the quality features according to the ownership of the requirements. For example, the invisibility feature conflicts with the adaptable behavior feature in a pair of requirements. There are 2 requirements that belong to the heterogeneity of devices feature and conflict with the safety quality feature. It is also noticed that Context Sensitivity does not conflict with Adaptable Behavior nor Fault Tolerance. Another fact that can be detected from this table is that the Device Hetero-geneity and Security features have the highest percentage of conflict relationships.

Table 4. Quality features conflicts [21].

Source \ Destination	AB	FT	HD	PT	QoS	SY	ST	Total
CS				1				1
EC				1				1
HD		1				2	1	4
IN	1							1
ST					3			3
SO			1	1				2
Grand Total	1	1	1	3	3	2	1	12

6 Conflict Resolution

A real challenge that faces the business analyst and software architect is to resolve the conflicts between the requirements. A simple and direct resolution strategy is to eliminate one requirement for the sake of the other as long as it is identified as a superseding one as follows:

1. Conf #1: Requirement #54 supersedes #19 in order to apply user-related rules on the user's devices properly.
2. Conf #2: Requirement #27 supersedes #10 because protecting the confidentiality and the privacy of the information is by far more important than capturing personal knowledge; otherwise, the probability of leaking information may increase.
3. Conf #3: Requirement #27 supersedes #53 because privacy of the user is more important as it is protected by law where an uninformative message may cause, in the worst case, a bad user experience.
4. Conf #4: Requirement #38 supersedes #18 because conflicts of the crucial shared resources may hinder the safety of the users and the system. Accordingly, the system must not allow those devices which are not well known and may cause troubles with shared resources.
5. Conf #5: Requirement #35 supersedes #18 because if the new technology will lead to expected or unexpected side effects which may risk the safety of the environment, then it is better to keep it away as the safety of humans, living creatures and the system itself is far more important.
6. Conf #6: Requirement #18 supersedes #14 because the benefit of increasing device technologies will shadow the faults that may appear in the environment since the system can handle them in different ways.
7. Conf #7: Requirement #44 supersedes #18 because security rules are more important for the sake of the whole environment even if the number of device technologies does not increase.
8. Conf #8: Requirement #45 supersedes #30 because an increase in the average processing capability due to securing transmitted data may be accepted if the system accepts joins from non-trusted devices.

9. Conf #9: Requirement #27 supersedes #5 because if the sensors are not controlled properly, this may lead to leakage of confidential data. This is a very high risk which shadows the benefit of the sensors.
10. Conf #10: Requirement #44 supersedes #30 because an environment is considered healthy if security rules are applied for the overall protection of the environment. The wise decision in this case is to accept any additional increase in the average processing time for the sake of the overall environment's health.
11. Conf #11: Requirement #49 supersedes #30 because the counter-measures help the system continue working normally and are of a great value even if the average processing time may decrease.
12. Conf #12: Requirement #3 supersedes #21 because keeping the users informed all the time with the changes, even if it entails more interactions, helps protect the overall safety of the environment.

The overall goal of the reference architecture is not met if conflicts are resolved by eliminating the requirements. Accordingly, it was decided to identify solutions for these conflicts in order to satisfy as many requirements as possible. By introducing functional and architectural solutions, it is guaranteed to enhance the decision making for the architect in order to generate concrete architectures out of the reference architecture and that in turn will make them more practical [24].

All the conflicts were reviewed, as explained in Sect. 3, and alternative solutions proposed. Some solutions were merged to achieve a higher balance. In some other conflicts, only a single solution is proposed or the superseding requirement is chosen (Fig. 1).

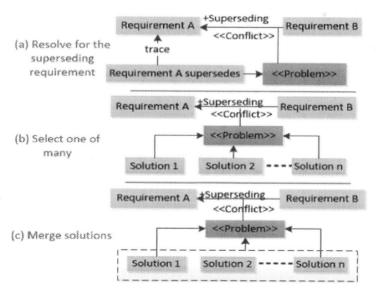

Fig. 1. Conflict resolution [21].

The alternative solutions were analyzed thoroughly and a relationship matrix built between the solutions and the requirements of the quality features within the scope of the conflict, maximize, and minimize relationships since this could be adopted as a cross-cutting concern [24]. The merged solution is designed so that the positive impact (maximize and minimize) of one solution shadows the negative impact (conflict) of the other solutions with the same quality feature requirement if it exists. The score of the solution is calculated using the feature weight of the quality feature in Table 2. The formula, as mentioned in [21], estimates the positive impact of the solution given the negative impact and as expressed in formula (2)

$$Score = R_+ * FR^+_{weight} - R_- * FR^-_{weight} \qquad (2)$$

R_+ is the percentage of the minimize (mi_f) and maximize (mx_f) relationships from all the relationships of the solution with the other requirements. R_- is the percentage of the conflict relationships (cf_f) of the solution with the other requirements. They are calculated using formulas (3) and (4), as mentioned in [21], respectively.

$$R_+ = \frac{\sum_{f=1}^{11} mi_f + mx_f}{\sum_{f=1}^{11} mi_f + mx_f + cf_f} \qquad (3)$$

$$R_- = \frac{\sum_{f=1}^{11} cf_f}{\sum_{f=1}^{11} mi_f + mx_f + cf_f} \qquad (4)$$

FR^+_{weight} is the weighted average, an average multiplied by its probability [25], of the minimize and maximize relationships of the solution with the requirements belonging to a single feature multiplied by the weight of this feature ($weight_f$) in Table 2. FR^-_{weight} is the weighted average of the number of conflict relationships of the solution with the requirements belonging to a single feature multiplied by the weight of the feature ($weight_f$) in Table 2. They are calculated using formulas (5) and (6) as cited in [21]

$$FR^+_{weight} = \sum_{f=1}^{11} \left(mx_f + mi_f\right) * weight_f \qquad (5)$$

$$FR^-_{weight} = \sum_{f=1}^{11} \left(cf_f\right) * weight_f \qquad (6)$$

The followed rules in order to devise the formula were that:

1. The generated solution score must be calculated based on the positive and negative relationships with the requirements of the quality features.
2. The maximize and minimize relationships impact the solution score positively, while the conflict relationships impact the solution score negatively.
3. The formula must generate a normalized score in order to analyze all the solutions for all the conflicts on the same scale.

4. The weights of the quality features, which are normalized already, must drive the score of the solution.

The solution score tables in the sub-sections below show only the number of relations for every feature and then the weighted score is given by applying the formula. A list of the proposed solutions was devised, as shown in Table 5, and the way solutions will be linked to conflicts is as explained above.

Table 5. Solutions list [21].

Sol ID	Solution	Sol ID	Solution
SO-001	Associate device with user	SO-002	Authenticate every time
SO-003	Delete unnecessary sensor data	SO-004	Disable sensors if not needed
SO-005	Increase shared resources	SO-006	Mediate access through a middleware
SO-007	Authorize access upon information request	SO-008	Classify personal information as a setting
SO-009	Define information access explicitly	SO-010	Teach the system (add to its knowledge base)
SO-011	Declare security rules for the devices willing to join the system	SO-012	Scan devices before joining the system
SO-013	Apply less strict security rules on the private smart environment	SO-014	Apply less strict security rules on trusted objects
SO-015	Log all changes for later access	SO-016	Notify for important changes only
SO-017	Transfer non-securely if possible	SO-018	Use a light-weight encryption algorithm
SO-019	Use compatible technologies	SO-020	A positive merge of solutions (7, 8, 9)
SO-021	A positive merge of solutions (10, 19)	SO-022	A positive merge of solutions (11, 12)
SO-023	A positive merge of solutions (13, 14)	SO-024	A positive merge of solutions (15, 16)
SO-025	A positive merge of solutions (17, 18)		

6.1 One Solution

Conflicts 3 and 11 are resolved for the superseding requirement. This decision is taken because partial fulfillment of the superseding requirements may risk the existence of the whole system. Conflict 6 is resolved using solution 21, which is used to resolve other conflicts in the coming sub-sections. It is meaningless to assign a score for the solution in this case.

6.2 Alternative Solutions

These are the type of problems that bare different solutions that may not be merged. A description for every solution is given and the number of relationships is counted between these solutions and the requirements of the quality features as shown in Table 6.

Table 6. Conflict 4 solutions score [18].

Solution	SO-005				SO-006				SO-019			
Feature	mi	mx	cf	Total	mi	mx	cf	Total	mi	mx	cf	Total
SY	1			1	2			2	2			2
ST												
SO		2		2							1	1
FT					1			1	1			1
HD		1		1		2		2		1		1
PT												
CS		1		1		1		1				
QoS	1			1								
AB		1		1		1		1				
EC												
IN												
Total	2	5		7	3	4		7	3	1	1	5
Score	0.7295				0.7419				0.4341			

The score equation was applied for every solution. For example, Conflict 4 is between requirement (Maximize the number of device technologies) and requirement (Minimize conflicting usage of shared resources) can be resolved by solution (Increase shared resources), solution (Mediate access through a middleware), or solution (Use compatible technologies).

1. **Solution SO-005 (Increase shared resources):** Increase the number of shared resources to decrease conflicts. For example, if there is X number of temperature sensors and they are not enough to serve the system and cause contention, then it may be possible to add more sensors to respond to the increased demand. The condition here is that they have to be from the same technology providers. This is a classical solution that works in case the devices are not fully tested and there is a high probability that they may cause problems in working systems. This solution has a positive impact on 6 features and zero negative impact.

2. **Solution SO-006 (Mediate access through a middleware):** Shared resources can be mediated using a middleware-software. The purpose of the middleware is to ensure proper access to the shared resources even if they are coming from different technology providers. The middleware has a main benefit which is hiding the complexity of the different technologies from service requesters leading to better handling of resources [26]. This solution has a positive impact on 2 features and zero negative impact.

3. **Solution SO-019 (Use compatible technologies):** There are technologies that were tested in common solutions and proven to be working with minimal conflicts, including shared resource conflicts. Hence, by using compatible technologies only, it will not be possible to add more devices from other technology providers unless they were tested with the existing ones in the system and proven to be working without major problems. This solution has a positive impact on 3 features and a negative impact on one feature.

The same approach was applied for conflicts 1 and 9 and that resulted in defining alternative solutions as shown in Table 7.

Table 7. Alternative solutions conflict matrix [21].

Conflict ID / Solution	1	4	9
SO-001	●		
SO-002	●		
SO-003			●
SO-004			●
SO-005		●	
SO-006		●	
SO-019		●	

6.3 Merged Solutions

The same approach was followed in defining alternative solutions for the same conflicts in Sect. 6.2. However, a more solid solution could be found if solutions could be introduced together. The merged solution eliminates the negative impact (conflict) only if there is one or more maximize or minimize relationships provided from at least one solution for the same requirement.

The adopted procedure to decide if a business requirement is satisfied by a merged solution is as follows:

1. Build a matrix of the solutions as columns and the requirements as rows.
2. Go over every piece of requirements and if there are positive and negative relationships, then ignore the negative relationship and inherit the positive ones. Hence, the merged solution will have a single positive relationship with that requirement.
3. If all the relationships of the alternative solutions are negative, then the merged solution will have a single negative relationship with that requirement.
4. This activity is repeated for all the requirements that are impacted by the alternative solutions.
5. The requirements that are not addressed by the alternative solutions are ignored.

For example, Conflict 8, as shown in Table 8, is between requirement (Ensure secure data transmission) and requirement (Minimize average processing time) can be resolved by solution SO-017 (Transfer non-securely if possible), solution SO-018 (Use light-weight encryption algorithm), or solution SO-025 which is a merged solution between them.

1. **Solution SO-017 (Transfer non-securely if possible):** There are some contexts that may not require secure transmission. For example, (a) Private systems that are not accessed from outsiders may transfer normally without encryption, (b) Transmission of an already encrypted material, and (c) public data. The overall response time in this case will be optimum. This solution has positive impacts on 5 features and negative impacts on 3 features.
2. **Solution SO-018 (Use light-weight encryption algorithm):** By using light-weight encryption algorithms, the system may be able to sustain for a longer period of time, does not degrade performance as much, and an acceptable level of security is achieved while transmitting data [27]. This solution has a positive impact on 4 features and zero negative impact.
3. **Solution SO-025 (merged solution):** a merged solution between the above two solutions. It has a positive impact on 6 features and zero negative impact.

Table 9 shows all the conflicts and the solutions that make the required balance.

Table 8. Conflict 8 merged alternative solutions [18].

Solution	SO-017				SO-018				SO-025			
Feature	mi	mx	cf	Total	mi	mx	cf	Total	mi	mx	cf	Total
SY			1	1		1		1		1		1
ST	1	1	1	3	1	1		2	2	1		3
SO		1		1						1		1
FT	1			1	1			1	1			1
HD												
PT												
CS												
QoS	1		1	2	1	1		2	1	1		2
AB		2		2						2		2
EC												
IN												
Total	3	4	3	10	3	3		6	4	6		10
Score	0.4219				0.8200				1.2667			

7 Evaluation

Different solutions for the same problem were introduced in order to enrich the selection process for the architect. They will be ultimately used in the concrete architecture of the pervasive system in some way or another based on the final decision.

Table 9. Merged alternative solutions score matrix [21].

Solution \ Conflict ID	2	5	7	8	10	12
SO-007	●					
SO-008	●					
SO-009	●					
SO-010		●				
SO-011			●			
SO-012			●			
SO-013					●	
SO-014					●	
SO-015						●
SO-016						●
SO-017				●		
SO-018				●		
SO-019		●				
SO-020	●					
SO-021		●				
SO-022			●			
SO-023					●	
SO-024						●
SO-025				●		

A solution that has a lower score is considered inferior within the scope of the selected requirements. It could be a good solution within another context which is driven by the weights of the quality features. If the weights of the quality features are changed, the scores of the solutions may change as well and the solution with the lower positive impact may score higher.

Table 10 reveals some facts about the solutions. It reveals that the highest score is 1.6550 for solution SO-020, which merges solutions SO-007, SO-008, and SO-009, for conflict 2 as shown in Table 10 and the lowest score is −0.1218 for solution SO-004 (Disable sensors if not needed) for conflict 9 as shown in Table 7. The mean of all the scores μ, is 0.6431 and the standard deviation σ, is 0.4805. Accordingly, it is inferred that the solutions that have scores above the mean have a higher positive impact and those that are below the mean have a lower positive impact. It is important to note that all the scores are on the same ratio scale and it is possible to calculate the central tendency of these solutions as will be explained in the next paragraph.

What makes this statistical evaluation powerful is that these solutions are normally distributed. The normality of the solution scores was tested according to [25] and was found to be normal with a P-value of 0.536 and confidence level 95% (Fig. 2). In the

Table 10. Scores of the conflict solutions [21].

Solution	FR^+_{weight}	FR^-_{weight}	R_+	R_-	Score
SO-001	1.123	0	1	0	1.123
SO-002	1.058	0.280	0.545	0.455	0.450
SO-003	0.563	0.330	0.636	0.364	0.238
SO-004	0.178	0.347	0.429	0.571	−0.122
SO-005	0.730	0	1	0	0.730
SO-006	0.742	0	1	0	0.742
SO-007	1.415	0.146	0.833	0.167	1.155
SO-008	0.674	0.310	0.818	0.182	0.495
SO-009	0.830	0.034	0.778	0.222	0.638
SO-010	0.936	0	1	0	0.936
SO-011	0.949	0	1	0	0.949
SO-012	1.210	0.046	0.875	0.125	1.054
SO-013	0.355	0.419	0.600	0.400	0.046
SO-014	0.355	0.210	0.750	0.250	0.214
SO-015	0.204	0	1	0	0.204
SO-016	0.118	0.210	0.750	0.250	0.036
SO-017	0.802	0.465	0.700	0.300	0.422
SO-018	0.820	0	1	0	0.820
SO-019	0.582	0.157	0.800	0.200	0.434
SO-020	1.753	0.017	0.944	0.056	1.655
SO-021	0.936	0	1	0	0.936
SO-022	1.577	0.046	0.900	0.100	1.415
SO-023	0.355	0.419	0.600	0.400	0.046
SO-024	0.265	0.210	0.857	0.143	0.197
SO-025	1.267	0	1	0	1.267

probability plot, if the P-Value is greater than 0.5, then it is an indication that the population is normally distributed. The distribution of the scores in Table 11 shows that the presented solutions are capable of resolving the conflicts as the model's capability index, (Cpk = 1.17), is greater than 1 (and the upper bound is 2.23 and the lower bound is −0.8). Being normally distributed gives an edge for the architects to:

1. Simplify the decision for alternative solutions by measuring them using the statistical model as a reference.
2. Standardize the solution scores as z values and use the standard z-table [25]. Z values simplify the interpretation of the scores as the z-value of zero or more has a higher positive impact than the negative z-values. Z-values could be obtained by using Eq. (7) [24].

$$z = \frac{score - \mu}{\sigma} \tag{7}$$

3. Allow the solutions to follow the system goal which could be controlled by the weights of the quality features.

The architect can maximize the positive impact of the solutions if he/she selects the solutions with the highest scores for every problem. The architect must revisit his/her selections if the weights of the quality features changed.

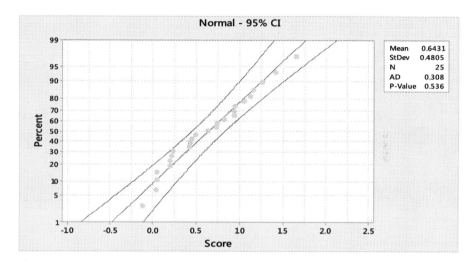

Fig. 2. Probability plot of the solutions' scores [21].

Since the weights of the quality features are considered quite important for the correct scores of the solutions, they were validated before starting to analyze the conflicts. A survey containing the list of all the requirements was published (as shown in the Appendix), in which some users were asked to give their subjective decision about the importance of every requirement. The survey received responses from 17 respondents who have different experiences in software development within different business industries. The responses were grouped by the quality features and the average importance was then computed, which is equivalent to the complexity weight, for every quality feature. The responses showed close proximity to our conclusions about the weights of the quality features with a relatively small standard deviation, 2.3741 [20].

It was interesting to compare our results for the ranking of the quality features (Table 11) with the results reported by Spínola and Travassos [22], the guiding research work which lists most of the mentioned quality features. Spínola and Travassos's approach was to review the literature and run surveys and workshops with users to reach for the outcome conclusion. However, our trade-off analysis was made using pure technical analysis and statistical approaches after the requirements for the quality features were collected.

Table 11. Comparison between our priority results and Spínola and Travassos' priority results with respect to the business quality features [18].

Key comparison	This research work	Spínola and Travassos's research work
Service omnipresence	Service omnipresence is ranked as one of the top priority features	Service Omnipresence is a key characteristic that is found in all ubiquitous projects
Classification of the Business Quality Features	Quality features are classified as *enablers* and *constraints*	Classified quality features as *functional* and *restrictive*
Enabler vs. Functional Categories	Enabler features are Adaptable Behavior, Context Sensitivity, Heterogeneity of Devices, and Service Omnipresence	Functional characteristics are context sensitivity, adaptable behavior, service omnipresence, heterogeneity of devices, and experience capture
Constraint vs. Restrictive Categories	Constraint features are Privacy and Trust, Quality of Service, Safety, Security, Fault Tolerance, and Experience Capture	Restrictive characteristics are privacy and trust, fault tolerance, quality of service, and universal usability
Invisibility Quality Feature	*Invisibility* cannot be classified as enabler or constraint feature and it is ranked as the lowest in priority	Invisibility was ranked the lowest with respect to pertinence level

8 Discussion

Product Line Architecture tools can embed this statistical model in their frameworks to automate the generation of the concrete architectures. The weights of the quality features drive the recommendations of the solutions. It is a kind of a goal-driven architecture which the architect can control according to the context by which the concrete architecture will be used. Similar approaches are applied successfully in product-line architectures as stated in [28, 29].

The statistical model can be used at runtime to enable or disable solutions according to the context. This can be applied either by the administrator of the system or by allowing the system to send feedback about its performance to the adaptation engine in order to recalculate the weights of the quality features and the solutions subsequently. Additionally, the architect should further study the rippled effect of the solution variations on the different architecture components [30].

This approach can be scaled over any number of requirements. It becomes very difficult to review all the requirements with all the stakeholders all the time. Accordingly, it is also an excellent choice for agile projects that have large number of requirements, limited access to the required stakeholders, or constrained implementation time. The presented heuristic approach can provide fast decisions with high confidence levels in such situations.

On the other hand, the architect may use a simple binary (Boolean) approach to rank the solutions against the quality features based on their positive and negative impact within a limited scope to make a quick evaluation. However, this simple model may increase the probability of errors if it is used with the Product Line Architecture to adopt different solutions at runtime. This statistical model is more accurate because it starts the analysis from the requirements level which reduces the subjectivity of the decisions because the selected requirements are proven to be a representative sample of the population of the requirements in the selected quality features.

9   Conclusion

In this paper, a conflict resolution approach is presented between conflicting requirements. We applied this approach in our research project of building a reference architecture for pervasive computing systems. A basic list of requirements for 11 quality features was presented. The weights of the quality features were calculated according to a statistical analysis of the relationships between the requirements. The identified conflicting relationships between the requirements were addressed by proposing functional or architectural solutions. We analyzed these solutions statistically and proved they are normally distributed, which gave an early validation about the correctness of these solutions as design decisions.

This work is a practical guide for architects who are willing to produce systems categorized as pervasive, ubiquitous, or Internet of Things (IoT). The approach can be applied in general to solutions in other domains even with a different set of requirements.

The scope of the solutions can grow if the conflicts increase. The solutions complement the requirements by filling the gaps created by the conflicting requirements. The list of presented solutions provides guidance to only start a concrete architecture and may include other future requirements and solutions as well.

The requirements model can be woven inside the software system at runtime. It will be useful to attribute the performance of the system to the statistical model of the requirements. It is possible to achieve it by linking the performance indicators of the system to the quality features and the requirements and the collected statistics are used to further improve the architecture of the system.

Acknowledgement. We would like to thank the following experts for their help and support in this research work: Ahmed Ibrahim and Hassan Ali (IBM Egypt), Hany Ouda, (Etisalat Egypt Telecommunications), Mohamed Hassan Abdelrahman (Vodafone Egypt Telecommunications), and Soumaia Al-Ayyat (AUC).

Appendix

The following list is a high level summary of the quality features' requirements as referenced from [21]:

(a) *Adaptable Behaviour (AB):* In order to fulfil this feature [31], the system is required to (1) evaluate/improve adaptive actions (actions taken in response for the context change), (2) have smart decision rules, (3) notify users with changes, and (4) possess actuation capabilities.

(b) *Context Sensitivity (CS):* In order to fulfil this feature [14], the system is required to (5) have sensors, (6) locate interacting objects, (7) provide analytical capability, (8) provide interpretation rules, and (9) record the object's lifetime.

(c) *Experience Capture (EC):* In order to fulfil this feature [22, 32, 33], the system is required to (10) capture Knowledge about users, (11) correlate information and knowledge, and (12) capture/change behavioural patterns.

(d) *Fault Tolerance (FT):* In order to fulfil this feature [34, 35], the system is required to (13) detect faults quickly, (14) minimize faults, (15) minimize the probability of a device going offline, (16) reduce error consequences, (17) display a proper error message, and (18) take the proper corrective action.

(e) *Heterogeneity of Devices (HD):* In order to fulfil this feature [36, 37], the system is required to (18) maximize the number of device technologies, (19) provide a unique identifier for every object, and (20) render content on a maximum number of devices.

(f) *Invisibility (IN):* In order to fulfil this feature [33], the system is required to (21) minimize unneeded interactions, (22) remove unnecessary motions, (23) conceal the system devices and (24) minimize the use of explicit input.

(g) *Privacy and Trust (PT):* In order to fulfil this feature [38, 39], the system is required to (25) certify trusted entities, (26) classify Information, (27) reveal Information controllably, and (28) track Information.

(h) *Quality of Service (QoS):* In order to fulfil this feature [14, 40], the system is required to (29) declare service/quality feature boundaries, (30) minimize average processing time, (31) monitor and improve QoS boundaries, and (32) specify hard/soft deadlines.

(i) *Safety (SY):* In order to fulfil this feature [23, 34], the system is required to (33) alert the user if safety is about to be/or is compromised, (34) allow the user to override/cancel system decisions, (35) avoid conflicting side effects (e.g. contradicting actions), (36) avoid invalid operational directives (e.g. wrong directives set by the users that may cause safety hazards to people and devices), (37) ensure that generated rules do not conflict with the system's policy, (38) minimize conflicting usage of shared resources, (39) override system rules by the regulator (an authorized entity to set/change the rules of the system), (40) provide maximum protection (protect the interacting users and devices from injury and damage) for the environment, (41) resolve conflicts among objects by an administrator, and (42) respect societal ethics.

(j) *Security (ST):* In order to fulfil this feature [14, 32, 41, 42], the system is required to (43) disallow anonymous usage of system, (44) enforce Security rules on all objects, (45) ensure secure data transmission, (46) maintain data integrity, (47) prevent data leakage, (48) provide data access rules, (49) take counter-measures to mitigate security threats, and (50) announce malfunctioning smart objects.

(k) *Service Omnipresence (SO):* In order to fulfil this feature [42], the system is required to (51) distribute computing power, (52) enrich the experience of the highly used scenarios, (53) provide Informative messages, (54) use a unique user identifier and (55) utilize the user's cell phone.

References

1. Chakraborty, A., Kanti Baowaly, M., Arefin, A., Newaz Bahar, A.: The role of requirement engineering in software development life cycle. J. Emerg. Trends Comput. Inf. Sci. **3**(5), 723–729 (2012)
2. A Guide to the Business Analysis Body of Knowledge, 1.6. International Institute of Business Analysis (2006)
3. IIBA Business Analysis Competency Model, 3.0. International Institute of Business Analysis, Toronto, Ontario, Canada, March 2011
4. Mendizabal, O.M., Spier, M., Saad, R.: Log-based approach for performance requirements elicitation and prioritization. In: 2012 20th IEEE International Requirements Engineering Conference (RE), pp. 297–302 (2012)
5. Kolos-Mazuryk, L., Poulisse, G.-J., van Eck, P.: Requirements engineering for pervasive services. In: Second Workshop on Building Software for Pervasive Computing (2005)
6. Afridi, A.H., Gul, S.: Method assisted requirements elicitation for context aware computing for the field force. Lect. Notes Eng. Comput. Sci. (2008)
7. Muñoz, J., Pelechano, V.: Building a software factory for pervasive systems development. In: Pastor, O., Falcão e Cunha, J. (eds.) CAiSE 2005. LNCS, vol. 3520, pp. 342–356. Springer, Heidelberg (2005). https://doi.org/10.1007/11431855_24
8. Pérez, F., Valderas, P.: Allowing end-users to actively participate within the elicitation of pervasive system requirements through immediate visualization. In: 2009 Fourth International Workshop on Requirements Engineering Visualization, pp. 31–40 (2009)
9. Khaled, O.M., Hosny, H.M., Shalan, M.: A survey of building robust business models in pervasive computing. In: The Proceedings of the 2014 World Congress in Computer Science, Computer Engineering, and Applied Computing, Las Vegas, Nevada, USA (2014)
10. Salado, A., Nilchiani, R.: The tension matrix and the concept of elemental decomposition: improving identification of conflicting requirements. IEEE Syst. J. **PP**(99), 1–12 (2015)
11. Sadana, V., Liu, X.F.: Analysis of conflicts among non-functional requirements using integrated analysis of functional and non-functional requirements. In: 31st Annual International Computer Software and Applications Conference (COMPSAC 2007), vol. 1, pp. 215–218 (2007)
12. Oster, Z.J., Santhanam, G.R., Basu, S.: Scalable modeling and analysis of requirements preferences: a qualitative approach using CI-Nets. In: 2015 IEEE 23rd International Requirements Engineering Conference (RE), pp. 214–219 (2015)
13. Galster, M., Eberlein, A.: Facilitating software architecting by ranking requirements based on their impact on the architecture process. In: 2011 18th IEEE International Conference and Workshops on Engineering of Computer-Based Systems, pp. 232–240 (2011)
14. Coulouris, G., Dollimore, J., Kindberg, T., Blair, G.: Distributed Systems: Concepts and Design, 5th edn. Addison-Wesley Publishing Company, Boston (2011)
15. Gunasekaran, A., Kobu, B.: Modelling and analysis of business process reengineering. Int. J. Prod. Res. **40**(11), 2521–2546 (2002)
16. Mohapatra, S.: BPR and automation. In: Mohapatra, S. (ed.) Business Process Reengineering: Automation Decision Points in Process Reengineering, pp. 213–219. Springer, Boston (2013). https://doi.org/10.1007/978-1-4614-6067-1_10
17. Liu, J., Li, J., Jiang, T.: Research on the reengineering of warehousing process based on Internet of Things. In: 2014 IEEE International Conference on Progress in Informatics and Computing, pp. 567–571 (2014)

18. Khaled, O.M.: Pervasive Computing reference architecture from a software engineering perspective. Ph.D. thesis dissertation, The American University in Cairo, Cairo, Egypt (2017)
19. Salado, A., Nilchiani, R.: The concept of order of conflict in requirements engineering. IEEE Syst. J. **10**(1), 25–35 (2016)
20. Khaled, O.M., Hosny, H.M., Shalan, M.: A pervasive computing business reference architecture: the basic requirements model. Int. J. Softw. Eng. IJSE **10**(1), 17–46 (2017)
21. Khaled, O.M., Hosny, H.M., Shalan, M.: A statistical approach to resolve conflicting requirements in pervasive computing systems. Presented at the 12th International Conference on Evaluation of Novel Approaches to Software Engineering (ENASE 2017), Porto, Purtogal, p. 12 (2017)
22. Spínola, R.O., Travassos, G.H.: Towards a framework to characterize ubiquitous software projects. Inf. Softw. Technol. **54**(7), 759–785 (2012)
23. Yang, H.I., Helal, A.: Safety enhancing mechanisms for pervasive computing systems in intelligent environments. In: 2008 Sixth Annual IEEE International Conference on Pervasive Computing and Communications (PerCom), pp. 525–530 (2008)
24. Galster, M., Avgeriou, P., Weyns, D., Männistö, T.: Variability in software architecture: current practice and challenges. SIGSOFT Softw. Eng. Notes **36**(5), 30–32 (2011)
25. Moore, D.S., McCabe, G.P., Craig, B.A.: Introduction to the Practice of Statistics: Extended Version, 6th edn. W.H. Freeman, New York (2009)
26. Dubois, D.J., Bando, Y., Watanabe, K., Holtzman, H.: ShAir: extensible middleware for mobile peer-to-peer resource sharing. In: Proceedings of the 2013 9th Joint Meeting on Foundations of Software Engineering, New York, NY, USA, pp. 687–690 (2013)
27. Petroulakis, N.E., Askoxylakis, I.G., Tryfonas, T.: Life-logging in smart environments: challenges and security threats. In: 2012 IEEE International Conference on Communications (ICC), pp. 5680–5684 (2012)
28. Losavio, F., Ordaz, O.: Quality-based heuristic for optimal product derivation in Software Product Lines. In: 2015 Internet Technologies and Applications (ITA), pp. 125–131 (2015)
29. Murwantara, I.M.: Hybrid ANP: quality attributes decision modeling of a product line architecture design. In: 2012 2nd International Conference on Uncertainty Reasoning and Knowledge Engineering, pp. 30–34 (2012)
30. Oliveira, E., Allian, A.P.: Do reference architectures can contribute to standardizing variability management tools? In: 2015 1st International Workshop on Exploring Component-based Techniques for Constructing Reference Architectures (CobRA), pp. 1–4 (2015)
31. Dobson, S., Sterritt, R., Nixon, P., Hinchey, M.: Fulfilling the vision of autonomic computing. Computer **43**(1), 35–41 (2010)
32. Internet of Things Architecture IoT-A Project Deliverable D6.2 – Updated Requirements. European Lighthouse Integrated Project, January 2011
33. Viana, J.R.M., Viana, N.P., Trinta, F.A.M., de Carvalho, W.V.: A systematic review on software engineering in pervasive games development. In: 2014 Brazilian Symposium on Computer Games and Digital Entertainment, pp. 51–60 (2014)
34. Khaled, O.M., Hosny, H.M., Shalan, M.: On the road to a reference architecture for pervasive computing. In: 2015 International Conference on Pervasive and Embedded Computing and Communication Systems (PECCS), pp. 98–103 (2015)
35. Sommerville, I.: Software Engineering, 9th edn. Addison-Wesley Publishing Company, Boston (2010)
36. Purao, S., Paul, S., Smith, S.: Understanding enterprise integration project risks: a focus group study. In: 18th International Workshop on Database and Expert Systems Applications (DEXA 2007), pp. 850–854 (2007)

37. Nosrati, M., Karimi, R., Hasanvand, H.A.: Mobile computing: principles, devices and operating systems. World Appl. Program **2**(7), 399–408 (2012)
38. Joinson, A.N., Reips, U.-D., Buchanan, T., Schofield, C.B.P.: Privacy, trust, and self-disclosure online. Hum. Comput. Interact. **25**(1), 1–24 (2010)
39. Kostakos, V., O'Neill, E., Penn, A.: Designing urban pervasive systems. Computer **39**(9), 52–59 (2006)
40. Wang, X., Khemaissia, I., Khalgui, M., Li, Z., Mosbahi, O., Zhou, M.: Dynamic low-power reconfiguration of real-time systems with periodic and probabilistic tasks. IEEE Trans. Autom. Sci. Eng. **12**(1), 258–271 (2015)
41. Ray, A., Cleaveland, R.: An analysis method for medical device security. In: Proceedings of the 2014 Symposium and Bootcamp on the Science of Security, New York, NY, USA, pp. 16:1–16:2 (2014)
42. Addo, I.D., Ahamed, S.I., Yau, S.S., Buduru, A.: A reference architecture for improving security and privacy in Internet of Things applications. In: 2014 IEEE International Conference on Mobile Services, pp. 108–115 (2014)

Assisting Configurations-Based Feature Model Composition
Union, Intersection and Approximate Intersection

Jessie Carbonnel[1], Marianne Huchard[1(✉)], André Miralles[2],
and Clémentine Nebut[1]

[1] LIRMM, CNRS and Université de Montpellier,
161 rue Ada, 34095 Montpellier Cedex 5, France
{jessie.carbonnel,marianne.huchard,clementine.nebut}@lirmm.fr
[2] TETIS, IRSTEA, 500 rue Jean-François Breton,
34093 Montpellier Cedex 5, France
andre.miralles@teledetection.fr

Abstract. Feature Models (FMs) have been introduced in the domain
of Software Product Lines (SPL) to model and represent product variability. They have become a de facto standard, based on a logical tree
structure accompanied by textual cross-tree constraints. Other representations are: (product) configuration sets from concrete software product lines, logical representations, constraint programming, or conceptual
structures, coming from the Formal Concept Analysis (FCA) framework.
Modeling variability through FMs may consist in extracting them from
configuration sets (namely, doing FM synthesis), or designing them in
several steps potentially involving several teams with different concerns.
FM composition is useful in this design activity as it may assist FM iterative building. In this paper, we describe an approach, based on a configuration set and focusing on two main composition semantics (union,
intersection), to assist designers in FM composition. We also introduce
an approximate intersection notion. FCA is used to represent, for a product family, all the FMs that have the same configuration set through a
canonical form. The approach is able to take into account cross-tree constraints and FMs with different feature sets and tree structure, thus it
lets the expert free of choosing a different ontological interpretation. We
describe the implementation of our approach and we present a set of
concrete examples.

Keywords: Software product line · Feature Model
Feature Model Composition · Feature model merging
Formal Concept Analysis · Union models · Intersection models

1 Introduction

Software Product Line Engineering (SPLE) is a development paradigm which
aims to develop a set of related and similar software systems as a single entity

© Springer International Publishing AG, part of Springer Nature 2018
E. Damiani et al. (Eds.): ENASE 2017, CCIS 866, pp. 116–140, 2018.
https://doi.org/10.1007/978-3-319-94135-6_6

rather than developing individually each software system [1]. From a development point of view, the core of this methodology is a generic architecture where off-the-shelf reusable artifacts can be plugged depending a given set of requirements, and from which can easily be derived a set of software variants. SPLE is composed of two phases. *Domain engineering* consists in analyzing and representing the domain, developing the off-the-shelf artifacts and implementing the generic architecture. *Application engineering* consists in giving the final user the opportunity to select the characteristics she/he wants in her/his software product, and then to derive the corresponding software variant composed with the matching artifacts.

Variability modeling is a task that takes place during domain representation. It consists in modeling what varies in the software variants, and how it varies. It is central to SPLE paradigm, as a substantial part of the method is based on the variability representation, as for instance designing the generic architecture, or guiding the user to select characteristics. The most common approaches model variability in terms of *features*, where a feature is a distinguishable characteristic which is relevant to one or several stakeholders. *Feature models* (FMs) are considered the standard to model variability with these approaches. They are a family of visual/graphical languages which depict a set of features and dependencies between these features. FMs are used, amongst others, to derive selection tools for the end product designer.

Nowadays, practitioners have to cope with product lines which are more and more complex. Managing one, huge feature model representing the whole product line is unrealistic. A solution to ease the application of the SPLE approach in these cases is to divide the product line according to various concerns and to manage a separate and specific feature model for each concern. However, even though it is easier to manage separate FMs, for some design activities it can be useful to merge these FMs, as for commonalities analysis between different concerns. Therefore, defining operations that enable feature model composition is necessary. Feature model composition also has other purposes, in the context of Software Product Line *reengineering*, for feature model reuse and adaptation.

Several approaches for FM composition have been proposed in the past, that are reported in [2]. The main directions for feature model composition in the literature are using operators on the feature model structure, or propositional logic computation. Although these approaches have their advantages, either they tend to confine the designer in a predefined ontological view, or they produce approximate results, or they need a significant work to build a feature model from the result (when the result is a logic formula). Besides, operators on feature model structure hardly take into account the textual cross-tree constraints.

In this paper, we investigate feature model composition in the contexts where the product configuration set is known (or can be obtained) and where the entities to be composed are either several feature models, or a feature model and a product configuration set, or several product configuration sets. The paper extends previous research presented in [3]. The approach uses the framework of Formal Concept Analysis [4] which provides relevant tools for variability representation.

This framework ensures the production of sound and complete compositions, taking into account the cross-tree constraints. Our approach exploits Formal Concept Analysis properties to produce intermediate canonical and graphical representations (Equivalence Class Feature Diagrams, or ECFDs) which give assistance to a designer to manually derive a feature model. The ECFD contains all the possible ontological links and avoids confining the designer in a specific ontological view. Two main composition operations are defined (union and intersection), and, in this paper, we also study the problem of common sub-configuration extraction (approximate intersection), which arises when the intersection is empty, but the feature models have some similarities. Except in extreme cases, the approximate intersection is not empty. We present a prototype tool which computes union, intersection, and approximate intersection, and we conduct an evaluation on real feature models. The results allow us to show concrete situations where the approach is scalable, to draw its scope of applicability and to compare the different operations.

Next Sect. 2 defines feature models and gives an overview of the approach. Section 3 introduces the main composition operations (union and intersection). Section 4 introduces Formal Concept Analysis and shows how the framework helps to build an intermediate canonical and graphical representation with the aim to assist a designer in feature model composition. The section also proposes an assisting approach for the extraction of common sub-configurations (approximate intersection) which is based on the conceptual structure. The prototype tool and the evaluation are presented in Sect. 5. Related work and a discussion are developed in Sect. 6. Section 7 summarizes the approach and provides perspectives for this research.

2   Context and Overview

In this section, we define feature models (Sect. 2.1), then we provide an overview of the compositional approach (Sect. 2.2).

2.1   Feature Models

The most common SPLE approaches model variability in terms of features, where a feature is a distinguishable characteristic which is relevant to some of the involved stakeholders. Feature Models (FMs) are considered the standard to model variability with these approaches [5]. They are a family of visual languages which depict a set of features and dependencies between these features [6]. In this way, they define the legal combinations of these features, namely the possible software variants of the product line (also called product configurations or simply configurations). In FMs, the features are organized in a hierarchy, where each feature represents a characteristic or a concept at several levels of increasing details, and where each edge represents an ontological relation as "is-a-kind-of", "refines", "is-a-part-of", "implements", etc. Dependencies are expressed on the edges of the tree with graphical decorations, or in textual cross-tree constraints. Figure 1 gives an example of an FM representing an SPL about e-commerce applications, in the most common formalism (FODA [5]). The example states that e_commerce (root feature) requires a catalog. This mandatory relation is indicated through an edge ending with a black disk. Also, it shows that e_commerce optionally possesses a basket, and this is indicated by an edge ending with a white circle. In FMs, the children of a feature may also be grouped into *xor groups* (meaning that if the parent feature belongs to a configuration, exactly one child feature of the group is also present) or into *or groups* (meaning that if the parent feature belongs to a configuration, one or more child features of the group are also present). An *xor group* is indicated by a black line connecting the edges going from the parent to the children of this group. In the example, one can see that an e_commerce application proposes a catalog presentation as a grid or as a list (but not both simultaneously). An *or group* is indicated by a black filled zone connecting the edges going from the parent to the children of this group. We can see in the example that the proposed payment_method may be credit_card, or check, or both. In Fig. 1, two cross-tree constraints, shown in the figure caption, indicate a mutual dependency between payment_method and basket.

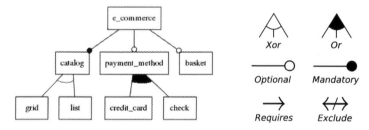

Fig. 1. Left-hand side: An FM describing the variability in a family of e commerce applications in FODA formalism. Two cross-tree constraints come along: payment_method requires basket (and reversely). Right-hand side: Main feature tree annotations.

An FM owns an *ontological semantics*. Closeness and correspondences between FMs and ontologies are studied in [7]. The ontological semantics is the domain knowledge expressed by the feature tree along with the other feature dependencies (groups, mutex and constraints). For instance, we can read in the e-commerce FM that catalog is a mandatory characteristic that refines the concept of e_commerce, and that (pay with) check implements the concept of payment_method. In our work, we also are interested in another semantics of feature models, the *configuration semantics*. It is given by the set of valid configurations, which are the combinations of features (feature sets) which respect all the dependencies given by the FM. The set of configurations of an FM f is denoted by $[\![f]\!]$. Our e-commerce FM here has 8 valid configurations, which correspond to the description of the 8 possible software variants of the product line. Equation 1 shows $[\![e\_commerce]\!]$.

$$Ec, Ca, G \qquad Ec, Ca, L$$
$$Ec, Ca, G, Pm, Cc, B \qquad Ec, Ca, L, Pm, Cc, B$$
$$Ec, Ca, G, Pm, Ch, B \qquad Ec, Ca, L, Pm, Ch, B \tag{1}$$
$$Ec, Ca, G, Pm, Cc, Ch, B \qquad Ec, Ca, L, Pm, Cc, Ch, B$$

2.2   Compositional Approach Overview

Figure 2 illustrates the proposed composition operations. The input can be: two feature models (top left), one feature model and one configuration set (bottom left), or two configuration sets (not illustrated). The configuration sets are computed for each input feature model, and then represented in the form of formal contexts. The composition operations (union and intersection) are made on the formal contexts. A conceptual structure (here an AC-poset, namely a structure only containing the concepts introducing the features) is built for the union (resp. intersection) formal context. The ECFD, which is a canonical and graphical structure is then extracted from the AC-poset; it supports the designer to compose a new FM. All these notions are explained in the next sections.

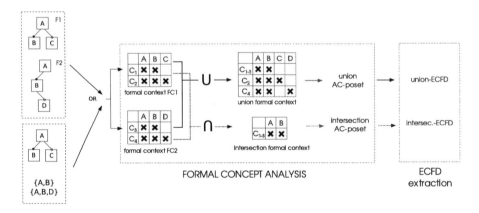

Fig. 2. An overview of the FM composition process. The FMs F_1 and F_2 (top left) have resp. FC1 and FC2 as associated configuration sets/formal contexts.

3   Feature Model Composition

In this section, we define the union and intersection of feature models (Sect. 3.1), then we discuss the main existing approaches to implement them in order to motivate ours (Sect. 3.2).

3.1   Intersection/Union Based Composition

Nowadays, practitioners have to cope with product lines which are more and more complex, and managing one, huge feature model representing the whole product line is unrealistic. To ease the application of the SPL approach in these cases, a solution is to divide the product line according to separate concerns and to manage a distinct and more specific feature model for each one of these concerns. However, even though it is easier to manage, for some design activities it can be necessary to merge these feature models (or part of them), and therefore we need operations that enable feature model composition [8]. Among the various composition operations shown in [8], merge-union and merge-intersection have a special place for managing FMs that give different views of a system. Merge-union is an integrated view, while merge-intersection allows to highlight the common core. They are defined using the configuration semantics as follows.

Definition 1 (Merge-intersection[2]). *The merge-intersection operation, denoted by $\cap$, builds a feature model FM_3 from two feature models FM_1 and FM_2 such that $[\![FM_3]\!] = [\![FM_1]\!] \cap [\![FM_2]\!]$.*

Definition 2 (Merge-union [2]). *The merge-union operation, denoted by $\cup^{\sim}$, builds a feature model FM_3 from two feature models FM_1 and FM_2 such that $[\![FM_3]\!] \supseteq [\![FM_1]\!] \cup [\![FM_2]\!]$. This is an approximate union.*

Definition 3 (Merge-strict-union [2]). *The merge-strict-union operation, denoted by $\cup$, builds a feature model FM_3 from two feature models FM_1 and FM_2 such that $[\![FM_3]\!] = [\![FM_1]\!] \cup [\![FM_2]\!]$.*

By definition, the merge-strict-union is a restriction of the merge-union. Figure 2 illustrates merge-intersection and merge-strict-union on a simple example, with $[\![F_1]\!] = \{\{A, B\}, \{A, B, C\}\}$ and $[\![F_2]\!] = \{\{A, B\}, \{A, B, D\}\}$. Thus intersection and strict union are as follows: $[\![F_1]\!] \cap [\![F_2]\!] = \{\{A, B\}\}$ and $[\![F_1]\!] \cup [\![F_2]\!] = \{\{A, B\}, \{A, B, C\}, \{A, B, D\}\}$. An example of a merge-union is given in next Sect. 3.2.

3.2   Comparing Main Implementations of Composition Operations

Several methods have been proposed for implementing merge-union and merge-intersection. The two main approaches are based on the feature tree structure or on the logic formula associated with the FMs [8]. Both take as input two feature models.

The approach based on logic formulas consists in using the logic formulas that are equivalent to the FMs to be merged. In our case, a formula for F_1 can be $(A \wedge B) \vee (A \wedge B \wedge C)$, while a formula for F_2 can be $(A \wedge B) \vee (A \wedge B \wedge D)$. In [8], the proposed formula for the merge-intersection (resp. merge-strict-union) is given by Eq. 2 (resp. Eq. 3). While the approach is sound and complete, and can be implemented using the FM to derive the logic formula as defined in [9], it needs to be completed by a second step consisting in FM extraction from the logic formula, for example, using the approach given in [10].

$$(((A \wedge B) \vee (A \wedge B \wedge C)) \wedge (\neg D)) \wedge (((A \wedge B) \vee (A \wedge B \wedge D)) \wedge (\neg C)) \quad (2)$$

$$(((A \wedge B) \vee (A \wedge B \wedge C)) \wedge (\neg D)) \vee (((A \wedge B) \vee (A \wedge B \wedge D)) \wedge (\neg C)) \quad (3)$$

For discussing the structural approach based on the feature tree, we need to introduce a slightly more complicated example, and we use a follow up of the e-commerce example. Figure 3 presents two feature models representing e-commerce applications and that are to be merged. Table 1 presents their respective sets of valid configurations. These configurations are given an identifier (such as FM_1C_1) for later use in the paper. The structural approach is based on a set of composition rules which compute the merge-intersection and the merge-union. These rules are listed in [8]. Their result is shown in Fig. 4. For example, a rule for merge-union composition establishes that the *xor group* below `Catalog` of FM_2, when merged with the mandatory `grid` feature of `Catalog` in FM_1, gives an *or group* below `Catalog` in the merge-union (see right-hand side of Fig. 4). An underlying hypothesis in this approach is that the same set of features is shared by the two FMs to be merged. In our case, this is not the case and the rules sometimes produce a non-strict merge-union, as for example configuration $\{Ec, Ca, G, L, Pm, Ch\}$ is not in the merge-strict-union of the configurations appearing in Table 1: this configuration indeed contains L which is not available in FM_1, and Ch which is not available in FM_2. A main characteristic of this approach is that the rules do not reconsider all the ontological semantics and

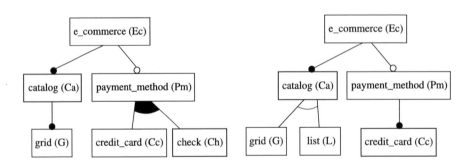

Fig. 3. Two feature models (left-hand, FM_1 and right-hand, FM_2) representing e-commerce applications and that are to be merged.

Table 1. Configuration sets of FM_1 and FM_2 from Fig. 3.

	Ec	Ca	G	Pm	Cc	Ch		Ec	Ca	G	L	Pm	Cc
FM_1C_1	x	x	x				FM_2C_1	x	x	x			
FM_1C_2	x	x	x	x	x		FM_2C_2	x	x		x		
FM_1C_3	x	x	x	x		x	FM_2C_3	x	x	x		x	x
FM_1C_4	x	x	x	x	x	x	FM_2C_4	x	x		x	x	x

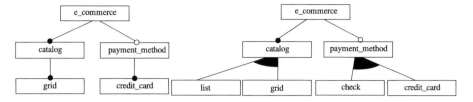

Fig. 4. Merge-intersection (left-hand side) and merge-union (right-hand side) of FM_1 and FM_2 from Fig. 3 using the structural approach of [8].

especially the child-parent relationships. In our example, two different solutions for attaching `payment_method` may be considered: below `e_commerce`, as it is preserved by the structural rule or below `catalog`, which is an alternative that can be considered by a designer (with a "part-of" semantics in the associated software components), but is not proposed by the rule. Besides, it is important to underline that this approach does not take into account the cross-tree constraints, if some exist.

This is why, despite the qualities of these approaches, it is useful to have a complementary point of view, based on the configuration set, which ensures the soundness and completeness of merge-intersection and merge-strict-union operations, is able to take into account cross-tree constraints and FMs with different feature sets, and does not confine the designer in a specific ontological view (if a FM is badly designed, but its configuration set is correct, our approach produces a correct result), while assisting her/him in the FM construction. We propose such a solution in the following section. The solution can be used for merging two feature models, or one feature model and a configuration set, or two configuration sets.

4   Formal Concept Analysis for Feature Model Composition

In Sect. 4.1, we briefly present the notion of *formal context*. A formal context is an input data for Formal Concept Analysis (FCA). We define (merge) intersection and strict union in terms of operations on formal contexts and illustrate the definitions in the context of variability modeling. The *conceptual structures* that are built by FCA are presented in Sect. 4.2. Then, we introduce an intermediate structure, the *Equivalence Class Feature Diagram (ECFD)* in Sect. 4.3. The ECFD associated with a configuration set is a canonical, graphical representation of variability: all FMs having the same configuration set have a projection in the ECFD (and can be extracted from it). We show how the ECFD can assist the designer in building feature models which are consistent with the domain. At last, we extend the scope of the study by an approach for extracting the *common sub-configurations* in Sect. 4.4.

4.1 Formal Contexts for Intersection and Strict Union

Formal Concept Analysis (FCA) is a mathematical data analysis framework for hierarchical clustering and rule extraction [4]. In its basic form, it concentrates on a restricted application of Galois connection and Galois lattice theory to binary relationships [11–13]. As input, it takes a set of objects described by a set of attributes, arranged in a tabular form called a formal context.

Definition 4 (Formal Context). *A formal context K is a 3-tuple (G, M, I), where G is an object (configuration) set, M is an attribute (feature) set, and $I \subseteq G \times M$ is a binary relation which associates objects (configurations) with attributes (features) they own. Given a context $K = (G, M, I)$, for $g \in G$ we will denote by $I(g)$ the set of features of g, i.e. the set $\{m \in M | (g, m) \in I\}$.*

The two binary relationships of Table 1, which presents the configuration sets of FM_1 and FM_2, are formal contexts. Each row corresponds to an object (a configuration) and each column corresponds to an attribute (a feature). The left-hand side formal context indicates that configuration FM_1C_1 comprises the attributes Ec, Ca, G. We present in the next Sect. 4.2 the conceptual structures that are extracted from a formal context.

For defining the intersection and strict union formal contexts, we first introduce the notion of equality of objects (configurations), denoted by $\triangleq$, as objects having the same set of attributes. In tables and figures, which are generated by tools, when applicable, $\triangleq$ is denoted by "=".

Definition 5 (Equality of Objects, $\triangleq$).

$$g_1 \triangleq g_2 \Leftrightarrow g_1 \in G_1, g2 \in G_2 \text{ and } I_1(g_1) = I_2(g_2)$$

We then define the formal context associated with intersection as the rows that are present in the two initial formal contexts (Definition 6). A labeling of rows is added to indicate their origin. Table 2 shows the formal context associated with the intersection of FM_1 and FM_2 formal contexts from Table 1.

Table 2. Formal context associated with the intersection of FM_1 and FM_2 formal contexts from Table 1.

	Ec	Ca	G	Pm	Cc
$FM_1C_1 = FM_2C_1$	x	x	x		
$FM_1C_2 = FM_2C_3$	x	x	x	x	x

Definition 6 (Intersection Formal Context). *The formal context of intersection $Inter(K_1, K_2)$ is*
$K_{Inter(K_1,K_2)} = (G_{Inter(K_1,K_2)}, M_{Inter(K_1,K_2)}, I_{Inter(K_1,K_2)})$ *such that:*

- $G_{Inter(K_1,K_2)} = \{g_{g_1 \triangleq g_2} \mid \exists (g_1, g_2) \in G_1 \times G_2, g_1 \triangleq g_2\}$
- $M_{Inter(K_1,K_2)} = M_1 \cap M_2$

$- \ I_{Inter(K_1,K_2)} \quad = \quad \{(g_{g1 \triangleq g2}, m) \quad | \quad m \quad \in \quad M_{Inter(K_1,K_2)}, g_{g1 \triangleq g2} \quad \in$
$G_{Inter(K_1,K_2)}, (g1, m) \in I_1(or \ equivalently \ (g2, m) \in I_2)\}$

Definition 7 introduces the formal context associated with strict union. Table 3 shows the formal context associated with the strict union of FM_1 and FM_2 formal contexts from Table 1. It highlights the two common configurations (first two rows) and the configurations that are specific to one FM (next four rows).

Definition 7 (Strict Union Formal Context). *Let us consider:*

- *the set of common configurations (from Definition 6) $G_{Inter(K_1,K_2)}$ and the corresponding relation $I_{Inter(K_1,K_2)}$*
- *the set of configurations specific to G_1:*
  $SPE(G_1) = \{g1 \mid g1 \in G_1 \ and \ \nexists g2 \in G_2, with \ g_{g1 \triangleq g2} \in G_{Inter(K_1,K_2)}\}$
- *the set of configurations specific to G_2:*
  $SPE(G_2) = \{g2 \mid g2 \in G_2 \ and \ \nexists g1 \in G_1, with \ g_{g1 \triangleq g2} \in G_{Inter(K_1,K_2)}\}$

The formal context of strict union $Union(K_1, K_2)$ is:
$K_{Union(K_1,K_2)} = (G_{Union(K_1,K_2)}, M_{Union(K_1,K_2)}, I_{Union(K_1,K_2)}) \ such \ that:$

- $G_{Union(K_1,K_2)} = G_{Inter(K_1,K_2)} \cup SPE(G_1) \cup SPE(G_2)$
- $M_{Union(K_1,K_2)} = M_1 \cup M_2$
- $I_{Union(K_1,K_2)} = I_{Inter(K_1,K_2)}$
  $\cup \{(g, m) \mid g \in SPE(G_1), m \in M_{Union(K_1,K_2)}, (g, m) \in I_1\}$
  $\cup \{(g, m) \mid g \in SPE(G_2), m \in M_{Union(K_1,K_2)}, (g, m) \in I_2\}$

Table 3. Formal context associated with the strict union of FM_1 and FM_2 formal contexts from Table 1.

	Ec	Ca	G	L	Pm	Cc	Ch
$FM_1C_1 = FM_2C_1$	x	x	x				
$FM_1C_2 = FM_2C_3$	x	x	x		x	x	
FM_1C_3	x	x	x		x		x
FM_1C_4	x	x	x		x	x	x
FM_2C_2	x	x		x			
FM_2C_4	x	x		x	x	x	

4.2   Conceptual Structures

From a formal context, specialized algorithms of the FCA framework build *formal concepts*. A formal concept is a maximal group of objects associated with the maximal group of attributes they share. It can be read in the table of the context as a maximal rectangle of crosses (modulo permutations of rows and columns).

Definition 8 (Formal Concept). *Given a formal context $K = (G, M, I)$, a formal concept associates a maximal set of objects with the maximal set of attributes they share, yielding a set pair $C = (Extent(C), Intent(C))$ such that:*

- *$Extent(C) = \{g \in G | \forall m \in Intent(C), (g, m) \in I\}$ is the extent of the concept (objects covered by the concept).*
- *$Intent(C) = \{m \in M | \forall g \in Extent(C), (g, m) \in I\}$ is the intent of the concept (shared attributes).*

For example, $(\{FM_1C_1 = FM_2C_1, FM_1C_2 = FM_2C_3, FM_1C_3, FM_1C_4\}, \{Ec, Ca, G\})$ is a formal concept in strict union of Table 3.

The formal concepts are ordered using inclusion of their extent (or reverse inclusion of their intent). Given two formal concepts $C_1 = (E_1, I_1)$ and $C_2 = (E_2, I_2)$ of K, the concept specialization/generalization order $\preceq_C$ is defined by $C_2 \preceq_C C_1$ if and only if $E_2 \subseteq E_1$ (and equivalently $I_1 \subseteq I_2$). C_2 is a specialization (a subconcept) of C_1. C_1 is a generalization (a superconcept) of C_2. Due to these definitions, C_2 intent inherits (contains) the attributes from C_1 intent, while C_1 extent inherits the objects from C_2 extent. For example, concept $(\{FM_1C_1 = FM_2C_1, FM_1C_2 = FM_2C_3, FM_1C_3, FM_1C_4\}, \{Ec, Ca, G\})$ is a superconcept of concept $(\{FM_1C_3, FM_1C_4\}, \{Ec, Ca, G, Pm, Ch\})$ in strict union of Table 3.

Definition 9 (Concept Lattice). *If we denote by $\mathcal{C}_K$ the set of all concepts of K, $\mathcal{L}_K = (\mathcal{C}_K, \preceq_C)$, is the concept lattice associated with K.*

The graphical representation of the conceptual structures (as concept lattices) exploits the inclusion property to avoid representing in the concepts the top-down inherited attributes (features) and the bottom-up inherited objects (configurations). An attribute appears in the highest concept that possesses this attribute. We say that this concept introduces the attribute, and it is then an Attribute-Concept. An object appears in the lowest concept that possesses this object. We say that this concept introduces the object, and it is then an Object-Concept. A concept is represented in this document by a three-parts box. The upper part is the concept name; the middle part contains the simplified intent (deprived of the top-down inherited attributes); the bottom part contains the simplified extent (deprived of the bottom-up inherited objects).

Specific suborders, that contain only some concepts, can be isolated in the concept lattice. In these structures, configurations are organized depending on the features they share, and dually, the features are structured depending on the configurations in which they are. Thus, these structures permit to emphasize and extract information about variability. The difference is that some of them keep only some of this variability information. The AOC-poset (Attribute Object Concept partially ordered set) contains only the concepts introducing at least one object (configuration), or at least one attribute (feature), or both. In the AOC-poset (as in the concept lattice) a configuration (resp. a feature) appears only once, thus we have a maximal factorization of configurations and features. Another interesting conceptual structure to address our problem is the AC-poset (Attribute-Concept poset) where one configuration may appear several times (and be introduced by several lowest concepts), but features remain maximally factorized revealing an even more simple structure, focusing on the representation of the feature hierarchy. The AC-poset is the minimal conceptual structure necessary to extract logical dependencies between features. The four structures: formal context, concept lattice, AOC-poset and AC-poset are equivalent, in the sense that each one can be rebuilt from any other one, without ambiguity.

Left-hand side of Fig. 5 shows the AC-poset associated with the formal context of Table 3. It emphasizes: *co-occurring features*, e.g. e_commerce and catalog always appear together in any configuration; *implication between features*, e.g. when a configuration has the feature list it always has the feature catalog; *mutually exclusive features*, e.g. list and grid never appear together in any configuration; and *feature groups*, e.g. when payment_method is in a configuration, there is at least check or credit_card, or they are both present. As this kind of information is rather difficult to read in an AC-poset, in the next section, we propose an canonical diagrammatic representation that we have called the Equivalence Class Feature Diagram (ECFD) and which is closer to the FM.

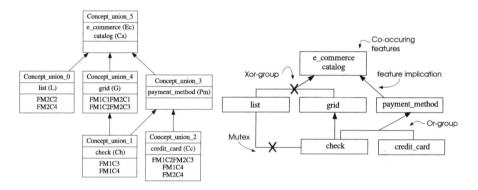

Fig. 5. Left-hand side: AC-poset associated with the strict union formal context of Table 3. Right-hand side: ECFD extracted from the AC-poset.

4.3   Equivalence Class Feature Diagram (ECFD)

The ECFD seeks to be more intuitive than the AC-poset to read variability information. It depicts the feature dependencies extracted from the initial set of configurations that are summarized in the AC-poset, in a representation close to a feature model but without explicit ontological semantics. Therefore it includes all equivalent feature models, hence its name.

Figure 5 shows the ECFD (right-hand side) extracted from the AC-poset (left-hand side). Co-occurring features (as e_commerce and catalog) are in a same box. Arrows between boxes represent feature implications (like check implies grid). Groups of boxes connected by horizontal lines rooted in an upper feature summarize feature groups (like list and grid rooted in box e_commerce-catalog, or check and credit_card rooted in box payment_method). *Xor groups* are marked with a cross. A cross also represents mutually exclusive features, also called *mutex* (like list and check) when they do not belong to a group. The constructs and the semantics of the ECFD are more generally given in Table 4 and a construction algorithm is available in [14].

If we consider an AC-poset corresponding to a set of feature models with the same configuration set, all these FMs *conform* to the AC-poset. This means that each dependency expressed in these feature models matches a dependency expressed in the corresponding AC-poset. For instance, if there is a child-parent (f_c, f_p) in one FM, it belongs to the AC-poset in this way: let C_c be the concept introducing f_c and let C_p be the concept introducing f_p, we have $C_c \preceq_C C_p$.

The ECFD structures the variability information extracted from the configuration set, and it can guide the expert in assigning ontological semantics on its logical dependencies. Figures 6 and 7 show the guidance process. The two FMs at the right-hand side of the figures have the same configuration-semantics. To obtain them, first the designer has to choose between e_commerce and catalog. One is the root (e.g. e_commerce), and the other (e.g. catalog) is a mandatory feature connected to the root. The *xor group* list and grid has to be connected to e_commerce or to catalog. The designer here chooses catalog as the parent of the group. Then payment_method is connected either to catalog (Fig. 6) or

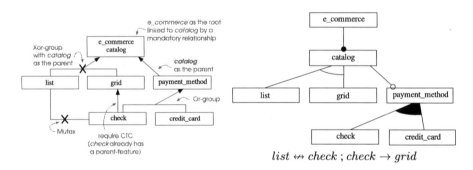

Fig. 6. Left-hand side: ECFD for the strict union formal context of Table 3 annotated with designer choices. Right-hand side: First extracted FM.

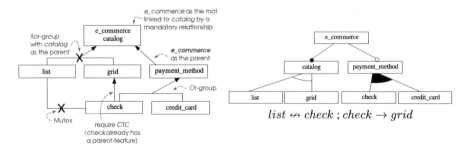

Fig. 7. Left-hand side: Reminder of the ECFD for the strict union formal context of Table 3 annotated with designer choices. Right-hand side: Second extracted FM.

Table 4. Equivalence class feature diagram (ECFD): constructs and semantics [3]. The third column is an example of conform feature model with $n_A = n_B = 3$ and $n_C = 2$.

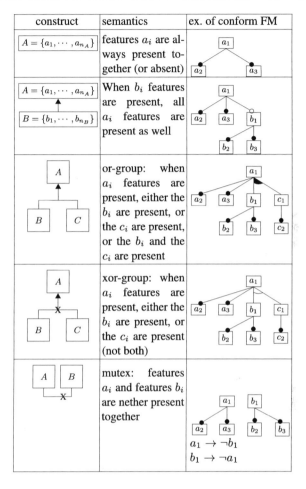

to e_commerce (Fig. 7). Feature check can be a child of grid, or it can belong to the *or group* (check, credit_card, rooted in payment_method). The second choice is made. The cross-tree constraints list ↔ check and check → grid are added to the FMs.

The left-hand side of Fig. 8 shows the ECFD extracted from the intersection AC-poset, built from Table 2. In this very simple case, the difference between the AC-poset and the ECFD is only that in the AC-poset, the nodes (concepts) also contain the list of configurations. The right-hand side shows a possible FM extracted from the ECFD. The top box of co-occurring features gives rise to mandatory feature grid refining mandatory feature catalog refining root e_commerce. With the bottom box, the designer chooses to insert

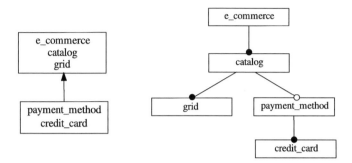

Fig. 8. Left-hand side: ECFD for the intersection formal context of Table 2. Right-hand side: An extracted FM.

payment_method as an optional sub-feature of catalog, and credit_card as a mandatory feature refining payment_method.

4.4   Extraction of Common Sub-configurations

As we noticed during our evaluation (reported in the next section), while FM strict union is always informative, FM intersection is often empty, even when the initial FMs have similarities. We illustrate this issue with a slight modification of the e-commerce example. To the configurations of FM_1, we add UserManagement (Um) as a mandatory sub-feature of e_commerce (Ec) (the new FM is denoted by FM_{1_e}). To the configurations of FM_2, we simply add Paypal (Pp) as a mandatory sub-feature of Credit_Card (Cc) (the new FM is denoted by FM_{2_e}). After these additions, there is no more common configuration to FM_{1_e} and FM_{2_e}. Table 5 shows the extended formal contexts for FM_{1_e}, FM_{2_e} and the strict union formal context. Figure 9 shows the AC-poset built from the union formal context.

Concepts in the AC-poset highlight different types of information on common parts and differences between the FMs. Their study allows us to determine a common core in feature combinations and to categorize the sub-configurations:

- *(Specific sub-configuration)* When the (complete) extent only contains configurations from one feature model, the intent is a sub-configuration or a valid configuration for this feature model only. In both cases, it is specific to this feature model and does not belong to a common core.
- *(Core sub-configuration)* When the (complete) extent contains configurations from both feature models, the intent is a partial common configuration (in a broad meaning, namely it can be a valid configuration) and:
  - *(Configuration)* If the simplified extent contains one configuration of both feature models, the intent is a valid configuration for both and it is in the intersection which is not empty (it was the case for Concept_Union_4 in Fig. 5).

Table 5. Top: Configuration sets of FM_{1_e} and FM_{2_e} from FM_1 and FM_2 of Fig. 3 extended with UserManagement (Um) and Paypal (Pp). Bottom: Strict union formal context $FM_{1_e} \bigcup FM_{2_e}$.

FM_{1_e}	Ec	Ca	G	Pm	Cc	Ch	Um
FM_1eC_1	x	x	x				x
FM_1eC_2	x	x	x	x	x		x
FM_1eC_3	x	x	x	x		x	x
FM_1eC_4	x	x	x	x	x	x	x

FM_{2_e}	Ec	Ca	G	L	Pm	Cc	Pp
FM_2eC_1	x	x	x				
FM_2eC_2	x	x		x			
FM_2eC_3	x	x	x		x	x	x
FM_2eC_4	x	x		x	x	x	x

$UnionExt$	Ec	Ca	G	L	Pm	Cc	Ch	Um	Pp
$FM1eC1$	x	x	x					x	
$FM1eC2$	x	x	x		x	x		x	
$FM1eC3$	x	x	x		x		x	x	
$FM1eC4$	x	x	x		x	x	x	x	
$FM2eC1$	x	x	x						
$FM2eC2$	x	x		x					
$FM2eC3$	x	x	x		x	x			x
$FM2eC4$	x	x		x	x	x			x

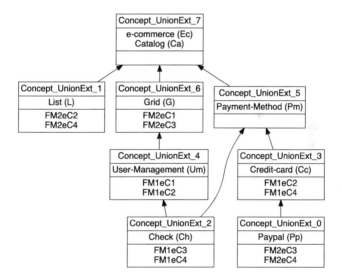

Fig. 9. AC-poset associated with the strict union of the configuration sets of FM_{1_e} and FM_{2_e}.

– *(Strict semi-partial sub-configuration)* If the simplified extent only contains configurations from one feature model (as for Concept_UnionExt_6 in Fig. 9, whose simplified extent only contains configurations from FM_{2_e}), the intent is a strict partial configuration for the feature model which has no configuration in the simplified extent (here FM_{1_e}) and a valid configuration for the other (here FM_{2_e}).

– *(Strict partial sub-configuration)* If the simplified extent is empty (as for `Concept_UnionExt_7` and `Concept_ UnionExt_5` in Fig. 9), the intent is a strict partial configuration. It is not valid for neither of the feature models, but it is contained inside some of the configurations of both feature models and it highlights a similarity between them.

When the intersection is small or empty, the concepts of the core category are especially useful for exploring more deeply the commonalities between the two feature models. They represent possibly incomplete configurations, from which specific features present in only one FM (like `Um` to `Pp`), or specific combinations have been removed. From these concepts, we can build an approximate intersection (denoted by $\bigcap^{\sim}$). The corresponding formal context is built by keeping the intents of the core concepts and assigning them arbitrary configuration names (as common sub-configurations, possibly incomplete).

Figure 10 show the formal context (left-hand side) and the AC-poset (right-hand side) associated with $FM_1 \bigcap^{\sim} FM_2$ and $FM_{1_e} \bigcap^{\sim} FM_{2_e}$. These two examples were constructed in such a way that the approximate intersections are identical in order to simplify the writing. The difference lies in the fact that when considering $FM_1 \bigcap^{\sim} FM_2$, the formal context contains the configurations of $FM_1 \bigcap FM_2$ (which is not empty).

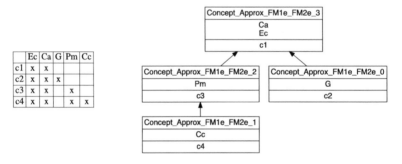

Fig. 10. Left-hand side: Formal context of $FM_1 \bigcap^{\sim} FM_2$ and $FM_{1_e} \bigcap^{\sim} FM_{2_e}$. Right-hand side: The corresponding AC-poset.

Figure 11 shows the ECFD extracted from this AC-poset. This is not appropriate in this case to build the groups and the mutex. For example, in the intents of the core concepts, features `G` and `Pm` never appear together, while they may appear together in complete valid configurations. Appropriate information that can be read is: co-occurring features, mandatory features, optional features and implications. In this example, two possible FMs can be derived by an expert. In this specific case, she/he will preferably choose the FM where `e_commerce` is the root. Here, the approximate intersection is simple, but in the general case, complex ECFDs can be found and the expert benefits from their full potential: compared to a logic-based approach, building an FM for an approximate

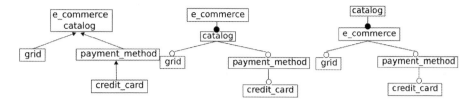

Fig. 11. Left-hand side: ECFD of the approximate intersection. Right-hand side: Two possible FMs extracted from the ECFD.

intersection is guided; compared to a feature tree structure-based approach, no presupposition is made about the ontological relations.

5 Implementation and Assessment

The approach has been implemented as presented in Fig. 12. It uses two existing tools. Familiar[1] [15] is an executable Domain Specific Language, provided with an environment allowing to create, modify and reason about FMs. In the current project, we use it to build the configuration set of an FM. rcaexplore[2] is a framework for Formal Concept Analysis which offers a variety of analysis kinds. It is used to build the AC-poset from which the ECFD structure (nodes and edges) is extracted. We also developed specific tools for this project: ConfigSet2FormalContext builds a formal context (within input format of rcaexplore) from a configuration set extracted with Familiar; ComputeInterAndUnion builds the intersection and strict union formal contexts; ComputeGroupsAndMutex computes the groups *Xor*, *Or* and the mutex

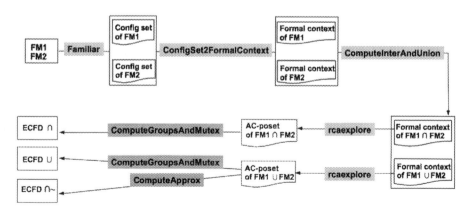

Fig. 12. The implemented process (extended from [3]).

---

[1] https://nyx.unice.fr/projects/familiar/.

[2] http://dolques.free.fr/rcaexplore/.

of the ECFD. To obtain the approximate intersection, an additional tool, ComputeApprox computes the core concepts of the AC-poset and an ECFD without groups or mutex, which are not appropriate in this case.

We apply the approach on several feature models that own from 4 to 864 configurations, and from 6 to 26 features. Some are taken from the SPLOT repository[3] [16], from the Familiar[4] website, or from the literature, and we also made some variants of these feature models. In Table 6, we give the number of features, configurations, *xor groups*, *or groups* and constraints of each selected FM. We also compute the ECFD and indicate the number of *xor groups*, *or groups*, mutex, situations where a box in the ECFD has several direct parents (*multi-par.*), and nodes. The number of groups, e.g. *xor groups*, may vary between the FM and the ECFD. For example, one *xor group* of the ECFD may combine several *xor groups* of the FM when there are additional constraints, or the ECFD may reveal more possible *xor groups* than initially indicated in the FM.

Table 7 presents information about intersection, approximate intersection and strict union. The built ECFDs have reasonable size compared to the input FMs,

Table 6. FMs (and the corresponding ECFDs) used for testing the approach [3]. *var.* stands for *variant*. *Cst* stands for *Constraint*. e-commerce FMs are the examples of this paper, Eshop FMs come from SPLOT, Wiki FMs come from FAMILIAR documentation (or are variants), Bicycle FMs are variants of Mendonca SPLOT FMs.

FM	Feature model					ECFD				
	#feat.	#conf.	#Xor	#Or	#Cst.	#Xor	#Or	#mutex	#multi-par.	#nodes
FM1 (e-com.)	6	4	0	1	0	0	1	0	0	3
FM2 (e-com.)	6	4	1	0	0	1	0	0	0	4
Martini Eshop	11	8	1	1	1	1	2	1	1	6
Tang Eshop	10	13	1	1	2	1	2	1	1	7
Toacy Eshop	12	48	1	2	0	1	2	0	0	9
Wiki-V1	14	10	4	0	4	3	2	5	2	9
Wiki-V2 (V1 var.)	17	50	4	1	4	6	13	1	1	13
Wiki-V3 (V1 var.)	18	120	3	2	6	2	2	1	0	13
Bicycle1	19	64	2	0	2	1	0	0	0	10
Bicycle2	22	192	5	0	1	6	1	6	0	17
Bicycle3	25	576	4	0	2	5	1	8	0	19
Bicycle4	26	864	5	0	2	6	1	8	0	21

---

[3] http://www.splot-research.org/.
[4] http://familiar.variability.io/.

Table 7. Merge-intersection, approximate intersection, and merge-strict union ECFDs (extended from [3]). #conf. (resp. #subconf) is the number of different configurations for intersection and strict-union (resp. sub-configurations for approximate intersection). NA stands for "Non Applicable".

FM	Formal context		ECFD					% diff with ∩~	
	#feat.	#(sub)conf.	#Xor	#Or	#mutex	#multi-par.	#nodes	#feat.	#nodes
FM1 ∩ FM2	5	2	0	0	0	0	2	-0%	-50%
FM1 ∩~ FM2	5	4	NA	NA	NA	0	4	.	
FM1 ∪ FM2	7	6	1	1	1	1	6	+40%	+50%
Martini∩Tang	0	0	0	0	0	0	0	-100%	-100%
Martini ∩~ Tang	9	6	NA	NA	NA	0	6	.	
Martini∪Tang	12	21	1	2	3	1	8	+33%	+33%
Martini∩Toacy	0	0	0	0	0	0	0	-100%	-100%
Martini ∩~ Toacy	9	6	NA	NA	NA	0	6	.	
Martini∪Toacy	14	56	1	1	4	0	10	+56%	+67%
Tang∩Toacy	8	5	1	2	0	0	5	-11.1%	-16.7%
Tang ∩~ Toacy	9	6	NA	NA	NA	0	6	.	
Tang∪Toacy	13	56	1	1	4	1	10	+44%	+67%
WikiV1∩WikiV2	0	0	0	0	0	0	0	-100%	-100%
WikiV1 ∩~ WikiV2	11	7	NA	NA	NA	0	7	.	
WikiV1∪WikiV2	20	60	5	9	26	0	16	+82%	+129%
WikiV1∩WikiV3	0	0	0	0	0	0	0	-100%	-100%
WikiV1 ∩~ WikiV3	9	5	NA	NA	NA	0	5	.	
WikiV1∪WikiV3	23	130	3	4	42	0	18	+156%	+260%
WikiV2∩WikiV3	14	50	0	6	0	0	6	-0%	-45.5%
WikiV2 ∩~ WikiV3	14	11	NA	NA	NA	0	11	.	
WikiV2∪WikiV3	21	120	0	16	8	1	17	+50%	+55%
Bicycle1∩Bicycle2	14	8	1	0	0	0	6	-6.7%	-40%
Bicycle1 ∩~ Bicycle2	15	10	NA	NA	NA	0	10	.	
Bicycle1∪Bicycle2	26	248	6	1	32	2	21	+73%	+110%
Bicycle3∩Bicycle4	23	288	5	1	8	0	18	-4.2%	-5.3%
Bicycle3 ∩~ Bicycle4	24	19	NA	NA	NA	0	19	.	
Bicycle3∪Bicycle4	27	1152	6	1	8	0	22	+13%	+16%

with node number ranging from 2 to 22, mutex from 0 to 32, *xor* and *or groups* from 0 to 16, and very few multi-parent situations. This is encouraging if we consider that experts have to extract FMs, guided by the ECFDs.

The last two columns of Table 7 respectively show the difference between: intersection and approximate intersection; strict union and approximate intersection. For example, if we consider FM1 ∩~ FM2, we can notice that union FM1 ∪ FM2 feature number (7) is 40% more than the FM1 ∩~ FM2 feature number (5). FM1 ∪ FM2 sub-configurations (or AC-poset node number) (6) are 50% more than the FM1 ∩~ FM2 feature number (4). Intersection FM1 ∩ FM2 feature number (5) is 0% less than the FM1 ∩~ FM2 feature number (5). FM1 ∩ FM2 sub-configurations (or AC-poset node number) (2) are 50% less than the FM1 ∩~ FM2 feature number (4). When intersection is empty, a relatively low difference between approximate intersection and strict union (like the Martini-Tang case, with 33%) indicates a good similarity between the FMs, not highlighted by the configuration-semantics. Reversely, when intersection is empty, but the difference between approximate intersection and union is high (like the WikiV1-WikiV3 case, with more than 150% for features, and 260% for common sub-configurations) reveals a low similarity. When approximate intersection is close to intersection (like the Bicycle3-Bicycle4 example), this means that the configuration-semantics is well captured by the common sub-configurations and features. When approximate intersection feature number is close to intersection feature number (like the Bicycle1-Bicycle2 example, with −6.7%), but this is not the case for node number (−40%), this means that there are many common features, but the configuration-semantics is not well captured by the common sub-configurations. This information also can guide an expert in her/his composition process.

6   Related Work and Discussion

Formal Concept Analysis has many applications in software engineering as was summarized in [17] for the period 1992–2003. Since this period new applications appeared, that range from fault localization [18] to bad smells and design patterns detection [19], suggest appropriate refactorings to correct some design defects [20], or analyzing software version control repositories [21]. In the domain of SPLE, FCA serves as a foundation for different approaches. Loesch and Ploederer [22] analyze the concept lattice between configurations and features to find variability information such as the co-occurring features, groups of features that are never present together, etc. This analysis helps extracting constraints or reorganizing features, e.g. by merging or removing some of them. These ideas are deepen and reused in feature model analysis or synthesis in [23–26]. Another available tool in the framework of FCA is the notion of implicative systems, used in [24]. This is another logical encoding of the formula which is equivalent to a concept lattice (or to a feature model), which can be rather compact. The relationship between scenarios, functional requirements and quality requirements is studied in [27]. FCA-based identification of features in source code has been studied for software product line in [28,29], where they use the description of software variants by source code elements. Finding traceability links between features and the code is more specifically studied in [30]. In [31], authors analyze source code parts and scenarios which execute them and use features, with the purpose to identify parts of the code which correspond to feature implementation. Carbonnel et al. analyze PCMs from Wikipedia or randomly generated to evaluate the scale up of FCA on this type of data in [32] and the associated ECFDs in [14].

Several approaches for FM composition are compared in [2,33]. In [34,35] the input feature models are maintained separately and links are established between them through constraints. The approach of [8] establishes, in a first phase, the matching between similar elements, then an algorithm recursively merges the feature models with structural rules. Catalogs of local transformation rules are proposed in [36,37]. Other approaches encode the FMs into propositional formulas [9], then compute the formula representing the intersection (resp. the union), then synthesize a FM from the boolean formula [10]. The logic and structural approaches have been illustrated and discussed in Sect. 3.2 and our approach was illustrated with the example used for illustrating the structural approach.

Compared to the logic approach, our approach also is sound and complete, and we produce a structure (the ECFD with all feature groups and mutex) which assists the expert in the extraction of the composed FM. Compared to the structural approach, ours does not make any presupposition about which relations are ontological, allowing to fix possible mistakes in the initial FMs. In our approach, the configuration-semantics and the non-contradictory ontological child-parent edges are preserved. We accept FMs with different feature sets, and we take into account cross-tree constraints. Our approach computes the merge-strict-union, the merge-intersection, and we also compute an approximate intersection, which is useful when the configuration sets to be merged have an empty, or small, intersection, and in general, for having a core description of the two FMs. When there are hierarchy mismatches, the AC-poset manages this information but the vocabulary (feature names) has to be the same (it can be aligned before the merge operations).

Our approach needs to know the list of configurations, thus as such, the proposed solution is restricted to some contexts: FMs that have limited number of configurations; real-world product lines given with configuration sets. Many FMs have a very large configuration set, as Video player FM from SPLOT, with 71 features and more than 1 billion configurations. We do not address these cases, as we more specifically address the contexts where the FMs have a reasonable number of configurations, which corresponds in particular to FMs coming from real-world product lines. Concerning product lines inducing a number of configurations not tractable by FCA, our approach also could benefit from product line decomposition: dividing a feature model according to scopes, concerns or teams into less complex interdependent feature models. Besides, the paper [38] gives a procedure to derive (in a polynomial time) an implicative system directly from a feature model, thus without using the configuration set which may be an obstacle in some cases as noticed by [24]. The logical semantics is guaranteed by the FCA framework. The computational complexity is polynomial for AC-posets, in the size of the number of configurations and the number of features. Thus this is very different from the complexity of concept lattices, which may be exponential in worst cases. As detailed by [24], ECFD group and *mutex* computation might be exponential in the number of configurations or features but remains reasonable in typical situations, with an optimized implementation.

7   Conclusion

We have proposed an approach to assist designers in configurations-based FM composition. We focused on strict union, intersection and approximate intersection. FCA was used to represent all the FMs with the same configuration semantics through a canonical form, the ECFD (Equivalence Class Feature Diagram). Our approach may take into account different feature sets and structures, as well as cross-tree constraints. It allows to reset the ontological relationships. We have implemented our approach and we have tested it on concrete examples.

As future work, we would like to investigate more the approximate intersection. More specifically, from the intersection and union AC-posets, we would like to define similarity metrics, e.g. based on the size of intents and the number of concepts of each category (strict partial, strict semi-partial, configuration). We also would like to define a composition approach based on implicative systems, to discard the limit imposed by the current need to have the configuration set. Let us notice that having the configuration set is not always a limit, as in concrete product line, this is the standard data.

References

1. Pohl, K., Böckle, G., van der Linden, F.J.: Software Product Line Engineering: Foundations, Principles, and Techniques. Springer Science & Business Media, Heidelberg (2005). https://doi.org/10.1007/3-540-28901-1
2. Acher, M., Collet, P., Lahire, P., France, R.B.: Comparing approaches to implement feature model composition. In: 6th European Conference on Modelling Foundations and Applications (ECMFA), pp. 3–19 (2010)
3. Carbonnel, J., Huchard, M., Miralles, A., Nebut, C.: Feature model composition assisted by formal concept analysis. In: 12th International Conference on Evaluation of Novel Approaches to Software Engineering (ENASE), pp. 27–37 (2017)
4. Ganter, B., Wille, R.: Formal Concept Analysis - Mathematical Foundations. Springer, Heidelberg (1999). https://doi.org/10.1007/978-3-642-59830-2
5. Kang, K.C., Cohen, S.G., Hess, J.A., Novak, W.E., Peterson, A.S.: Feature-Oriented Domain Analysis (FODA): Feasibility Study. Technical report CMU/SEI-90-TR-21 - ESD-90-TR-222 (1990)
6. Achtaich, A., Roudies, O., Souissi, N., Salinesi, C.: Selecting SPL modeling languages: a practical guide. In: 3rd IEEE World Conference on Complex Systems (WCCS), Marrakech, Morocco (2015)
7. Czarnecki, K., Kim, C.H.P., Kalleberg, K.T.: Feature models are views on ontologies. In: 10th International Conference on Software Product Lines (SPLC), pp. 41–51 (2006)
8. Acher, M., Collet, P., Lahire, P., France, R.: Composing feature models. In: van den Brand, M., Gašević, D., Gray, J. (eds.) SLE 2009. LNCS, vol. 5969, pp. 62–81. Springer, Heidelberg (2010). https://doi.org/10.1007/978-3-642-12107-4_6
9. Batory, D.S.: Feature models, grammars, and propositional formulas. In: 9th International Conference on Software Product Lines (SPLC), pp. 7–20 (2005)
10. Czarnecki, K., Wasowski, A.: Feature diagrams and logics: there and back again. In: 11th International Conference on Software Product Lines (SPLC), pp. 23–34 (2007)
11. Birkhoff, G.: Lattice theory. Volume 25 of Colloquium publications. American Mathematical Society (1940)
12. Barbut, M., Monjardet, B.: Ordre et Classification, vol. 2. Hachette (1970)
13. Davey, B.A., Priestley, H.A.: Introduction to Lattices and Order. Cambridge University Press, Cambridge (1990)
14. Carbonnel, J., Huchard, M., Nebut, C.: Analyzing variability in product families through canonical feature diagrams. In: 29th International Conference on Software Engineering and Knowledge Engineering (SEKE), pp. 185–190 (2017)

15. Acher, M., Collet, P., Lahire, P., France, R.B.: FAMILIAR: a domain-specific language for large scale management of feature models. Sci. Comput. Program. (SCP) **78**, 657–681 (2013)
16. Mendonca, M., Branco, M., Cowan, D.: S.P.L.O.T.: Software Product Lines Online Tools. In: 24th ACM SIGPLAN Conference Companion on Object Oriented Programming Systems Languages and Applications (OOPSLA), pp. 761–762. ACM (2009)
17. Tilley, T., Cole, R., Becker, P., Eklund, P.: A survey of formal concept analysis support for software engineering activities. In: Ganter, B., Stumme, G., Wille, R. (eds.) Formal Concept Analysis. LNCS (LNAI), vol. 3626, pp. 250–271. Springer, Heidelberg (2005). https://doi.org/10.1007/11528784_13
18. Cellier, P., Ducassé, M., Ferré, S., Ridoux, O.: DeLLIS: A data mining process for fault localization. In: 23rd International Conference on Software Engineering and Knowledge Engineering (SEKE), pp. 432–437 (2009)
19. Arévalo, G., Ducasse, S., Gordillo, S., Nierstrasz, O.: Generating a catalog of unanticipated schemas in class hierarchies using formal concept analysis. Inf. Softw. Technol. **52**, 1167–1187 (2010)
20. Moha, N., Hacene, A.R., Valtchev, P., Guéhéneuc, Y.: Refactorings of design defects using relational concept analysis. In: 6th International Conference on Formal Concept Analysis (ICFCA), pp. 289–304 (2008)
21. Greene, G.J., Esterhuizen, M., Fischer, B.: Visualizing and exploring software version control repositories using interactive tag clouds over formal concept lattices. Inf. Software Technol. **87**, 223–241 (2017)
22. Loesch, F., Ploedereder, E.: Restructuring variability in software product lines using concept analysis of product configurations. In: 11th European Conference on Software Maintenance and Reengineering (CSMR), pp. 159–170 (2007)
23. Yang, Y., Peng, X., Zhao, W.: Domain feature model recovery from multiple applications using data access semantics and formal concept analysis. In: 16th Working Conference on Reverse Engineering (WCRE), pp. 215–224 (2009)
24. Ryssel, U., Ploennigs, J., Kabitzsch, K.: Extraction of feature models from formal contexts. In: 15th International Conference on Software Product Lines (SPLC) Workshop Proceedings, vol. 2, p. 4 (2011)
25. Al-Msie'deen, R., Huchard, M., Seriai, A., Urtado, C., Vauttier, S.: Reverse engineering feature models from software configurations using formal concept analysis. In: 11th International Conference on Concept Lattices and Their Applications (CLA), pp. 95–106 (2014)
26. Shatnawi, A., Seriai, A.D., Sahraoui, H.: Recovering architectural variability of a family of product variants. In: 14th International Conference on Software Reuse (ICSR), pp. 17–33 (2015)
27. Niu, N., Easterbrook, S.M.: Concept analysis for product line requirements. In: 8th International Conference on Aspect-Oriented Software Development (AOSD), pp. 137–148 (2009)
28. Xue, Y., Xing, Z., Jarzabek, S.: Feature location in a collection of product variants. In: 19th Working Conference on Reverse Engineering (WCRE), pp. 145–154 (2012)
29. Al-Msie'deen, R., Seriai, A., Huchard, M., Urtado, C., Vauttier, S., Salman, H.E.: Mining features from the object-oriented source code of a collection of software variants using formal concept analysis and latent semantic indexing. In: 25th Conference on Software Engineering and Knowledge Engineering (SEKE), pp. 244–249 (2013)

30. Salman, H.E., Seriai, A., Dony, C.: Feature-to-code traceability in a collection of software variants: combining formal concept analysis and information retrieval. In: 14th Conference on Information Reuse and Integration (IRI), pp. 209–216 (2013)
31. Eisenbarth, T., Koschke, R., Simon, D.: Locating features in source code. IEEE Trans. Softw. Eng. **29**, 210–224 (2003)
32. Carbonnel, J., Huchard, M., Gutierrez, A.: Variability representation in product lines using concept lattices: Feasibility study with descriptions from wikipedia's product comparison matrices. In: 1st International Workshop on Formal Concept Analysis and Applications, FCA&A 2015, co-located with 13th International Conference on Formal Concept Analysis (ICFCA), pp. 93–108 (2015)
33. Acher, M., Combemale, B., Collet, P., Barais, O., Lahire, P., France, R.B.: Composing your compositions of variability models. In: Moreira, A., Schätz, B., Gray, J., Vallecillo, A., Clarke, P. (eds.) MODELS 2013. LNCS, vol. 8107, pp. 352–369. Springer, Heidelberg (2013). https://doi.org/10.1007/978-3-642-41533-3_22
34. Schobbens, P., Heymans, P., Trigaux, J., Bontemps, Y.: Generic semantics of feature diagrams. Comput. Netw. **51**, 456–479 (2007)
35. Heymans, P., Schobbens, P., Trigaux, J., Bontemps, Y., Matulevicius, R., Classen, A.: Evaluating formal properties of feature diagram languages. IET Software **2**, 281–302 (2008)
36. Segura, S., Benavides, D., Cortés, A.R., Trinidad, P.: Automated merging of feature models using graph transformations. In: Generative and Transformational Techniques in Software Engineering II, International Summer School (GTTSE 2007), Revised Papers, pp. 489–505 (2007)
37. Alves, V., Gheyi, R., Massoni, T., Kulesza, U., Borba, P., de Lucena, C.J.P.: Refactoring product lines. In: 5th International Conference on Generative Programming and Component Engineering (GPCE), pp. 201–210 (2006)
38. Carbonnel, J., Bertet, K., Huchard, M., Nebut, C.: FCA for software product lines representation: mixing product and characteristic relationships in a unique canonical representation. In: 13th International Conference on Concept Lattices and Their Applications (CLA), pp. 109–122 (2016)

A Cloud-Based Service
for the Visualization and Monitoring
of Factories

Guillaume Prévost[(✉)], Jan Olaf Blech, Keith Foster, and Heinrich W. Schmidt

RMIT University, Melbourne, Australia

Abstract. With standard networking technologies gaining access to the factory floors, remote monitoring and visualization of the collected information is an important topic in the field of industrial automation. Information may be used for remote operation of a production plant, for planning and conducting maintenance, for incident analysis, and for optimization purposes.

In this paper, we present a framework for the collection and visualization of data streaming from industrial automation devices such as machines in factories or robots. An important part of our framework is the use of cloud-based services to collect data from programmable logic controllers (PLCs). PLCs are used to control machines such as grippers and conveyor belts. PLCs send data to our services and clients such as analysis or visualization services can subscribe to these data channels in accordance with customer needs. Here, we focus on the visualization services themselves. In our work, data from industrial automation facilities is associated with formal semantic models. For example, a formal semantic model can be a mathematical representation of the material flow in a production plant. In general, the formal semantic models are used to represent interdependencies between entities, their functionality and other descriptive elements. Formal semantic models are in the visualization and for reasoning about systems. In order to complement the visualization and cloud-based services work, we present our demonstrator. Our demonstrator comprises an example factory, we are using Raspberry Pi-based controllers as PLCs. These are connected with each other and to the internet using standard ethernet technology.

This paper is an extended version of a previously published paper [18] by the same authors.

Keywords: Industrial automation · Cloud-based services
Data visualization

1   Introduction

The connection of controllers in factories such as programmable logic controllers or robots to internet services can provide a variety of benefits for operation and maintenance for these facilities. Recent trends are frequently summarized terms such as Industry 4.0 [14] or smart factories (e.g., [25, 26]). Factory automation controllers communicating with centralized cloud-based services can not only be used for classical supervisory control and data acquisition (SCADA) tasks, but can also be a basis for services that are orthogonal to SCADA functionality. These services can comprise data analytics and longer-term health monitoring. Visualization and an adequate presentation of findings is a key component to the success of our remotely interacting with industrial facilities. Web-based front ends seem an adequate solutions due to their independence of concrete platforms.

In our work, we are focused on remote monitoring, operation and maintenance of production plants. For example the support of mining site operations, e.g., in the Australian outback is a target area (see [4,5]). The main contributions of this paper are

- The introduction of a cloud-based framework to gather data from controllers and visualize the data using a web-based frontend.
- The use of semantic carrying data models.
- The presentation of a demonstrator using a real example factory.

The paper extends a previously published paper [18] by the same authors. We have added some new figures, extended explanations and a separate related work section. Both papers feature the use of semantic data models for industrial automation in combination with our cloud-based visualization platform. In addition, both papers present our demonstrator combining these technologies. Our demonstrator can be used to analyze production plant operations remotely.

Overview

Section 2 gives an overview on related work. Our data modeling language and framework is introduced in Sect. 3. The cloud-based data visualization platform is presented in Sect. 4. Section 5 gives an overview on our demonstrator. A conclusion and ideas for future work are presented in Sect. 6.

2   Related Work

In this paper, we introduce a cloud-based framework to gather data from controllers and visualize the data using a web-based frontend. While a variety of products already exist for visualizing industrial facilities such as Dassault Systèmes' Delmia and Enovia [9, 10], we focus on the cloud-based architecture and on a more abstract data visualization view. Visualization is based on formal models. In particular, we are interested in models that express spatio-temporal relationships between entities. A variety of formalisms for spatio-temporal models have been developed. More process algebra-like approaches [7,8] can have benefits when investigating concurrency. On the modeling side, our approach is similar to the qualitative predicates of the Region Connection Calculus (RCC) [2] that can express inclusion, neighborhood and similar spatial properties. Furthermore, the cardinal direction calculus [22], the rectangle algebra [1], and the cross calculus [23] use comparable means of abstracting from concrete geometric objects in models. On the other hand, semantic descriptions of services in the industrial automation area have been discussed (see, e.g., [17]) as well as ontologies for factory automation (e.g. [16]).

Platforms for additional data analytics and visualization functionality such as ABB's service port framework[1] go beyond traditional SCADA functionality and are used in industrial practice. Furthermore, we have worked on approaches such as remote health monitoring (see, e.g., [24]) and cloud-based monitoring of industrial applications [19] that go into a similar direction. Additional means for visualization of industrial automation data has been investigated by us in the virtual reality context [21] and large screen visualization [20].

3   BeSpaceD-Based Data-Models

Semantic models as well as data in production plants play an important role in our work. Dependencies and data need an adequate representation, our formalization is created using the BeSpaceD framework [6] which has been developed by us. In this section, we briefly introduce the language then describe the data structures used in the models.

3.1   Spatio-Temporal Modeling and Reasoning

Our BeSpaceD framework is a key ingredient for spatio-temporal modeling and reasoning. The framework comprises:

- A language for modeling spatio-temporal systems and representing data. The language serves as a domain specific language (DSL) and is realized using abstract datatype constructors provided by the Scala programming language. The language comprises logical operators such as conjunctions, disjunctions and implications as well as operators for time and space as basic entities.
- A library-like collection of operations to reason about the BeSpaceD models as well as import and export functionality. Typical operations comprise abstractions and property detection (such as collisions in time and space).

In the past, BeSpaceD was successfully applied to domains such as train systems [13], industrial automation [5], industrial robots [11], communication infrastructure [12] and smart energy systems [3]. Some of this work integrates with model-based development tools.

3.2   Representing Industrial Plants

Most of our models for production plants are represented as mathematical graphs (L, E). Graphs comprise a set of locations L and a set of edges E. Typically L

---

[1] http://new.abb.com/process-automation/process-automation-service/advanced-services/serviceport.

can refer to machines, sensors and actuators in a plant while the elements of E comprise connections between elements of L. They represent interdependencies such as physical connections, material flow, distances, communication channels. Both edges and locations can be annotated. To give a look and feel, we have realized the constructors for graphs in BeSpaceD/Scala which are shown in Fig. 1.

```
class BeGraphAnnotated[+N, +A]
  (terms: List[EdgeAnnotated[N, A]])
   extends BIGAND[EdgeAnnotated[N, A]](terms)

class EdgeAnnotated[+N, +A]
      (val source : N, val target : N,
          val annotation: Option[A])
      extends ATOM
```

Fig. 1. Graph definition in BeSpaceD (see [18]).

For example, we have modeled different aspects of our factory demonstrator. In the evaluation of our framework, we are particularly interested in the *material flow* topology. This represents the expected flow – between sensors and actuators – of material through the factory. We created a specialized subclass of our graph. The following provides a small excerpt of our graph-based formal model. The listing below shows the definition of an edge in a graph and its use in a very small graph definition comprising a set of two edges. The topology does not need to be static, it can change over time. To represent this, we can annotate the graphs with time constraints. This is shown in Fig. 2.

```
def edge(s: FestoSensor, t: FestoSensor) =
    EdgeAnnotated(s, t, Some(ProcessSequence))

BeGraphAnnotated[FestoSensor,
      TemporalFestoConnection] (
  edge(CapDispenser.StackEjectorRetracted,
    CapDispenser.StackEjectorExtended)    ^
    edge(CapDispenser.StackEjectorExtended,
      CapDispenser.StackEmpty)
)
```

Fig. 2. Graph in BeSpaceD (see [18]).

The nodes (e.g. `StackEjectorRetracted`) are objects that uniquely identify a sensor in the demonstrator.

3.3   Representing Sensor Data

In addition to the static nature of the plant models, we use BeSpaceD to treat live sensor data. Sensor data comprises a sensor identifier that should have a corresponding node in the plant model. Furthermore, it is associated with a timestamp and the actual sensor value. For example, we use the following construct is used to specify that the sensor StackEjectorRetracted has the value Obstructed(High) at a timepoint 1479976418130

```
INSTATE(StackEjectorRetracted, 1479976418130,
     Obstructed(High))
```

The long integers for the time point are recording milliseconds since Epoch (12:00am, Jan 1st, 1970). Sensor data can be sent using the JSON format. The example above is encoded as shown in Fig. 3:

```
{"type": "IMPLIES",
"premise":{"type": "BIGAND", "terms": [
  {"type": "Component",
   "id": "Stack Ejector Retracted"},
  {"type": "TimePoint",
   "timepoint": 1479976418130}
  ]},
"conclusion": {"type": "Obstructed",
     "signal": High}
}
```

Fig. 3. JSON Encoding of graphs (following [18]).

4   Cloud-Based Reporting and Visualization

This section describes the cloud-based software platform for the report generation and visualization of production plant data and data-models. Data-models are formalized using the BeSpaceD framework.

4.1   eStoRED Overview

eStoRED is an open source data evaluation and visualization platform that is used for industrial decision support and risk assessment. Its architecture is shown in Fig. 4. It enables the joint-visualization of data from various data sources or workflows in the cloud. The visualization is realized using a scalable platform, to make sense of the various pieces of data as a whole, and to provide a way of collaboratively telling a meaningful story about the data. The eStoRED tool offers a way to connect to data sources, retrieve data and visualize it along with the possibility to attach metadata.

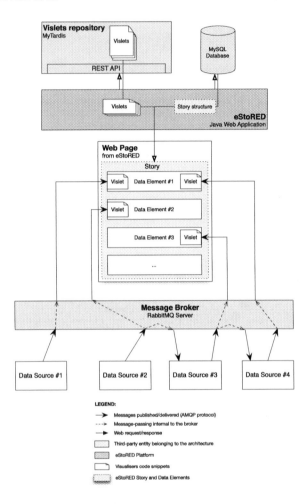

Fig. 4. eStoRED software architecture (cf. [18]).

Possible data sources comprise streamed data (such as sensor data delivered over a network connection), web-services, relational databases and file systems. In eStoRED, users can add their own analysis and risk definition assessment, thereby enriching and adding further value to the data displayed. This allows building data-backed comprehensive reports. The eStoRED system can handle static data extracted from files or databases as well as live data - such as data coming from sensors - given that there exist a connector to the data source.

Before it was lifted up as a more versatile platform, eStoRED originated as a decision-support platform for early-stages climate risk assessment and climate change adaptation training/planning for Australian and south Pacific seaports. It was gathering data from multiple public authorities and government agencies sources, such as the Bureau of Meteorology (BOM), the Commonwealth

Scientific and Industrial Research Organisation (CSIRO), the Australian Bureau of Statistics (ABS) and the Bureau of Infrastructure, Transport and Regional Economics (BITRE) to enable climate change experts manipulating and presenting this data according to their needs, thus supporting organizational climate risk management strategies needed by decision-makers.

The platform is currently used within RMIT University to enrich and visualize large research data collections coming from live data sources like Twitter streaming API feed providing millions of data points, or recorded tracking of actual movement of couriers from a UK-based delivery company.

eStoRED covers a wide range of possible applications, but we focus on the role it plays in the context of industrial automation, for visualizing plant data and data model. In the following, we examine its architecture.

4.2   eStoRED Architecture

In eStoRED, the main entities created by users are called *Stories*. *Stories* contain different *Elements*: *Data Elements* are the connected elements visualizing data, *Input Elements* are the analysis parts written by the users. At its core, the eStoRED platform is composed of a web application backed by a relational database, a message broker and a repository of snippets of code for visualizing data, called *Vislets*. We describe eStoRED's components and how they interact together:

- On one end, the data sources are the processes, applications and systems that produce the data. They publish data into messages handled by a *publish/subscribe* system that orchestrates and distributes messages to the processes that have subscribed. The third-party system chosen for this role is RabbitMQ[2], an open-source, secure, robust and scalable system for software messaging, using the AMQP protocol[3].
- The Java web application is using the Spring MVC framework, Hibernate ORM to map its data model to a MySQL database storing the internal eStoRED data (*Stories, Data Elements, Input Elements*, etc.). When working on a *Story*, a user can create *Data Elements* and define one or more *Subscriptions* for each of them.
- A *Subscription* is composed of a subscription expression, the expected format of the data to be received and the snippet of code, called *Vislet* that will handle and visualize the data once it is received. eStoRED is connected via a REST API to a curated repository of *Vislets* and can filter them according to some metadata attached to each *Vislet*. The eStoRED graphical user interface automatically filters the *Vislets* to only show those that can handle the expected data format.
- The *topic* subscription mechanism of RabbitMQ is used for subscribing. The mechanism uses *routing keys* to match publishers and subscribers. The subscription expression defined in eStoRED is used as the RabbitMQ routing key,

---

[2] https://www.rabbitmq.com.

[3] https://www.amqp.org/.

a sequence of characters up to 255 bytes, defining dot-separated words and allowing the wildcards characters * (star) substituting for exactly one word and # (hash) substituting for zero or more words. This enables a powerful and flexible mechanism to easily create subscription expressions spanning a wide range of data sources. For example: *australia.2016.rainfall, australia.2016.*, #.rainfall* are valid routing keys.

Data sources can also use this mechanism to subscribe to each other via the messaging system, and this way create data workflows. This is illustrated at the bottom of Fig. 4 where Data Source #3 is subscribed to Data Source #2, and Data Source #4 is subscribed to Data Source #3.

Once *Data Elements* have been defined, whenever a Story is loaded, the following steps happen, as shown in Figure 4:

1. eStoRED retrieves the *Story* and the *Data Elements* it contains.
2. It connects to the *Vislet* repository and retrieves the *Vislets* defined in the *Subscriptions* of each *Data Element*.
3. The web application then generates a web page where the *Vislets* are included.
4. On the web page, a JavaScript client for RabbitMQ is executed directly into the client's web browser to subscribe to the expression.

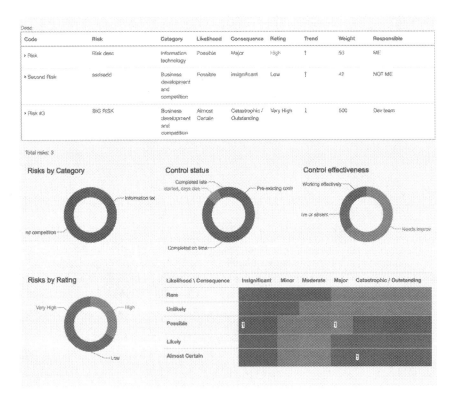

Fig. 5. Some visualized diagrams.

5. When a Data source publishes a message, if a *Data Element* is subscribed to it, the message broker passes it on, and the *Vislet* code is called to interpret the data contained in the message, and act on it by displaying it or performing specific computations on them.

To provide a look-and-feel, some diagrams visualized by eStoRED are shown in Fig. 5.

5   Demonstrator and Evaluation

We have created a factory demonstrator and connected it to our framework. An extended description of a BeSpaceD-based formalization of the factory demonstrator can be found in [15].

5.1   The Factory Demonstrator

Figure 6 shows an overview of our food-processing factory demonstrator. The conveyor belt circle for pallets in the middle part and the bottling machinery in the lower left of the picture are visible.

Fig. 6. Food processing plant demonstrator (cf. [18]).

One of our Raspberry Pi-based controllers is shown in Fig. 7. It features a Raspberry Pi including network connectivity as well as IO-boards to communicate with the sensor and actuator world.

Fig. 7. Raspberry Pi-based controller (cf. [18]).

5.2   eStoRED - Factory Connection

The Fig. 8 shows how the eStoRED architecture is used in the context of visualizing that demonstrator. The topology of the food processing plant demonstrator is formalized in BeSpaceD as part of the configuration of the program monitoring the plant. It is converted into the JSON format and sent to the message broker at initialization. Whenever the sensors' statuses change over time, the sensors send signals to their respective Raspberry Pi-based controller. A program to monitor this is deployed on the Raspberry Pi. After converting these into the BeSpaceD language, the corresponding events are sent to the message broker via a simple AMQP client.

At the other end, a *Data Element* is created in the eStoRED platform, with two *Subscriptions*: one for the topology, and one for the sensor events. The specific visualizers are retrieved and loaded into the web browser. Being in the same data element, both visualizers are acting on the same graph visualization. The topology visualizer draws the nodes and edges of the graph representing the process, and the sensors visualizer re-draws the status of the sensors by colouring the nodes whenever they get updated.

Figure 9 shows an eStoRED *Data Element* which has received both topology data and sensor data. A timeline control can be observed at the top of the *Data Element*, which is updated when receiving new sensor data. Since each sensor signal encompasses the exact time when it happened, the visualizer enables scrolling through signals received in the past, using this timeline control. At the bottom of the *Data Element* are displayed metadata that can optionally be added to AMQP messages as key-value pairs. Here it only shows metadata as an example, but this could be important data such as the factory location or

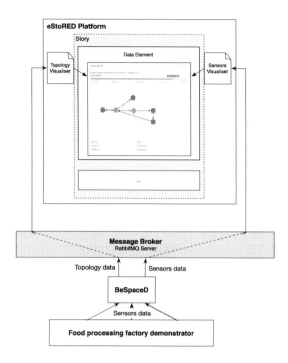

Fig. 8. eStoRED in the factory data visualization context (cf. [18]).

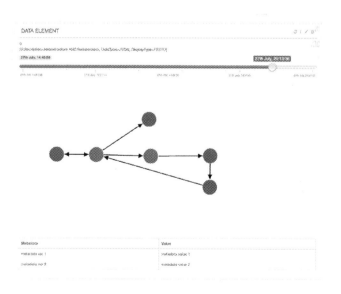

Fig. 9. Example of an eStoRED data element including topology and sensor data (cf. [18]).

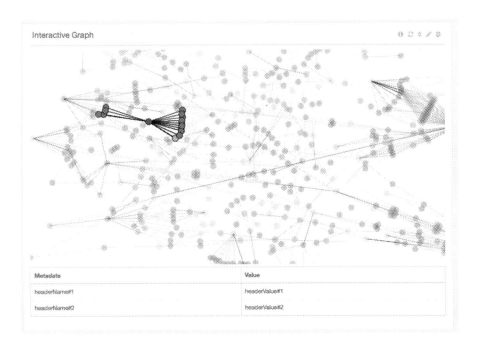

Fig. 10. Selection of a node in a graph visualized with eStoRED.

staff responsible for it. To provide a look and feel, Fig. 10 shows the selection of
a node and its connections in a larger graph visualized using eStoRED.

An excerpt of the semantic model represented as a topology in the JSON
format is shown in Fig. 11.

Two edges representing material flow are shown with their annotations in
the excerpt.

A series of figures show another graphical representation factory elements.
These are presented in Figs. 12, 13 and 14. Only a limited number of edges are
shown for readability proposes.

The dashed lines represent parts of the factory and these correspond to their
relative spatial position and size. Squares represent actuators and circles represent sensors.

Some meta data is shown that is used for configuration, debugging and automatic decision support. Of note is the General Purpose Input Output (GPIO)
Pin number of the Raspberry Pi-based PLC that is mapped to the actuator that
controls and actuator: it extends a stack ejector. The signal mapping defines the
binary voltage level (e.g. zero or 24 volts) that the actuators or sensors accept
or emit. This relates to sensor states in our model (e.g. [de]activate actuator;
[un]obstructed light sensor). Spatial measurements for a tube that holds bottling caps are shown to illustrate the annotation of geometric information. The
symbols are reference points and intermediate values used to formulate absolute
measurements.

```
{"type":"BIGAND","terms":[    {
        "type" : "EdgeAnnotated",
        "source" : {"type":"Component",
        "id":"Stack Ejector Retracted"},
        "target" : {"type":"Component",
        "id":"Stack Ejector Extended"},
        "annotation" : "ProcessSequence"
        } , {
    "type" : "EdgeAnnotated",
        "source" : {"type":"Component",
        "id":"Stack Ejector Extended"},
        "target" : {"type":"Component",
        "id":"Stack Empty"},
        "annotation" : "ProcessSequence"
        } , ...
```

Fig. 11. JSON Example (following [18]).

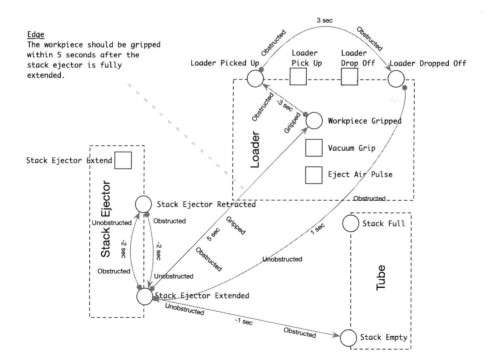

Fig. 12. Partial model of a factory element (material flow). (Color figure online)

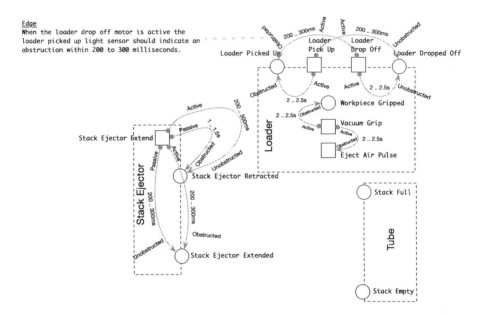

Fig. 13. Partial model of a factory element (interdependency). (Color figure online)

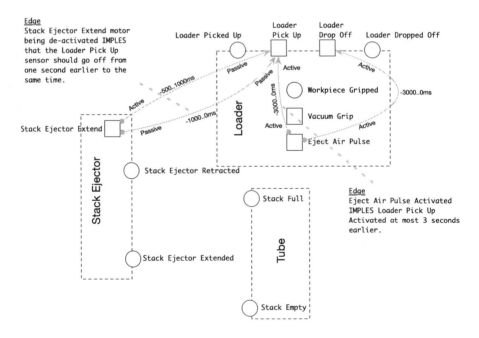

Fig. 14. Partial model of a factory element (safety). (Color figure online)

There are three different qualitative topological aspects that can be distinguished in our factory model. One edge from each aspect is added to the diagrams to illustrate them.

- Material Flow Topology (green)
  In the example, this edge is asserting that the stack empty sensor becomes obstructed exactly one second before the stack ejector extended sensor becomes unobstructed. In other words, it takes one second to eject the last cap from the stack.
- Interdependency aspects (blue)
  This edge is asserting that the stack ejector extended sensor becomes unobstructed between 200 to 300 milliseconds after the stack ejector extend actuator is inactivated (passive). In other words, it takes 200–300 ms for the light sensor to indicate retraction after the actuator starts retracting the stack ejector.
- Safety aspects (red)
  This edge is asserting a constraint that we want the loader to move to the pick-up position from half a second before to one and a half seconds after the stack ejector starts extending in order to avoid a collision.

6   Conclusion

This paper described our eStoRED framework with a focus on an industrial automation application. It extends a previous paper on the same topic [18]. In particular, we presented a cloud-based data collection and visualization solution for industrial automation. The framework incorporates spatio-temporal models from our BeSpaceD framework. Furthermore, we discussed some detailed examples in the paper and introduced a demonstrator and a visualization application. The cloud-based software framework and the example factory are integrated with each other. They serve as a demonstrator platform for our lab.

Our work intends to facilitate monitoring, operation and maintenance of production plants and mining operations. In particular remote plants and sites such as mining operations in the Australian outback are a targeted application area. These remote sites are sometimes more than 1000 km away from larger population centers and thus are characterized by difficulties to keep a large number of staff on-site due to limited accessibility, high on-site living costs, costs of bringing staff to and from the sites and similar reasons.

On the technical side, future work will connect additional services to the AMQP server in order to establish a common interchange platform for factory data. Larger demonstrators and advances on the BeSpaceD formalisms could be another promising direction.

References

1. Balbiani, P., Condotta, J.-F., del Cerro, L.F.: A new tractable subclass of the rectangle algebra. In: Proceedings of the 16th International Joint Conference on Artifical Intelligence, vol. 1, pp. 442–447 (1999)
2. Bennett, B., Cohn, A.G., Wolter, F., Zakharyaschev, M.: Multi-dimensional modal logic as a framework for spatio-temporal reasoning. Appl. Intell. **17**(3), 239–251 (2002)
3. Blech, J.O., Fernando, L., Foster, K., Abhilash, G., Sudarsan, Sd.: Spatio-temporal reasoning and decision support for smart energy systems. In: Emerging Technologies and Factory Automation (ETFA). IEEE (2016)
4. Blech, J.O., Peake, I., Schmidt, H., Kande, M., Ramaswamy, S., Sudarsan, Sd., Narayanan, V.: Collaborative engineering through integration of architectural, social and spatial models. In: Emerging Technologies and Factory Automation (ETFA). IEEE (2014)
5. Blech, J.O., Peake, I., Schmidt, H., Kande, M., Rahman, A., Ramaswamy, S., Sudarsan, SD., Narayanan, V.: Efficient incident handling in industrial automation through collaborative engineering. In: Emerging Technologies and Factory Automation (ETFA). IEEE (2015)
6. Blech, J.O., Schmidt, H.: BeSpaceD: Towards a Tool Framework and Methodology for the Specification and Verification of Spatial Behavior of Distributed Software Component Systems. http://arxiv.org/abs/1404.3537. arXiv.org (2014)
7. Caires, L., Cardelli, L.: A spatial logic for concurrency (Part I). Inf. Comput. **186**(2), 194–235 (2003)
8. Caires, L., Cardelli, L.: A spatial logic for concurrency (Part II). Theor. Comput. Sci. **322**(3), 517–565 (2004)
9. DS DELMIA V6R2013x - Fact Sheet: 3DEXPERIENCES of Global Production Systems for all stakeholders in the extended supply chain. Dassault Systèmes (2013)
10. ENOVIA V6R2013x - Fact Sheet. Dassault Systèmes (2013)
11. Han, F., Blech, J.O., Herrmann, P., Schmidt, H.: Towards verifying safety properties of real-time probabilistic systems. In: Formal Engineering approaches to Software Components and Architectures, vol. 147. EPTCS (2014)
12. Han, F., Blech, J.O., Herrmann, P., Schmidt, H.: Model-based engineering and analysis of space-aware systems communicating via IEEE 802.11. In: CompSac 2015. IEEE (2015)
13. Hordvik, S., Oseth, K., Blech, J.O., Herrmann, P.: A methodology for model-based development and safety analysis of transport systems. In: Evaluation of Novel Approaches to Software Engineering (2016)
14. Kagermann, H., Wahlster, W., Helbig, J. (eds.): Recommendations for implementing the strategic initiative INDUSTRIE 4.0 - Final report of the Industrie 4.0 Working Group. Acatech (2013)
15. Foster, K., Blech, J.O., Prevost, G.: Towards the Formalization of a Factory Demonstrator in BeSpaceD. http://arxiv.org/abs/1612.05316. arXiv.org (2016)
16. Lin, H.K., Harding, J.A.: A manufacturing system engineering ontology model on the semantic web for inter-enterprise collaboration. Comput. Ind. **58**(5), 428–437 (2007)
17. Loskyll, M., Schlick, J., Hodek, S., Ollinger, L., Gerber, T., Pirvu, B.: Semantic service discovery and orchestration for manufacturing processes. In: 16th Conference on Emerging Technologies & Factory Automation (ETFA). IEEE (2011)

18. Prévost, G., Blech, J.O., Foster, K., Schmidt, H.W.: An architecture for visualization of industrial automation data. In: Evaluation of Novel Approaches to Software Engineering (2017)
19. Peake, I., Blech, J.O.: A candidate architecture for cloud-based monitoring in industrial automation. In: IEEE International Conference on Software Quality, Reliability and Security (Companion). IEEE (2017)
20. Peake, I., Blech, J.O., Fernando, L., Schmidt, H., Sreenivasamurthy, R., Sudarsan, Sd.: Visualization facilities for distributed and remote industrial automation: VxLab. In: Emerging Technologies and Factory Automation (ETFA). IEEE (2015)
21. Peake, I.D., Blech, J.O., Watkins, E., Greuter, S., Schmidt, H.W.: The virtual experiences portals — a reconfigurable platform for immersive visualization. In: De Paolis, L.T., Mongelli, A. (eds.) AVR 2016. LNCS, vol. 9768, pp. 186–197. Springer, Cham (2016). https://doi.org/10.1007/978-3-319-40621-3_14
22. Skiadopoulos, S., Koubarakis, M.: On the consistency of cardinal direction constraints. Artif. Intell. **163**(1), 91–135 (2005)
23. Van de Weghe, N., Kuijpers, B., Bogaert, P., De Maeyer, P.: A qualitative trajectory calculus and the composition of its relations. In: Rodríguez, M.A., Cruz, I., Levashkin, S., Egenhofer, M.J. (eds.) GeoS 2005. LNCS, vol. 3799, pp. 60–76. Springer, Heidelberg (2005). https://doi.org/10.1007/11586180_5
24. Wenger, M., Zoitl, A., Blech, J.O., Peake, I.: Remote monitoring infrastructure for IEC 61499 based control software. In: 8th International Congress on Ultra Modern Telecommunications and Control Systems. IEEE (2016)
25. Westkämper, E., Jendoubi, L.: Smart factories–manufacturing environments and systems of the future. In: Proceedings of the 36th CIRP International Seminar on Manufacturing Systems (2003)
26. Zuehlke, D.: SmartFactory–towards a factory-of-things. Ann. Rev. Control **34**(1), 129–138 (2010)

An Operational Semantics of UML2.X Sequence Diagrams for Distributed Systems

Fatma Dhaou[1]([✉]), Ines Mouakher[1], J. Christian Attiogbé[2], and Khaled Bsaies[1]

[1] Lipah, Faculty of Sciences Tunis, Tunis, Tunisia
[2] LS2N, University of Nantes, Nantes, France
dhaoufatma@gmail.com

Abstract. UML2.X sequence diagrams (SD) are equipped with high structures: the combined fragments (CF) that permit to model complex behaviours of systems. CF can be nested to allow more sophisticated behaviours, however they complicate the interpretation of the SD and the computation of precedence relations between the events.

In a previous work, we proposed a causal semantics for UML2.X SD. It is based partial order theory, its well-defined relations allow the computation of all precedence relations for the events of UML2.X SD with nested CF. We considered the most popular CF of control-flow ALT, OPT, LOOP, SEQ allowing to model respectively alternative, optional, iterative and sequential behaviours. In this work, we improve that previous work to consider a PAR CF allowing to model parallel behaviours, and we propose an operational semantics that is based on the causal semantics. The proposed operational semantics is a substantial step towards the refinement checking and the analysis of some properties of SD.

Keywords: UML2.X sequence diagrams · Operational semantics
Causal semantics · Nested combined fragments

1 Introduction

Context. The speed of design, the intuition and the ease of graphical representation make UML2.X sequence diagrams (SD) a privileged language often used by the engineers in the software industries. Although the Object Management Group (OMG) [1] has defined an official standard semantics for UML2.X SD, some shortcomings still persist. For instance, we report that the definitions of the standard semantics are not well suited for an exhaustive computation of all possible traces of basic SD modelling the behaviours of distributed systems this is a shortcoming. Moreover, they are not formalized which yields, in some cases, to the ambiguities of interpretations.

Motivation. The defined rules by the OMG for deriving partial order of a given basic SD impose to order the events along each lifeline, even if they are received

© Springer International Publishing AG, part of Springer Nature 2018
E. Damiani et al. (Eds.): ENASE 2017, CCIS 866, pp. 158–182, 2018.
https://doi.org/10.1007/978-3-319-94135-6_8

from independent lifelines, which do not allow the computation of all possible valid behaviours. This leads to the emergence of unspecified behaviours in the implementation. Although we can add coregion operator and additional messages to establish the required order, however we obtain an overcrowded graphical representation that can lead to the interpretation ambiguities. With UML2.X, the combined fragments allow the modelling of several kind of behaviours. We focus especially on a subcategory of CF: ALT, OPT, LOOP, SEQ and PAR; they permit a compact syntactic representation of behaviours. In contrast, they cause challenges for the determination of precedence relations between the events. To compute traces for SD equipped with these CF, the OMG standard recommends to compute the traces of each components of the SD independently then the traces are composed by the WEAK SEQUENCING operator. This processing is equivalent in other approaches [2–5] to the flattening of the SDs that are semantically equivalent. However, the benefits of the compact syntactic representation are lost.

Moreover, the ALT and the LOOP CF have a different meaning than in the structured programming languages; although, to ease the processing of these CF, the existing approaches [5–7], restrict their use by interpreting them in the same way. However, in the standard they have much more flexible interpretations allowing to model more complex behaviours; for instance the ALT CF is not equivalent to the $IF-Then-Else$ structure, and in the LOOP CF, weak sequencing between the iterations is applied, rather than strict sequencing, permitting the interleaving of the occurrence of the events of different iterations.

In the practical cases, CF can be nested to model more sophisticated behaviours. All the cited problems are increasing. In the standard semantics, the notion of nested CF is briefly mentioned. In literature, few works [5–7] deal with nested CF. In [6] the authors study the issues resulting of the nesting of some kinds of CF (different of those considered in this paper), and by limiting the nesting levels of CF [5,6], or by proposing a complicated formalization very close to the target formalism [7].

Although the existing semantics that are proposed for UML2.X SD are various [3,8–10], but they are usually based on the definitions of the standard semantics for the computation of traces of the SD, thus they are not suitable for SD modelling behaviours of distributed systems. These shortcomings have motivate our proposal for a causal semantics dedicated for UML2.X SD with nested CF that models behaviours of distributed systems. Most of the existing semantics of different kinds (denotational, operational, algebraic) are based on the definitions of the standard semantics for the computation of precedence relations between the events, hence they present the same shortcomings as the standard semantics. Defining an operational semantics for SD facilitates their operational analysis and permits a better understanding of the language.

Contribution. This paper extends our previous works [11,12]; in [11] we have extended the semantics that is proposed for UML1.X SD [13]; we have proposed several formal rules, to compute directly the partial order between the events of SD with the most popular combined fragments (ALT, OPT, LOOP) that are sequential, by processing the SD as a whole. In [12], we have extended the formalization to deal with the nesting of (ALT, OPT and LOOP) CF, and we have generalized the precedence relations of the causal semantics that suit for UML2.X SD modelling the behaviours of distributed systems and equipped with nested CF.

We now propose additional contributions that consist in covering an other important CF that is the PARALLEL[1] CF, and we propose an operational semantics permitting a better understanding of the behaviour of the SD by defining the rules of occurrences of the events.

Organization. The remainder of the article is structured as follows. In Sects. 2 and 3, we provide an overview on our previous work: we explain the formalization of UML2.X SD and the precedence relations of the causal semantics. Section 4 is devoted to the operational semantics. Before concluding in Sect. 6, we present some related works in Sect. 5.

2   Causal Semantics

To overcome the shortcomings of the standard semantics, we considered an existing semantics [13] that is suitable for basic SD modelling behaviours of distributed systems. Its rules take into account the independence of the components, (modelled by lifelines), involved in the interactions. Indeed, in contrast with the standard semantics that totally order the events on each lifeline even for the receiving events from independent lifelines, the causal semantics imposes slighter scheduling constraints on the behaviour of lifelines results in more expressive SDs, since each SD describes a larger number of acceptable behaviours. This larger expressive power facilitates the task of the designer since a great number of cases have to be considered, and permits to prevent the issue of the emergence of unspecified behaviours in the implementation. The causal semantics is founded on a partial order theory. Intuitively, the causal semantics [14] is based on the idea of ordering events if there is a logical reason to do so. We present the relations of the causal semantics as defined in [13] in informal way as follows.

Synchronization Relationship $<_{SYNC}$. Each message m is received only if it was sent previously.

Reception-Emission Relationship $<_{RE}$. Receiving a message causes the sending of the message that is directly consecutive to it.

Emission-Emission Relationship $<_{EE}$. If two messages are sent by the same lifeline their sending events are ordered.

Causal order Relation $<_{caus}$. This relation is defined as follows:

$$<_{caus} = (<_{SYNC} \bigcup <_{RE} \bigcup <_{EE})$$

---

[1] The parallelism is logic, which mean that two events occur in any order.

The transitive closure of the relation $<_{caus}$ that we note $<^+_{caus}$ permits to obtain all the causal dependencies between the events of the SD. The event occurrence depends on the partial order relationship $<_{caus}$.

The causal semantics is mainly proposed for basics UML1.X SD modelling behaviours of distributed systems, and the application of its rules causes some inconsistencies (aberrant relations, deadlock and inadvertent triggers of some events [11]). Hence in our previous work [12], we proposed a new formalization of UML2.X SD with nested CF that is based on set theory and the tree structure. Then, based on this formalization, we proposed the extension of the causal semantics whose its relations permit the computation of precedence relations for each event that belong to an UML2.X SD with nested CF modelling behaviours of distributed systems.

3   Overview on Previous Extension of the Causal Semantics

3.1   Formalization of UML2.X SD with Nested CF

We consider a sub-set of SD containing combined fragment of control-flow ALT, OPT, LOOP and SEQ CF. The considered CF are sequential, and can be nested to model more sophisticated behaviours. We assume that the operands of the CF do not overlap, but can be nested. For the formalization of sequence diagrams equipped with nested CF, we choose, on the one hand, the set theory notations[2] that is a privileged way due to its several advantages. For instance, although it is founded on first order logic, it permits to manipulate objects of high order such as sets and relations of any depth (that is, sets and relations built themselves on sets and relations, and so on) [15]. On the other hand, we use the tree structure that is hierarchic by nature and it is convenient to capture the nested structure of SD, and allow to represent them in an intuitive way.

Sequence Diagram Definitions

Definition 1 *(Sequence Diagram)*
A sequence diagram SD is a tuple
$SD : \langle L, M, EVT, FCT\_s, FCT\_r, FCT\_l, OP, F, <_{caus}, tree\_OP \rangle$ *where:*

- *L is a set of not empty lifelines, and $card(L) \geq 2$,*
- *M is a set of asynchronous messages which is well formed and not empty. The set M is well formed if every message is identified by a pair of events: a sent event and a received event,*
- *$EVT = E\_s \cup E\_r$ is a set of events such that $card(EVT) \geq 2$[3], E_s and E_r denotes respectively the set of sent events and the set of received events such that $E\_s = \{!m \mid m \in M\}$[4] and $E\_r = \{?m \mid m \in M\}$[5], and $E\_s \cap E\_r = \emptyset$,*

---

[2] N.B we use the same set theory notation as those of Event-B method.
[3] Cardinal of a set E.
[4] $!m$ denote the sent event of the m message.
[5] $?m$ denote the received of the m message.

- *for a set of message M we define two bijective functions FCT_s and FCT_r that permit to associate to each message respectively one sent event and one received event: $FCT\_s : M \rightarrowtail E\_s$[6], and $FCT\_r : M \rightarrowtail E\_r$*
- *$FCT\_l : EVT \twoheadrightarrow L$[7] a total surjective function that associates to each event one lifeline, the transmitter or the receiver,*
- *$F = \{F_1, F_2, ..., F_n\}$ is the set of n CF, where $F_i = \langle OP_i, operator_i, L_i \rangle$ is a CF that is identified by its operands, an operator, and the set of lifelines that are covered by it,*
- *$<_{caus} \subseteq EVT \leftrightarrow EVT$ denotes the partial order relationship,*
- *OP: the SD is considered as a set of operands,*
- *tree_OP is a partial function that allows to structure the SD in the form of a tree of operands.*

To obtain the local order within each lifeline noted $<_{SD,l}$, we project the causal order relation $<_{caus}^{+}$[8] on the lifeline l.

Operands of CF. An SD is abstracted as a tree of operands. Intuitively, a combined fragment will be viewed as an operator together with its operands; this will be detailed in the sequel. We consider the following CF SEQ, ALT, OPT and LOOP. The SD is represented as a set of operands. We associate a label to each operand. Two operands with the same index i belong to the same combined fragment: it's the case of the operands of an ALT and PAR CF for instance, in Fig. 1, OP_{21}, OP_{22} and OP_{23} belong to the same CF ALT.

The whole SD is transformed to a root operand that we note OP_{00}; the set OP is defined as $(\bigcup_{i=\{1..n\}} OP_i) \cup \{OP_{00}\}$; where n is the number of operands of the considered SD. Each operand in an SD has a weight. For instance, each operand of SEQ, ALT or OPT CF has a weight equal to 1; an operand of a LOOP CF has a weight equal to a value max, which is the maximum number of iterations of the considered LOOP CF. We assume that each operand of a CF has only one first event. The first events of the different operands of a same CF do not belong necessarily to the same lifeline, since some of them came from lower level when we built the tree.

The general definition of an operand in a combined fragment is given as follows.

Definition 2 (Operand in Combined Fragment)
We define a set of operands OP_i in a CF F_i as:

$$OP_i = \{OP_{i,j=\{1..k\}} \mid OP_{ij} = \langle guard_{ij}, weight_{ij}, EVT\_D_{ij} \rangle\}$$

where: (i) k is the number of operands in CF Fi, (ii) $guard_{ij}$ is the guard of the operand OP_{ij}, (iii) $weight_{ij}$ is the weight of the operand OP_{ij}, (iv) EVT_D_{ij} are the events that are directly contained in an operand OP_{ij}.

---

[6] $\rightarrowtail$ denotes a bijective function.

[7] $\twoheadrightarrow$ denotes a total surjection.

[8] R^{+}: the transitive closure of R.

We use the following functions to manipulate the operands:

- EVT_D returns the events that are directly contained in each operand[9]:

$$EVT\_D : OP \rightarrow \mathbb{P}(EVT)$$

- EVT_G returns all the events that are contained in an operand including those which are contained in its nested operands:

$$EVT\_G : OP \rightarrow \mathbb{P}(EVT)$$

- $weight$ returns the weight of each operand:

$$weight : OP \rightarrow NAT^+$$

- $first$ gets the first event of each operand. $first : OP \rightarrow EVT$; intuitively, a first event is an event that has not a preceding events in the considered operand.

$$\textbf{first} = \{(X, e)| X \in OP \ \wedge \ e \in EVT\_G(X) \ \wedge$$
$$(\forall \ e')[e' \in EVT \ \wedge \ e' <^*_{caus} e \Rightarrow e' \notin EVT\_G(X)]\}$$

The instantiation of the Definition 2 for SEQ, ALT, OPT and LOOP CF is intuitive and it given in detail in our previous paper [12].

We just present the instantiation of the definition for the PAR CF;

Definition 3 (Operands in the PAR Combined Fragment)
A parallel combined fragment F_i is composed of a set of k operands:

$$OP_i^{\text{PAR}} = \{OP_{i1}, ..., OP_{ik}\}$$

where $OP_{ij} = \langle True, 1, EVT\_D_{ij}\rangle$
the guard is true and the weight is equal to 1.

The semantics of interactions is explained with an interleaving semantics [1], i.e. two events may not occur at exactly the same time.

In the same way, we choose an interleaving semantics to support alternatives and concurrency behaviours, since it is more appropriate for SD modelling behaviours of distributed system. Indeed, if the semantics allows the occurrence of two events exactly in the same time (like in the true-concurrency semantics[10]), in the case of an ALT CF, we'll have a simultaneous occurrence of the events of different operands, this is not compliant with the standard semantics of this CF where at most one operand among several potential operands must be chosen.

---

[9] $\mathbb{P}(EVT)$ is the set of subsets E.

[10] True-concurrency semantics is a non-interleaving semantics, it supports the occurrence of two events in the same time.

Transformation of SD as a Tree of Operands. An SD is encoded as a tree that is composed by a set of linked operands, such that each operand has at maximum one direct ancestor. For instance, the Fig. 2 illustrates the associated tree for the SD of the Fig. 1. A naive way to transform an SD into a tree is to associate a node to each CF or operand. When building the tree of an SD, we always have a root node that represents the complete SD; the process is then breadth-first. Note that the operands of an ALT or a PAR CF are independent, i.e. they have disjoint executions. Therefore, to simplify the tree representation of the SD, we substitute the node which should stand for these fragments with the nodes representing their operands. They are moved to the upper level. However, to distinguish them, the operands of the same fragment have their indexes built with the same prefix (OP_{21}, OP_{22} and OP_{23}). From the node of a current SD, the consecutive fragments of the SD become the nodes of the current node. Each fragment is either represented as a node or it is represented by the nodes of its operands. A node is associated to each CF that has only one operand (for instance LOOP or OPT). A CF with more than one operand (for instance ALT or PAR) is replaced with the nodes associated to its operands.

We define the tree structure for SD operands as follows:

Definition 4 *(Tree Structure for SD Operands)*
The tree structure tree_OP related to an SD is defined as a partial function: tree_OP : OP ↛ OP which is acyclic and non-reflexive. The root is the only operand that does not have a parent:

$$(\forall X)[X \in OP \,\wedge\, X \notin dom(tree\_OP) \,\wedge\, X \in ran(tree\_OP) \Rightarrow X = OP_{00}]$$

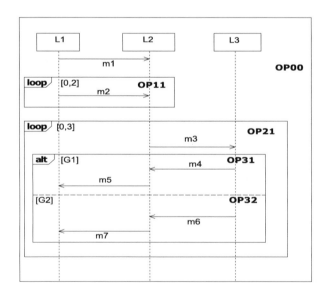

Fig. 1. Example of SD with nested CF.

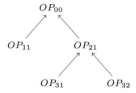

Fig. 2. Tree associated to the SD of the Fig. 1.

Once an SD is transformed to a tree of operands, we define relations that permit to get the locations of the operands that are required in the formalizations of precedence relations. To associate to each operand all the operands where it is nested (its ancestor operands in the $tree\_OP$), we introduce the relation $ancestor$. To identify the operands of the same CF ALT, PAR, we introduce the relation $brother$. We call brother operands those that belong to the same CF ALT, PAR. In a given tree: $tree\_OP = \{OP_{i1}....OP_{ij}\}$, the brother operands are the operands that belong to the same level and that have the same index i. Hence, the operands of the same sibling are not all necessarily brothers, since some of them came from lower level when built the tree.

- $ancestor$: a binary transitive relation[11] that is defined on OP.

$$ancestor : OP \leftrightarrow OP$$

For an operand X we compute its ancestors[12] as follows:

$$ancestor[\{X\}] = \bigcup_{s \in \{1,..,d\}} \{tree\_OP^s(X)\}$$

where d is the depth of the node X in the $tree\_OP$.

Illustration. In Fig. 2, $ancestor[\{OP_{00}\}] = \emptyset$, and $ancestor[\{OP_{31}\}] = \{OP_{21}, OP_{00}\}$.

- $brother$: a binary transitive relation that is defined on a set OP.

$$brother : OP \leftrightarrow OP$$
$$\mathbf{brother} = \{(OP_{ij}, OP_{tk})|(OP_{ij}, OP_{tk}) \in OP \times OP$$
$$\wedge (i = t \wedge j \neq k)\}$$

Illustration. In Fig. 1, the operands OP_{31}, OP_{32} belong to the same CF ALT, thus they are brothers. $brother[\{OP_{11}\}] = \emptyset$ and $brother[\{OP_{31}\}] = \{OP_{32}\}$

Weight of an Event. The function $weight$ was defined on an operand, We overload the function to associate the weight of the path between two operands.

$$weight_e : (OP \times OP) \rightarrow NAT^+$$

---

[11] $\leftrightarrow$ denotes a relation.

[12] $R[\{e\}]$: Relational image; gives the set of images.

For two operands X and Y, we compute the weight of their paths as follows:

$$\left\{ \begin{array}{l} weight_e(X,Y) = 1 \ if \ X = Y \\ weight_e(X,Y) = \displaystyle\prod_{s \in \{0,..,d\}} weight(tree\_OP^s(Y)) \end{array} \right\}$$

with d the *length* of the path between the operand X and the operand Y.

We overload the function *weight* that permits to associate to each event its maximal number of occurrence.

$$weight : EVT \rightarrow NAT^+$$

For an event evt of an operand X, such that $evt \in EVT\_D(X)$, we compute its weight as follows:

$$weight(evt) =$$
$$weight(X) * weight(tree\_OP(X))*$$
$$weight(tree\_OP^2(X) * ... * weight(\underbrace{tree\_OP^d(X)}_{OP_{00}}))$$

$$= \prod_{s \in \{0,d\}} weight(tree\_OP^s(X))$$
$$= weight_e(OP_{00}, X), (with \ d = depth \ of \ X)$$

The new formalization is used as a basis for the extension of the causal relationships that permits to compute the partial order between the events of the SD.

3.2   Extension of the Causal Semantics

The relations $<_{Sync}$, $<_{RE}$, $<_{EE}$ and $<_{RR}$ permit to compute the precedence relations for each event of an SD. The structuring of SD with nested CF in form of tree permits an obvious identification of the preceding events, they are grouped by operand, for each event that belongs to this kind of SD.

In this section, we generalize these relations. The synchronisation relationship ($<_{Sync}$) is unchangeable. The formalizations of $<_{RE}$ and $<_{EE}$ relationships permit to order two events that belong to the same lifeline and that are successive. We define a new relationship $<_{RR}$ to consider some particular cases of the ordering of receiving of events in the context of distributed components.

To detail a bit, and to alleviate the presentation of the formalization of $<_{RE}$ and $<_{EE}$ relationships, we introduce three binary relations *not_in_brother*, *succ1* and *succ2*. In the following, we first give the intuition of each of them before their formalizations.

Two successive events that belong to distinct operands of an ALT or a PAR CF must not be ordered. The relation *not_in_brother* expresses this intuition: the successive events of an ALT CF to be ordered must neither belong to brother operands nor to operands where in their respective ancestors exist a brother operands.

$$\textbf{not\_in\_brother} = \{(e, e') | (e, e') \in EVT^2 \wedge (\forall X)(\forall Y)$$
$$[X \in (ancestor[\{EVT\_D^{-1}(e)\}] \cup \{EVT\_D^{-1}(e)\})$$
$$\wedge Y \in (ancestor[\{EVT\_D^{-1}(e')\}] \cup \{EVT\_D^{-1}(e')\})$$
$$\Rightarrow (X, Y) \notin brother]\}$$

Illustration: In Fig. 1, the event $!m4 \in OP31$, the event $!m6 \in OP32$, however we have $OP32 \in brother[\{OP31\}]$, hence the events $!m4$ and $!m6$ should not be ordered.

Formally, we define that two events are successive in two manners with two distinct relations $succ1$ and $succ2$. These relations are used respectively in the formalization of $<_{EE}$ and $<_{RE}$ relationships. The relation $succ1$ relates two events that belong to the same lifeline and which are successive. Nevertheless, we admit between them, events that must necessarily belong to an operand that can be omitted (i.e. the events between successive events do not belong to any operand ancestor of the operands of the considered events).

$$\textbf{succ1} = \{(e, e') | (e, e') \in EVT^2 \wedge$$
$$(\exists l)[l \in L \wedge e <^*_{SD,l} e'$$
$$\wedge (\forall e")[e" \in EVT \wedge (e <^*_{SD,l} e" \wedge e" <^*_{SD,l} e')$$
$$\Rightarrow EVT\_D^{-1}(e") \notin (ancestor[\{EVT\_D^{-1}(e)\}]$$
$$\cup ancestor[\{EVT\_D^{-1}(e')\}])]]\}$$

The relation $succ2$ expresses the same conditions and effects as those defined in $succ1$ relationships, moreover it expresses that we admit between the successive events received events.

$$\textbf{succ2} = \{(e, e') | (e, e') \in EVT^2 \wedge$$
$$(\exists l)[l \in L \wedge e <^*_{SD,l} e' \wedge (\forall e")[e" \in EVT \wedge$$
$$(e <^*_{SD,l} e" \wedge e" <^*_{SD,l} e')$$
$$\Rightarrow e" \in ran(FCT\_r) \vee$$
$$EVT\_D^{-1}(e") \notin (ancestor[\{EVT\_D^{-1}(e)\}]$$
$$\cup ancestor[\{EVT\_D^{-1}(e')\}])]]\}$$

The relationship $<_{EE}$ permits to order two sent events that satisfy the conditions expressed in $not\_in\_brother$ and $succ1$ relations.

$$<_{EE} = \{(e, e') | [(e, e') \in (EVT)^2 \wedge$$
$$e \in ran(FCT\_s) \wedge e' \in ran(FCT\_s) \wedge$$
$$(e, e') \in not\_in\_brother \wedge (e, e') \in succ1]\}$$

The relationship $<_{RE}$ permits to order two events such that the first one is a received event and the second one is a sent event, and both of them satisfy the conditions expressed in $not\_in\_brother$ and $succ2$ relations.

$$<_{RE} = \{(e, e') | [(e, e') \in (EVT)^2 \wedge$$
$$e \in ran(FCT\_r) \wedge e' \in ran(FCT\_s) \wedge$$
$$(e, e') \in not\_in\_brother \wedge (e, e') \in succ2]\}$$

In a distributed system context, the components are independent and the communication between them is carried out according to protocols, each of them guarantees properties semantics concerning the reception of messages. In case the considered protocol ensures a First in First Out (FIFO) delivery order, the receptions of two messages coming from the same lifeline are received in the same order of their emission. The $<_{RR}$ relationship permits to compute these precedence relations.

$$<_{RR}=\{(e,e') \mid [(e,e') \in E_r^2 \; \wedge$$
$$(\exists e_1, \exists e_2)[(e_1,e_2) \in E_s^2 \; \wedge$$
$$Fct\_s^{-1}(e_1) = Fct\_r^{-1}(e) \; \wedge$$
$$Fct\_s^{-1}(e_2) = Fct\_r^{-1}(e') \; \wedge$$
$$e_1 <_{EE}^* e_2 \; \wedge \; Fct\_l(e_1) = Fct\_l(e_2)]\}$$

In the previous work [12], we showed that in LOOP CF as well as in nested CF that contains LOOP CF the determination of the precedence relations for each event is not obvious.

3.3   Hidden Precedence Relations in LOOP Combined Fragment

The events inside a LOOP operand can have as preceding events that can be located:

– for the first iteration: *(i)* either outside the LOOP operand and/or, *(ii)* inside the LOOP operand of the same iteration.
– from the second iteration: *(i)* either outside the LOOP operand and/or, *(ii)* inside the LOOP operand of the same iteration and/or of the previous iterations.

We call hidden relations the relations between the events of LOOP operand of the current iteration and the events of the previous iterations (Fig. 3). These relations appear when the LOOP operand is flatten at least one time. Hence, the necessity of defining a new relation $<_{Hcaus}$ in which we express the constraints of precedence between the events of the current iteration and the events of the previous iteration. In order to compute the hidden precedence relations, we propose the following steps: we flatten the LOOP operand only once whatever is the number of iterations; we obtain an intermediate sequence diagram SD'.

In SD', we rename the operands as well as the events of the second iteration with the same name as those of the preceding iteration by labelling them with a single quote (Fig. 3). We define the set EVT' to represent the events of the next iteration. $<_{RE}'$ and $<_{EE}'$ are respectively the reception-emission, and the emission emission relationships associated to the SD'. In an SD we can have several LOOP operand that can be sequenced or nested. In this case, the same processing is applied by computing for each LOOP operand its hidden relationships; we note $<_{HcausX}$, the hidden relations of a given LOOP operand named

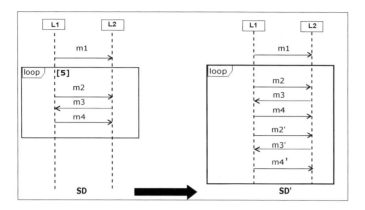

Fig. 3. Processing of an SD with LOOP operand.

X. The formalization of the hidden relationships for a LOOP operand X is given as follows.

$$<_{HcausX} =$$
$$\{(e, e') | e \in EVT \wedge e' \in EVT' \wedge$$
$$(e, e') \in <'_{RE} \vee (e, e') \in <'_{EE}\}$$

Illustration1. Consider the SD in Fig. 3, the SD' represents the flattening of the LOOP operand only once. In the SD', in the first iteration, the $!m2$ has as preceding event the event $!m1$ that is located outside the loop operand; the event $!m3$ has as preceding events, the event $?m1$ (that is located outside the loop operand) and the $?m2$ (that belongs to the same iteration). In the second iteration, the event $!m2'$ has as preceding event the event $!m4$ which belongs to the first iteration; the event $!m3'$ has as preceding events the events $?m4$ and $?m2'$, which belong respectively to the first and the second iteration.

Illustration2. As aforementioned, for an ALT CF, only one operand must be executed, hence the events that belong to distinct operands must not be ordered, otherwise we'll have deadlocks of some events.

However, in some particular cases of nested structure, especially for an ALT that is nested in a LOOP CF, we can face a problem that the events of distinct operands of the same ALT CF (brother operands) can have precedence relations. Figure 5 represents the flattening of the LOOP operand of the SD of Fig. 4. Figure 6 represents a possible execution of the SD (depicted in Fig. 4) containing nested CF. In the first iteration of the LOOP CF, the first operand of the ALT CF is executed; in the second iteration of the LOOP CF, the third operand of the ALT CF is executed. According to the $<_{EE}$ relationship, the event $!m2$ precedes the event $!m7'$, although they respectively belong to brother operands $OP21$ and $OP22$. Likewise for the events $!m3$ and $!m6'$. This is problematic, since the events of brother operands should not be ordered. This justifies the renaming of the events and the operands of the next iteration to avoid this issue.

In an SD we can have several LOOP operand that can be sequenced or nested. In this case, the same processing is applied by computing for each LOOP operand

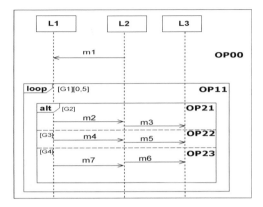

Fig. 4. SD with nested CF.

its hidden relationships; the entire hidden relation is the union of the hidden relations of each LOOP operand. Now, the causal relationships is computed as follows.

$$<_{caus} = <_{SYNC} \cup <_{RE} \cup <_{EE} \cup <_{RR} \cup <_{Hcaus}$$

That means the ordering of events depends on the cumulative rules of the relationships. The valid traces are those which can be generated satisfying these orders.

The defined rules ($<_{RE}$, $<_{EE}$, $<_{RE}$ and $<_{Hcaus}$) may be applied to the standard semantics by restoring the constraints that we relaxed. In the same way, these rules can be adapted for any kind of semantics by strengthening or weakening some constraints. The causal semantics can be exploited for several purposes, it can used as basis for the computation of all possible valid traces of SD modelling behaviours of distributed systems as it can be the basis for the definition of an operational semantics that facilitates its implementation and then the analysis of the SD and several properties of systems for instance safety, liveness, fairness or reachability properties.

4   Operational Semantics

The most of the existing semantics are trace-based semantics, they require a meticulous work that consists in generating all possible traces of an SD then in their categorisation depending on the aim of the semantic, and they do not propose tools to ensure this task [3,16]. Moreover, most of them ignore interaction constraint that guards combined fragments, which are essential to ensure soundness of refinement relation [16]. In the approach of [16], the authors consider the interaction constraint in a non-intuitive way. Indeed, they propose to include the guard as an element in the standard definition of trace.

The motivation behind the definition of an operational semantics is the intention of the use of existing refinement relations that are well defined on transition

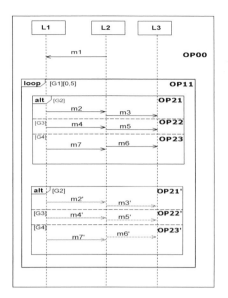

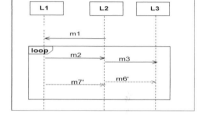

Fig. 5. Processing of the OP11 LOOP operand of Fig. 4.

Fig. 6. Possible execution of the SD of Fig. 4.

systems, since an operational semantics is concretely given as a transition system. Moreover, in the operational semantics, we define execution strategies of the events of an SD with nested CF. They include on the one hand, the order of the occurrence of the events in a nested structure (CF) as well as the conditions under which those executions can take place, on the other hand their execution effects that they produce. These strategies allow for better understanding and analysis of the behaviour of a sequence diagram.

Moreover, the guard is straightforwardly expressed. Formally, it is given as a guarded transition system:

$$Sem(SD) = \langle S, S^0, \triangle \rangle$$

where S is the set of possible states of the SD, S^0 is the initial state and $\triangle$ is the transition relation.

4.1   State

Each state of an SD is expressed with two variables (*state, current_instance*): *state* expresses the states of all events of SD, *current_instance* expresses the lifeline of the current event.

The state of an Event. An event which belongs to a basic SD can have two obvious basic states: executed or not yet executed. In our semantics, we support sequence diagrams with sequential CF that can be nested. The basic states are not sufficient to express the state of an event in an SD with sophisticated structures (nested CF). Indeed, each event in such SD can be: not yet occurred, occurred, consumed one or several times. Then, the variable *state* is defined as follows.

$$state : EVT \rightarrow NAT$$

The state of an event is decreased whenever it is occurred or ignored. To describe the state of an event e, we use the following vocabulary:

– not yet occurred: when $state(e) = weight(e)$,
– occurred: if the event e is executed or ignored one or several times and $0 < state(e) < weight(e)$,
– consumed: when $state(e) = 0$.

During its execution, an SD can be in one state among the following states:

– an initial state S^0, when all its events are not yet occurred,
– an intermediate state of S,
– a final state, when all its events are consumed: $state = EVT \times \{0\}$.

The notion of state is very important, indeed, it constraints the occurrence of a given event (for instance we decrement the state of an event whenever it is occurred, or if we want to prohibit its occurrence); it also serves to indicate the location of the considered event; this information is useful especially when we have several nested LOOP CF.

4.2   Transition Rules

For each event *evt* in an SD we associate the following transition:

$$p \xrightarrow{[g]evt} q \stackrel{def}{\equiv} ((p, [g] \; evt, \; q) \in \triangle \; \wedge \; g)$$

An event is enabled only when its trigger conditions, (labelled **TCi**), hold. When the enabled event occurs, it produces execution effects (labelled **EEi**) that update the SD from the state p to the state q.

In the following, we define rules for the guarded transition system which constraint the occurrence of the events (the trigger conditions and the executions effects). The rules of our operational semantics have the following shape.

$$evt = \frac{CD1 \wedge CD2 \wedge ...CDi}{EE1, EE2, ..., EEi}$$

4.3   Occurrence of the Events

For each event the trigger conditions must be checked conjointly and the executions effects are produced simultaneously.

Trigger Conditions. Some trigger conditions have a simple shape: they are atomic formulas where others trigger conditions are composed by the conjunction of several conditions. Indeed, some conditions must be strengthened in order to take into account of some particular cases and to prevent some issues that result of the presence, the disposition of the nesting of some CF (for instance the nesting CF that contains LOOP CF that induces hidden relations).

- First trigger condition related to satisfaction of precedence constraints

In our causal semantics, we first transform the considered SD in the form of a tree of operands. This transformation allows us to identify easily the preceding events of each event that are grouped by operand. Then the defined relations permit the computation of the precedence relations between the events.

The first trigger condition **TC1** necessary to the occurrence of each event consists in checking that its preceding events were occurred. This is made by comparing the states of the considered event and those of its preceding events. Remind that each event has a state which is initialized to its weight corresponding to its maximal number of occurrence. Depending on the kind of combination of CF ((ALT-LOOP), (ALT -LOOP), (LOOP-LOOP)....) to nest and the location of the considered events (these informations is given in the states of the events), the shape of the first trigger condition varies.

Consider an event evt that belongs to an UML2.X SD. To facilitate the reasoning, we assume that the event evt has only one preceding event e. The occurrence of the event evt depends on the state of the event e.

If the considered events e and evt have the same weight, then the trigger condition is simply expressed in the form of an inequality on the respective states of evt and e, hence it is enough to check that:

$$state(e) < state(evt)$$

However, in an SD, we can have several combinations of different kinds of CF. The combinations and the nesting of some kinds CF, especially those that contain LOOP CF complicate the form of the first trigger condition. Indeed if the events have distinct weights that are >1, it is the case where the events belong to nested CF that contain loop CF. The weight is a term making the product from the root to the event. The weight of an intermediate operand is a multiplicative factor of the events contained in the child operands.

Therefore, the comparison of the states of two events is based on their weights relative to a common node (operand) or the first shared node that encompasses the events, which is the lowest common ancestor (LCA). Indeed, the terms of the weight derived from the ancestors are the multiplicative factors common.

For instance in the Fig. 9, consider the events $?m1$ and $!m2$ that belong respectively to $OP21$ and $OP11$ operands, the LCA is the operand $OP11$, hence $weight(?m1) = 3 * 5$ and $weight(!m2) = 5$. In the Fig. 13, consider the events $!m1$ and $!m2$ that belong respectively to $OP21$ and $OP31$ operands, the LCA is the operand $OP11$, hence $weight(!m1) = 5 * 3$ and $weight(!m2) = 5 * 4$.

Consider the operands X et Y of the events e and evt: $X = EVT\_D^{-1}(e)$, $Y = EVT\_D^{-1}(evt)$ and Z is the lowest common ancestor of the operands X

and Y: $Z = LCA(X, Y)$. Depending on the weights of the events of e and evt, we distinguish the following cases:

1. **Case1:** each of the event e and evt has a weight that is equal to 1. In this case None of the operands X Y or Z is a LOOP operand. Moreover their respective ancestors are not LOOP operands.
2. **Case2:** each of the events e et evt has a weight that is different of 1. In this case, we have to argue with regard to the lowest common ancestor (Z) of the operands X and Y of the events e and evt. Indeed, we distinguish 4 possible cases:
   2.1 **Case2.1:** There is no LOOP operand neither in the path from the operand Z to the operand X nor in the path from the operand Z to the operand Y (i.e. $weight(Z, X) = 1$ and $weight(Z, Y) = 1$),
   2.2 **Case2.2:** there is a LOOP operand only in the path from the operand Z to the operand X (i.e. $weight(Z, X) > 1$ and $weight(Z, Y) = 1$),
   2.3 **Case2.3:** there is a LOOP operand only in the path from the operand Z to the operand Y (i.e. $weight(Z, X) = 1$ et $weight(Z, Y) > 1$),
   2.4 **Case2.4:** in each path from the operand Z to the operand X and from the operand Z to the operand Y there is a LOOP operand (i.e. $weight(Z, X) > 1$ et $weight(Z, Y) > 1$).

In the sequel, we illustrate each case with an example et we give the appropriate trigger condition.

• **Case1.** The weight of event e and evt is equal to 1. We distinguish two possible cases: *(i)* both events e and evt are located in the same operand: $X = EVT\_D^{-1}(e) = EVT\_D^{-1}(evt)$ (see Fig. 7(a)), and *(ii)* the events are located in distinct operands: $EVT\_D^{-1}(e) \neq EVT\_D^{-1}(evt)$ (see Fig. 7(b)).

In this case it is enough to check that:

$$CD11 : state(e) = 0 < state(evt) = 1$$

Illustration: In both Fig. 7(a) and (b), according to the $< EE$ relation, the events $!m1$ and $!m2$ are ordered, they are respectively located in the same operand (Fig. 7(a)) and in distinct operands 7(b). Both events have a weight equal to 1. The event $!m2$ can occur only if the event $!m1$ was consumed. Hence we must check the condition

$$state(!m1) = 0 \ \wedge \ state(!m2) = 1$$

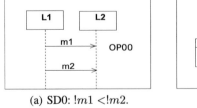

(a) SD0: $!m1 < !m2$.

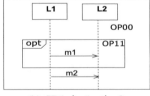

(b) SD1: $!m1 < !m2$.

Fig. 7. Illustration case1.

• **Case2.1.** The weight of the events e and evt are different of 1. We distinguish two cases: *(i)* the events are located in the same operand:

$X = EVT\_D^{-1}(e) = EVT\_D^{-1}(evt)$ (see Fig. 8(a)), and *(ii)* the events evt and e are located in distinct operands: $EVT\_D^{-1}(e) \neq EVT\_D^{-1}(evt)$ (Fig. 8(b)). We consider only the case where the paths from the operand Z to the operand X and from the operand Z to the operand Y did not contain a LOOP operand (i.e. $weight(Z, X) = 1$ and $weight(Z, Y) = 1$). In this case, either the operand Z or at least one of its ancestors is a LOOP operand.

Illustration1: In the Fig. 8(a), the weight of each event $!m1$ and $?m1$ is equal to 4, hence each of them can occur 4 times. For each iteration, the message $m1$ can be received only if it is sent (the event $!m1$ was occurred) This conditions constraints the occurrence of the event $?m1$, it is expressed as follows:

$$state(!m1) < state(?m1)$$

Illustration2: In the Fig. 8(b), the weight of each event $!m1$ and $?m1$ is equal to 4, hence each of them can occur 4 times. For each iteration, the event $?m2$ can occur only if the event $!m1$ was occurred. This condition constraints the occurrence of the event $?m1$, it is expressed as follows:

$$state!(m1) < state(!m2)$$

Hence in these cases the trigger condition can be expressed as follows:

$$CD12 : \ state(e) < state(evt)$$

• **Case2.2.** The weights of the events e and evt are different of 1. Moreover, they are located in distinct operands: $EVT\_D^{-1}(e) \neq EVT\_D^{-1}(evt)$. We have only a LOOP operand in the path from the operand Z to the operand X (i.e. $weight(Z, X) > 1$ and $weight(Z, Y) = 1$)

Illustration: Consider the Fig. 9, for each iteration of the operand $OP11$, the event $!m2$ can occur only if the event $?m1$ was occurred 3 times. The table represented in Fig. 10 illustrates the 5 states for which the event $!m2$ can occur.

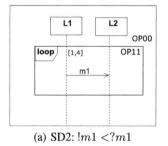

(a) SD2: $!m1 <?m1$ (b) SD3: $!m1 <!m2$

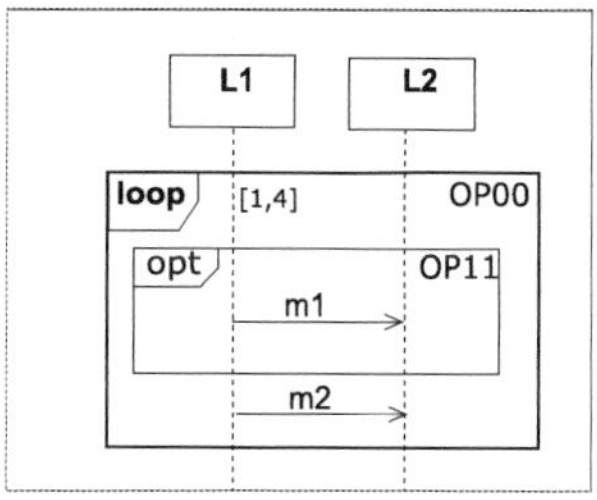

Fig. 8. Illustration case2.1.

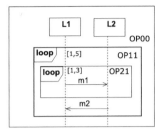

n° iteration	$state(?m1)$	$state(!m2)$
1	12	5
2	9	4
3	6	3
4	3	2
5	0	1

Fig. 9. SD5: $?m1 <!m2$.

Fig. 10. Variation of states values with iteration of the SD of Fig. 9.

$$[state(?m1)/3 < state(!m2)] \ \wedge \ [(state(?m1)mod\ 3 = 0)]$$

In this case, the trigger condition of the event evt is expressed in form of a conjunction of predicates. Such that the first predicate is an inequality on states of the event evt and its preceding event e where the state of the preceding event is weighted with the coefficient $1/weight(Z, X)$. The second predicate permits to the event evt iterate once the event e was occurred $weight(Z, X)$ times.

$$CD13 : [state(e)/weight(Z, X) < state(evt)] \wedge [(state(e) \bmod weight(Z, X) = 0)]$$

• **Case2.3.** The weights of the events e and evt are different of 1. Moreover, they are located in distinct operands: $EVT\_D^{-1}(e) \neq EVT\_D^{-1}(evt)$.

We have only a LOOP operand in the path from the operand Z to the operand Y (i.e. $weight(Z, X) = 1$ et $weight(Z, Y) > 1$).

Illustration: In the Fig. 11, the event $?m1$ precedes the event $!m2$. For each iteration of the operand $OP11$, the event $!m2$ occurs 4 times. For each occurrence of the event $?m1$, the event $!m2$ occurs 4 times. The table represented in Fig. 12 illustrates the 20 states for which the event $!m2$ can occur. Hence the trigger condition of the event $!m2$ can be expressed as follows.

$(state(!m2) \bmod 4 = 0) \implies (state(?m1) < state(!m2)/4)$

Hence, in this case, the trigger condition of the event evt is expressed as follows.

$CD14 : (state(evt) \bmod weight(Z, Y) = 0) \implies (state(e) < state(evt)/weight(Z, Y))$

• **Case2.4.** The weights of the events e and evt are different of 1. Moreover, they are located in distinct operands: $EVT\_D^{-1}(e) \neq EVT\_D^{-1}(evt)$.

In each path (from the operand Z to the operand X and from the operand Z to the operand Y), it exists a LOOP operand (i.e. $weight(Z, X) > 1$ et $weight(Z, Y) > 1$).

Illustration: In the Fig. 13, the event $!m1$ precedes the event $!m2$. For each execution of the operand $OP11$ the event $!m2$ occurs 4 times. After each 3

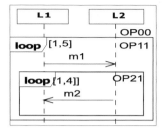

Fig. 11. SD8: $?m1 <!m2$.

n° iteration	state(?m1)	state(!m2)
1	4	20..17
2	3	16 ..13
3	2	12 ..9
4	1	8..5
5	0	4 ..1

Fig. 12. Variation of states values with iteration of the SD of Fig. 11.

occurrences of the event $!m1$, the event $!m2$ occurs 4 times. The table represented in Fig. 14 illustrates the 20 states where the event $!m2$ can occur.

$$state(!m2) \bmod 4 = 0 \Rightarrow state(!m1)/3 < state(!m2)/4 \wedge (state(!m1) \bmod 3 = 0)$$

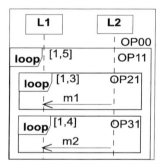

Fig. 13. SD7: $!m1 <!m2$.

n° iteration	state(!m1)	state(!m2)
1	12	20..17
2	9	16 ..13
3	6	12 ..9
4	3	8..5
5	0	4 ..1

Fig. 14. Variation of states values with iteration of the SD of Fig. 13.

In this case, the trigger condition of the event evt is expressed as follows.

$$CD15 : \ (state(evt) \bmod weight(Z,Y) = 0) \Rightarrow$$
$$[state(e)/weight(Z,X) < state(evt)/weight(Z,Y)] \wedge$$
$$[(state(e) \bmod weight(Z,X) = 0)]$$

Generalization of the Trigger Condition $TC1$. Thenceforth, we can deduce the general form of the first trigger condition. We check the occurrence of the preceding events that are computed receptively from the relation $(<_{caus} \setminus <_{Hcaus})$ and from the relation $<_{Hcaus}$ independently in two distinct trigger conditions.

- $(e, evt) \in (<_{caus} \setminus <_{Hcaus}) \ (TC1)$
- $(e, evt) \in <_{Hcaus} \ (TC1')$

- Hence, when we have:
$\forall(e)(\exists X)(\exists Z)[(e, evt) \in (<_{caus} \setminus <_{Hcaus}) \land X = EVTD^{-1}(e)$
$\land \; Y = EVTD^{-1}(evt) \land \; Z = LCA(X, Y)$
Then, the first trigger condition is expressed as follows:

> **TC1:**
> $(state(evt) \bmod weight(Z, Y) = 0) \Longrightarrow$
> $((state(e)/weight(Z, X) < state(evt)/weight(Z, Y)$
> $\land \; (state(e) \bmod weight(Z, X) = 0)))$

- For each event *evt* of a LOOP operand or that belong to a nested CF that contains a LOOP operand and that has hidden preceding events that appear from the second iteration.
    Hence, when we have: $(\forall e)(\exists X)(\exists Z)[(e, evt) \in <_{Hcaus} \land X = EVTD^{-1}(e)$
$\land \; Y = EVTD^{-1}(evt) \land \; Z = LCA(X, Y)$ We define the following trigger condition **TC1'**.

> **TC1':**
> $(state(e) \bmod (weight(Z, Y) * weight(Z) <> 0)) \Longrightarrow$
> $((state(e)/weight(Z, X) = state(evt)/weight(Z, Y)$
> $\land \; (e, evt) \in not\_in\_brother))$

- the second trigger condition consists in checking that the event can still be occurred: it is not yet consumed (**TC2**). It is formally defined as follows:

$$\textbf{TC2}: \; state(evt) \geq 1$$

- for the events that belong to a guarded CF we add a third trigger condition that permits to check the value of the guard.

Execution Effects. The execution effects of an event should simultaneously:

- update the state of the current event by decreasing its state (**EE1**);
  the execution effect **EE1** is to update the state with: **EE1**: $state(evt) - 1$
- update the lifeline of the current event (**EE2**); the execution effect **EE2** is to set *current_instance* with: **EE2**: *current_instance* := $FCT\_l(evt)$ Remind the $FCT\_l(evt)$ gives the lifeline of the event.

Particular Cases: for the guarded ALT, we assume that the evaluation of the guard is made on the first event. If the guard is evaluated to true (**TC3**) then the first event must synchronize the events of the other operands of the same CF by decrementing their states (remind that the standard semantics of the ALT CF impose that only one operand must be executed among several potential operands having simultaneously a true guard). Otherwise, if the guard is evaluated to false (**TC3'**), the first event must decrement the states of the events of the same operand in order to prohibit their occurrence. Hence, in addition to the trigger conditions **TC1** and/or **TC1'**, we must add a third trigger condition **TC3** for the first event of each operand of an ALT CF.

$$\textbf{TC3} : guard := true$$

$$\textbf{TC3'} : guard := false$$

If the guard is evaluated to true, in addition to the executions effects **EE1** and **EE2**, we must add a third execution effect **EE3** to modify the states of the events of the brother operands. When we have $[evt \in EVT\_D(X) \ \wedge \ e \in EVT\_D(Y) \ \wedge \ e \in EVT\_G(Z)]$,

EE3: $state(e) - weight(Z, Y)$, where $Z = brother(X)$ If the guard is evaluated to false, in addition to the executions effects **EE1** and **EE2**, we must add a third execution effect **EE3'** to decrement the states of the events of the same operand. When we have $evt \in EVT\_D(X) \wedge e \in EVT\_D(Y) \wedge e \in EVT\_G(X)$, then **EE3':** $state(e) - weight(X, Y)$

All the operands of any kind of CF can be guarded, in this case in addition to the trigger conditions **TC1** and/or **TC1'**, we must add a third trigger condition **TC3** for the first event of the considered operand. If the guard is evaluated to false, in addition to the executions effects **EE1** and **EE2**, we must add a third execution effect **EE3'** to decrement the states of the events of the same operand. N.B In a nested CF, we assume that the guard evaluation of a child operand should be made after a *True* guard evaluation of the parent operand. This is compliant with the hypothesis we made in Subsect. 3.1, which states that each operand has one first event. Moreover, if the guard of the parent operand is evaluated to *False*, its events including the events of its child operands are ignored.

All these rules define the operational semantics of UML2.X SD with nested combined fragments. They are not linked to any target formalism and they can be implemented in various ways and by any formalism doted with tools for its checking.

5   Related Works

In the literature, there are several semantics approaches to define a semantics for UML2.X SD. Among them we cite the most popular: *(i)* denotational semantics [3,16], *(ii)* transformational semantics [9], and *(iii)* operational semantics [10,17]. They are mainly proposed to overcome some issues of the standard semantics, or to adapt the use of the SD to the modelling of different systems, and for other purposes. For instance, in [3,16], the authors defined a trace semantics based on denotational semantics to distinguish between mandatory and required behaviours. In [10], the authors proposed a denotational semantics based on partially ordered multisets or pomsets that deals with language constructs for specifying negative traces. In the works of [9], the authors proposed a transformational semantics based on the translation of SD into Büchi automata in order to verify liveness and safety properties of reactive systems. In [17], the authors proposed an operational semantics for SD that supports negative behaviours and that distinguishes between possible and required behaviours. In [10], the authors proposed an operational semantics for SD, which is compliant with the semantics proposed in [18], for capturing the composition operators from High Message Sequence Charts (HMSC) and NEG ASSERT CF.

We underlined that a few of the existing semantics, [3,9,16,18], can be used to formalize the refinement relation while the others do not allow it [2,4,17,19,20].

For this purpose, the trace-based semantics, [3,9,16], are not very convenient, indeed they permit to verify only some kinds of refinement relations (trace inclusion, trace equivalence...), this require a meticulous preprocessing on all traces of the considered SD, knowing that most of them did not propose tools that ease this arduous task; moreover they ignore the guards of CF which are essential to ensure soundness of refinement relation. Although, in the work of [16], the proposed trace-based semantic refinement considers guard, but in a non-intuitive way, by modifying the standard definition of the trace.

In contrast to trace-based semantics, with an operational semantics several kinds of well-defined refinement relations can be expressed (simulation trace, inclusion trace, equivalence trace...). Moreover the operational facilitates the analysis of the behaviours of the modelled systems.

Most of the existing semantics [3,4,9,16–18] are usually based on the definitions of the standard for the computation of traces, thus they are not suitable for SD modelling behaviours of distributed systems. Moreover most of the work, [5,6,21,22] did not deal properly with some CF and the nested CF. Indeed they impose strict hypothesis to avoid inconsistencies due to the use of these CF. In our last work we have well explained these restrictions that limit the expressive power of these CF. To overcome these insufficiencies, we proposed an operational semantics that is, on the one hand, based on an extended causal semantics, suitable for UML2.X SD equipped with the most popular CF modelling distributed systems, on the other hand, it supports guards straightforwardly since it is given as a guarded transition system. The operational semantics can be easily implemented and can be used as a basis for refinement checking purpose for our ongoing work.

6   Conclusion

To help in preliminaries design steps of distributed systems, we have equipped UML2.X sequence diagrams with a causal semantics that is based on partial order theory and tree structure. Its relations permit the determination of the precedence relations straightforwardly for SD with nested CF that model behaviours of a distributed system, by avoiding its flattening, hence the compact syntactic representation is preserved. The causal semantics can serves for several purposes, in this paper we have proposed an operational semantics in which we define execution strategies of the events of an SD with nested CF. The proposed operational semantics is not linked to a specific target formalism. We currently implement the operational semantics with the Event-B method [11,23]. Transforming SD into corresponding B specifications enables rigorous model analysis using the formal techniques of Event B and its various tools Rodin: (with a theorem-prover, and with ProB model-checker). Meanwhile, the operational semantics serves as the basis of our ongoing work on the verification of the refinement relation between sequence diagrams. Indeed the operational semantics is concretely given as a transition system since refinement relations are well defined on the transition system as a simulation relation. This is used for investigating whether or not a sequence diagram specification is a correct refinement of another sequence diagram specification. In addition, we currently study theoretical properties that are derived from the proposed semantics.

References

1. Object Management Group. OMG Unified Modeling Language (OMG UML), Superstructure Version 2.2 (2015)
2. Knapp, A., Wuttke, J.: Model checking of UML 2.0 interactions. In: Kühne, T. (ed.) MODELS 2006. LNCS, vol. 4364, pp. 42–51. Springer, Heidelberg (2007). https://doi.org/10.1007/978-3-540-69489-2_6
3. Runde, R.K., Haugen, Ø., Husa, K.E.: STAIRS towards formal design with sequence diagrams. Softw. Syst. Model. **4**, 355–357 (2005)
4. Störrle, H.: Semantics of interactions in UML 2.0. In: HCC, pp. 129–136 (2003)
5. Hammal, Y.: Branching time semantics for UML 2.0 sequence diagrams. In: Najm, E., Pradat-Peyre, J.-F., Donzeau-Gouge, V.V. (eds.) FORTE 2006. LNCS, vol. 4229, pp. 259–274. Springer, Heidelberg (2006). https://doi.org/10.1007/11888116_20
6. Égel, Z., Kövi, A., Micskei, Z., Huszerl, G., Waeselynck, H. (eds.): Refined Design and Testing Framework, Methodology and Application Results (2008)
7. Shen, H.: A formal framework for analyzing sequence diagram. Ph.D. thesis (2013)
8. Harel, D., Maoz, S.: Assert and negate revisited: modal semantics for UML sequence diagrams. Softw. Syst. Model. **7**(2), 237–252 (2008)
9. Grosu, R., Smolka, S.A.: Safety-liveness semantics for UML 2.0 sequence diagrams. In: 5th International Conference on Application of Concurrency to System Design, pp. 6–14 (2005)
10. Cengarle, M.V., Graubmann, P., Wagner, S.: Semantics of UML 2.0 Interactions with Variabilities. Technische Universität München (2005)
11. Dhaou, F., Mouakher, I., Attiogbé, C., Bsaies, K.: Extending causal semantics of UML2.0 sequence diagram for distributed systems. In: ICSOFT-EA 2015 - Proceedings of the 10th International Conference on Software Engineering and Applications, Colmar, Alsace, France, pp. 339–347 (2015)
12. Dhaou, F., Mouakher, I., Attiogbé, C., Bsaïes, K.: A causal semantics for UML2.0 sequence diagrams with nested combined fragments. In ENASE 2017 - Proceedings of the 12th International Conference on Evaluation of Novel Approaches to Software Engineering, Porto, Portugal, 28–29 April 2017, pp. 47–56 (2017)
13. Sibertin-Blanc, C., Tahir, O., Cardoso, J.: A causality-based semantics for UML sequence diagrams. In: 23rd IASTED International Conference on Software Engineering, pp. 106–111. Acta Press (2005)

182   F. Dhaou et al.

14. Sibertin-Blanc, C., Tahir, O., Cardoso, J.: Interpretation of UML sequence diagrams as causality flows. In: Ramos, F.F., Larios Rosillo, V., Unger, H. (eds.) ISSADS 2005. LNCS, vol. 3563, pp. 126–140. Springer, Heidelberg (2005). https://doi.org/10.1007/11533962_12

15. Abrial, J.-R.: The B Book. Cambridge University Press, Cambridge (1996)

16. Kim, D.-K., Lu, L.: Required behavior of sequence diagrams: semantics and refinement. In: 16th IEEE International Conference on Engineering of Complex Computer Systems (ICECCS), pp. 127–136 (2011)

17. Lund, M.S., Stølen, K.: A fully general operational semantics for UML 2.0 sequence diagrams with potential and mandatory choice. In: Misra, J., Nipkow, T., Sekerinski, E. (eds.) FM 2006. LNCS, vol. 4085, pp. 380–395. Springer, Heidelberg (2006). https://doi.org/10.1007/11813040_26

18. Cengarle, M.V., Alexander, K.: UML 2.0 interactions: semantics and refinement, pp. 85–99. Technische Universitat Munchen (2004)

19. Aredo, D.B.: A framework for semantics of UML sequence diagrams. PVS J. Univ. Comput. Sci. (JUCS) 8(7), 674–697 (2002)

20. Cho, S.M., Kim, H.H., Cha, S.D., Bae, D.H.: A semantics of sequence diagrams. Inf. Process. Lett. 84(3), 125–130 (2002)

21. Cavarra, A., Küster-Filipe, J.: Formalizing liveness-enriched sequence diagrams using ASMs. In: Zimmermann, W., Thalheim, B. (eds.) ASM 2004. LNCS, vol. 3052, pp. 62–77. Springer, Heidelberg (2004). https://doi.org/10.1007/978-3-540-24773-9_6

22. Maoz, S., Harel, D., Kleinbort, A.: A compiler for multimodal scenarios: transforming LSCs into AspectJ. ACM Trans. Softw. Eng. Methodol. 20(4), 1–41 (2011)

23. Dhaou, F., Mouakher, I., Attiogbé, C., Bsaïes, K.: Refinement of UML2.0 sequence diagrams for distributed systems. In: Proceedings of the 11th International Joint Conference on Software Technologies (ICSOFT 2016) - Volume 1: ICSOFT-EA, Lisbon, Portugal, 24–26 July 2016, pp. 310–318 (2016)

Fast Prototyping of Web-Based Information Systems Using a Restricted Natural Language Specification

Jean Pierre Alfonso Hoyos$^{(\boxtimes)}$ and Felipe Restrepo-Calle$^{(\boxtimes)}$

Department of Systems and Industrial Engineering,
Universidad Nacional de Colombia, Bogotá, Colombia
{jpalfonsoh,ferestrepoca}@unal.edu.co

Abstract. Early phases of the Software Development Life Cycle (SDLC) like requirements elicitation and model design are often critical for the project success. These phases are also linked to several project problems and failure causes, delaying the project finalization and increasing its total cost. Several strategies to mitigate the effects of errors in these early stages have been proposed. Some of these include: GUI based fast prototyping; agile software development methodologies; and, as in this work, automatic model (or source code) generation from a natural language specification. Although these approaches can reduce production time and costs, they can also be slow and imprecise leading to development difficulties. This work proposes an approach to obtain a functional prototype of a web-based process-oriented information system, using only a restricted natural language specification as an input. This approach allows the processing of the input to be faster and more precise than the approaches proposed previously. Two case studies are presented in order to validate the proposal and demonstrate its applicability.

Keywords: Fast prototyping · Software requirements
Natural language specification · Compilers
Software construction automation · Restricted natural language
Web applications · BPMN · E-R

1 Introduction

Requirements elicitation tasks induce errors in the Software Development Life Cycle (SDLC) mainly due to incompleteness, ambiguities or incongruence in the written requirements [1]. Developers lack of knowledge about the customer application domain and business operations, and limited communication with the stakeholders are some of the causes of this situation [1,2]. Errors in these early phases usually have large impact in the project duration and budget [1].

To mitigate some of the effects of these problems, various strategies like fast prototyping and agile software development methodologies have been proposed [3]. However, agile methodologies are more suitable for small teams

© Springer International Publishing AG, part of Springer Nature 2018
E. Damiani et al. (Eds.): ENASE 2017, CCIS 866, pp. 183–207, 2018.
https://doi.org/10.1007/978-3-319-94135-6_9

and small-scale value-oriented software projects, and left behind big scale or mission critical software [4,5]. Moreover, fast prototyping approaches attempt to make SDLC faster, less prone to human errors, and less sensible to natural language inherent ambiguities and specification incompleteness. Therefore, they can reduce production costs, time to market delivery and prototyping costs [6]. In exchange of this speed, elements like technical debt, used languages and tools, and project quality are often not taken into account rigorously. Some examples of these fast prototyping tools are: *Bizzagi*[1], which uses graphical interactions and model-based specification languages to develop information systems; *JustInMind*[2] that creates interactive UI prototypes of mobile applications and web pages; *OpenXava*[3] that creates web applications from a set of Java classes. In addition, other approaches use a specification written in natural language (restricted or unrestricted) to automate the construction of models from texts [7,8]. These approaches permit a fast validation of the software models, obtaining feedback from stakeholders more frequently [9,10].

This chapter presents a fast prototyping scheme that uses a restricted natural language specification and generates the source code of a web application. This is a functional prototype that is capable of executing process tasks over some domain data classes definition. This prototyping scheme is meant to be used during a live meeting with the stakeholders, showing and validating results in very short time and in an interactive way. To achieve this purpose, a transformation is proposed between two well-known modeling languages (i.e., BPMN[4] and E-R[5]) and a new restricted natural language that is proposed as the input of the prototyping scheme. This allows the scheme to use the expressiveness and concepts of the two modeling languages, and also to complement their capabilities.

This work extends the paper recently published in [11], which presents some preliminary results. The main contributions of this chapter are:

- A new specification language for software requirements: *restricted natural language*.
- A fast prototyping method for web applications running business processes using a *restricted natural language* specification.
- An automated source code generation method from the proposed specification language.

The rest of this chapter is structured as follows. Next section describes the background of the work including the related works. Section 3 presents the proposed fast prototyping scheme. Section 4 explains the implementation details. Later, Sect. 5 presents and discusses the results of two different case studies. Finally, Sect. 6 summarizes some concluding remarks and suggests the future works.

---

[1] https://www.bizagi.com/.
[2] https://www.justinmind.com/.
[3] http://openxava.org.
[4] Business Process Model and Notation.
[5] Entity-Relationship.

2   Background

2.1   Software Requirements

The collection and analysis of requirements are the initial steps for any software development process. Requirements are usually written in natural language and they can be seen as the first model of the system to be built. A requirement is defined as follows [12]: "*a condition or capability that must be met or possessed by a system, system component, product, or service to satisfy an agreement, standard, specification, or other formally imposed documents*". The process of writing this specification or document is the requirements elicitation.

A taxonomy of software requirement errors is presented in [13]. It classifies errors in three categories: *people errors*, which are failures of the people involved in the project; *process errors* that are caused by errors in the way of achieving objectives, and are mainly related to the requirements elicitation stage; and *documentation errors*, which are errors in the specification.

In addition, [14] describes the types of ambiguities that are present in the requirements documents as follows: lexical, terms with more than one meaning; syntactical, more than one syntax tree per requirement; semantical, more that one meaning in a context; pragmatical, the meaning of a phrase depends on where it is placed; induced by vagueness, no analysis can assign a meaning; and induced by generality, the phrase can not be interpreted precisely.

Moreover, several strategies to aid the requirements elicitation process and to reduce errors associated with it have been proposed. Some of these are: to use software tools [15]; to use requirements templates [16]; to use restricted languages [17,18]; to use translations to formal specification languages [19]; to use Natural Language Processing (NLP) techniques to enhance the requirements quality [20,21]; and to use requirements elicitation methodologies [22].

2.2   Related Works

Many work has been done on the extraction of software models from texts. Efforts have been mainly focused on: design attributes mining from texts written in natural language, the use of templates to write requirements, and specification languages inspired by natural languages. Figure 1 shows the three main ways that are commonly used to achieve this goal.

At the top of Fig. 1 is shown a schema aimed at extracting design information from textual specifications written in unrestricted natural language. Abbott [9] and Saeki et al. [23] originally proposed manual procedures back in the 80's. Words in the description matching certain parts of speech and phrase structures were used to build a model. This procedure latter was extended and automatized using natural language processing tools. Some general steps of this method include: stemming, Part-Of-Speech (POS) tagging, sentence splitting, resolve references and anaphoras, use ontologies to determine implicit relationships, use wordnet to find synonyms and not explicit stated relationships, rule based design information extraction, and finally, a production of a model (or a set of models).

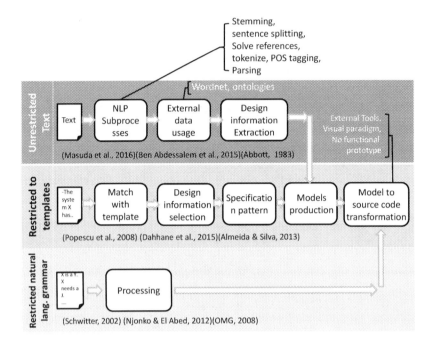

Fig. 1. Alternatives to generate models from natural language texts.

Some works within this field include: [24–27]. Furthermore, [28] recently proposed a transformation framework between natural language to domain specific languages (DSLs) using machine learning techniques to generate a set of possible programs.

This group of approaches facilitates to any person the description of the desired functionality of software. Even with a few writing errors, information still can be used [7]. In the downside, it is necessary some predefined knowledge (ontologies, wordnet, . . .) in order to properly extract relationships between terms [29]. Sometimes a training data set [24] and/or a set of ontologies [30] might be needed to achieve acceptable results. Moreover, current NLP tools can be imprecise sometimes leading to induce misinterpretations of the specification [24]. In addition, this method is the slowest of the three types of approaches due to its high processing requirements [24].

At the middle of Fig. 1 is shown the general approach where authors restrict the way requirements are written using templates. This approach keeps design information stored in a way that can be easily extracted from requirements lists to generate a model [31–37]. Table 1 shows some examples of templates used in these works.

Although using templates to write the specification of the software is more difficult, when done, it is as easy to understand by the stakeholders as in the first approach [38]. The use of templates facilitates processing tasks, making this approach faster than the first one. However, its main disadvantage is that

Table 1. Templates examples for requirements specification.

Proposal	Template example

Nishida et al. [10]	`<procedure sentence>::= <procedure predicate verb> <term>`
	`[(to|from|with) <term>]* [in <format>] [by <procedure name>]`
	`<procedure sentence>, and store the result in <term>`

Zapata [33]	A `<ESTA_CONFORMADO_POR>` B
Zeaaraoui et al. [36]	`As a <role>, I want to <action-1> and <action-2> <action-n>` `<object> so that <business value>`
Videira et al. [34]	`<EntityInheritanceDefinition> : <Entity> is a <Entity>`
Konrad and Cheng [32]	`"it is always the case that " (durationCategory|periodicCategory` `| realtimeOrderCategory)`
Dahhane et al. [37]	`[Role] <Source Object> <is composed of> <Cardinality>` `[Role] <Target Object>`

designers must be very careful writing requirements or some information may be lost. It is necessary to define each template in order to extend the proposed solution, and requirements not matching any template will be discarded leaving information outside of the final model [39].

The bottom of Fig. 1 corresponds to approaches that restrict the grammar of a natural language such as English. That restriction can lead to overcome the ambiguity and imprecision of such languages. For instance, Attempto [40] is an executable specification language in which the English grammar is restricted to only a few grammar elements. In this way, writing requirements is very similar to work with a programming language, which avoids ambiguities and facilitates the processing effort [41]. Nonetheless, having to learn an artificial language is an inconvenient for the designers and the stakeholders [40]. This approach is slower generating code than the second one but faster than the first one.

We propose the use of templates within the context of an specification language, this is, a hybrid between the second and the third approaches explained before.

3   Fast Prototyping of Web Applications Running Business Processes

This work proposes a fast prototyping method for web applications running business processes using a restricted natural language specification. To do so, we use the model-view-controller design pattern, implementing business processes operating over a set of domain classes, using only the restricted specification.

Figure 2 presents a general schema of the proposed workflow. Firstly, during a live meeting with stakeholders, a designer writes down a software specification using the restricted English grammar, which is proposed in this paper (restricted natural language). This process will be supported by an IDE and auto completion tools to avoid common mistakes. Although the specification in restricted natural language could be understood by a non-technical user, the target user of the proposed method is a designer with technical background. This is needed because the relationships and concepts expressed within the restricted language are not easy to understand to a non-technical stakeholder due to the required abstraction level. Secondly, our code generation engine produces the source code of the web application. Next, the stakeholders are able to revise and validate the generated application prototype. If a modification is required then the specification is changed, the code is generated and validated again in an iterative way. In this way, it is possible to obtain direct feedback from the stakeholders and achieve fast validation of the software prototype.

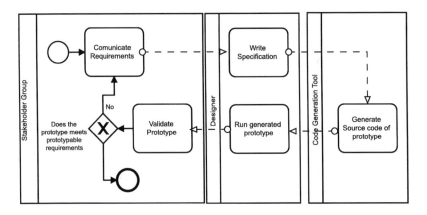

Fig. 2. General workflow proposed for fast prototyping of web applications.

3.1   Restricted Natural Language - RNL

To work with a Restricted Natural Language (RNL) to generate web application prototypes without human intervention, we focus only on the English constructs of interest for this task. To do so, we use the reasoning presented previously in [11], which is as follows: we first consider two different transformations from commonly used software design models, i.e. E-R diagrams and BPMN models, to a restricted natural language. Next, we build a language capable of defining the operations and combine the previous two specifications. This is illustrated in Fig. 3, where T_{e-r} is the transformation of E-R diagrams, T_{BPMN} is the transformation of BPMN models, and T_N is the part of the language responsible for mixing both. These are the three parts of the RNL language.

BPMN is a graphical specification language designed to show the flow of activities, decisions and events that occur in an organization in order to generate some form of business value.

Equations (1) to (6) were previously published in [11] and can be explained as follows. Let $BPMN$ be the set of all well constructed BPMN models. Also,

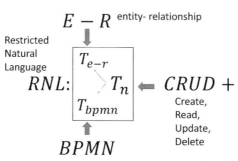

Fig. 3. Restricted Natural Language - RNL - components.

let $b \in BPMN$. $f(b) = S_1$ (Eq. 1) will be a function that maps b to source code in some destination language (s_1). In addition, note that a generalization of several works like [42, 43] can be made, resulting in a function of the form $g(t_1) = b$ where t_1 is a restricted (or unrestricted) natural language specification and g is a function transforming the input text into a BPMN model (Eq. 2).

$$f(b) = s_1 \tag{1}$$

$$g(t_1) = b \tag{2}$$

Moreover, for this work we will also use E-R diagrams. These are graphical models that show the relationships between information entities and its contents. A model is always in the context of a single system and in a single knowledge domain.

Similarly, let $E-R$ be the set of all well constructed E-R models and $e \in E-R$ a representative of that set. Let $h(e)$ (Eq. 3) a function that generates source code (s_2) from the original model e. A generalization of some works can also be done here. Works like [44–46] try to get a model from texts and can be expressed in an abstract way as $j(t_2) = e$ (Eq. 4). With j being a function that maps some natural language text t_2 to an E-R model e.

$$h(e) = s_2 \tag{3}$$

$$j(t_2) = e \tag{4}$$

Using the Eqs. 1, 2, 3, and 4, we get that the evaluation of functions $f(g(t_1))$ and $h(j(t_2))$ will return source code from two independent restricted natural language specifications. Note that t_1 and t_2 could also be unrestricted specifications and the general formula could still be true. However, for the purposes of this paper, we will restrict the natural language constructs to avoid ambiguities and different context-dependent interpretations. Also, the proposed language will focus on a single knowledge domain to avoid using several external sources of information that can induce more ambiguities.

Suppose the existence of a pair of inverse functions: $g^{-1}(b)$ and $j^{-1}(e)$. This means that there is a projection of the design models into natural language (Eqs. 5 and 6). The construction of these functions can be viewed as a "design or construction" process starting from the model space to the natural language space.

$$g^{-1}(b) = t_1 \tag{5}$$

$$j^{-1}(e) = t_2 \tag{6}$$

Although there is no reason to these projections to be unique, some subset of natural language constructs and grammar elements can be selected in a way that it is not ambiguous and can be used to transform both models to a single common representation.

By having both models in the same space, it is possible to combine them in a way that exceeds the code generation capabilities of both models separately. Moreover, in this case we will extend the language obtained by merging the languages g^{-1} and j^{-1} by adding a set of task definition non terminals. Furthermore, with no ambiguity restrictions, a traditional parser can be used to process the natural language specification.

It is worth mentioning that unrestricted natural language is not used because the process described in Sect. 2.2 will induce errors or generate more than one system [28], making difficult to validate every possible system.

From E-R Diagrams to Restricted Natural Language $(j^{-1}(e))$. To achieve a textual representation of an E-R diagram, we propose to restrict the natural language constructs as shown in Fig. 4.

```
terminal FID : '^'?('A'..'Z'|'_') ('a'..'z'|'A'..'Z'|'_'|'0'..'9')*;
Identifier : parts+=FID (parts+=FID)*;
DefinitionItem: arity=('a'|'an'|'many') specName=Identifier 'named' intanceName=Identifier
        'with' defaultName=Identifier 'as' 'default';
Definition: childname=Identifier 'is' 'an' specName=Identifier
    ('which' 'exist' 'in' contextName=Identifier)?
    'and' 'needs' ':' definitions+=DefinitionItem (',' definitions+=DefinitionItem)* '.';
```

Fig. 4. Grammar for the Restricted Natural Language representing E-R diagrams, presented originally in [11].

To define an entity, an entity name (*childname*) is required. Also, a set of relationships and a set of properties (*DefinitionItem*) are defined. Note that the *entity name* can be in singular and plural forms, thus, needing a mechanism to identify them both as the same noun. This grammar fragment can be used to generate a class diagram including properties, relationships, and also, the forms associated with this class at the visualization time.

Furthermore, notice that some defaults need to be configured including both data types and their respective memory size. For instance, properties having a VARCHAR data type are assumed to be maximum of 255 in length.

From BPMN to Restricted Natural Language $(g^{-1}(b))$. In order allow our restricted natural language and code generation tool to represent and execute business processes, we propose to use the following BPMN representation transformed in grammar elements. Note that these representations include the most common BPMN constructs and some are left behind, also, only the processes diagrams are translated. Figure 5 shows the mappings from a BPMN model to EBNF grammar rules written in Xtext[6] format.

```
//------Process and Start Event------
Tasklist: taskList+=Asignedtask ((',' taskList+=Asignedtask)* 'and,' taskList+=Asignedtask)? '.';
Process: 'the' name=Identifier 'process' 'starts' ',' 'then' ':' taskList=Tasklist;
//------End Event------
EndEvent: 'the' 'process' name='ends';
//------Tasks------
SimpleTask: name=Identifier;
GotoJump:'go' 'back' 'to' returnTo=Identifier;
Task:task=(SimpleTask|AfterEvent|WaitSignalEvent|WaitMessageEvent|GotoJump|EndEvent|
SubprocessendEvent|SubprocessCall|JumpToAsk|QuestionRedirect|EventRedirect|ParallelRedirect);
//------Exclusive Gateways------
QuestionRedirect: 'ask' 'if' redirectTo=Identifier;
QuestionControl : 'if' 'the' 'answer' 'to' questionName=Identifier 'is' answer=FID 'then' ':'
taskList=Tasklist ;
//------Parallel Gateways------
ParallelRedirect: 'do' 'at' 'the' 'same' 'time' 'the' redirectTo=Identifier 'tasks';
ParallelControl: 'for' redirectName=Identifier 'tasks' ('also')? 'do':' taskList=Tasklist;
//------Event Gateways------
EventRedirect: 'check' 'the' redirectTo=Identifier 'event';
EventControl : 'if' 'the' 'event' eventName=Identifier 'is'
eventCatched=Identifier ('signal'|'message'|'timer')
'then' ':' taskList=Tasklist ;
//------Subprocess------
SubprocessCall:'the' subprocessName=Identifier 'is' 'made';
Subprocess: 'the' name=Identifier 'subprocess' 'starts' ',' 'then' ':' taskList=Tasklist;
//------Events------
WaitMessageEvent:'wait' 'for' 'the' messageName=Identifier 'message';
AfterEvent:'wait' 'duration=INT unit=('week'|'weeks'|'hour'|'hours'|'minutes'|
'minute'|'days'|'day');
WaitSignalEvent:'wait' 'for' 'the' signalName=Identifier 'signal';
//------Lanes------
Asignedtask: task=Task ('(by' assignee=Identifier ')')?;
//------Frontier events------
FronterEvent: 'if' 'the' name=Identifier ('signal'|'message'|'timer') 'arrives' 'while' 'doing'
task=Identifier ('stop' 'it'|'wait' 'to' 'complete')  'and' 'then' ':' taskList=Tasklist;
```

Fig. 5. Grammar for the Restricted Natural Language representing BPMN models, presented originally in [11].

Notice that for the gateway and frontier event elements, the rule is split in two parts: one defined within task list rule, and another defined in a separated paragraph. This allows the specification to take more than a paragraph in the textual representation. Finally, observe that returning to a previously defined task is done with a special rule "go back to".

Task Definition Language. This part of the grammar emerges due to in previous works was identified that some method to define the actions to be performed in each task was necessary. The previous approach was to generate controllers an views based in a template-per-verb approach. This was difficult

---

[6] http://www.eclipse.org/Xtext/.

to maintain and required many templates to be executed properly and generate a prototype as near to the final product as possible.

This part of the grammar involves the definition of each task in each process to generate the views and controllers for the desired system prototype. This definition must involve some sort of operations in some of the defined domain classes. The approach used to define this operations is using one of the four CRUD (Create, Read, Update or Delete) operations. In addition, two extra operations ("single selection" and "multiple selection") are included as well. This operations solve problems like showing a single instance (that must be selected beforehand), and selecting a list of instances to operate over them.

Furthermore, operations like creation and edition over multiple instances of the domain classes may be useful in several applications. The grammar created to fulfill these requirements is shown in Fig. 6.

```
TaskRedefinition:taskName=Identifier 'is' 'a' 'task' 'where' ':' partslist=ViewPartsList;
ViewPartsList: list+=AbstractOperation+;
AbstractOperation: operation=(Creation|MultipleView|SingleView|FieldView);
FieldRestrictor : ',' 'only' fields+=Identifier (',' fields+=Identifier)* 'are' 'shown';
Operations :'edition'|'deletion'|'multiple' 'selection'| 'single' 'selection';
OperationAdition: ',' 'with' permisions+=(Operations) (('','|'and')
permisions+=(Operations))* 'capabilities';
Creation: '-' arity=('multiple'|'a') name = Identifier ('are'|'is') 'created'
(restriction=FieldRestrictor)? '.';
MultipleView: '-' 'all' 'the' child = Identifier ('in' parent = Identifier)? 'are' 'shown'
(restriction= FieldRestrictor)? (operations=OperationAdition)? '.';
SingleView : '-' 'a' name = Identifier 'is' 'shown' (operations=OperationAdition)? '.';
FieldView : '-' 'the' fields+=Identifier (('','|'and') fields+=Identifier)* 'in'
parent = Identifier 'are' 'shown' (operations=OperationAdition)? '.';
```

Fig. 6. Grammar for task definition, presented originally in [11].

The previous two grammar fragments $g^{-1}(b)$ and $j^{-1}(b)$ can be functionally merged using this new fragment. This is done by making relationships between tasks in a process and domain classes defined previously, and performing some action in the instances of these classes. This is more efficient at the maintainability level than using a single template per each verb.

Overall, the Restricted Natural Language permits to specify not only structural information, but also functional requirements of the software. Thus, it allows the designer to build a textual specification of the required software in conjunction with the stakeholders.

3.2   Code Generation Approach

After the software specification is written in Restricted Natural Language, the source code of the target web application is generated as depicted in Fig. 7.

The input of the code generation process is a file or string with the textual specification of the software written in the Restricted Natural Language. The first steps consist of traditional lexical and syntactic analyses performed to the specification. Next, the phase of design information extraction is performed,

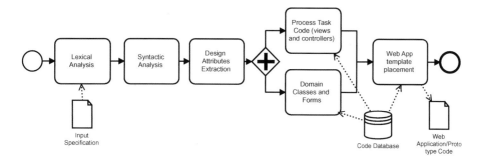

Fig. 7. Code generation process.

where the names of the parts of the system are extracted. Then, this information and its context are used to generate source code for the web application.

Previous to this process, a database containing code templates must be developed. The content of this database is a series of specification types related to several templates. These templates represent a code fragment to be executed during a task, front-end HTML fragments, complete view examples, controllers for the different BPMN elements and fields of domain classes with its respective representations for the selected frameworks. Also this database contains the web application template that will be used as the final destination of all the generated source code.

Thanks to the Restricted Natural Language, the lexer, parser, and payload extraction phases can be performed using a traditional top-down parser. This avoids the inherent ambiguity of natural languages, having to validate multiple solutions or interpretations [28] or simply getting an incomplete model [47].

After this processing, the code for the domain classes and forms is created. To match expected relationships, we check for the following cases: (1) an attribute has a known data type (its in the database its a database field); (2) an attribute references another class in the specification (previously defined in the input file, a many-to-one relationship); (3) a class has an attribute of the form *many* (a one to many relationship); and (4) a class has an attribute of the form *many* and the another class has the first class referenced back in other attribute of the form *many* (a many to many relationship); (5) an attribute references another class of the specification and that class references back the first class both of the singular (a, an) way (a one-to-one relationship).

In the first case (1), we use the code database to generate the desired field; in the second case (2), we assign the data type of the attribute to a foreign key referencing the class. In third case (3), we understand this as an one-to-many relationship, thus, we alter the referenced class inserting a foreign key attribute referencing the class that has *a set of* the other class. For the fourth case (4), this is interpreted as a many-to-many relationship, therefore, we insert an additional table referencing the two involved classes and the respective foreign keys in each class. Finally for the fifth case (5) we insert references in one of the classes and a foreign key and a reference in the other one.

Next, the code for the process is generated. For each element of each process a template in the database is fetched and resolved. If the controller generated needs a view the file is generated also. If the process element is a *SimpleTask* then the following process is performed:

1. Check for the definition in other paragraph of the specification.
2. If the definition exists, then resolve the controller and view code.
3. If it is not defined, use a default controller and view.

This *SimpleTask* definition methods use the *"TaskRedefinition"* non-terminal to generate the code for its view and controller. It uses code fragments defined in the database to generate only the needed code to query, update, create or delete the domain classes instances.

From previous experiences developing this idea, we determined that is easier to control the flow of activities and elements using a centralized control method. This method will be in charge of determining the path to follow given the current task/element. It will use the information of order of elements present in the *TaskList* non-terminals across the paragraphs in the specification. Also, this will help to solve the gateways by validating that the conditions for each output path are met.

The code for the exclusive gateways will be a method where a snippet of HTML is rendered asking the defined question. Then, after a POST request to a controller, use the previously defined controller method to determine the task to be done next.

Finally, these pieces of code are placed in a template prepared to execute the web application as desired in the specification.

4   Implementation

To explain the implementation that was performed for this proposal, we should first clarify the boundaries between the source code generation/prototyping tool and the final result of the execution of it over an input. Both of them use different languages and tools to execute its required tasks. For the source code generation tool, we use a set of Java based tools, and for the prototype itself we use a set of Python based tools.

This implementation is the second that was made. The first one evidenced serious limitations at the code production level because it depended on several templates made for each one of the verbs of a single specification. This weakness was solved by implementing the T_n grammar fragment. Also, limitations were shown at the start of the process because some domain class instances needed to be selected and there was not a way to select the instance, this was solved by introducing the "single selection" and "multiple selection" capabilities. In addition, the tool set was changed for this second implementation to generate an IDE integration.

For the code generation tool we used the *Xtext* (See footnote 6) toolkit including the *Xtend* language, adding a database of specifications and code templates using SqlLite, and a micro ORM framework called OrmLite[7]. Code templates stored in this database were created using the Freemarker[8] engine.

According to the process illustrated in Fig. 8, which is the specialization of the general code generation process shown in Fig. 7. We use Xtext to generate the lexical analyzer, the parser, and the design information extractor. We implement the previously shown grammars. Also, Xtext creates a set of classes containing the required design information from each rule.

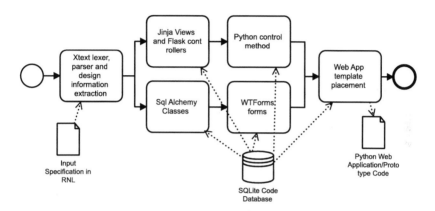

Fig. 8. Implementation work flow.

Prior to generate code for domain classes, the fields that reference another specifications are resolved, determining the case they belong (as described previously), or simply fetched and resolved from the code template database. Notice that it is necessary to take into account the respective transformations between the plural and singular forms of the nouns (*entity names*) to find the relationships. This can be done having a predefined set of rules and a dictionary for irregular nouns.

When the references are determined, a set of previously written code templates is used to transform the design information into the target code. For the *entities*, a *SQLalchemy*[9] (an *ORM* system) class, and also to class in a *WTForms*[10] (a web forms processor). Note that more than one code fragment can be generated in one template and this can be useful to generate code that requires the same design information. An example of the templates used to generate the domain classes code is shown in Fig. 9.

After this code is ready, the views and controller methods for each task are created. Again using templates (but this time several of them), we generate code for each one of the non-terminals that are options of the non-terminal "Task".

---

[7] http://ormlite.com/sqlite_java_android_orm.shtml.
[8] http://freemarker.org/.
[9] http://www.sqlalchemy.org/.
[10] https://wtforms.readthedocs.io/.

```
class ${spec.childname.asClassName()}(Base):
    __tablename__ = '${spec.childname.asVariableName()}'
    id = Column(Integer, primary_key=True)
    <#list definitions as child>
${child}
    </#list>
    def __str__(self):
        return getattr(self,'name',str(self.id))
class ${spec.childname.asClassName()}Form(ModelForm):
    class Meta:
        model = ${spec.childname.asClassName()}
<#list spec.definitions as d>
<#if d.inSpec()>
    def ${d.specName.asClassName()}_helper_method():
        return session.query(${d.specName.asClassName()}).all()
    ${d.intanceName.asVariableName()}_id = QuerySelectField2(
        query_factory=${d.specName.asClassName()}_helper_method,
        allow_blank=True
    )
</#if>
</#list>
```

Fig. 9. Domain class template example.

The process of generating a view changes if there is a redefinition for a "SimpleTask" non-terminal. Then, the process uses information given in the "TaskRedefinition" non-terminal. It uses the information within its parse tree to determine the code result in both controller and view. To do so, we use templates to generate partial results of the source code of the method, and then, merge them in a helper template.

Moreover, there must be templates used to generate edition controllers with or without selections, and only to show previously created elements. It is also possible to create a template that takes into account all the possibilities but it will soon render too complex to be treated by a template engine. Following the same idea, we use templates to create the HTML template that the web application needs to render its UI. This UI rendered code can also be a template, but this time for the result system engine.

Furthermore, we iterate over the "Process" non-terminal instances again to create the helper method. This task is carried out with recursive calls of the "Tasklist" non-terminal within the process and gateway definitions. It generates a single method which takes as an input the URL of the current task and returns the next task.

After all the source code is generated, using the same template system, the resultant strings are placed directly into a web application template assuming that the needed imports and dependencies are resolved.

The template system used to render the views of the result web application was *Jinja2*[11]. Moreover, a small database in SQLite3[12] is used to deploy and test the result of the proposed method.

---

[11] http://jinja.pocoo.org/docs/dev/.
[12] https://www.sqlite.org/.

In summary, the tool chain used for the implementation of our proposal is comprised of: Programming languages: *Python 2.7, Xtend*; Parser generator: *Xtext*; Template systems: *Jinja 2, Freemarker*; Web framework: *Flask*; *ORM* systems: *SqlAlchemy, OrmLite*; Web forms processor: *WTforms*; *HTML, CSS,* and *JS* framework for developing responsive applications on the web: *Bootstrap*[13], and the *SB Admin 2 Bootstrap*[14] admin theme; Database: *SQLite3*.

5   Results and Discussions

In order to validate and demonstrate the applicability of the proposal, this section includes the presentation of the results of two case studies, and the comparison of this work to related works. The case studies are titled: *Question Cycle*, and *Odoo Sales Clone*.

5.1   Case Study: *Question Cycle*

The objective of the prototype presented in this section is to work as a quiz generator in an academic context. In this application an anonymous user generates the quiz by selecting questions from a list. The BPMN process that models this behavior is presented in Fig. 10.

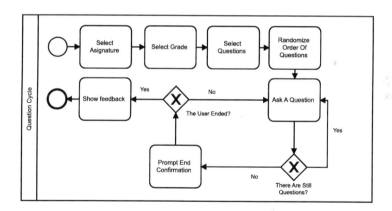

Fig. 10. BPMN model for "Question Cycle".

Initially the user selects a course and a level, after this a set of questions is shown, each one with n possible answers. The original requirement stated that the questions must be filtered by the course and level selected beforehand. Each question also belongs to an extra classification called "DBA" o "Basic Learning Right". The user selects the questions, and then, the first one of the selected

---

[13] getbootstrap.com/.

[14] https://startbootstrap.com/template-overviews/sb-admin-2/.

questions is asked. The questions could contain math equations and should be showed in LATEX format. When there is no more questions to answer, the user is asked if he/she really wants to leave. Finally, after the quiz is complete, the feedback is shown.

The representation in Restricted Natural Language of this process is shown in Fig. 11. In addition, some resultant screen-shots are shown in Fig. 12.

Nevertheless, this prototype has some limitations with respect to the original requirements. These include: questions are not filtered as requested; the gateways can be replaced by source code that determines these conditions automatically; the question order randomization cannot be achieved using our restricted language; equations are not shown in LATEX format. Therefore, these requirements

```
1   Subject is a Domain Class and needs: a String named Name and a String named Code Value.
2   Dba is a Domain Class and needs: a String named Code and a String named Dba Name.
3   Answer is a Domain Class and needs: a String named Text Value.
4   Level is a Domain Class and needs: a Number named Course Number.
5   Question is a Domain Class and needs: a Dba named Dba, many Answer named Answers, a Level named Level
6   and a String named Heading Text.
7
8   the Question Cycle process starts, then: Select Subject, Select Level,
9   Select Questions, Ask One Question and, ask if Are There Unanswered Questions.
10  Select Subject is a task where:-all the Subject are shown, with single selection capabilities.
11  Select Level is a task where:-all the Level are shown, with single selection capabilities.
12  Select Questions is a task where:-all the Question are shown, with multiple selection capabilities.
13  Ask One Question is a task where:-a Question is shown.
14  -all the Answer in Question are shown, with single selection capabilities.
15
16  if the answer to Are There Unanswered Questions is Yes then: go back to Ask One Question.
17  if the answer to Are There Unanswered Questions is No then: Prompt End Confirmation and, ask if The User Ended.
18  if the answer to The User Ended is Yes then: Show Questions Answer and, the process ends.
19  if the answer to The User Ended is No then: go back to Ask One Question.
20
21  Show Questions Answer is a task where:-a Question is shown.-a Answer is shown.|
```

Fig. 11. Restricted Natural Language representation for *Question Cycle*.

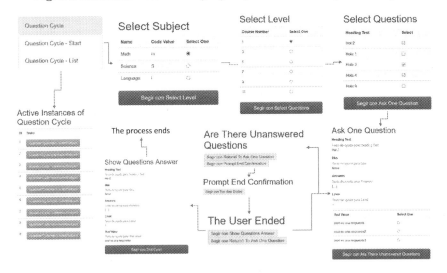

Fig. 12. Question Cycle result screen-shots.

should be implemented manually by the developers after the prototyping cycle is completed.

5.2 Case Study: *Odoo Clone*

Odoo[15] is an open ERP and CRM system. For the purpose of this work, some modules of this system are developed using our restricted language. The selected modules are: sales and projects. The selected version of Odoo is 9.0. To support these modules, some core features of Odoo must be implemented first, which include: user management, language, and sales teams configurations.

The sales module has five processes. Each one of them consists in a couple of tasks. There are three creation processes including: Client, Opportunity, and Product; and two additional processes to list opportunities and products, and select and edit them.

The project module consists in a series of projects, each one with a set of associated tasks. Also there are processes for the selection, presentation, and creation of tasks and projects.

The resultant software requirements can be specified using the Restricted Natural Language as shown in Fig. 13.

Resulting in a set of views linked as shown in Fig. 16. These views contain the creation processes and the two selection and posterior detail processes. In addition, as an example of the generated code, the controller for the "Show Selected Project" task is shown in Fig. 14. This controller renders the view shown in Fig. 15, which is also a template written to be compatible with the Jinja2 template system. In this view, each one of the fields of the "project" domain class and all the "tasks" associated with the selected "project" are shown.

Some of the limitations of the generated prototype include: the card-like layout of the original Odoo is lost in the transcription, the same happens with its state based card list; the images of the products are not shown but they are uploaded; the project labels and their auto-complete field are omitted; and the labels of the form fields are not configurable without editing the source code. These are general limitations of this scheme, these configurations (and also GUI customizations) would require a bigger RNL language.

On the other hand, the fast processing of the specification and its prototype generation allows the stakeholders to see within seconds changes made to the project. The textual specification permits to the designer a rapid specification and its corresponding validation after learning the restricted language constructs. Results can be seen in short time after a live meeting starts with the stakeholders, and changes to specifications at this stage are painless and economical. Furthermore, some tools like auto-completion, highlight syntax, and IDE integration were integrated to facilitate the prototyping process.

---

[15] https://www.odoo.com/.

```
1   Language is an Domain Class and needs: a String named Name.
2   Contact Type is an Domain Class and needs: a String named Type.
3   Contact is an Domain Class and needs: a Contact Type named Type, a String named Name, a String named Address,
4   a String named Address2, a String named City, a String named State, a Number named Zip Code, a String named Country,
5   a Website named Homepage, a String named Work Desk, a Phone named Personal Phone, a Phone named Mobile Phone,
6   a Phone named Fax, a Email named Personal Email, a String named Title and a Language named Language.
7
8   User is an Domain Class and needs: a String named Name and an Email named Username.
9   Sales Team is an Domain Class and needs: a String named Name, a Number named Code and a User named Team Leader.
10  Activity is an Domain Class and needs: a String named Message Type, a Number named Number Of Days and
11  a Sales Team named Assigned Sales Team.
12
13  Opportunity State is an Domain Class and needs: a String named Name.
14  Opportunity Phase is an Domain Class and needs: a String named Name.
15  Opportunity is an Domain Class and needs: a String named Description, a Number named Income, a Number named Probability,
16  a Contact named Client, an Activity named Next Activity, an Email named Contact Email, a Phone named Contact Phone,
17  a Date named Provided Closing, a User named Seller, a Sales Team named Responsible Sales Team, a Number named Rating,
18  an Opportunity Phase named Phase and a Opportunity State named State.
19
20  Product Type is an Domain Class and needs: a String named Name.
21  Product is an Domain Class and needs: an Image named Photo, a String named Name, a Product Type named Type,
22  a String named Bar Code, a Number named Price and a Number named Cost.
23
24  Project State is a Domain Class and needs: a String named Name.
25  Project is an Domain Class and needs: a String named Name, a String named Task Label, a Contact named Client and
26  a Project State named State.
27
28  Task is a Domain Class and needs: a String named Name, a String named Description, a Date named Limit Date,
29  a User named Assigned and a Project named Project.
30
31  the Client Creation process starts, then: Create Contact and, the process ends.
32  Create Contact is a task where: -a Contact is created.
33
34  the Opportunity Creation process starts, then: Create Opportunity and, the process ends.
35  Create Opportunity is a task where: -a Opportunity are created.
36
37  the Opportunity List process starts, then: Show Opportunities, Show Opportunity and, the process ends.
38  Show Opportunities is a task where:-all the Opportunity are shown, with single selection capabilities.
39  Show Opportunity is a task where:-a Opportunity is shown, with edition capabilities.
40
41  the Product List process starts, then: Show Product List, Product Detail and, the process ends.
42  Show Product List is a task where: -all the Products are shown, only Name, Price are shown, with single selection capabilities.
43  Product Detail is a task where:-a Product is shown.
44
45  the Product Creation process starts, then: Create Product and, the process ends.
46  Create Product is a task where:-a Product is created.
47
48  the Project Creation process starts, then: Create Project and, the process ends.
49  Create Project is a task where:-a Project is created.
50
51  the Project List process starts, then: List Projects, Show Selected Project and, the process ends.
52  List Projects is a task where: -all the Projects are shown, with single selection capabilities.
53  Show Selected Project is a task where: -a Project is shown. -all the Tasks in Project are shown.
54
55  the Task Creation process starts, then: Create Task and, the process ends.
56  Create Task is a task where: -a Task is created.
57
58  the Task List process starts, then: List Tasks, Show Task and, the process ends.
59  List Tasks is a task where: -all the Tasks are shown, with single selection capabilities.
60  Show Task is a task where:-a Task is shown, with edition capabilities.
```

Fig. 13. Restricted Natural Language representation for *Odoo Clone*.

```
@app.route('/projectList/<pid>/showSelectedProject',
methods=['GET','POST'])
def projectList_showSelectedProject(pid):
    viewparams={}
    data = get_instance_data(pid)
    formdata = request.form.copy()
    for file in request.files:
        formdata[file] = request.files[file].filename
    request.form = formdata
    project = session.query(Project).filter(
      Project.id==data.get("selected_Project",0)
    ).first()
    viewparams['project']=project
    task_list = session.query(Task).filter(
        Task.project_id==data.get('selected_Project',0)
    ).all()
    viewparams['task_list']=task_list
```

Fig. 14. Code example of a generated controller.

```
<div class="panel-heading">Show Selected Project</div>
<div class="panel-body">
{% for field in project.__table__.columns._data.keys()%}
<div class="form-group">
        <b>{{field}}</b><br /> {{project[field]}}
</div>
{% endfor %}
<div class="col-lg-12">
<div class="table-responsive">
<table class="table">
<tr>
{% for prop in task_list[0].__mapper__.columns.keys() %}
<th>{{prop}}</th>
{% endfor %}
</tr>
{% for ent in task_list %}
<tr>
{% for prop in ent.__mapper__.columns.keys() %}
<td>{{ent[prop]}}</td> {% endfor %}
</tr>
{% endfor %}
</table></div></div></div>
```

Fig. 15. Code example of a generated view.

Fig. 16. Odoo clone result views.

5.3   Comparative to Similar Works

Table 2 presents a comparative of related works, including this proposal. It includes: the main differences with respect to the starting point of the workflow, i.e., templates, (un)restricted natural language, or specification language;

Table 2. Comparison to related works.

Work	Start point	Result	Human intervention	Type of processing	Intermediate representation
[40]	Specification language	Executable	No	Compiler (Prolog)	AST
[48]	Unrestricted natural language	UML diagrams	Rewriting	Stanford Parser + Rule Matching	-
[42]	Unrestricted natural language	BPMN diagram	No	Stanford Parser (factored model)	-
[49]	Templates	UML class and sequence diagrams	Completes missing information	Match Template	Use case table
[9]	Unrestricted natural language	ADA Executable (manual process)	Manual process	Manual	-
[44, 46]	Unrestricted natural language	E-R diagram	No	Grammar parsing	XML
[29]	Templates	UML class diagram	Review final model	Match Template	Textual OAAM
[26]	Unrestricted natural language	OSMs	No	Shallow parser	-
[27]	Unrestricted natural language	UML class diagram	Chose classes and attributes	POS tagging	-
[28]	Unrestricted natural language	DSLs	Select Best Fit	Machine Learning	Ml features
[38]	Unrestricted paragraphs	SBVR	No	GATE	Multiple SBVR
[36]	Sentences From Templates	UML (classes)	No	Match Template	User history
[50, 51]	Sentences From Templates	UML (states, classes)	Write in tabular notation and enclose certain words	Match Template	-
[52]	Sentences From Templates	LSC or UML (sequence)	Resolve ambiguities	Match Template + POS tagging	LSC
[53]	Unrestricted paragraphs	UML (classes)	No	Stanford Parser (Deep parse)	-
[47]	Unrestricted paragraphs	UML (classes)	No	Pattern matching	XML
[6]	Unrestricted sentences	Verilog	No	Recursive descent syntactic parser	-
[54]	Unrestricted sentences	State chart	Manual process	Manual	Table representation
This Work	Restricted natural language + Templates	Executable Web application prototype	No	LL(*) Parser	AST

the final result of each work, e.g., executable program, UML models, E-R diagrams, etc.; if the work needs human intervention after the computational process stars; the type of computational tool used to process the input of the process; and finally, if the processing requires an intermediate representation in order to be completed.

One can see that most related works manage some form of natural language as starting point for the process. In addition, most of the works end up with a model constructed in some specification language like BPMN, UML (some subset of the possible diagrams), or E-R. Further translations are limited for external tools like *Rational Rose* or *Visual Paradigm*. Furthermore, some of the works also need a manual intervention of the user to select the design attributes and even rewriting requirements or complete missing information. It is also common in these works that the processing of the input text is a NLP parser or a traditional compiler depending on the input text features. Intermediate representations are often present in works that pretend to do this job with aid of external software, multiple stages or, using a special capability of this intermediate representation. In this work, we obtain a working prototype closer to a final product without intervention from the user or external software using as intermediate representation the abstract syntax tree of the written specification produced by Xtext.

Only a few proposals obtain executable programs as an output. Among them, the work in [9] involve a manual process, and the proposal in [40] requires to work with previously defined code fragments in order to obtain a command-line based program, just like the work presented in this chapter.

6 Conclusions

In this paper a fast prototyping method was presented. This method produces a web application that implements the business processes ideas present in BPMN. As input, it only uses a specification written in a Restricted Natural Language to generate the source code of a prototype. To achieve this restricted representation two transformations were proposed between design models (E-R and BPMN) and a common natural language (English). With this approach, the expressiveness and ideas behind this two languages are maintained and, by putting them in a single common representation they can be merged to overcome limitations regarding to source code generation capabilities.

The source code template usage in order to generate a prototype resulted in a very useful approach when maintenance and construction of the prototyping tool should be taken into account. This template approach also helped to extend the available fields of the T_{e-r} model. As a downside, templates can get complex very fast in order to extend the functionality of a single template.

Moreover, the previously discussed limitations show a relationship between the complexity of the specification and the proximity of the prototype with the final product. This trade-off affects the difficulty of generating source code. A more complex specification language will have more design details and non-terminal types to generate more details in the prototype. Also, there is a relation between complexity in language and learning difficulties.

The most relevant advantages of the proposed approach are related to prototyping speed and specification expressiveness. These allow the designer to generate and execute software prototypes in a very short time, which permits the software development process to be performed in a live meeting with the stakeholders. Specification modifications and additions can generate results almost instantly thanks to the code generation approach selected. In addition, the IDE integration and support of auto-completion and highlight syntax tools facilitate the development of the specification. The result of this prototyping method is the source code of a prototype ready to be used as part of the final product. Overall, this approach can reduce common errors associated with requirements and design stages in the software development life cycle.

Finally, we can devise some paths to be followed in order to achieve a better fast prototyping schema in the future works. Some of these include: to propose a sub-grammar/method for automatic gateway resolution; to add more models to the restricted representation using the same translate and mix schema; to alter task execution based on previous tasks; to add a language/method to generate statistics and reports; to generate new visualizations of special types of fields (geo-references, videos, special types of images, etc.); and finally, to add restrictions between domain classes (arity restrictions, restrictions involving queries).

References

1. Walia, G.S., Carver, J.C.: A systematic literature review to identify and classify software requirement errors (2009)
2. Fairley, R.E.: Managing and Leading Software Projects. IEEE Computer Society/Wiley, Los Alamitos/Hoboken (2009)
3. Augustine, S., Martin, R.C.: Managing Agile Projects. Robert C. Martin Series. Prentice Hall Professional Technical Reference, Upper Saddle River (2005)
4. Githens, G.: Managing agile projects by Sanjiv Augustine. J. Prod. Innov. Manag. **23**(5), 469–470 (2006)
5. Fowler, M., Highsmith, J.: The agile manifesto. Softw. Dev. **9**, 28–35 (2001)
6. Harris, I.G.: Extracting design information from natural language specifications. In: Proceedings of the 49th Annual Design Automation Conference on - DAC 2012, p. 1256 (2012)
7. Ibrahim, M., Ahmad, R.: Class diagram extraction from textual requirements using natural language processing (NLP) techniques. In: 2nd International Conference on Computer Research and Development, ICCRD 2010, pp. 200–204 (2010)
8. Bhatia, J., Sharma, R., Biswas, K.K., Ghaisas, S.: Using grammatical knowledge patterns for structuring requirements specifications. In: 2013 3rd International Workshop on Requirements Patterns, RePa 2013 - Proceedings, pp. 31–34 (2013)
9. Abbott, R.J.: Program design by informal English descriptions. Commun. ACM **26**(11), 882–894 (1983)
10. Nishida, F., Takamatsu, S., Fujita, Y., Tani, T.: Semi-automatic program construction from specifications using library modules. IEEE Trans. Softw. Eng. **17**(9), 853–871 (1991)
11. Hoyos, J.P.A., Restrepo-Calle, F.: Automatic source code generation for web-based process-oriented information systems. In: Proceedings of the 12th International Conference on Evaluation of Novel Approaches to Software Engineering - Volume 1: ENASE, pp. 103–113. INSTICC, ScitePress (2017)
12. ISO/IEC and IEEE: ISO/IEC/IEEE 24765:2010 - Systems and Software Engineering - Vocabulary. ISO/IEC IEEE, vol. 2010, p. 410 (2010)
13. Walia, G.S., Carver, J.C.: A systematic literature review to identify and classify software requirement errors. Inf. Softw. Technol. **51**(7), 1087–1109 (2009)

14. Ferrari, A., Spoletini, P., Gnesi, S.: Ambiguity and tacit knowledge in requirements elicitation interviews. Requir. Eng. **21**(3), 333–355 (2016)
15. Li, K., Dewar, R., Pooley, R.: Computer-assisted and customer-oriented requirements elicitation. In: 13th IEEE International Conference on Requirements Engineering (RE 2005), pp. 479–480. IEEE (2005)
16. Fatwanto, A.: Specifying translatable software requirements using constrained natural language. In: 2012 7th International Conference on Computer Science & Education (ICCSE), no. ICCSE, pp. 1047–1052 (2012)
17. Fockel, M., Holtman, J.: ReqPat: efficient documentation of high-quality requirements using controlled natural language. In: IEEE International Requirements Engineering Conference, vol. 23, pp. 280–281 (2015)
18. Aiello, G., Di Bernardo, R., Maggio, M., Di Bona, D., Re, G.L.: Inferring business rules from natural language expressions. In: Proceedings - IEEE 7th International Conference on Service-Oriented Computing and Applications, SOCA 2014, pp. 131–136 (2014)
19. Yan, R., Cheng, C.-H., Chai, Y.: Formal consistency checking over specifications in natural languages. In: Design, Automation Test in Europe Conference Exhibition (DATE), pp. 1677–1682 (2015)
20. Arora, C., Sabetzadeh, M., Briand, L., Zimmer, F.: Automated checking of conformance to requirements templates using natural language processing. IEEE Trans. Softw. Eng. **41**(10), 944–968 (2015)
21. Dzung, D.V., Ohnishi, A.: Evaluation of ontology-based checking of software requirements specification. In: Proceedings - International Computer Software and Applications Conference, pp. 425–430 (2013)
22. Soares, H.A., Moura, R.S.: A methodology to guide writing Software Requirements Specification document. In: Proceedings - 2015 41st Latin American Computing Conference, CLEI 2015 (2015)
23. Saeki, M., Horai, H., Enomoto, H.: Software development process from natural language specification. In: Proceedings of the 11th International Conference on Software Engineering, pp. 64–73 (1989)
24. Bellegarda, J.R., Monz, C.: State of the art in statistical methods for language and speech processing. Comput. Speech Lang. **35**, 163–184 (2015)
25. Cambria, E., White, B.: Jumping NLP curves: a review of natural language processing research [Review Article]. IEEE Comput. Intell. Mag. **9**, 48–57 (2014)
26. Chioac, E.V.: Using machine learning to enhance automated requirements model transformation. In: Proceedings - International Conference on Software Engineering, pp. 1487–1490 (2012)
27. Overmyer, S., Benoit, L., Owen, R.: Conceptual modeling through linguistic analysis using LIDA. In: Proceedings of the 23rd International Conference on Software Engineering, ICSE 2001, pp. 401–410 (2001)
28. Desai, A., Gulwani, S., Hingorani, V., Jain, N., Karkare, A., Marron, M., R, S., Roy, S.: Program synthesis using natural language. In: Proceedings of the 38th International Conference on Software Engineering, ICSE 2016, pp. 345–356. ACM (2016)
29. Popescu, D., Rugaber, S., Medvidovic, N., Berry, D.M.: Reducing ambiguities in requirements specifications via automatically created object-oriented models. In: Paech, B., Martell, C. (eds.) Monterey Workshop 2007. LNCS, vol. 5320, pp. 103–124. Springer, Heidelberg (2008). https://doi.org/10.1007/978-3-540-89778-1_10
30. Zhou, N., Zhou, X.: Auto-generation of class diagram from free-text functional specifications and domain ontology, no. 2, pp. 1–20 (2008)

31. Smith, R., Avrunin, G., Clarke, L.: From natural language requirements to rigorous property specifications. In: Workshop on Software Engineering for Embedded Systems (SEES 2003) From Requirements to Implementation, pp. 40–46 (2003)

32. Konrad, S., Cheng, B.H.C.: Facilitating the construction of specification pattern-based properties. In: 13th IEEE International Conference on Requirements Engineering RE05, no. August, pp. 329–338 (2005)

33. Zapata, C.M.: UN Lencep: Obtención Automática de Diagramas UML a partir de un Lenguaje Controlado. Memorias del VII Encuentro Nacional de Computación ENC 2006, pp. 254–259 (2006)

34. Videira, C., Ferreira, D., Da Silva, A.R.: A linguistic patterns approach for requirements specification. In: Proceedings - 32nd Euromicro Conference on Software Engineering and Advanced Applications, SEAA, vol. 2004, pp. 302–309 (2006)

35. Ilić, D.: Deriving formal specifications from informal requirements. In: Proceedings - International Computer Software and Applications Conference, vol. 1, no. Compsac, pp. 145–152 (2007)

36. Zeaaraoui, A., Bougroun, Z., Belkasmi, M.G., Bouchentouf, T.: User stories template for object-oriented applications. In 2013 3rd International Conference on Innovative Computing Technology, INTECH 2013, pp. 407–410 (2013)

37. Dahhane, W., Zeaaraoui, A., Ettifouri, E.H., Bouchentouf, T.: An automated object-based approach to transforming requirements to class diagrams. In: 2014 2nd World Conference on Complex Systems, WCCS 2014, pp. 158–163 (2015)

38. Selway, M., Grossmann, G., Mayer, W., Stumptner, M.: Formalising natural language specifications using a cognitive linguistic/configuration based approach. Inf. Syst. **54**, 191–208 (2015)

39. Granacki, J.J., Parker, A.C.: PHRAN-SPAN: a natural language interface for system specifications. In: 24th ACM/IEEE Conference Proceedings on Design Automation Conference - DAC 1987, pp. 416–422 (1987)

40. Schwitter, R.: Attempto-from specifications in controlled natural language towards executable specifications. Arxiv preprint cmp-lg/9603004 (1996)

41. Bryant, B.R., Lee, B.S.: Two-level grammar as an object-oriented requirements specification language. In: Proceedings of the Annual Hawaii International Conference on System Sciences, vol. 2002-Janua, no. c, pp. 3627–3636 (2002)

42. Friedrich, F., Mendling, J., Puhlmann, F.: Process model generation from natural language text. In: Mouratidis, H., Rolland, C. (eds.) CAiSE 2011. LNCS, vol. 6741, pp. 482–496. Springer, Heidelberg (2011). https://doi.org/10.1007/978-3-642-21640-4_36

43. Steen, B., Pires, L.F., Iacob, M.-e.: Automatic generation of optimal business processes from business rules, pp. 117–126 (2010)

44. Geetha, S., Mala, G.: Extraction of key attributes from natural language requirements specification text. In: IET Chennai Fourth International Conference on Sustainable Energy and Intelligent Systems (SEISCON 2013), pp. 374–379. Institution of Engineering and Technology (2013)

45. Meziane, F., Vadera, S.: Obtaining E-R diagrams semi-automatically from natural language specifications, pp. 638–642 (2004)

46. Geetha, S., AnandhaMala, G.S.: Automatic database construction from natural language requirements specification text. ARPN J. Eng. Appl. Sci. **9**(8), 1260–1266 (2014)

47. Ben Abdessalem Karaa, W., Ben Azzouz, Z., Singh, A., Dey, N., Ashour, A.S., Ben Ghazala, H.: Automatic builder of class diagram (ABCD): an application of UML generation from functional requirements. Softw. Pract. Exp. **39**(7) (2015)

48. Deeptimahanti, D.K., Sanyal, R.: Semi-automatic generation of UML models from natural language requirements. In: Proceedings of the 4th India Software Engineering Conference on - ISEC 2011, pp. 165–174 (2011)

49. Liu, D., Subramaniam, K., Eberlein, A., Far, B.H.: Natural language requirements analysis and class model generation using UCDA. In: Orchard, B., Yang, C., Ali, M. (eds.) IEA/AIE 2004. LNCS (LNAI), vol. 3029, pp. 295–304. Springer, Heidelberg (2004). https://doi.org/10.1007/978-3-540-24677-0_31

50. Fatwanto, A.: Software requirements translation from natural language to object-oriented model. In: Proceedings of 2012 IEEE Conference on Control, Systems and Industrial Informatics, ICCSII 2012, pp. 191–195 (2012)

51. Fatwanto, A.: Translating software requirements from natural language to formal specification. In: Proceeding - 2012 IEEE International Conference on Computational Intelligence and Cybernetics, CyberneticsCom 2012, pp. 148–152 (2012)

52. Gordon, M., Harel, D.: Generating executable scenarios from natural language. In: Gelbukh, A. (ed.) CICLing 2009. LNCS, vol. 5449, pp. 456–467. Springer, Heidelberg (2009). https://doi.org/10.1007/978-3-642-00382-0_37

53. Vidya Sagar, V.B.R., Abirami, S.: Conceptual modeling of natural language functional requirements. J. Syst. Softw. **88**(1), 25–41 (2014)

54. Rui, S.: Translating software requirement from natural language to automaton. In: Proceedings 2013 International Conference on Mechatronic Sciences, Electric Engineering and Computer (MEC), pp. 2456–2459 (2013)

Model-Based Analysis
of Temporal Properties

Maria Spichkova[✉]

RMIT University, Melbourne, Australia
maria.spichkova@rmit.edu.au

Abstract. In our previous work, we introduced a framework for property-based testing applied on formal models with temporal properties. In this paper, we discuss model-based approaches for analysis of temporal properties of safety-critical systems more deeply. We also discuss the core features of FOCUS^{ST}, framework for formal specification and analysis of temporal and spatial properties of safety-critical systems. To illustrate the feasibility of the framework, we demonstrate how to implement on its basis time-triggered and event-based view on systems with temporal properties.

Keywords: Formal methods · Verification · Testing
Temporal properties

1 Background

Safety-critical systems, e.g., in the automotive domain [18], become more and more software-intensive with every year. While specifying such systems, a precise formal model, i.e., a mathematical model at some level of abstraction, might be essential to eliminate ambiguity and to detect possible errors early in the software development life-cycle (SDL). Verification and testing of the temporal aspects is crucial, as the properties of safety-critical systems have to be analysed in relation to the time in many cases.

In this paper, we are going to focus of the analysis of temporal properties using Formal Methods (FMs). Despite all the advantages of FMs, software engineers are not keen to include them into the software development process. This problem was discussed 15–20 years ago, e.g., in [16]. This problem is still unsolved now. Lack of readability and usability is one of the reasons for very limited use of FMs in industrial projects [38]. However, in some cases even simply implementable improvements can make an FM more readable and understandable, cf. [22].

In our previous work [3,4], we presented a framework for property-based testing applying for temporal formal models. *Property-based testing* allows for the use of randomly generated tests based on systems properties to test systems against their specifications, where one test case can be executed hundreds of

© Springer International Publishing AG, part of Springer Nature 2018
E. Damiani et al. (Eds.): ENASE 2017, CCIS 866, pp. 208–223, 2018.
https://doi.org/10.1007/978-3-319-94135-6_10

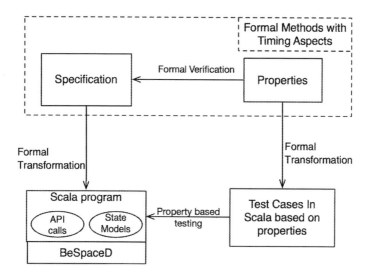

Fig. 1. Framework for property-based testing that we proposed in [4].

times with different input values. An example of such library in Haskell programming language is QuickCheck [12].

The core idea of the framework proposed in [4] is illustrated by Fig. 1. We start by specifying the system using human-oriented formal modelling techniques. The model can be also verified wrt. system properties. The system under test is then designed according to this formal model. The framework then generates random test cases (based on system properties) to check that the system runs according to the specification. If a test fails, the corresponding parts of the system and specification have to be analysed to identify the error. If the test passes, the system under test meets the specification.

The workflow within the framework includes the following steps:

– To specify system requirements using natural language;
– To transform the requirements specification to a formal specification (model) of the system, e.g., in Focus^{ST} [30];
– To verify formal model, e.g., using Isabelle/HOL theorem prover [20];
– To translate the formal model to Scala using the provided translation schema;
– To add the specified in Scala model to the extended ScalaCheck library;
– To check the extended ScalaCheck library against the behaviour generated from the formal specification.

In our current work, we would like to discuss the first steps of the workflow in more details, focusing on readability of formal models with timing aspects.

Outline: The rest of the paper is structured as follows. Section 2 discusses the core features of Focus^{ST} language and presents time-triggered view on systems with temporal properties. Section 3 presents event-based view on systems with temporal properties. Section 4 concludes the paper by highlighting the main contributions, and introduces the future work directions.

2   Time-Triggered View: FocusST

The FocusST [30] language was inspired by Focus [8], a framework for formal specification and development of interactive systems. In both languages, specifications are based on the notion of *streams*. However, in the original Focus input and output streams of a component are mappings of natural numbers $\mathbb{N}$ to single messages, whereas a FocusST stream is a mapping from $\mathbb{N}$ to lists of messages within the corresponding time intervals. Moreover, the syntax of FocusST is particularly devoted to specify spatial (S) and timing (T) aspects in a comprehensible fashion, which is the reason to extend the name of the language by ST.

The FocusST specification layout is similar to Focus (which layout was inspired by Z specification language, cf. [34,35]), but it has many new features to increase the readability and understandability of the specification. The FocusST specification layout is based on human factor analysis within formal methods [22,23,31]. It allows to create concise but easily understandable specifications and is appropriate for application of the specification and proof methodology presented in [27]. This methodology allows to create specifications in a way that carrying out proofs is quite simple and scalable to practical problems. In particular, a specification of a system can be translated to a Higher-Order Logic and verified by the interactive semi-automatic theorem prover Isabelle [20] also applying its component Sledgehammer [5]. Sledgehammer employs resolution based first-order automatic theorem provers and satisfiability modulo theories solvers to discharge goals arising in interactive proofs. Other advantages of *Focus on Isabelle* are

- well-developed theory of composition;
- representation of processes within a system [29];
- feasibility demonstrated by number of auto motive case studies, also formalising the core aspects of the FlexRay communication protocol [11,13,14,17,19,24–26,32].

In FocusST specifications, input and output streams of a component are always timed, as spatio-temporal aspects are the core of the framework. The (timed) streams are mappings from $\mathbb{N}$ to lists of messages within the corresponding time intervals. Thus, these streams are infinite per default, but they could be empty completely or from a certain point which is represented by empty time intervals $\langle \rangle$. More precisely, FocusST has streams of two kinds:

- *Infinite timed streams* (denoted by M^{∞}) are used to represent the input and the output streams;
- *finite timed streams* (denoted by M^{*}) are used to argue about a timed stream that was truncated at some point of time.

Infinite timed streams of type T are defined by a functional type

$$\mathbb{N} \rightarrow T^{*}$$

Finite timed streams of type T are defined by list of lists over this type, i.e.,

$$(T^*)^*$$

where T^* denotes a list of elements of type T.

We specify every component using assumption-guarantee-structured templates, to avoid the omission of unnecessary assumptions about the system's environment: the component has to fulfil the guarantee part of the specification only if its environment behaves in accordance with the assumption part of the specification.

To make our formal language better understandable for programmers, we use in FOCUS^{ST} so-called *implicit else-case* constructs: If a variable is not listed in the guarantee part of a transition, it implicitly keeps its current value, cf. also [29]. An output stream not mentioned in a transition will be empty.

Specifying a component we often have that for some cases both hold: local variables (i.e., the current system state) still be unchanged and there is no output. This can occur, e.g., if at this time interval the component receives no input or if some preconditions (that are necessary to produce the corresponding output) don't hold. In classical FOCUS we need to specify such cases explicitly, otherwise we get an underspecified component that has no information how it must act if it gets no input or if some preconditions don't hold. However, this optimization is not applicable to component representing functionality of timers or counters, because a counter-variable must be also changed even if the component gets no input.

The formal background on FOCUS^{ST} is presented in [27,30], but we would like to mention very shortly a small number of operators we used in the paper:

- $\langle\rangle$ – denotes an empty stream,
- $\langle x \rangle$ – denotes one element stream consisting of the element x,
- ft.l – returns the first element of an untimed stream l (e.g., the first element of a list),
- s^i – returns the ith time interval of the stream s,
- $\text{msg}_n(s)$ – returns *true*, if the stream s has at most n messages at each time interval (an *n-bounded stream*),
- $\text{ts}(r)$ – returns *true*, if the stream r has exactly one message at each time interval (so called *time-synchronous* stream).

To represent real objects that can physically change their location in space, we define so-called *sp-objects*. An sp-object is defined not only by its behavioural specification but also by a tuple

$$<location, speed, direction, radius, occupied space>$$

In FOCUS^{ST} this tuple is specified using

- a special global (in the scope of the system specification) constant *rad* associated with an elementary so-object to represent the radius of the maximal space the sp-object can "cover" in the worst case; In the case an sp-object S is a composition (system) of a number of other sp-objects, we calculate its *rad* by analysing which space its subcomponents can occupy in the worst case:

$$S.rad = max(WCX, WCY)/2$$

WCX and WCY being the maximum extensions of all of the subcomponents of S in direction x respective y;

– four special global (in the scope of the system specification) variables to store for each sp-object its
  - current *location* $\in$ *Space* (i.e., central point of the sp-object),
  - current *speed* $\in \mathbb{N}$,
  - current *direction* $\in$ *Directions*, and
  - current *rzone* $\in$ *Zone*.

The type *Space* is a tuple of two Cartesian coordinates defined over $\mathbb{N}$:

$$Space \overset{\text{def}}{=} \mathbb{N} \times \mathbb{N}$$

The type *Directions* represents an angle in the Cartesian coordinate system:

$$Directions \overset{\text{def}}{=} \{0, \dots, 359\}$$

The type *Zone* is a tuple of Cartesian coordinates of two spatial points X and y ($minX, minY, maxX, maxY$) defined over $\mathbb{N}$, where X correspond to the upper left corner and Y corresponds to the upper right corner of the corresponding zone.

$$Space \overset{\text{def}}{=} \mathbb{N} \times \mathbb{N} \times \mathbb{N} \times \mathbb{N}$$

The behavioural specification of the corresponding component can contain constrains on the speed, direction, and location of the so-object as well as on spatio-temporal dependencies among the so-objects in the system. While verifying the corresponding properties we can ensure, for example, that the object does not exceed its speed limit, does enter specific areas or does not collide with another so-object.

For composite so-objects we also have additional constraints:

$\forall S, C : C \in subcomp(S) \rightarrow$
$\quad (S.rzone.minX \leq S.C.rzone.minX \wedge S.rzone.minY \leq S.C.rzone.minY) \wedge$
$\quad (S.rzone.maxX \geq S.C.rzone.maxX \wedge S.rzone.maxY \geq S.C.rzone.maxY)$

$\forall k, S, C : C \in subcomp(S) \rightarrow$
$\quad (k \leq S.rzone.minX \rightarrow (k + S.C.rad) \leq S.C.location.xx)$

2.1 TSTD

Alur and Dill [1,2] introduced timed automata that are nowadays one of the most well-established models for the specification and verification of real-time system design. Timed automata have many advantages and many application areas, but they assume perfect continuity of clocks which may not suit to specification of embedded system with instantaneous reaction times. Timed automata also do not prevent Zeno runs [15]: an infinite number of transitions in a finite period of time cannot be excluded. This problem was solved in an extended version of timed automata presented [7,21]. Focus^{ST} provides a completely different solution to this problem: the Zeno runs are excluded on the syntactical level.

The Focus^{ST} specifications are a special form of timed automata that we name *Timed State Transition Diagrams* (TSTDs). A TSTD can be described in both diagram and textual form. For easier argumentation, we can further represent it by a special kind of tables including a number of new operators that work on time intervals.

For any real-time system S with syntactic interface $(I_S \rhd O_S)$, where I_S is a set of input timed streams $i_1 \in I_1^\infty, \ldots, i_m \in I_m^\infty$, and O_S is a set of output timed streams $o_1 \in O_1^\infty, \ldots, o_n \in O_n^\infty$, we can define the corresponding timed state transition diagram $TSTD(S)$ by a tuple

$$(State, state_0, I_S, O_S, \rightarrow),$$

where $State$ is a set of states, $state_0 \in State$ is the initial state, and the function $\rightarrow$ $\subseteq State \times I_S \times State \times O_S$ represents the transition function of the TSTD.

Thus, an input action for a TSTD is the set of current time intervals of the input streams of the system, where the output action is the set of corresponding time intervals of the input streams of the system: in the case of a weak-causal system the output must be produced within the same time interval the input is consumed, but in the case of a strongly causal system the output must be produced within a delay in at least one time unit – this delay must be defined according to the timing requirements on the specified system.

A tiTable for a system S looks in general as follows:

tiTable $STable$ (univ $u_1, \ldots, u_k$) : $\forall\, t \in \mathbb{N}$ where $a_1, \ldots, a_w$

	i_1	$\ldots$	i_m	o_1	$\ldots$	o_n	v_1'	$\ldots$	v_p'	Preconditions
1										
2										
$\ldots$										
N										

N is here the number of table lines in the table, $v_1, \ldots, v_p$ denote the local variables of the system S, while $u_1, \ldots, u_k$ and $a_1, \ldots, a_w$ represent respectively universal variables and some abbreviations used within the system. By v_i' we denote the value of the local variable v_i after the transition, i.e., the value at the time interval $t + 1$.

If it is not enough to use the weak causality and the *strong causality* is needed, i.e., a component should have a delay of k ($k > 0$) time units, the following notation for the tiTable-head must be used: if the column of an output stream o_i is labelled by o_i^k, then the corresponding output will be produced with the delay k. Arguing about time intervals we can ensure the causality property of a defined component (or system), specifying time interval values of output streams via input and local values from the previous (in the case of strong causality) or the same (in the case of weak causality) time intervals.

A TSTD can be also rewritten in a purely textual manner: each table line (in the case of a diagram, each transition) can be specified as a single formula in the gar-part of the specification, the rewriting scheme is straightforward.

Example 1. Let us discuss a simple timer specification. The component *Timer* is strongly-causal with a delay of one time unit, and has two input channels, both of type $\mathbb{N}$: *set* to set the timer, and *dataIn* to get the input data: if the timer is off, the data can be transmitted via the output channel *dataOut*. The second output channel *resp* of type $\{timeout\}$ is used to signal the timeout. The FOCUS^{ST} specification of this component is presented in Fig. 2.

Timer		timed
in	$set, dataIn : \mathbb{N}$	
out	$resp : \mathbb{N}; \ dataOut : \{timeout\}$	
local	$locCounter \in \mathbb{N}$	
univ	$k \in \mathbb{N}, x \in \mathbb{N}^*$	
init	$locCounter = 0$	
asm	$\mathsf{msg}_1(set)$	
gar	tiTable $TimerTable$	

Fig. 2. FOCUS^{ST} specification of a simple timer.

At every time interval this component can receive at most one message of type $\mathbb{N}$ via the channel *set* and a finite sequence of natural numbers via the channel *dataIn*. If the timer receives a number k, $k > 0$ via the channel *set*, it waits k time intervals (counts down starting from k) and gives out the timeout signal *timeout*. During countdown the input data on channel *dataIn* are ignored. If any time a new *set*-message comes, the timer will be restarted, however, if this message is 0, timer is set to 0 and gives out the *timeout*-signal immediately. Below you can see the tiTable representation of *TimerTSTD*.

tiTable *Timer Table* (univ $x : \mathbb{N}^*, k : \mathbb{N}) : \forall t \in \mathbb{N}$

	set	*dataIn*	*resp*	*dataOut*	*locCounter′*	Preconditions
1	$\langle\rangle$	x	$\langle\rangle$	x	0	$locCounter = 0$
2	$\langle 0\rangle$	x	$\langle timeout\rangle$	x	0	
3	$\langle k\rangle$	x	$\langle\rangle$	x	k	$locCounter = 0,\ k > 0$
4	$\langle k\rangle$	x	$\langle\rangle$	$\langle\rangle$	k	$locCounter > 0,\ k > 0$
5	$\langle\rangle$	x	$\langle\rangle$	$\langle\rangle$	$locCounter - 1$	$locCounter > 1$
6	$\langle\rangle$	x	$\langle timeout\rangle$	x	0	$locCounter = 1$

Finally, we present the timer specification in textual style: Fig. 3 demonstrates a $\textsc{Focus}^{ST}$ specification *TimerInTextualStyle*, where Fig. 4 demonstrates how the same specification would look like without any optimisations discussed at the beginning of Sect. 2 (the additional Formulas 1 and 2 in the guarantee-part of this specification, define initial output values).

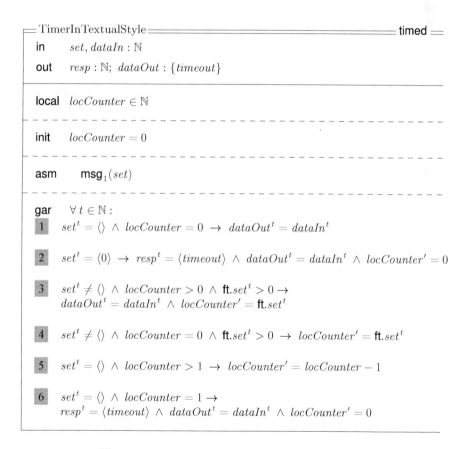

Fig. 3. $\textsc{Focus}^{ST}$ specification of a simple timer: Textual style with optimisation.

The component is strongly causal, therefore we need to define not only the initial value of the local variable, but also the output of the component during the first time interval. We can easily change the delay of the component to some natural number l, $l > 1$: we just replace $t + 1$ in the specification of the output streams by $t + l$ and add the specification of the initial outputs (component outputs at time intervals $0, \ldots, l - 1$). Moreover, we can define this delay as a parameter of the component.   □

Fig. 4. FocusST specification of a simple timer: Textual style without optimisation.

2.2   Operating over Time Intervals

Arguing over time intervals we can use predefined operators to make specification more readable. In this section we present only a small number of these operators to give a better feeling how our approach can be used to specify a system.

An often used operation over timed streams is *concatenation of a number of time intervals* ($\frown$ is a standard FOCUS operator to concatenate two sequences). The operator $\mathsf{ti}^k(s, n)$ denotes the sequence of messages that are present on the channel s at the time interval between ticks $n - 1$ and $n + k$:

$$\mathsf{ti}^k(s, n) = s^n \frown \ldots \frown s^{n+k}$$

We define this operator formally as follows:

$$\mathsf{ti}^k(s, n) \stackrel{def}{=} \begin{cases} s^n & if \quad k = 0 \\ \mathsf{ti}^{k-1}(s, n) \frown s^{n+k} & otherwise \end{cases} \tag{1}$$

The *timed merge operator* $\mathsf{merge}^{ti}(s, r)$ concatenates the sequences of messages that are present on the channels (streams) s and r at the same time interval:

$$\forall\, t.\ \mathsf{merge}^{ti}(s, r)^t = s^t \frown r^t \tag{2}$$

Example 2. Applying the timed merge operator to the timed streams s_1 and s_2,

$$s_1 = \langle\langle a_1\rangle, \langle a_2, a_3\rangle, \langle\rangle, \langle a_4, a_5, a_6\rangle, \langle a_7, a_8, a_9, a_{10}\rangle, \langle\rangle, \ldots\rangle, \quad \text{and}$$
$$s_2 = \langle\langle b_1, b_2\rangle, \langle\rangle, \langle b_3\rangle, \langle\rangle, \langle b_4\rangle, \langle\rangle, \langle b_5\rangle, \langle\rangle, \ldots\rangle,$$

we get the following timed stream

$$\mathsf{merge}^{ti}(s_1, s_2) = \langle\langle a_1, b_1, b_2\rangle, \langle a_2, a_3\rangle, \langle b_3\rangle, \langle a_4, a_5, a_6\rangle, \langle a_7, a_8, a_9, a_{10}, b_4\rangle, \langle\rangle, \ldots\rangle$$

Zeno runs are excluded in the streams s_1 and s_2 by definition. This holds also for a stream we get after applying the merge operator.   □

Using operators over time intervals we can also represent such properties as changing time granularity, (un)timed simulation, etc.

2.3   Changing Time Granularity

In many cases it is useful to change time granularity of the specification (also named *frequency of the streams* or *time raster*, see [9,10]).

The operator $s \wedge_n$ refines the time granularity splitting every time interval of the stream s into n time intervals in such a way that all messages from the original time interval belong to the first of the n new intervals:

$$\wedge \in M^{\underline{\omega}} \times \mathbb{N} \to M^{\underline{\omega}}$$
$$s \wedge_n^t \stackrel{def}{=} \begin{cases} s^{t/n} & \mathrm{mod}(t, n) = 0 \\ \langle\rangle & otherwise \end{cases} \tag{3}$$

Surely, ones can define other versions of time refinement, e.g., (i) all messages from the time interval of the original stream belong to the *last* of the n corresponding intervals; (ii) the messages from the time interval of the original stream are distributed to the n corresponding intervals. We choose this one because in our experience, the mostly used kind of streams are 1-bounded streams (which can have at most one message at each time interval).

The operator $s \curlyvee_n$ makes the time granularity more coarse – it joins n time intervals of the stream s into a single time interval:

$$\curlyvee \in M^{\underline{\omega}} \times \mathbb{N}_+ \to M^{\underline{\omega}}$$
$$s \curlyvee_n^t \stackrel{def}{=} \mathrm{ti}^{n-1}(s, n * t) \tag{4}$$

Theorem 1. *For any infinite timed stream x and for any natural number $n > 0$ the following equation holds:*

$$(x \curlywedge_n) \curlyvee_n = x \qquad \square$$

Example 3. Let discuss the case of duplication of the time raster illustrated by Fig. 5. It is easy to see that applying operators $\curlywedge$ and $\curlyvee$ we always get a timed stream where Zeno runs are excluded.

Streams x and y are defined here as simplification of Eqs. 3 and 4, i.e., the relations $y = x \curlywedge_2$ and $y \curlyvee_2 = x$ hold.

$$x \curlywedge_2^t \stackrel{def}{=} \begin{cases} x^{t/2} & \mathrm{even}(t) \\ \langle\rangle & \mathrm{otherwise} \end{cases}$$

$$y \curlyvee_2^t \stackrel{def}{=} y^{2*t} \frown y^{2*t+1} \qquad \square$$

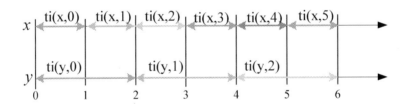

Fig. 5. Duplicated time raster.

2.4   Untimed Causal Simulation

Using the representation via time intervals we can also define a simulation relation defining the property of untimed equivalence of two streams. The *untimed causal simulation* of the streams x and y, denoted $x \dashrightarrow y$, in comparison to the equivalence of the untimed versions of these streams, takes into account the causality property.

We define the untimed causal simulation $x \dashrightarrow y$ of two streams x and y by

$$x \dashrightarrow y \overset{\text{def}}{=} x \overset{0}{\dashrightarrow} y \tag{5}$$

where $x \overset{i}{\dashrightarrow} y$ is defined for all $i \in \mathbb{N}$ as follows:

$$x \overset{0}{\dashrightarrow} y \ \wedge \ x^1 = \langle\rangle \ \Rightarrow \ y^1 = \langle\rangle \ \wedge \ x\uparrow_1 \overset{0}{\dashrightarrow} y\uparrow_1$$

$$x \overset{i}{\dashrightarrow} y \ \wedge \ x^1 = \langle\rangle \ \wedge \ i \neq 0$$

$$\Rightarrow \ y^1 = \langle\rangle \Rightarrow x\uparrow_1 \overset{i}{\dashrightarrow} y\uparrow_1 \ \wedge \ y^1 \neq \langle\rangle \Rightarrow x\uparrow_1 \overset{i-1}{\dashrightarrow} y$$

$$x \overset{i}{\dashrightarrow} y \ \wedge \ x^1 \neq \langle\rangle$$

$$\Rightarrow (y^1 = \langle\rangle \Rightarrow x \overset{i+1}{\dashrightarrow} y\uparrow_1) \wedge (y^1 \neq \langle\rangle \Rightarrow x\uparrow_1 \overset{i}{\dashrightarrow} y\uparrow_1 \wedge y^1 = x^1)$$

Theorem 2. *For any two infinite timed streams x and y the following relation holds ($\overline{x}$ and $\overline{y}$ denote the untimed versions of streams x and y respectively):*

$$x \dashrightarrow y \Rightarrow \overline{x} = \overline{y}$$

$\square$

Please note that the implication does not hold in the opposite direction, i.e., the relation $x \dashrightarrow y \Leftarrow \overline{x} = \overline{y}$ does not hold in general.

Theorem 3. *For any two infinite timed streams x and y the following relation holds:*

$$x \dashrightarrow y \wedge y \dashrightarrow x \Leftrightarrow x = y$$

$\square$

Example 4. Let x, y and z be infinite timed streams and let s_1, s_2, s_3 denote the sequences of message that represents some time intervals of these streams.

time interval	1	2	3	4	5	6	7	8	9	10	11	12	13	14	
x	$\langle\rangle$	s_1	$\langle\rangle$	s_2	$\langle\rangle$	s_3	$\langle\rangle$	$\langle\rangle$	s_1	$\langle\rangle$	s_2	$\langle\rangle$	s_3	$\langle\rangle$	...
y	$\langle\rangle$	$\langle\rangle$	$\langle\rangle$	s_1	s_2	$\langle\rangle$	s_3	$\langle\rangle$	$\langle\rangle$	$\langle\rangle$	s_1	s_2	$\langle\rangle$	s_3	...
z	s_1	$\langle\rangle$	s_2	$\langle\rangle$	$\langle\rangle$	$\langle\rangle$	s_3	s_1	$\langle\rangle$	s_2	$\langle\rangle$	$\langle\rangle$	$\langle\rangle$	s_3	...

The untimed versions of these streams are equal

$$\overline{x} = \overline{y} = \overline{z} = \langle s_1, s_2, s_3, s_1, s_2, s_3, \ldots \rangle$$

however, the untimed causal simulation holds only for the pair of streams x and y, and for the pair of streams z and y: $x \dashrightarrow y$ and $z \dashrightarrow y$, while the relations $x \dashrightarrow z$, $y \dashrightarrow x$, $y \dashrightarrow z$, and $z \dashrightarrow x$ do not hold. $\square$

3 Event-Based View: Focus^E

To deal with event based systems, we suggest inheriting the Focus^{ST} syntax accompanied with different semantics. For simplicity, we call the new version of the language Focus^E. In Focus^E, input and output streams of a component are mappings of natural numbers $\mathbb{N}$ to lists of messages, like in Focus^{ST}. However, in Focus^E these lists represent not the messages within the corresponding *time intervals*, but messages within the same *causality intervals*. We can see causality intervals as an abstract view of time intervals (cf. also Fig. 6):

- If messages belong to the same causality interval, this means that according to the system's clock these messages come simultaneously,
- If some message a belongs to the causality interval i (from the timed point of view it belongs to some time interval t), and some message b belongs to the causality interval $i + 1$, this does not necessary mean that B should belong to the time interval $t + 1$, because the causality property insure only the fact "event b happens after event a". Thus, b should belong to the time interval $t + \delta$, where $\delta > 0$.

In special case, a causality intervals of a stream can be equal to time interval of this stream.

Each message can be seen as a *single event*, but we can also have an additional view on the streams, where a set of messages (single events) from the same causality interval can be denoted as a *combined event*.

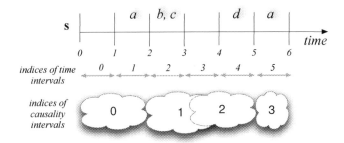

Fig. 6. Time intervals vs. causality intervals.

We suggest the following notation for Focus^E an additional operator $s^{(i)}$ to represent the ith time interval of the stream s.

For the example presented on Fig. 6, we have that

$$s^0 = \langle\rangle, \ s^1 = \langle a\rangle, \ s^2 = \langle b, c\rangle, \ s^3 = \langle\rangle, \ s^4 = \langle d\rangle, \ s^5 = \langle a\rangle,$$

and

$$s^{(0)} = \langle a\rangle, s^{(1)} = \langle b, c\rangle, s^{(2)} = \langle d\rangle, s^{(3)} = \langle a\rangle.$$

From purely syntactical point of view, if we take a timed (FOCUS^{ST}) stream and remove all empty timed intervals from it, we obtain an event (FOCUS^E) stream.

Correspondingly, we can define operators over events' causality, e.g., to denote that the ith causality interval of a stream s_1 occurs before the jth causality interval of a stream s_2, to denote that events of some type should occur in the stream always before some instances of messages of other type, etc.

4   Conclusions

In this paper, we discuss model-based approaches for analysis of temporal properties of safety-critical systems, to expand the ideas presented in our previous works [3,4] on property-based testing and its application on formal models with temporal properties.

One of the core parts of our approach for property-based testing, FOCUS^{ST}, framework for formal specification and analysis of temporal and spatial properties of safety-critical systems. In this paper we discuss the features of FOCUS^{ST} more deeply. To illustrate the feasibility of the framework, we demonstrate how to implement on its basis time-triggered and event-based view on systems with temporal properties.

The following directions of the future work might be especially promising:

- To combine the presented ideas with analysis of cloud computing tasks, e.g., with Chiminey Computing and Data Management Platform [37],
- To apply the framework for property-based testing to the analysis of cyber-virtual Systems [6], as well as
- To expand human-centred features of FOCUS^{ST} by combining with approaches presented in [28,33,36].

References

1. Alur, R., Madhusudan, P.: Decision problems for timed automata: a survey. In: Bernardo, M., Corradini, F. (eds.) SFM-RT 2004. LNCS, vol. 3185, pp. 1–24. Springer, Heidelberg (2004). https://doi.org/10.1007/978-3-540-30080-9_1
2. Alur, R., Dill, D.L.: A theory of timed automata. Theor. Comput. Sci. **126**, 183–235 (1994)
3. Alzahrani, N., Spichkova, M., Blech, J.O.: Spatio-temporal models for formal analysis and property-based testing. In: Milazzo, P., Varró, D., Wimmer, M. (eds.) STAF 2016. LNCS, vol. 9946, pp. 196–206. Springer, Cham (2016). https://doi.org/10.1007/978-3-319-50230-4_14
4. Alzahrani, N., Spichkova, M., Blech, J.O.: From temporal models to property-based testing. In: 11th International Conference on Evaluation of Novel Approaches to Software Engineering (ENASE), pp. 241–246. SCITEPRESS (2017)
5. Blanchette, J.C., Böhme, S., Paulson, L.C.: Extending Sledgehammer with SMT solvers. In: Bjørner, N., Sofronie-Stokkermans, V. (eds.) CADE 2011. LNCS (LNAI), vol. 6803, pp. 116–130. Springer, Heidelberg (2011). https://doi.org/10.1007/978-3-642-22438-6_11

6. Blech, J.O., Spichkova, M., Peake, I., Schmidt, H.: Visualization, simulation and validation for cyber-virtual systems. In: Maciaszek, L.A., Filipe, J. (eds.) ENASE 2014. CCIS, vol. 551, pp. 140–154. Springer, Cham (2015). https://doi.org/10.1007/978-3-319-27218-4_10

7. Bouyer, P., Markey, N., Sankur, O.: Robust model-checking of timed automata via pumping in channel machines. In: Fahrenberg, U., Tripakis, S. (eds.) FORMATS 2011. LNCS, vol. 6919, pp. 97–112. Springer, Heidelberg (2011). https://doi.org/10.1007/978-3-642-24310-3_8

8. Broy, M., Stølen, K.: Specification and Development of Interactive Systems: Focus on Streams, Interfaces, and Refinement. Springer, New York (2001). https://doi.org/10.1007/978-1-4613-0091-5

9. Broy, M.: Refinement of time. Theor. Comput. Sci. **253**(1), 3–26 (2001)

10. Broy, M.: Time, abstraction, causality and modularity in interactive systems: extended abstract. Electr. Notes Theor. Comput. Sci. **108**, 3–9 (2004)

11. Broy, M., Fox, J., Hölzl, F., Koss, D., Kuhrmann, M., Meisinger, M., Penzenstadler, B., Rittmann, S., Schätz, B., Spichkova, M., Wild, D.: Service-oriented modeling of CoCoME with Focus and AutoFocus. In: Rausch, A., Reussner, R., Mirandola, R., Plášil, F. (eds.) The Common Component Modeling Example. LNCS, vol. 5153, pp. 177–206. Springer, Heidelberg (2008). https://doi.org/10.1007/978-3-540-85289-6_8

12. Claessen, K., Hughes, J.: QuickCheck: a lightweight tool for random testing of haskell programs. SIGPLAN Not. **46**(4), 53–64 (2011)

13. Feilkas, M., Fleischmann, A., Hölzl, F., Pfaller, C., Rittmann, S., Scheidemann, K., Spichkova, M., Trachtenherz, D.: A top-down methodology for the development of automotive software. Technical report TUM-I0902 (2009)

14. Feilkas, M., Hlzl, F., Pfaller, C., Rittmann, S., Schtz, B., Schwitzer, W., Sitou, W., Spichkova, M., Trachtenherz, D.: A refined top-down methodology for the development of automotive software systems - the KeylessEntry-system case study. Technical report TUM-I1103, TU München (2011)

15. Gómez, R., Bowman, H.: Efficient detection of Zeno runs in timed automata. In: Raskin, J.-F., Thiagarajan, P.S. (eds.) FORMATS 2007. LNCS, vol. 4763, pp. 195–210. Springer, Heidelberg (2007). https://doi.org/10.1007/978-3-540-75454-1_15

16. Hinchey, M.G.: Confessions of a formal methodist. In: Safety Critical Systems and Software, pp. 17–20. ACS (2003)

17. Kühnel, C., Spichkova, M.: Upcoming automotive standards for fault-tolerant communication: FlexRay and OSEKtime FTCom. In: Proceedings of EFTS 2006 International Workshop on Engineering of Fault Tolerant Systems (2006)

18. Kühnel, C., Spichkova, M.: Fault-tolerant communication for distributed embedded systems. In: Pelliccione, P. (ed.) Software Engineering of Fault Tolerance Systems, vol. 19, p. 175. World Scientific Publishing, Singapore (2007)

19. Kühnel, C., Spichkova, M.: FlexRay und FTCom: Formale Spezifikation in FOCUS. Technical report TUM-I0601, TU München (2006)

20. Nipkow, T., Wenzel, M., Paulson, L.C. (eds.): Isabelle/HOL: A Proof Assistant for Higher-Order Logic. LNCS, vol. 2283. Springer, Heidelberg (2002). https://doi.org/10.1007/3-540-45949-9

21. Puri, A.: Dynamical properties of timed automata. Discrete Event Dyn. Syst. **10**(1–2), 87–113 (2000)

22. Spichkova, M.: Human factors of formal methods. In: IADIS Interfaces and Human Computer Interaction 2012 (2012)

23. Spichkova, M.: Design of Formal Languages and Interfaces: "Formal" Does Not Mean "Unreadable". IGI Global, Hershey (2013)

24. Spichkova, M.: Stream processing components: Isabelle/HOL formalisation and case studies. Arch. Formal Proofs, 1–142 (2013)
25. Spichkova, M.: Compositional properties of crypto-based components. Arch. Formal Proofs, 1–42 (2014)
26. Spichkova, M.: FlexRay: verification of the FOCUS specification in Isabelle/HOL. A case study. Technical report TUM-I0602, TU München (2006)
27. Spichkova, M.: Specification and seamless verification of embedded real-time systems: FOCUS on Isabelle. Ph.D. thesis, Technical University Munich (2007)
28. Spichkova, M.: Architecture: requirements + decomposition + refinement. Softwaretechnik-Trends **31**(4), 1–4 (2011)
29. Spichkova, M.: Focus on processes. Technical report (TUM-I1115), TU München (2011)
30. Spichkova, M., Blech, J.O., Herrmann, P., Schmidt, H.W.: Modeling spatial aspects of safety-critical systems with FOCUS^{ST}. In: MoDeVVa, pp. 49–58 (2014)
31. Spichkova, M., Liu, H., Laali, M., Schmidt, H.W.: Human factors in software reliability engineering. In: Workshop on Applications of Human Error Research to Improve Software Engineering (2015)
32. Spichkova, M., Simic, M.: Towards formal modelling of autonomous systems. In: Damiani, E., Howlett, R., Jain, L., Gallo, L., De Pietro, G. (eds.) Intelligent Interactive Multimedia Systems and Services, pp. 279–288. Springer, Cham (2015). https://doi.org/10.1007/978-3-319-19830-9_25
33. Spichkova, M., Zamansky, A., Farchi, E.: Towards a human-centred approach in modelling and testing of cyber-physical systems. In: 2015 IEEE 21st International Conference on Parallel and Distributed Systems (ICPADS), pp. 847–851. IEEE (2015)
34. Spivey, M.: Understanding Z - A Specification Language and Its Formal Semantics. Cambridge Tracts in Theoretical Computer Science, vol. 3. Cambridge University Press, Cambridge (1988)
35. Spivey, M.: The Z Notation: A Reference Manual. Prentice-Hall International Series in Computer Science, 2 Ausgabe edn. Prentice-Hall, New York (1992)
36. Vo, P.T.N., Spichkova, M.: Model-based generation of natural language specifications. In: Milazzo, P., Varró, D., Wimmer, M. (eds.) STAF 2016. LNCS, vol. 9946, pp. 221–231. Springer, Cham (2016). https://doi.org/10.1007/978-3-319-50230-4_16
37. Yusuf, I.I., Thomas, I.E., Spichkova, M., Androulakis, S., Meyer, G.R., Drumm, D.W., Opletal, G., Russo, S.P., Buckle, A.M., Schmidt, H.W.: Chiminey: reliable computing and data management platform in the cloud. In: 37th International Conference on Software Engineering (ICSE 2015). IEEE Press (2015)
38. Zamansky, A., Rodriguez-Navas, G., Adams, M., Spichkova, M.: Formal methods in collaborative projects. In: 11th International Conference on Evaluation of Novel Approaches to Software Engineering. IEEE (2016)

Towards a Java Library to Support
Runtime Metaprogramming

Ignacio Lagartos, Jose Manuel Redondo, and Francisco Ortin$^{(\boxtimes)}$

Computer Science Department, University of Oviedo, 33007 Oviedo, Spain
{uo196684, redondojose, ortin}@uniovi.es

Abstract. Statically typed languages such as Java offer two key advantages: robustness increase due to compile time error detection, and better runtime performance caused by the reduction of runtime type checking. However, dynamic languages are sometimes preferred in scenarios where runtime adaptability is a strong requirement, such as building software capable of adapting to runtime changing environments. The metaprogramming features of dynamic languages allow the runtime adaptation of class and object structures, modifying inheritance relationships, and the evaluation of dynamically generated code. In this position paper, we describe the steps we are following to add to Java some of the metaprogramming services provided by most dynamic languages. The objective is to provide the runtime flexibility of structural intercession, dynamic inheritance and dynamic code evaluation, without losing the robustness of compile-time type checking. The metaprogramming services are provided as a library so, unlike other existing systems, any standard virtual machine and language implementation could be used.

Keywords: Java · Metaprogramming · Structural intercession
Dynamic inheritance · Dynamic code evaluation · Static typing
Early type error detection · Reflection API · Introspection

1 Introduction

Dynamic languages have turned out to be suitable for specific scenarios such as rapid prototyping, Web development, interactive programming, dynamic aspect-oriented programming, and runtime adaptive software [1]. Most dynamic languages provide metaprogramming services that allow treating programs like data, and modify them at runtime [2]. Fields and methods can be added and removed dynamically from classes and objects (structural intercession), and new pieces of code can be generated and evaluated at runtime, without stopping the application execution [3]. These services make it easier to develop runtime adaptable software in dynamic languages [4].

In order to provide that runtime adaptability, dynamic languages commonly implement a dynamic type system, postponing type checking until runtime. One limitation of this approach is that every type error is detected at runtime. On the contrary, statically typed languages such as Java and C# commonly detect many type errors at compile time, when the programmer is writing the code. This lack has been recognized as one of the limitations of dynamically typed languages [5]. The absence of compile-time type

© Springer International Publishing AG, part of Springer Nature 2018
E. Damiani et al. (Eds.): ENASE 2017, CCIS 866, pp. 224–242, 2018.
https://doi.org/10.1007/978-3-319-94135-6_11

information also involves fewer opportunities for compiler optimizations, and the extra runtime type checking commonly implies performance costs [6].

In previous works, we have inferred type information at compile time to provide early type error detection in dynamically typed code [7, 8]. In this work, we aim to provide metaprogramming services to the statically typed Java language. The objective is to increase the runtime adaptability of Java, without losing the early type error detection and runtime performance of its static type system.

The main contribution of this position paper is the description of a Java library aimed at providing metaprogrammning services, maintaining its static type system. Particularly, we intend to add structural intercession of classes and its existing objects at runtime, allowing the dynamic modification of their structure. We also provide the evaluation of dynamically generated Java code and changing the base class and the interfaces implemented by another class. This paper is an extension of the one published in [9], including how we plan to provide dynamic inheritance and a modification of the Java reflection API.

The rest of the paper is structured as follows. Section 2 describes the library interface with some excerpts of an example program. The different elements of the API are depicted in Sect. 3. Section 4 describes the related work, and the conclusions and future work are discussed in Sect. 5.

2 Library Interface

The metaprogramming services are provided as a library of the Java platform. We modify neither the Java Virtual Machine (JVM) nor the language implementation. Thus, unlike other approaches [10, 11], any standard JVM and Java compiler can be used.

To describe the interface of the library, this section presents an example that dynamically modifies the structure of the class shown in Fig. 1 [9].

```
1.    public class Dog {
2.        public void bark(){
3.            System.out.println("Woof!!");
4.        }
5.        public void shake(){
6.            System.out.println("Shakes");
7.        }
8.    }
```

Fig. 1. Example Java class [9].

2.1 Structural Intercession

The code in Fig. 2 [9] modifies the Dog class at runtime using structural intercession (read and write reflection) [12]. We add a name field to every Dog instance at runtime,

```
1.  // Create transaction
2.  IntercessorTransaction transaction = new IntercessorTransaction();
3.  // Add field name
4.  transaction.addField(Dog.class, String.class, "name");
5.  // Add get/set
6.  transaction.addMethod(Dog.class, "getName", MethodType.methodType(String.class),
                          "return name;");
7.  transaction.addMethod(Dog.class, "setName", MethodType.methodType(void.class,
                          String.class),"name = value;", "value");
8.  // Modify existing methods
9.  transaction.replaceImplementation(Dog.class, "bark",
                          "System.out.println(this.name + \": Woof!!\");");
10. transaction.replaceImplementation(Dog.class, "shake",
                          "System.out.println(this.name + \": Shakes\");");
11. // Execute transaction
12. transaction.commit();
13. // Get invoker for 'setName'
14. BiConsumer<Dog, String> setName = Intercessor.getInvoker(Dog.class, "setName",
15.                               BiConsumer.class, Dog.class, String.class);
15. // Check name field
16. String name = readLine("Name: ");
17. Dog dog = new Dog();
18. setName.accept(dog, name);
19. dog.bark();
```

```
Name: Rufus
Buddy: Woof!!
```

Fig. 2. Example adaptation of the Dog class using a transaction collecting 5 intercesive operations [9].

evolving the structure of the class. Besides this new field, we also add two new getName and setName methods. Moreover, the implementation of the existing bark and shake methods are modified, so that they consider the new name field.

The proposed library allows performing the five operations individually. Additionally, it also provides the execution of all the operations at the same time with the concept of transaction. Figure 2 creates one transaction (line 2) with the five operations (lines 4 to 10). Then, the transaction is executed atomically in line 12. If all the operations can be executed, the program continues; otherwise, no operation is performed. For example, if the body of setName has a type error (line 7) a CompilationFailedException exception error will be thrown and none of the five operations will be executed.

If we want to invoke a newly added method (e.g., setName), we should provide a new mechanism because that method is added later, when the application is running. A direct invocation to setName will not be compiled because that method does not exist at compilation time. For this purpose, our library provides the getInvoker method (line 14). It returns the standard BiConsumer interface added to Java 8 [13]. Its accept method executes setName, which was added at runtime. Unlike the Java reflection API, we generate statically typed code (at runtime), so we expect to obtain a significant performance benefit [14].

2.2 Dynamic Code Evaluation

We have just shown how the library provides structural intercession; we now describe how to obtain dynamic code evaluation (i.e., the `eval` function in Lisp, Python and JavaScript languages). Figure 3 [9] shows this capability.

```
20. // Overload 'bark' method
21. Intercessor.addMethod(Dog.class, "bark",
        MethodType.methodType(void.class, int.class),
        "for (int i = 0; i < times; i++) bark();", "times");
22. // Evaluate the call to overloaded method
23. BiConsumer<Dog, Integer> barkN =
        Evaluator.generateEvalInvoker("dog.bark(nTimes)",
        BiConsumer.class, new String[] {"dog", "nTimes" },
        Dog.class, int.class);
24. // Invoke overloaded method         Times: 3
25. int nTimes = readNumber("Times: ");  Buddy: Woof!!
26. barkN.accept(dog, nTimes);           Buddy: Woof!!
                                         Buddy: Woof!!
```

Fig. 3. Dynamic evaluation of a single expression [9].

Line 21 first adds another implementation of the `bark` method. This line shows how to perform a single intercesive operation without using a transaction. It also shows that methods could be overloaded at runtime, without breaking the rules of the type system. The following statements in Fig. 3 (lines 23 to 26) perform the dynamic evaluation of the string "`dog.bark(nTimes)`". It is important to notice that the code is represented as a string, and hence it can be built dynamically, depending on the runtime environment. That is to say, the code is evaluated dynamically (`dog` refers to the dynamic state of the dog object created in line 19, the same as `nTimes`).

We have just seen how to evaluate an expression dynamically. The proposed library also provides the evaluation of multiple statements, and even the creation of a whole class. Figure 4 [9] shows an example of that. A new `TrainedDog` class is added at runtime (line 29). This class extends the existing `Dog` class, which was modified at runtime (Figs. 2 and 3).

Line 28 in Fig. 4 asks for the code to be evaluated. The user dynamically writes the code with gray background color, which generates the new `TrainedDog` class. This class implements the `train` method that receives a function as a parameter (the standard `Consumer` Java 8 interface allows passing lambda expressions as arguments). Those functions can later be asked to the trained dog with the `order` method.

Line 36 creates an instance of a trained dog, trains it with the "shake" order (line 42) and orders it to shake (line 43). The output in Fig. 4 shows how the actions of the dog depend on its training. It also shows how a newly added class can extend another class defined statically, which in turn was modified dynamically.

All the metaprogramming operations are statically typed. If the code has a type error, the library dynamically throws a `CompilationFailedException`

```
27. // Add a subclass
28. String sourceClass = readLine("Code: ");
29. Class<?> TrainedDog = Evaluator.exec(sourceClass);
30. // Obtain invokers for subclass methods
31. TriConsumer<Dog, String, Consumer> train = Interceptor.getInvoker(TrainedDog,
        "train", TriConsumer.class, TrainedDog, String.class, Consumer.class);
32. BiConsumer<Dog, String> order = Interceptor.getInvoker(TrainedDog, "order",
        BiConsumer.class, TrainedDog, String.class);
33. // New order to train
34. Consumer<Dog> shake = Evaluator.generateEvalInvoker("dog.shake()",
        Consumer.class, new String[] { "dog" }, Dog.class);
35. // Create a TrainedDog instance
36. Dog trainedDog = (Dog)
        TrainedDog.newInstance();
37. // Set dog name
38. name = readLine("Name: ");
39. setName.accept(trainedDog, name);
40. // Test new functionality
41. order.accept(trainedDog, "shake");
42. train.accept(trainedDog, "shake", shake);
43. order.accept(trainedDog, "shake");
```

```
1.   package example;
2.
3.   import java.util.Map;
4.   import java.util.HashMap;
5.   import java.util.function.Consumer;
6.
7.   public class TrainedDog extends Dog {
8.
9.       private Map<String, Consumer<Dog>> trainedOrders =
                new HashMap<String, Consumer<Dog>>();
10.
11.      public void train(String order,
                    Consumer<Dog> action){
12.          trainedOrders.put(order, action);
13.          System.out.println(this.name + " learned "
                    + order + " order");
14.      }
15.      public void order(String order){
16.          Consumer<Dog> action = trainedOrders.get(order);
17.          if(action != null) action.accept(this);
18.          else System.out.println(this.name + " does nothing");
19.      }
20.  }
```

```
Code:
Name: Toby
Toby does nothing
Toby learned shake order
Toby: Shakes
```

Fig. 4. Dynamic evaluation of a Java file [9].

describing the compiler error. Besides, the dynamically generated code does not use reflection, so we avoid its runtime performance cost [15].

2.3 Dynamic Inheritance

Figure 5 shows how to use the some of the dynamic inheritance features provided by our library. We first create a transaction to both make Dog implement the Compa-rable <Dog> interface (line 48) and override the compareTo(Dog) method (line 50). The transaction is executed with no type errors. Since Dog instances are now Comparable, they can be ordered by name with Collections.sort (line 56).

The second paragraph of code in Fig. 5 changes the base class of Dog with the setSuperclass method (line 58). In this case, the Pet class is known statically, but it could be generated after executing the program. Class.forName should be used in that case. Since Dog now inherits age from Pet, lines 60-62 sort the dogs collection by age.

2.4 Introspection API

To provide the metaprogramming services, our library creates new versions of the existing classes at runtime (detailed in Sect. 3). Unfortunately, this implementation technique does not follow the programmer abstraction that classes are actually

```
45. // Create transaction
46. IntercessorTransaction addInterfaceTransaction = new IntercessorTransaction();
47. //Adds the Comparable<Dog> interface, specifying generic types
48. addInterfaceTransaction.addInterface(Dog.class, (Class<Comparable<Dog>>)Comparable.class);
49. //Adds a compareTo() method compatible with the Comparable<Dog> interface
50. addInterfaceTransaction.addMethod(Dog.class, "compareTo", MethodType.methodType(int.class,
                    Dog.class), "return this.name.compareTo(otherDog.name);", "otherDog");
51. // Execute transaction
52. addInterfaceTransaction.commit();

53. //Obtain a Dog list
54. List<Dog> dogs = getDogList();
55. //Sort as a Comparable (by dog name)
56. Evaluator.generateEvalInvoker(
        "Collections.sort(dogs);",
        Consumer.class, new String[] { "dogs" },
        List.class).accept(dogs);

57. //Change the superclass of Dog
58. Intercessor.setSuperclass(Dog.class, Pet.class);
59. //Lambda expression to sort using pet age
60. Comparator<Pet> sortCriteria = (pet1, pet2) -> pet1.getAge() - pet2.getAge();
61. //Sort using Pet attributes, since now is our parent class
62. Evaluator.generateEvalInvoker("Collections.sort(pets, criteria);", BiConsumer.class,
        new String[] { "pets", "criteria" }, List.class, Comparator.class).accept(dogs, sortCriteria);
```

```
1.  public class Pet {
2.      private String ownerName;
3.      public String getOwnerName() {…}
4.      public void setOwnerName(
5.                          String ownerName) {…}
6.      private int age;
7.      public int getAge() {…}
8.      public void setAge(int age) {…}
9.  }
```

Fig. 5. Dynamic inheritance.

modified. Although we modify the class implementation to provide the expected abstraction, the implementation details (i.e., different class versions) are shown when the programmer uses the Java reflection API.

We support an alternative reflection API to allow the use of introspection, maintaining the abstraction provided to the user. Figure 6 shows an example use. The Introspector class returns a Class instance reflecting the structure of the modified Dog. The rest of the code prints the interface implemented (Comparable) and its super class (Pet). As shown in Fig. 6, the code is the same as with the Java reflection API except for line 64. Besides, if the programmer needs to use the original reflection API, it is still available.

```
63. //Access a dog class information
64. Class dogClass = Introspector.getClass(dogs.get(0));
65. try {
66.     //Get current Dog implemented interfaces
67.     Class [] introspectionInterfaces = dogClass.getInterfaces();
68.     System.out.println(introspectionInterfaces[0]);
69.     //Get current Dog superclass
70.     Class introspectionSuperclass = dogClass.getSuperclass();
71.     System.out.println(introspectionSuperclass);
72. } catch (Exception e) {
73.     e.printStackTrace();
74. }
```

```
interface java.lang.Comparable
class Pet
```

Fig. 6. Alternative reflection API.

3   Elements of the Library

3.1   Metaprogramming Services

After presenting an example, we detail the functionalities of the proposed library. Regarding the dynamic modification of class structures, we provide:

- Adding, deleting and updating fields of classes and, thus, of all their running instances. The update action means changing the field type.
- Replacing method implementations. Without modifying their signature, the body of methods (their code) is replaced with a new one.
- Adding, deleting and updating methods (including their implementations). As with fields, updating means changing the method signature. Adding methods include overloading their implementation (as in Fig. 3).
- Adding and removing interfaces implemented by a class. To successfully add an interface, the class must implement all the declared methods in the interface. If so, the class type will promote to the interface type (polymorphism).
- Changing and removing the super class of a concrete class. After changing the base class, the compiler dynamically ensures that the type system rules are fulfilled (e.g., avoid accessing the methods inherited from its previous base class). Removing a base class means changing the existing one to `Object`.
- Introspection. All these primitives are complemented by an additional implementation of the Java reflection API, which considers the new fields, methods, base class and implemented interfaces of the classes adapted at runtime.

The metaprogramming services are applied to classes. Evolving a class implies the dynamic adaptation of its instances. Since Java is a class-based language [16], we do not provide the dynamic adaptation of a single object. That possibility is not included in the Java type system and, as mentioned, we want to take advantage of the benefits of its static type system.

Regarding dynamic code evaluation, our library provides the following services:

- Dynamic evaluation of expressions. This is the traditional `eval` functionality provided by most dynamic languages. Only one single expression is evaluated, and its value is returned. The expression may access any element of the running application.
- Dynamic execution of Java code. We provide the execution of either a sequence of statements or the contents of a Java file. As before, the code may depend on the runtime environment.

3.2   Runtime Adaptation

To describe the elements of the library, we explain how the system behaves at runtime, when the example in Sect. 2 is executed. Figure 7 [9] shows the runtime steps for that example.

One of the issues when implementing the proposed library is that the JVM does not allow reloading classes dynamically [17]. Once a class is loaded into memory, its code

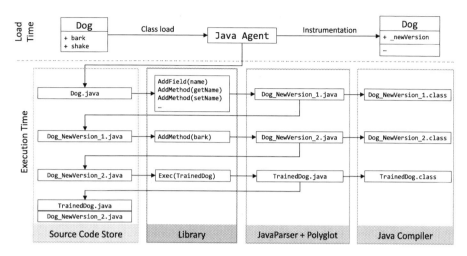

Fig. 7. Runtime steps for adapting the Dog class [9].

cannot be changed. The only exception is the capability of modifying method implementations, added in Java 5 with the `instrument` package (HotSwap). For this
reason, we propose a system based on creating new class versions at runtime.

Every time a class is modified with our library, a new class version is created and
loaded at runtime. The new class version holds all the changes made to the previous
version. If those changes are collected in one transaction, only one new version is
created regardless the number of class modifications.

Every class should provide a link to its last updated version, so we add a
`_newVersion private` field to all the classes (Fig. 7). To perform this field
addition transparently to the user, we customize the Java `ClassLoader` with new
`ClassFileTransformers` to modify all the classes at load time, using the Java
Agents API added to Java 5 [18]. This process is done at load time, so there is no
runtime performance penalty when the JVM reaches a steady state [19].

The first prototype of our library requires the source code of the applications (once
it is mature enough, we will work at the JVM binary code level). Figure 7 shows how
the source code of every class version is stored. Using this source code storage,
changes to the classes are implemented by changing the source code, recompiling and
loading them into memory.

When the user modifies the Dog class, a new version Dog_NewVersion_1 is
generated. This new class holds the last version of the original Dog class. The
`_newVersion` field of Dog instances will be updated at runtime. This field update is
performed lazily, when the object is first accessed after class adaptation. In that
moment, the `_newVersion` reference is updated, and the object state is transferred to
the new class version (Dog_NewVersion_1). This process consumes extra execution time, but it is performed only once per instance.

One issue is how we manage to replace the existing code accessing Dog fields with
code that accesses the corresponding fields in the last class version. This is done by
using the `invokedynamic` bytecode added to Java 7 [20]. Our `ClassLoader`

replaces all the field access bytecodes with `invokedynamic`. Therefore, we can change the functionality of field access with Java 7 `MutableCallSites`. We use the JINDY API to utilize `invokedynamic` from the Java language, getting rid of writing JVM assembly code [15].

Another issue is how we manage to replace method invocations with invocations to the new class version (recall that the last version holds the actual state of the objects, i.e. the appropriate `this`). We first modify the implementation of every method in `Dog`, using the `instrument` Java 5 package. The new code will simply invoke another method in `Dog_NewVersion_1`: `bark` calls `_bark_invoker`, `shake` calls `_shake_invoker`, and so on (see Fig. 8). The purpose of those `invoker` methods is to implement the lazy object state transfer and `_newVersion` update described above. After doing this update (only once per instance), the last method version (e.g., `bark` and `shake`) is called in `Dog_NewVersion_1`. In this way, if a method in an updated class is called, it will call the corresponding `invoker` in the last class version; if necessary, object state is transferred; and then the last method version is called.

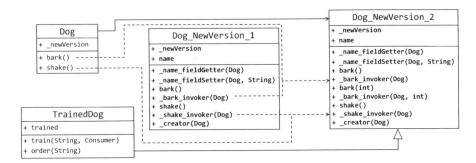

Fig. 8. Runtime structure of the existing class versions after using structural intercession [9].

When the programmer adapts an already adapted class (e.g., Fig. 3) a new `Dog_NewVersion_2` is created, compiled and loaded (Fig. 7). The `_newVersion` of both the original `Dog` and `Dog_NewVersion_1` will be lazily updated to the last class version. Similarly, all the method bodies will be replaced with direct invocations to the invokers in the last class version. The purpose is that, once instance states have been transferred, the runtime performance cost does not depend on the number of class versions. Figure 8 [9] shows the runtime structure of classes after performing the two class modifications in Figs. 2 and 3. After updating all the instances of the first version, `Dog_NewVersion_1` is useless.

3.3 Dynamic Code Evaluation

Figures 3 and 4 show how our library provides dynamic code evaluation. If we just need the dynamic evaluation of an expression (Fig. 3), the library creates a temporary class with a method that implements that expression. We need to provide a mechanism to execute that dynamically generated code, following the Java type system. For this purpose, we make the dynamically generated class to implement one of the "functional" interfaces added in Java 8 (`function` package) [13]. In this way, the interface provides the specific type of the expression to be evaluated.

For evaluating a sequence of statements, we follow a similar approach: the method body is the code provided by the user, and `void` is the returned type. For a whole class (Fig. 4), we just place the code in a Java source file and compile it.

As mentioned, class adaptation is achieved by modifying the application source code. However, code manipulation is not an easy task. To distinguish the elements in a program, code should be represented with tree- or graph-based data structures such as AST (Abstract Syntax Trees) [21]. To manipulate classes (add, remove or update fields and methods) we used the JavaParser tool (Fig. 7) [22]. It allows us to take Java code, obtain its AST, modify it, and regenerate the output Java code. Then, we simply call the `JavaCompiler` class added in Java 6.

In the dynamic evaluation of code, there is an important issue that should be considered. When programmers are writing code to be evaluated dynamically, they are not aware of the different class versions. Our library provides programmers the abstraction that the `Dog` class is being dynamically changed. For example, the programmer may be interesting in running the code `dog.setName("Rufus")`. However, if this code is evaluated, it will prompt a type error since `Dog` has no `setName` method (`Dog_NewVersion_1` does).

Therefore, we need to perform some changes in the code to be evaluated at runtime. Those changes are related to the types: if the code is accessing a new member added to a type, its last version must be used instead of the original one. We, thus, need to know the type of every expression to be evaluated dynamically (the type of `dog` in our example). At the implementation level, we just replace `setName` with `setName_invoker`, since the latter method always calls the last version.

To perform these changes when code is about to be dynamically evaluated, we use the Polyglot front-end compiler for building Java language extensions [23]. Following the Visitor design pattern [24], we traverse the AST and replace those method invocations which types have evolved. Finally, we generate the modified code, compile it and load it into memory.

3.4   Dynamic Inheritance

Dynamic inheritance allows changing both the interfaces implemented by one class and its super class. We implement these two functionalities by extending the class versioning mechanism described in the previous section.

Figure 9 shows the runtime adaptation for the code in Fig. 5. When the `addInterface` method is called, a new `Dog` version (`Dog_NewVersion_3`) implementing `Comparable` is created. `Dog` instances will be updated to this new version, using the lazy state transfer mechanism described in Sect. 3.2. The new `Dog` version now promotes to `Comparable`. Dynamically evaluated code uses this last version, utilizing the Polyglot source code program transformations described in the previous section.

removeInterface is implemented following the same mechanism. The Java type system ensures that a class does not promote to an interface that is no longer implemented.

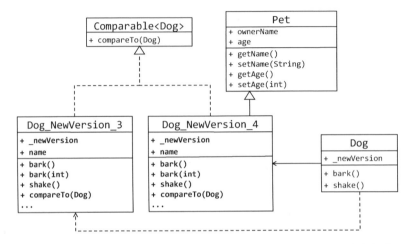

Fig. 9. Runtime structure of the existing class versions after using dynamic inheritance.

Figure 9 also shows how the Dog super class is changed to Pet. Its version 4 is implemented with another new class, inheriting from Pet. This new version can access and override the inherited members. The new fields are initialized with the default values described in the Java language specification [25].

3.5   Introspection Services

We create a new version when a class is modified, giving the abstraction that the class structure is actually changed. However, the Java reflection API reflects the implementation level of existing classes. If the Java reflection API is used to inspect an adapted class, different class versions will be reflected instead of the last version of the modified class.

We propose a new introspection API supporting the high-level abstraction of modifiable classes. To this aim, we use the Decorator design pattern that provides the same classes as the original API (e.g., Class, Field and Method) with an extended behavior (Fig. 10). Our reflection API provides its services through the Introspector class, which consults the information of the existing class versions in memory. Once the last version of the class is obtained, its runtime structure is consulted with the Java reflection API. If the class has not been modified, the decorator simply calls the original class representation in the Java reflection API, following the Proxy design pattern [24].

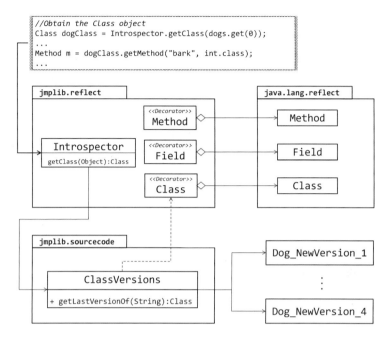

Fig. 10. Alternative reflection API.

4 Related Work

4.1 Structural Intercession

There are different works aimed at adding structural intercession to Java. Most of them are based on modifying the implementation of the JVM.

Würthinger *et al.* modify the JVM to allow the dynamic addition and deletion of class members [26]. They also support changing the class hierarchy at runtime. They ensure the type rules of the Java type system, and they verify the correct state of the program execution. After the adaptation, runtime performance is penalized by 15%, but this value converges to 3% when the JVM reaches a steady state [10]. This is currently the reference implementation of the HotSwap functionality included in JSR 292, which was not finally included in the standard platform [27].

JVOLVE is another implementation of the JVM to support evolving Java applications to fix bugs and add features [28]. JVOLVE allows adding, deleting and replacing fields and methods anywhere within the class hierarchy. They modify the class loader, JIT compiler and garbage collector of the JVM to provide those services. To adapt the running applications, JVOLVE stops program execution in a safe point and then performs the update. Class adaptation is controlled by *transformer* functions that can be customized by the user.

Iguana/J extends the JVM to provide behavioral reflection at runtime [29]. The programmer may intercept some Java operations such as object creation, method invocation and field access. The new behavior is specified by the user, and a

Meta-Object Protocol (MOP) adapts the application execution at runtime. When a MOP is associated to an object, it handles the operations against that object and provides the services to adapt its execution. Each modifiable operation is represented with one MOP class that the programmer has to extend to define the expected runtime adaptations. The MOP classes and objects are compiled following the Java type system.

Java Distributed Runtime Update Management System (JDRUMS) is a client-server system that allows changing a runtime program and adding more functionality to it [30]. Servers provide the update services to the clients, which run in the JDRUMS virtual machine. That virtual machine is a JVM extension that provides distributed dynamic updates [31]. Those updates modify the existing classes distributed as a deployment kit. For each updated class, a new version is created. Every time an instance of an old version is used, a new instance of the new version is created, its state is transferred to the new object, and the reference is updated. Object migration is controlled by a class that is included in the deployment kit.

In [32], class structures are dynamically modified, by changing the implementation of the JVM and creating a new `ClassLoader`. That new class loader provides the dynamic loading of modified classes, replacing the existing ones (a functionality that is not included in the standard JVM). The instances of the adapted classes can evolve in three different ways: no instance is modified, some of them are (depending on user-defined criteria), and all of them are adapted.

The following works provide some runtime adaptability with frameworks, without modifying the JVM. Pukall *et al.* propose unanticipated runtime adaptation, adapting running programs depending on unpredictable requirements [17]. They propose a system based on class wrappers and two roles: *caller* (service clients) and *callee* (service providers). A callee is a class wrapper that provides runtime adaptation. They provide services to access the original class. The implementation of those services are changed using the `instrument` Java 5 package. The callers are aimed at replacing invocations to an object with invocations to the appropriate callee wrapper.

DUSC (Dynamic Updating through Swapping of Classes) is a technique is based on the use of proxy classes, requiring no modification of the runtime system [33]. As in the previous paragraph, the main Java technology used to change method implementation at runtime is HotSwap. DUSC performs the static modification of classes to allow its later adaptation (making them *swapping-enabled*). They allow adding and deleting classes, but modified ones must maintain their interface (`private` methods and fields can be modified). Another noteworthy limitation is that non-public fields cannot be accessed from outside the class.

Rubah is another framework for the dynamic adaptation of Java applications [34]. When a new dynamic update is available, they load the new versions of added or changed classes at runtime, and perform a full garbage collection (GC) of the program to modify the running instances. The JVM is not modified. Instead, they implement an application-level GC traversal using reflection and some class-level rewriting. To update an application with Rubah, the programmer has to specify the update points, write the control flow migration, and detail the program state migration.

JRebel is a tool to skip the time-consuming build and redeploy steps in the Java development process, allowing programmers to see the result of code changes instantly, without stopping application execution [35]. Modified classes are recompiled and reloaded in the running application. JRebel allows changes in the structure of classes. Classes are instrumented with a native Java agent using the JVM Tool Interface, and a particular class loader. Each class is changed to a master class and different support anonymous classes that are dynamically JIT compiled [36]. JRebel does not check that the whole application has no type errors. Thus, application execution crashes when changes in a class imply errors in a program (e.g., a method is removed and it is later invoked).

MetaML is a statically typed programming language that supports program manipulation [37]. It allows the programmer to construct, combine and execute code fragments in a type safe manner. In this way, dynamically evaluated programs do not produce type errors. MetaML does not support the manipulation of dynamically evaluated code; i.e., evaluation of code represented as a string, unknown at compile time. Therefore, its metaprogramming features cannot be used to adapt applications to new requirements emerged after their execution.

4.2 Dynamic Inheritance

CLOS (Common Lisp Object System) is a Lisp extension for object-oriented programming. It is part of the ANSI Common Lisp and provides intercession and dynamic inheritance [38]. Classes can be redefined by evaluating a new `defclass` form. When a class is redefined, the changes are propagated to its instances and to the instances of any of its subclasses. Class redefinition provides the functionality of changing the inheritance tree by declaring a different parent. Instance updating occurs using an eager or a lazy approach depending on the language implementation [39].

The Smalltalk approach to implementing class-based dynamic inheritance is quite similar to that of CLOS. The `superclass:` message is used to dynamically modify the class inheritance tree [40]. When a class definition changes, the existing instances are also structurally modified (by the `Class-Builder` class) in order to match the definition of their new class. Smalltalk also provides the functionality to change the type of an object with the `changeClassTo` method. However, this semantics is not followed in every implementation. Both VisualWorks [41] and Dolphin Smalltalk [42] impose the same restriction on the type change primitive: both the new and old classes must define the same physical structure for their instances [43].

The concept of wide classes is an extension of the class-based model, allowing instances to be temporarily widened, extending their structure and behavior [44]. The widening operation on a single instance allows it to be temporarily transformed into an instance of a special subclass (a wide class). This approach also defines the opposite operation (shrinking an instance), which reshapes the instance to its original class. Widened objects preserve the subtyping relationship, since wide classes are always derived from the original class of the instance. It is possible to widen an object with two disjoint sets of messages and, depending on runtime values, to pass those recently added messages. Since wide classes should be explicitly declared, the type of an instance cannot be widened to an arbitrary subclass. This approach was implemented in the Bigloo programming language, an open implementation of Scheme [45].

Fickle$_{\text{II}}$ is a small class-based language that supports the type change primitive of dynamic inheritance to demonstrate how this feature could be introduced in an imperative, statically typed, class-based, object-oriented language [46]. They define a type change primitive as dynamic object reclassification: a programming language feature that allows an object to change its class membership at runtime while retaining its identity. In Fickle$_{\text{II}}$, a class definition may be preceded by the keywords root or state. Class reclassification can only occur within a hierarchy rooted with a root class. state classes are subclasses of root classes and they are the only ones that can be reclassified. Classes that are neither root nor state are respected by reclassification [47]. The Fickle$_{\text{II}}$ implementation of object reclassification offers an advantage over similar approaches (such as wide classes): Fickle$_{\text{II}}$ is type-safe, i.e., any type-correct program (in terms of the type system) is guaranteed never to attempt to access non-existing fields or methods [48].

ЯRotor [16] extends the object model of an efficient class-based virtual machine with prototype-based semantics, so that it can directly support both prototype- and class-based object oriented languages. Consequently, an important runtime performance improvement is obtained by using the virtual machine JIT compiler, while providing a direct interoperation between languages. By using this hybrid object model this virtual machine allows modifying the structure of both classes and objects. Additionally, dynamic inheritance primitives such as changes in the class inheritance tree and instance type changes are also implemented for both class- and prototype-based languages. Any language can take benefit of these additional VM features when implemented over this virtual machine. Access to these functionalities are provided to legacy languages using a library [6].

4.3 Java Reflection API

There exist some projects that enhance the capabilities of the Java reflection API. Reflections is able to scan a project classpath to perform queries against class metainformation at runtime [49]. These queries allow managing class information in ways that are not provided by the standard reflection API. Examples are getting the subtypes of a certain class, the types and members annotated with a concrete annotation, the resources matching a regular expression, and the methods with a specific signature, parameters, annotations and return type.

XStream is a library to serialize and deserialize Java objects to XML documents [50]. The developers detected that the Java reflection API does not provide all the information required to allow the later deserialization of classes and objects. For that reason, they implemented an enhanced version of the Java API. This enhanced version uses undocumented internal Java runtime classes to recreate more types of instances. Its implementation access internal native representations of the JVM, making it specific to a few virtual machine versions and implementations [50].

Cglib is a high-level library to generate and transform Java byte code [51]. It has been used to implement some AOP and testing tools. Its Enhancer class provides the dynamic generation of new classes deriving from existing classes, aimed to modify the behavior of the types overridden. The new dynamically generated classes allow method interception by means of the dynamic binding implemented by the Java platform. The reflection API is replicated by another one that provides similar types (e.g., `FastClass` and `FastMethod`) with better runtime performance [52].

5 Conclusions

We propose the design of a library aimed at providing structural intercession, dynamic inheritance, and dynamic code evaluation services for the Java platform and language. Our approach uses standard Java libraries, so we modify neither the Java virtual machine nor the language implementation. The metaprogramming services increase the runtime adaptability of Java without losing the benefits of its static type system. In this way, our library allows programmers to adapt their running applications while maintaining the robustness of the Java type system. Runtime adaptation has a runtime performance penalty that we are now measuring. We think that penalty will nearly negligible when the JVM reaches a steady state after application adaptation.

We have already implemented a proof-of-concept prototype that successfully executes the structural intercession and dynamic code evaluation examples shown in this article. Currently, it requires the use of Java source code.

Our next step is to add dynamic inheritance allowing the runtime adaptability of class hierarchies, and add the proposed modifications to the reflection API. Then, apply heavy optimizations to improve its steady state execution. The last step of the project is to allow the dynamic adaptation of whole applications that have been modified and recompiled, adapting running Java applications with a new recompiled version.

Acknowledgements. This work has been funded by the European Union, through the European Regional Development Funds (ERDF); and the Principality of Asturias, through its Science, Technology and Innovation Plan (grant GRUPIN14-100). We have also received funds from the Banco Santander through its support to the Campus of International Excellence.

References

1. Redondo, J.M., Ortin, F.: A comprehensive evaluation of widespread python implementations. IEEE Softw. **32**(4), 76–84 (2015)
2. Ortin, F., Cueva, J.M.: Implementing a real computational-environment jump in order to develop a runtime-adaptable reflective platform. ACM SIGPLAN Not. **37**(8), 35–44 (2002)
3. Ortin, F., Cueva, J.M.: Non-restrictive computational reflection. Comput. Stand. Interfaces **25**(3), 241–251 (2003)
4. Paulson, L.D.: Developers shift to dynamic programming languages. IEEE Comput. **40**(2), 12–15 (2007)
5. Meijer, E., Drayton, P.: Dynamic typing when needed: the end of the cold war between programming languages. In: Proceedings of the OOPSLA Workshop on Revival of Dynamic Languages (2004)
6. Ortin, F., Labrador, M.A., Redondo, J.M.: A hybrid class- and prototype-based object model to support language-neutral structural intercession. Inf. Softw. Technol. **56**(2), 199–219 (2014)

7. Garcia, M., Ortin, F., Quiroga, J.: Design and implementation of an efficient hybrid dynamic and static typing language. Softw. Pract. Experience **46**(2), 199–226 (2016)
8. Quiroga, J., Ortin, F., Llewellyn-Jones, D., Garcia, M.: Optimizing runtime performance of hybrid dynamically and statically typed languages for the .Net platform. J. Syst. Softw. **113**, 114–129 (2016)
9. Lagartos, I., Redondo, J.M., Ortin, F.: Towards the integration of metaprogramming services into Java. In: Proceedings of the 12th International Conference on Evaluation of Novel Approaches to Software Engineering (ENASE), Porto, Portugal, pp. 277–284 (2017)
10. Würthinger, T., Wimmer, C., Stadler, L.: Unrestricted and safe dynamic code evolution for Java. Sci. Comput. Program. **78**(5), 481–498 (2013)
11. Redondo, J.M., Ortin, F., Cueva, J.M.: Optimizing reflective primitives of dynamic languages. Int. J. Softw. Eng. Knowl. Eng. **18**(6), 759–783 (2008)
12. Ortin, F., Diez, D.: Designing an adaptable heterogeneous abstract machine by means of reflection. Inf. Softw. Technol. **47**(2), 81–94 (2005)
13. Oracle, function package, Java Platform SE 8 https://docs.oracle.com/javase/8/docs/api/java/util/function/package-summary.html. Accessed 23 June 2017
14. Ortin, F., Conde, P., Fernandez-Lanvin, D., Izquierdo, R.: The runtime performance of invokedynamic: an evaluation with a Java library. IEEE Softw. **31**(4), 82–90 (2014)
15. Conde, P., Ortin, F.: Jindy: a Java library to support invokedynamic. Comput. Sci. Inf. Syst. **11**(1), 47–68 (2014)
16. Redondo, J.M., Ortin, F.: Efficient support of dynamic inheritance for class- and prototype-based languages. J. Syst. Softw. **86**(2), 278–301 (2013)
17. Pukall, M., Kästner, C., Saake, G.: Towards unanticipated runtime adaptation of Java applications. In: 15th Asia-Pacific Software Engineering Conference, pp. 85–92 (2008)
18. Oracle, instrument package, Java Platform SE 8. https://docs.oracle.com/javase/8/docs/api/java/lang/instrument/package-summary.html. Accessed 23 June 2017
19. Georges, A., Buytaert, D., Eeckhout, L.: Statistically rigorous Java performance evaluation. In: Object-Oriented Programming Systems and Applications, OOPSLA 2007, NY, USA, pp. 57–76 (2007)
20. Oracle, Java Virtual Machine Support for Non-Java Languages. http://docs.oracle.com/javase/7/docs/technotes/guides/vm/multiple-language-support.html. Accessed 23 June 2017
21. Ortin, F., Zapico, D., Cueva, J.M.: Design patterns for teaching type checking in a compiler construction course. IEEE Trans. Educ. **50**(3), 273–283 (2007)
22. JavaParser, Process Java code programmatically. http://javaparser.org. Accessed 23 June 2017
23. Polyglot, A compiler front end framework for building Java language extensions. https://www.cs.cornell.edu/projects/polyglot. Accessed 23 June 2017
24. Gamma, E., Helm, R., Johnson, R., Vlissides, J.: Design Patterns: Elements of Reusable Object-Oriented Software. Addison-Wesley Professional (1994)
25. Oracle, Java Language and Virtual Machine Specifications. https://docs.oracle.com/javase/specs. Accessed 23 June 2017
26. Würthinger, T., Wimmer, C., Stadler, L.: Dynamic code evolution for Java. In: Proceedings of the 8th International Conference on the Principles and Practice of Programming in Java, NY, USA, pp. 10–19 (2010)
27. Oracle, JSR 292, supporting dynamically typed languages on the Java platform. https://www.jcp.org/en/jsr/detail?id=292. Accessed 23 June 2017

28. Subramanian, S. Hicks, M., McKinley, K.S.: Dynamic software updates: a VM-centric approach. In: Proceedings of the 30th ACM SIGPLAN Conference on Programming Language Design and Implementation, NY, USA, pp. 1–12 (2009)

29. Redmond, B., Cahill, V.: Supporting unanticipated dynamic adaptation of application behaviour. In: Magnusson, B. (ed.) ECOOP 2002. LNCS, vol. 2374, pp. 205–230. Springer, Heidelberg (2002). https://doi.org/10.1007/3-540-47993-7_9

30. Andersson, J., Ritzau, T.: Dynamic code update in JDrums. In: Proceedings of the ICSE 2000 Workshop on Software Engineering for Wearable and Pervasive Computing (2000)

31. Andersson, J.: A deployment system for pervasive computing. In: International Conference on Software Maintenance Proceedings, pp. 262–270 (2000)

32. Malabarba, S., Pandey, R., Gragg, J., Barr, E., Fritz Barnes, J.: Runtime support for type-safe dynamic Java classes. In: Bertino, E. (ed.) ECOOP 2000. LNCS, vol. 1850, pp. 337–361. Springer, Heidelberg (2000). https://doi.org/10.1007/3-540-45102-1_17

33. Orso, A., Rao, A., Harrold, M.J.: A technique for dynamic updating of Java software. In: Proceedings of the International Conference on Software Maintenance, pp. 649–658 (2002)

34. Pina L., Hicks, M.: Rubah: efficient, general-purpose dynamic software updating for Java. In: The 5th Workshop on Hot Topics in Software Upgrades (2013)

35. JRebel, Zero Turnaround JRebel, Reload code changes instantly, https://zeroturnaround.com/software/jrebel. Accessed 23 June 2017

36. Kabanov, J.: Reloading Java Classes 401: HotSwap and JRebel — Behind the Scenes. Zero Turnaround. https://zeroturnaround.com/rebellabs/reloading_java_classes_401_hotswap_jrebel. Accessed 23 June 2017

37. Taha, W., Sheard, T.: MetaML and multi-stage programming with explicit annotations. Theor. Comput. Sci. **248**(1–2), 211–242 (2000)

38. DeMichiel, Linda G., Gabriel, Richard P.: The common lisp object system: an overview. In: Bézivin, J., Hullot, J.-M., Cointe, P., Lieberman, H. (eds.) ECOOP 1987. LNCS, vol. 276, pp. 151–170. Springer, Heidelberg (1987). https://doi.org/10.1007/3-540-47891-4_15

39. Miller, F.P., Vandome, A.F., McBrewster, J.: Common Lisp: Lisp (programming language). In: Programming Language, American National Standards Institute, Specification (Technical Standard), Free and Open Source Software, Programming Paradigm. Alphascript publishing, Mauritius (2010)

40. Goldberg, A., Robson, D.: Smalltalk-80: The Language and its Implementation. Addison-Wesley Longman Publishing Co. Inc., Boston (1983)

41. Cincom, Visualworks Smalltalk Homepage. http://www.cincomsmalltalk.com/main/products/visualworks. Accessed 23 June 2017

42. ObjectArts, Dolphin Smalltalk Official Homepage. http://www.object-arts.com. Accessed 23 June 2017

43. Rivard, F.: Smalltalk: a reflective language. In: Proceedings of Reflection 1996, pp. 21–38 (1996)

44. Serrano, M.: Wide classes. In: Guerraoui, R. (ed.) ECOOP 1999. LNCS, vol. 1628, pp. 391–415. Springer, Heidelberg (1999). https://doi.org/10.1007/3-540-48743-3_18

45. Serrano, M.: Bigloo: A Practical Scheme Compiler. User Manual for Version 3.8a (2012). http://www-sop.inria.fr/mimosa/fp/Bigloo/doc/bigloo.pdf

46. Drossopoulou, S., Damiani, F., Dezani-Ciancaglini, M., Giannini, P.: *Fickle*: dynamic object re-classification. In: Knudsen, J.L. (ed.) ECOOP 2001. LNCS, vol. 2072, pp. 130–149. Springer, Heidelberg (2001). https://doi.org/10.1007/3-540-45337-7_8

47. Ancona, D., Anderson, C., Damiani, F., Drossopoulou, S., Giannini, P., Zucca, E.: A type preserving translation of Flickle into Java. Electron. Notes Theor. Comput. Sci. **62**, 69–82 (2002)
48. Ancona, D., Anderson, C., Damiani, F., Drossopoulou, S., Giannini, P., Zucca, E.: A provenly correct translation of Fickle into Java. ACM Trans. Program. Lang. Syst. **29**, 1–67 (2007)
49. Reflections, Java runtime metadata analysis. https://github.com/ronmamo/reflections. Accessed 23 June 2017
50. XStream, XStream Homepage. http://x-stream.github.io/index.html. Accessed 23 June 2017
51. Cglib, Byte Code Generation Library Homepage. https://github.com/cglib/cglib. Accessed 23 June 2017
52. Winterhalter, R.: Cglib: the missing manual. http://mydailyjava.blogspot.com.es/2013/11/cglib-missing-manual.html. Accessed 23 June 2017

Design Approaches for Critical Embedded Systems: A Systematic Mapping Study

Daniel Feitosa[1], Apostolos Ampatzoglou[1], Paris Avgeriou[1(✉)],
Frank J. Affonso[2], Hugo Andrade[3], Katia R. Felizardo[4],
and Elisa Y. Nakagawa[5]

[1] Department of Mathematics and Computer Science,
University of Groningen, Groningen, The Netherlands
{d.feitosa,a.ampatzoglou}@rug.nl, paris@cs.rug.nl
[2] Department of Statistics, Applied Mathematics and Computation,
São Paulo State University (UNESP), Rio Claro, Brazil
frank@rc.unesp.br
[3] Department of Computer Science and Engineering,
Chalmers University of Technology, Göteborg, Sweden
sica@chalmers.se
[4] Department of Computing, Federal Technological University of Paraná,
Cornélio Procópio, Brazil
katiascannavino@utfpr.edu.br
[5] Department of Computer Systems, University of São Paulo, São Carlos, Brazil
elisa@icmc.usp.br

Abstract. Critical Embedded Systems (CES) are systems in which failures are potentially catastrophic and, therefore, hard constraints are imposed on them. In the last years the amount of software accommodated within CES has considerably changed. For example, in smart cars the amount of software has grown about 100 times compared to previous years. This change means that software design for these systems is also bounded to hard constraints (e.g., high security and performance). Along the evolution of CES, the approaches for designing them are also changing rapidly, so as to fit the specialized needs of CES. Thus, a broad understanding of such approaches is missing. Therefore, this study aims to establish a fair overview on CESs design approaches. For that, we conducted a Systematic Mapping Study (SMS), in which we collected 1,673 papers from five digital libraries, filtered 269 primary studies, and analyzed five facets: design approaches, applications domains, critical quality attributes, tools, and type of evidence. Our findings show that the body of knowledge is vast and overlaps with other types of systems (e.g., real-time or cyber-physical systems). In addition, we have observed that some critical quality attributes are common among various application domains, as well as approaches and tools are oftentimes generic to CES.

Keywords: Systematic mapping study · Critical embedded system
Design

© Springer International Publishing AG, part of Springer Nature 2018
E. Damiani et al. (Eds.): ENASE 2017, CCIS 866, pp. 243–274, 2018.
https://doi.org/10.1007/978-3-319-94135-6_12

1 Introduction

Critical Embedded Systems (CESs) are among the most significant types of software-intensive systems, since they are extremely pervasive in modern society, being used from cars to power plants [1]. CESs are embedded systems in which runtime errors can potentially be catastrophic [2], causing serious damage to the environment or to human lives, or non-recoverable material and financial losses [3, 4]. Due to the criticality of such systems, the satisfaction of multiple quality constraints must be guaranteed. This is far from trivial, as it entails complex trade-offs, which to a large extent concern safeguarding the levels of critical against other non-critical qualities [5, 6]. As critical quality attributes (CQAs), we characterize qualities that, when not satisfied, may lead to catastrophic failures, as the aforementioned ones; typical examples are performance, security and reliability.

Engineering CES is particularly challenging, since it needs to guarantee the satisfaction of various critical qualities. One of the key solutions to alleviate this challenge is to design a sound architecture and validate it against the critical quality attributes. To this end, multiple approaches have been proposed, solving a variety of specific design problems. However, the plethora and diversity of available solutions has led to a difficulty on understanding, applying or even extending and combining such approaches. Thus, in order to support researchers and practitioners on CES design, it is important to have a comprehensive understanding of this field. To contribute towards a better understanding of design approaches for CES, we have conducted a systematic mapping study; this is a commonly used approach for assessing and describing the state of the art in a specific domain or problem (see Sect. 3 for more details). The contributions of this study are the following: (a) a classification of the existing approaches to design CES; (b) a list of tools for supporting existing approaches; (c) a list of domains for which approaches have been developed and used; (d) a list of the most commonly identified CQAs in the CES design; and (e) a classification of these approaches, based on the level of their empirical evidence.

2 Related Work

This section describes related Systematic Literature Reviews (SLRs) or Systematic Mapping Studies (SMSs), also known as secondary studies. To the best of our knowledge, there are no studies that focus on exactly the same topic as ours, i.e., designing of CESs. Thus, we searched for related work such as SMSs and SLRs that cover the entire software development process of CES, or a specific phase.

2.1 Development Processes

We identified two studies that discuss software development processes and are related to CESs [7, 8]. Although such processes do not focus or limit themselves to the design phase, they do have impact on the design phase. Cawley et al. [7] investigated Lean/Agile development processes on safety-critical systems, focusing on medical devices. For this purpose, an SLR based on the guidelines of Kitchenham and Charters

[9] was performed. The results of the SLR suggest that Lean/Agile methodologies are appropriate for the development of safety-critical systems, as they support several practices for regulated safety-critical domains (e.g., traceability and testing). However, the results also suggest a lack of adoption of Lean/Agile methods in these domains. This is not surprising as regulated environments typically involve activities that are not commonly used in these processes. Eklund and Bosch [8] investigated a holistic model for aligning software development processes with the architecture of embedded software. As part of this study, an SMS on development approaches for embedded systems was performed (based on the guidelines of Kitchenham and Charters [9]). The results of the study suggest that there is no single most common approach (or set of approaches) but, approaches are tailored for specific domains or products and may have different characteristics (e.g., incorporating agile practices). Despite the high customization of processes, the authors have been able to identify some similarities, e.g. activities are often executed sequentially and follow a V-model - [10] or stage-gate-like [11] process. In addition, the architectures created from these processes are often focused on supporting specific quality attributes, which are typically domain-specific (e.g., dependability for the space domain). Based on the identified approaches, the authors derived five archetypical developments processes, with their respective characteristics, aiming to support selection or migration between concrete archetypal development approaches.

2.2   Verification and Validation

Not all activities in the verification and validation of critical embedded software (V&V) are related to its design. However, a significant part concerns the verification and validation of design and are, therefore, relevant to the design phase. We identified two secondary studies that discuss aspects of V&V and are related to CES [12, 13]. Barbosa et al. [12] investigated software testing of CESs, checking the compliance level with the standard DO-178B, for the aviation industry. The aim was to identify primary studies that could be used to create a methodology for testing of CES. For this purpose, a SLR, based on Dybå and Dingsøyr [14], was performed to identify studies that implemented or applied V&V techniques in the context of CES. The results suggest that four techniques (functional, structural, mutation and model-based testing) are widely applied for testing of CES, from which the most recurrent technique is functional testing. In addition, all testing requirements of DO-178B have been investigated, with "structural coverage analysis" (e.g., dead code and deactivated code) being the most addressed requirement, likely due to its inherent complexity. Elberzhager et al. [13] investigated quality assurance techniques (i.e., analysis or test approaches) applied to Matlab Simulink models. These models are used in embedded software design, especially in critical domains. The aim was to develop an approach able to integrate different quality assurance techniques. For this purpose, an SMS was performed based on the guidelines of Petersen et al. [15], which presented different analysis and test techniques as well as some combined approaches. The results of the study suggest that formal methods, properties checking (e.g., rule-based analysis) and automatic test generation are the most common approaches for performing quality assurance for embedded systems. The results also suggest a lack of research on combining analysis techniques with testing techniques for such models.

2.3   Software Architecture

The activity of architecture design for embedded systems was investigated by Antonio et al. [16], which aimed at establishing the state of the art on the topic by analyzing proposed architectures, available on the literature. For that, a SMS based on the guidelines of Petersen et al. [15] was performed. To understand the activity, various characteristics were collected from the architectures, and used for classifying them. Firstly, the architectures were grouped according to the type of modeling technique used to design them, namely formal, semi-formal and informal. Next, further classes were identified based on recurrent characteristics, e.g., level of abstraction and whether it is domain-specific. The results of the SMS suggest that the Architecture Analysis and Design Language (AADL) is the most used formal modeling approach, whereas UML stands out among the semi-formal and informal approaches. In addition, the most recurrent characteristic of these architectures is that they are designed to specific application domains.

Similar to the previous study, Guessi et al. [17] investigate the modeling of software architectures for embedded systems. However, this study focuses on architecture description languages (ADLs), as well as the concerns (e.g., quality attributes) being addressed and information (e.g., components, events) being represented in the designed architectures. The investigation was performed via a SLR based on the guidelines of Kitchenham and Charters [9]. The results suggest that UML is the most common language, while safety is the concern that is more often addressed. Despite the variety of approaches that currently exist, the results also suggest that more attention should be placed on the description of embedded system architectures. Among the reasons, Guessi et al. argue that there is a lack of consensus about the most adequate approach (es) for describing architecture, as well as whether existing approaches are sufficient for representing the variety of embedded systems.

Nakagawa et al. [18] present the state of the art on architecting approaches for systems of systems[1] (SoS), of which CES are among the most common examples. For that, an SLR based on the guidelines of Kitchenham and Charters [9] was performed, investigating the creation, representation, evaluation and evolution of these architectures. The results suggest the existence of several approaches, although most of them lack maturity and are neither adequately adapted nor widely adopted. In addition, several application domains (e.g., avionics and space) and quality attributes (e.g., security, reliability and performance) are common between SoS and CES.

---

[1] SoS are integrated solutions comprising operationally independent (non-trivial) systems, which are orchestrated in order to provide a more complex functionality.

2.4   Comparative Analysis

After presenting related work, it is important to highlight the differences between these studies and our work. To illustrate these differences, we compare them w.r.t. six characteristics (Table 1): review type; number of included primary studies; whether the study focuses on CES or is only indirectly related (i.e., with partial applicability to CES); whether it considered quality attributes (QA) in the investigation; whether it considered application domains in the investigation; and the main topic of the investigation. The review type is an indication of whether the study presents an overview or a detailed analysis over the main topic (SMS) or it examines more in-depth research questions (SLR). As presented in Table 1, three other SMSs were performed, although they were focused in different, yet related, topics. However, these three studies were not focused on CESs, which reinforces the purpose of our study, as it complements existing knowledge. Other important aspects of our study include the larger body of knowledge that has been investigated (due to the broader topic of research), as well as the consideration of quality attributes and application domains in the investigation. CESs are used in a variety of application domains and multiple factors affect the decision-making to select or reuse a design approach. Quality constraints are among the most relevant factors, as also suggested by related work [8, 17, 18]. Application domains may also play an important role, as each domain groups a set of common requirements, that are in turn related to specific quality attributes [8].

Table 1. Comparison between related work and our study.

Study	Review type	Number of studies	Focus on CES?	Investigated QAs?	Focus on domains	Main topic
[7]	SLR	19	Yes	No	No	Development process
[8]	SMS	23	No	Yes	Yes	Development process
[12]	SLR	97	Yes	No	No	Verification and validation
[13]	SMS	44	No	No	No	Verification and validation
[16]	SMS	104	No	No	No	Software architecture
[17]	SLR	24	No	Yes	No	Software architecture
[18]	SLR	60	No	Yes	Yes	Software architecture
Ours	SMS	258	Yes	Yes	Yes	Design

3 Review Methodology

Systematic Mapping Studies (SMSs) and Systematic Literature Reviews (SLRs) have been broadly adopted as systematic research methods to aggregate knowledge. As this study aims to outline the state-of-the-art on design approaches for CES in a broad sense, we decided to perform an SMS [15]. The rest of this section describes the protocol of our SMS, based on the guidelines of Petersen et al. [15].

3.1 Research Scope

The goal of this SMS is described using the Goal-Question-Metrics (GQM) approach [19], as follows: "**analyze** existing software engineering literature **for the purpose of** characterizing the state of the art **with respect to** approaches (e.g., processes, methods and tools) for designing critical embedded systems **from the point of view of** researchers and practitioners **in the context of** software-intensive systems engineering". Based on the goal we defined the following research questions (RQs):

RQ_1 - What are the proposed approaches for designing CES?
$RQ_{1.1}$ - Is the nature of these approaches industrial, academic or mixed?
$RQ_{1.2}$ - What is the purpose of the approach?
RQ_2 - What are the application domains where these approaches are applied?
RQ_3 - What are the most common critical quality attributes identified in CES design?
RQ_4 - What tools have been used to support CES design?
RQ_5 - What are the types of evidence provided in CES design research?

To achieve the aforementioned goal, we must analyze and present the existing body of knowledge from different perspectives. The most important outcome of this SMS is the identification and characterization of the approaches that were created and/or used to design CES (RQ_1). As a first step in characterizing the approaches, we consider their nature and purpose. Next, we look at the application domain (RQ_2) which influences CES design as it often imposes a number of constraints. For example, several application domains are bounded by international standards (e.g., DO-178B for aviation). In addition, these constraints commonly aim at defining critical quality values (e.g., safety); thus, design approaches are often targeting those values (e.g., fault tree analysis). Therefore, investigating the addressed quality attributes (RQ_3) is of paramount importance. Furthermore, multiple tools have been proposed or tailored to support the design of CES. As the number of CES grows, it is interesting to investigate how this reflects on the tooling (RQ_4), e.g., leading to news tools and adaptation of existing ones. Finally, it is important to not only classify the approaches, but also assess their maturity level to inform researchers and practitioners. For that, we analyze the types of evidence provided within the literature (RQ_5).

3.2   Search Strategy

Considering the research questions, we defined the search strategy, which comprises the selection of sources for collecting primary studies, as well as the definition of the scope for the collection.

Sources Selection. We decided to perform an automated search, as a manual search would be very time-consuming, thus not allowing us to search as many venues. In addition, by considering digital libraries (through an automated search) we might also include venues that otherwise we would not be aware of. The following criteria were adopted to select search sources (i.e., digital libraries): content update (publications are regularly updated); availability (full text of the papers is available); quality of results (accuracy of the results returned by the search); and versatility export (since a lot of information is returned through the search, a mechanism to export the results is required). These criteria are also discussed by Dieste et al. [20]. The selected sources for our SMS are: ACM Digital Library, IEEE Xplore, Science Direct, Springer Link and Scopus. According to Dybå et al. [21], the first four digital libraries are sufficient to conduct SMSs in the context of software engineering. Furthermore, Scopus was added, since it is considered to be the largest database of abstracts and citations [9].

Search Scope. As CESs have been the subject of research for a long time, we decided to not limit the start of the search period based on date of publication. However, we limit the end date of the search period in order to measure influence of the primary studies (see Sect. 3.5), considering primary studies published up to two years before the date of collection. We performed the data collection on March of 2015 and, thus, collected primary studies published up to March of 2013. Moreover, only primary studies written in English will be processed in this SMS. Due to automated search, we also defined a search string for filtering the studies to those that can be potentially included in the SMS. As we are interested in approaches for CES design, we selected two main keywords, "Critical Embedded System" and "Approach", with the respective related terms. The keywords were chosen to be simple enough to yield a large number of results and, at the same time, rigorous to cover only the desired research topic. The final search string is: *("Critical Embedded System" OR "Critical Embedded Systems" OR "Critical Embedded Software") AND ("Approach" OR "Approaches" OR "Method" OR "Methods" OR "Framework" OR "Frameworks" OR "Technique" OR "Techniques" OR "Process" OR "Processes" OR "Tool" OR "Tooling" OR "Guideline" OR "Guidelines").*

We clarify that we do not include terms such as "real-time", "hard real-time" or "cyber-physical systems", as they describe a broader range of systems, which extrapolates the scope of this SMS, and would make the paper selection process impractical. To validate the search string and, consequently, the papers collected by the automated search, we performed a manual search in a small number of venues, similarly to determining a *quasi-gold* standard as proposed by Zhang and Babar [22]. We selected the venues for the manual search based on their likelihood to publish studies on CES design: Real-time Systems journal, Digital Avionics Systems Conference (DASC), and International Conference on Computer Safety, Reliability, and Security (SAFECOMP). To filter the primary studies for the *quasi-gold standard*, we considered the metadata (i.e., title, keywords and abstract) and full text (when necessary), resulting in the collection of 23 primary studies. Based on the *quasi-gold standard*, we adapted the search string to ensure that all 23 primary studies were included.

3.3   Study Selection

Based on the previously mentioned search strategy, we defined the procedure for filtering the results of the automated search, selecting the primary studies to be analyzed in the SMS. The study selection comprises the definition of the criteria for filtering the papers, both inclusion and exclusion criteria, as well as steps for applying them. We include a primary study if it: (a) proposes an approach to design CESs; (b) reports on the use of an approach to design CESs; (c) evaluates an approach to design CESs; or (d) discusses approach(es) to design CESs. A primary study is excluded if it is an editorial, position paper, keynote, opinion paper, tutorial, poster or panel. To promote a common understanding of the selection criteria among the three involved researchers, we performed a pilot selection on a small subset (50) of the papers collected from the sources. In this pilot, during a first review round, all researchers analyzed title, keywords and abstract of all papers and Cohen's Kappa was calculated between every pair of researchers (see Fig. 1). We clarify that no previous discussion was performed in order to evaluate the inclusion and exclusion criteria. Next, all researchers and authors discussed the criteria and their interpretation. Main points of this discussion included the boundaries of the design phase, hardware design and the inclusion of papers that do not propose approaches (e.g., use or discussion). Finally, in a second review round, the papers are analyzed again, but this time also considering introduction and conclusion sections (if necessary), and a new calculation of Cohen's Kappa was performed (see Fig. 1).

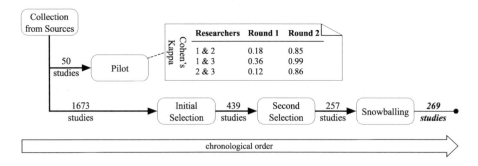

Fig. 1. Study selection.

To select the primary studies, we defined a three-step procedure. In every step, the papers were divided into three sets and three researchers were responsible for reviewing the papers of two sets. By doing this, we guarantee that every paper was reviewed by two different people while avoiding all three having to read all papers. When an inclusion/exclusion decision was conflicting or dubious (e.g., one or both reviewers were not confident), the case was discussed among all authors. The selection steps were the following: (1) *Initial selection:* the search string was customized and applied to each publication source listed in Sect. 3.2. The string terms were searched in the title, abstract and keywords of all primary studies available in each database and search engine. As a result, a set of primary studies possibly related to the research topic was obtained. Based on this set, the title and the abstract of each primary study were read and evaluated based on the inclusion and exclusion criteria. The introduction and the conclusion may also be considered when necessary; (2) *Second selection:* each of the previously selected primary studies were read in full-text and analyzed according to inclusion and exclusion criteria. This step also included the data extraction, which is discussed in Sect. 3.5; and (3) *Snowballing:* the references of the studies selected in step 2 were used to identify extra literature, for which steps 1 and 2 are repeated.

3.4 Keywording

During the first two steps of the selection procedure (see Sect. 3.3), a set of keywords was collected from each primary study. As proposed by Petersen et al. [15], the keywording process occurs in two steps:

(1) *Identification of Context*: While reading the paper, the reviewer identifies any keywords and concepts that are relevant to describe that particular study. For example, words that describe the purpose of the approach, code of standards and names of quality attributes or tools were collected. During this step, reviewers share topics of keywords (e.g., code of standards) to maintain consistency and optimize the collection. Differently from Petersen et al. [15], we extended the searching of keywords to the whole paper, as some relevant keywords have been identified within the full text at early stages of the study.

(2) *Summarization*: The keywords are combined in order to create abstractions that support understanding the body of knowledge under investigation. Examples of such abstractions are the topics mentioned in the previous step (e.g., standards). The abstractions also support identifying categories and create a classification scheme for the primary studies.

We applied keywording not only to classify the primary studies but also to identify relevant concepts for all research questions, e.g., purpose of tools, application domains standards and safety integrity levels (SILs).

3.5 Data Extraction and Mapping

During the *second selection* procedure (see Sect. 3.3), a set of variables were collected from each primary study to answer the research questions. Similar to selection procedure, the data collection of every paper involved two researchers and conflicts were discussed among all authors. The extracted variables are described in Table 2.

The mapping between variables and research questions is provided in Table 3, accompanied by the analysis method used on the data. The type of evidence (V14) evaluates the level of evidence of the proposed approach. For that, we adopted the classification proposed by Alves et al. [23] in order to make the assessment more

Table 2. Extracted variables.

Variable	Description	Variable	Description
V1	Author(s)	V8	Type of paper (conference/journal/book)
V2	Year	V9	SMS keywords
V3	Title	V10	Approaches to design CES
V4	Source	V11	Application domain(s)
V5	Venue	V12	Critical quality attributes
V6	Author(s) keywords	V13	Nature of the approaches (industrial/academic/mixed)
V7	Number of citations per year	V14	Tools to support the approaches
		V15	Type of evidence used to develop the approach

Table 3. Mapping of variables to RQs.

Research question	Variables used	Analysis method
RQ$_1$ (Approaches)	V1–V3, V6, V7, V9–V10	Descriptive Statistics (sum, average, frequency analyses, etc.) Classification based on keywording Heatmap based on classification and year Crosstabs on classification vs. nature
RQ$_2$ (Application domains)	V1–V3, V10, V11	Descriptive Statistics (sum, average, frequency analyses, etc.) Heatmap based on application domain and year Crosstabs on application domain vs. approaches (classification)
RQ$_3$ (Critical quality attributes)	V1–V3, V9–V12	Descriptive Statistics (sum, average, frequency analyses, etc.) Heatmap based on critical quality attribute and year Bubble chart on critical quality attribute vs. approaches (classification) vs. application domain Spearman correlation between critical quality attribute and approaches (classification), and application domain
RQ$_4$ (Tools)	V1–V3, V9, V10, V14	Descriptive Statistics (sum, average, frequency analyses, etc.) Classification based on keywording
RQ$_5$ (Evidence type)	V1–V3, V9, V10, V15	Descriptive Statistics (sum, average, frequency analyses, etc.) Heatmap based on type of evidence and year Bubble chart on type of evidence vs. approaches (classification) vs. application domain Spearman correlation between type of evidence and approaches (classification), and application domain

practical. From weakest to strongest, the classes are: (i) no evidence; (ii) evidence obtained from demonstration or working out toy examples; (iii) evidence obtained from expert opinions or observations; (iv) evidence obtained from academic studies (e.g., controlled lab experiments); (v) evidence obtained from industrial studies (i.e., studies are done in industrial environments, e.g., causal case studies); and (vi) evidence obtained from industrial application (i.e., actual use in industry).

4   Results

In this section, we present the results of the mapping study, highlighting the most important observations. We note that the complete information from data extraction is publicly available as part of the supplementary material for this paper [24]. We clarify that, when necessary, we cite specific primary studies using an "S" (e.g., [S134]). Due to space limitations, we do not provide the list the primary studies in this manuscript, but we have made it available as a supplementary material [24].

4.1   Demographic Overview

The distribution of studies, per year, among the different types of publication (conference, journal and book) is depicted in Fig. 2. We clarify that we collected studies published up to March of 2013 (see Sect. 3.2), resulting on the observed smaller number in that year. We notice a linear growth in the number of conference papers. The number of journal articles experiences a growth as well, but not as high. We note that conference proceedings published as books were counted as conferences, explaining the small number of book chapters in the chart.

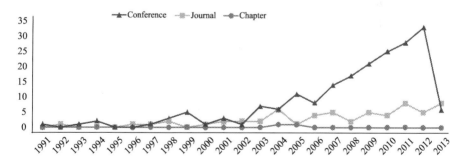

Fig. 2.   Number of filtered studies per year, per type of paper.

To investigate further potential reasons for the aforementioned growth, we looked at the venues and checked whether they focus on CES alone, or have a broader scope (e.g., embedded systems) and only include CES as one of the topics of interest. We observed that, although a few venues do focus on CES (e.g., Brazilian symposium on CES), most of the studies were published in other venues, suggesting a shift or growing interest of the respective (broad) communities towards CES. In addition, we can try to identify the most relevant venues, by looking at their distribution according to two metrics: number of included studies (Fig. 3a), and number of citations (Fig. 3b). We chose these metrics, because they reflect distinct features that may draw the attention of researchers to venues: the size of the CES community within the venue, and the potential visibility of the study. To investigate the venues, we analyzed how they are distributed statistically, identifying the high outliers, which in this case indicate popular venues for CES. We used the software IBM SPSS Statistics to create the box-plots as well as to identify the outliers, using the stem-and-leaf diagram.

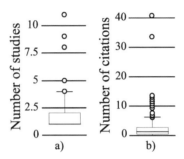

Fig. 3. Box-plot of venues based on (a) number of studies and (b) citations per paper per year.

On the one hand, Fig. 3a shows that the vast majority of venues contributed with one or two papers only, respectively 111 (approx. 70%) and 28 (17.5%). The analysis suggests that venues that contributed with four papers or more (nine venues) are exceptional in our dataset. On the other hand, Fig. 3b shows that most venues (85%) exhibit a maximum average of four citations per paper per year. The analysis of this metric suggests that venues with an average citation rate of 6.2 or more (15 venues in total) are also exceptional. Thus, we identified a set of 22 exceptional venues, which, due to space limitations, is presented in the supplementary material [24].

4.2   Design Approaches

As shown in the previous section we were able to collect a large number of studies. Therefore, it is infeasible to present all collected approaches here. For that reason, we decided to present the results as a summary based on the types of approaches that were found, which are based on a classification scheme (presented below). In addition, we present some details on the most relevant approaches, i.e., those with the most citations, identified by using the number of citations according to Google Scholar. To avoid omitting relatively new papers (i.e. those that did not have enough time to receive citations), we considered the number of citations per year. In the next subsections, we elaborate on this classification scheme and results.

Classification Scheme. The design phase in a development lifecycle is often elusive, in the sense that it is typically hard to determine the boundaries of design with respect to the other lifecycle phases. In embedded systems development, including systems with harder constraints such as CES, this is no exception. However, in order to classify the design approaches, it is necessary to identify the parts of the development lifecycle that approaches belong to, i.e., their purpose. It is widely accepted that the design phase includes activities that translate requirements into software/hardware elements, with their respective responsibilities, excluding the actual implementation of these elements (source code) [1, 25, 26]. To initialize our classification scheme, we collected the keywords obtained from the keywording process (see Sect. 3.4) and filtered those that regard the purpose of approaches. Next, we grouped the keywords by similarity, trying to organize them in a hierarchical fashion, also creating a generic design flow[2]. However, it was not possible to derive such hierarchical organization, as we were not able to identify or define a flow that was sufficiently generic to accommodate the extracted approaches. This is due to the high heterogeneity of domains, requirements, and platforms for which CES are designed [1]. Therefore, we decided to organize our keywords based on a simplified design flow proposed by Marwedel [1], which is meant to generically represent the design activities of an ES.

To create our classification scheme, we successfully mapped the identified keywords into some elements of the design flow proposed by Marwedel [1], and assessed whether or not the relationship between the keywords were consistent with the description of the simplified design flow. By the end of the keyword mapping, we were able to derive five types of activity representing general purposes, as well as scope them and their relationships. The final classification scheme is presented in Fig. 4, in which rectangles represent each general purpose, and arrows show the flow of design artifacts. Moreover, smaller rectangles (i.e., Optimization and Test) represent auxiliary purposes that are special for the design of embedded systems. The approaches are grouped according to how they modify the system's design, rather than based on a logical sequence of activities. In addition, common activities in embedded system design are also clearly placed within the classification (e.g., scheduling is placed within Application mapping). The main characteristic of this kind of classification is that it is artifact-centric, i.e., the artifacts dictate what activities may be performed (i.e., what

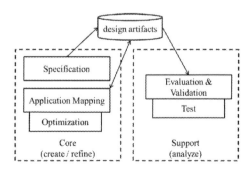

Fig. 4. Classification scheme.

---

[2] A design flow is the sequence of specific activities (with respective approaches) to design a system.

purposes they serve), rather than the other way around [1]. The five general purposes are described as follows:

- **Specification:** these activities formalize constraints (e.g., safety requirements) in the design. They define the scope/boundaries of the design. To draw a parallel, this type of activity is similar to the analysis in a software architecture design flow [27]. Common examples are formal specification languages, such as Z.
- **Application Mapping:** these activities generate new (partial) design information. A series of mappings are applied in order to refine the design from a more abstract representation to platform-specific design. In a software architecture design flow, this type of activity is similar to architecture synthesis [27]. Common approaches encompass: mapping of operations to concurrent tasks; mapping of operations to HW/SW; compilation; or scheduling.
- **Evaluation & Validation:** similarly to the evaluation in a software architecture design flow [27], these activities evaluate design elements w.r.t. the objectives (e.g. provide a proper scheduling of tasks) and validate a design description against other descriptions. Examples of approaches are algorithms or analysis frameworks for comparing models that tackle different quality attributes, as well as simulations.
- **Optimization:** these activities perform design tuning according to stated objectives. Examples of approaches are HL transformation and energy optimizations.
- **Test:** these activities include test generation and testability evaluation. They are included in design iterations if testability issues are already considered during the design steps. Tests are run after the design phase.

This classification is sufficiently robust for expressing different software, hardware and SW/HW design flows, including prominent ones such as the V-Model [28] and the design flow provided with SpecC [29]. Finally, it is important to clarify that approaches may serve several purposes. For example, some architecture modeling languages are able to perform both application mapping and specification.

Summary of Design Approaches. To analyze the extracted approaches, we classified each of them into one or more of the aforementioned general purposes. In addition, some studies presented entire design flows and, therefore, we also considered it as a category for the classification. Figure 5 depicts a heat map that shows the number of studies, per year, discussing approaches from each category.

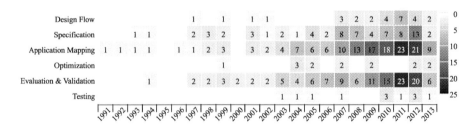

Fig. 5. Number of studies, per year, containing approaches from each category.

In this heat map, darker shades of grey represent bigger numbers, which are presented as well. For example, in 2011, 23 studies that contain approaches for application mapping were published. One can notice that most attention has been given to approaches for Application Mapping and Evaluation & Validation, which is understandable because approaches that serve this purpose encompass most of the design flow of an embedded system. Approaches for Specification of CES design were also presented in a considerable number of studies. Such interest is explained by the necessity of unambiguously representing the different aspects of CES (e.g., safety, components, security) in a variety of platforms (e.g., time/event-triggered and mixed architectures, and communication protocols). Table 4 presents the number of studies in each category, grouped by nature (i.e., academic, industrial or mixed). The table also presents the number of citations per year, for the entire set of studies. By exploring this table, one can notice that most of the studies were performed in an academic setting, followed by mixed and industrial settings, respectively; this is understandable as the included venues are more academic than industrial. In addition, solutions are normally proposed and explored in academic studies before they are applied in industry. However, there is one interesting observation to highlight. The mixed setting does not follow the same trend of the academic and industrial settings (which are in accordance to Fig. 5): studies performed in collaboration between academia and industry were mostly focused on Evaluation & Validation approaches, rather than Application Mapping, suggesting that the main interest of academic-industrial collaborations may be for evaluation & validation approaches. This finding may be partially explained by analyzing the number of citations per year. This number tends to follow the number of studies in the categories (i.e., more studies would result in more citations). However, there is one exception to that: industrial studies have more citations than mixed studies, w.r.t. approaches for Application Mapping, possibly due to increased industrial interest. By investigating the approaches we observed that: (a) almost all studies propose or consider formal approaches; (b) model-driven and component-based approaches are

Table 4. Classification of included studies by type of activity and nature.

Type of activity	Metric	Nature			Total
		Academic	Industrial	Mixed	
Design flow	Number of studies	16	6	6	28
	Citations/year	65,05	8,71	18,48	92,25
Specification	Number of studies	44	11	16	71
	Citations/year	181,84	31,30	39,50	252,64
Application mapping	Number of studies	97	21	32	150
	Citations/year	298,42	85,97	72,33	456,72
Evaluation & validation	Number of studies	74	17	36	127
	Citations/year	232,66	22,33	73,50	328,49
Optimization	Number of studies	11	1	2	14
	Citations/year	28,81	0,12	3,19	32,11
Testing	Number of studies	7	2	4	13
	Citations/year	31,96	2,40	6,83	41,19

preferred for tackling CES problems, specially due to the facilitation of (semi-) automatic verification and code generation; and (c) one of the most prominent challenges in designing CES, is the design of systems with mixed-criticality (i.e., critical and non-critical elements co-existing within the same system). In the following, we present the most important observations regarding each of the categories.

Multiple *design flows* have been proposed so far, which is in accordance to the high heterogeneity of CES. Each design flow aims at tackling specific problems, such as multi-tasking in multi-periodic synchronization [S206] or reliability-driven design in CES with mixed criticality [S257]. The most important observation is that the majority of the design flows didn't provide a complete lifecycle. They rather described how to tackle the specific issue within the system design. These incomplete flows are not surprising because every single CES entails a rather unique set of requirements that are tackled by combining different approaches. The most relevant studies are a generic design flow (from 1997) that served as inspiration to other flows [S16] and a safety-oriented and component-based design flow for vehicular systems [S102]. Approaches for design *specification* consist mostly of (semi-)formal languages or notations for representing different types of problems, such as specific forms of scheduling [S117, S225], or classes of constraints (commonly related to quality attributes such as safety or reliability) [S87, S244]. We highlight that most studies presenting specification approaches (approx. 80%) also presented approaches with other purposes (e.g., application mapping or evaluation & validation). The most relevant studies include the specification of time constraints in systems with mixed criticality [S225] and formal specification of safety constraints on higher-level design [S180].

The majority of the studies involve a variety of approaches for *Application Mapping*. Among these studies, approx. 30% proposed architectural approaches, i.e., architectures [S35, S94] or approaches for designing architectures (e.g., styles or patterns) [S121, S166]. We highlight that in the context of CES, communication architecture (e.g., time-triggered architecture [S35]) is a more relevant kind of architecture, due to its relevance on evaluating the hard constraints CES are subject to. In fact, this relevance is also evident by another common topic: scheduling of tasks/components, which corresponds to approx. 21% of the studies. Scheduling poses several challenges, from guaranteeing of time allocation to specific components, to integration with other models (e.g., fault-tolerance) to provide more accurate scheduling. Another common topic is software patterns, corresponding to approx. 9% of the studies, among which, design patterns were the most investigated [S105, S106, S137, S160, S259], followed by architectural [S121, S201], fault-tolerance [S191] and process patterns [S240]. As for the remainder of the studies, other scattered topics can be observed, from which the most recent/recurrent encompass approaches for modeling components w.r.t. various critical constraints (e.g., safety) and integration of models. The most relevant studies include the time-triggered architecture [S35], remote agent architecture [S13], a component-based approach for modeling safety [S102] and an approach for scheduling of mixed-criticality workload [S164].

Approaches for *Evaluation & Validation* comprise mostly formal methods for evaluating specific aspects of the design, such as scheduling of tasks [S51, S140, S225], fault-tolerance [S151, S192] and safety requirements [S74, S102]. In addition, there is a growing interest on model-driven approaches and object-oriented design.

Classical approaches for verifying safety and reliability (e.g., fault-tree analysis – FTA – and failure mode and effects analysis) have been adapted to new design paradigms. For example, a component-based FTA was proposed in [S128] aiming at facilitating the certification of systems by reusing certified components. In addition, exploratory-based evaluation approaches (e.g., prototyping and simulation) are also broadly explored in order to evaluate designs [S21, S102, S168, and S216]. The most relevant studies present formal approaches for evaluating reliability and safety [S8, S225], as well as safety evaluation based on simulation [S102].

Finally, regarding *Optimization* and *Testing* approaches, the approaches are used for the same reason: improving the evaluation & validation of the designed systems [S51, S186, and S261]. Most of the approaches, including the most relevant approaches, tackle time constraints [S51, S248] and fault-tolerance issues [S48, S151].

4.3   Application Domains

The results on application domains suggest that the most studies (approx. 57%) report generic approaches, from which approx. 9% showed examples on specific application domains, e.g., automotive [S149, S257] and avionics [S225, S166]. Figure 6 presents the distribution of the studies, per year, according to the application domains. For comparison purposes, we plot the amount of studies reporting generic approaches. We note that studies that report approaches for specific domains often refer to more than one domain, e.g., support the design of avionic and space systems [S161].

By observing Fig. 6, we notice that, besides constituting the majority, the number of studies reporting generic approaches is growing more than for any specific domain. This may suggest a trend or intention to work on unified technologies for developing CES. However, we also notice that the combined number of studies that focus on specific domains comprise almost half (approx. 48%) of the papers. Among the specific domains: avionics and automotive present the biggest growth. On the one hand, avionics is historically among the first application domains of CES and contains special regulations, which make the interchange of approaches more difficult. On the other hand, the automotive industry has been going through a series of technological innovations to provide several new features such as autonomous driving.

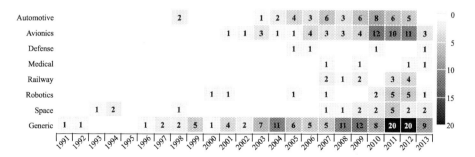

Fig. 6. Number of studies per application domain, per year.

To further analyze the influence of application domains on design approaches, we classified the primary studies according to their purpose. Table 5 presents the distribution of studies in each application domain among the five general purposes. We note that approaches serving more than one general purpose are counted for each of them. Based on Table 5, we observe that the distribution of studies on the application domains tend to be similar to the general distribution (Table 4). However, there is an exception for the medical and defense domains, as most studies report approaches for evaluation & validation rather than for application mapping. This may be either related to the low number of studies, or suggests a focus on this type of activity, perhaps motivated by specific industry standards or requirements of these domains. Another exception is that in the robotics domain the number of approaches for application mapping is quite higher (almost double) compared to evaluation & validation. Such disparity may be related to a larger variety of potential systems designs (large design space), which could result in more possibilities for mapping elements of the system. The disparity may also be related to a less regulated application domain that could in turn facilitate new design ideas to be implemented or experimented with.

Table 5. Classification of primary studies by domain and purpose.

Domain	Purpose					
	Design flow	Specification	Application mapping	Evaluation & validation	Optimization	Test
Automotive	7	11	31	22	2	2
Avionics	7	20	32	30	0	4
Defense	0	1	1	4	0	1
Medical	0	1	1	3	0	0
Railway	3	5	7	7	0	2
Robotics	2	3	13	6	0	1
Space	5	8	13	12	0	3
Generic	13	36	77	61	13	5

4.4 Quality Attributes

CES are subject to constraints on critical quality attributes (CQA). In this section, we report on the CQAs that are tackled within each primary study, using the original terms of CQAs that are used in the studies (i.e. those terms used by the authors). Even though some qualities are similar (e.g. dependability, fault-tolerance and reliability) we have not tried to merge them. Our goal is not to create a new quality model, but to simply present how authors express the hard-constraints of CES. However, we checked whether each term has the same or similar definition among the authors (e.g., if security is always used to convey the same concerns). We further discuss the relationship between CQAs and their definition in Sect. 5.1. We note that each study may tackle one or more CQAs. In Fig. 7, we present the number of studies, per year, tackling each critical quality attribute. We excluded two CQAs from this chart (power constraints and correctness) due to low number of papers (6 and 7, respectively).

Quality attribute	1991	1992	1993	1994	1995	1996	1997	1998	1999	2000	2001	2002	2003	2004	2005	2006	2007	2008	2009	2010	2011	2012	2013
Dependability								1	1	1			2	2	1	4	4	7	1	5	4	3	1
Fault-tolerance			1	1				2						3	5	2	2	4	3	5	6	3	2
Performance										1	2							2	2	7	4	1	
Reliability		1					1	1	1			1	1	4	4	2	5	7	7	7	10	8	5
Safety	1		1	1				2	4	2	1	2	7	7	5	7	6	12	18	22	29	33	7
Security																1	1	4	4	6	6	5	5
Timeliness	1			1				1	1		1	3	2	4	5	4	8	6	6	7	10	9	4

Timeliness includes *timing*, and *time-behavior*
Fault-tolerance includes *error-tolerance*

Fig. 7. Number of studies tackling quality attributes, per year.

By observing Fig. 7, one can notice that the interest in the different CQAs has grown in a similar fashion, except for safety, which shows higher growth. Such interest is not surprising, as safety is a very common and challenging concern among CQAs. In addition, the emergence and/or growth of application domains such as automotive, home automation, unmanned vehicles (e.g., drones) that are intrinsically centered on safety, have likely contributed to the observed growth. It is also relevant to point out that, although less intense, the interest in timeliness and reliability has also grown more than the remaining CQAs. The aforementioned arguments regarding safety, may also explain this observation. For example, the interest in multi-core platforms, as well as systems with mixed-criticality requires careful scheduling of tasks, and assurance that no interference between system parts with different criticality.

To further characterize the primary studies, we investigate them with respect to purpose and application domain. In Fig. 8, we present a bubble chart that depicts the distribution of the studies, based on CQAs (Y axis), with regards to the general purpose

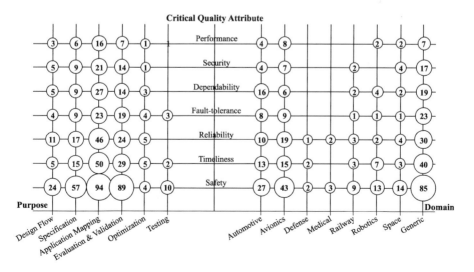

Fig. 8. Classification of studies based on quality attribute, purpose, and application domain.

(X axis—left side) and the application domain (X axis—right side). The size of the bubble represents the number of studies, which is shown inside the bubble. On the one hand, the distribution of studies among purposes, for each CQA, is similar compared to each other as well as compared to the general data (see Sect. 4.2). To confirm that, we calculated the spearman correlation between every pair of CQA and against the general data. All results were statistically significant and showed strong correlation (minimum coefficient of 0.899). This suggests that the distribution of research effort among different purposes is independent of CQAs. On the other hand, it is possible to observe a variation in the distribution of studies among application domains. For example, we notice that dependability displays a higher interest on the automotive domain (i.e., approx. 20% of the papers tackle this CQA), when compared against the average number of papers on dependability across domains (9%). We further investigated this observation by calculating the correlation between every pair of CQA, which showed that dependability has a weaker correlation with other CQAs (e.g., 0.667 with performance). This may suggest that these application domains are characterized by different constraints for the respective CQAs.

4.5   Tools

During the data extraction, we observed that approx. 53% of the papers either proposed or explicitly mentioned the use of specific tools. We also identified several Reference Technology Platforms (RTPs) [30], which consist of a set of approaches (e.g., methods, workflows) and tools providing a generic solution that can be tailored to various applications. The RTPs extracted in our study are all part of large projects involving multiple partners from both academia and industry. In total, we identified 147 tools of different kinds (e.g., CAD, model checkers, tool suites, etc.) and with various purposes (e.g., specification, application mapping, etc.). In addition, we noticed that some specification and/or modeling languages are an important part for many of these tools, e.g., serving as input format and base of the tool, or as exchange format between different tools. Therefore, we considered it relevant to include these languages in the results. Due to the number of identified tools, we summarized the results based on the general purposes presented in Sect. 4.2.

Table 6 shows the number of tools identified for each category (i.e., purpose). Within each category, we were able to define certain subcategories of tools representing specific purposes. We note that we include RTPs and IDEs (Integrated Development Environment), into the *Design Flow* category, as they support entire sets of activities. We also note that similar to approaches every tool may be classified in more than one category, e.g., a modeling tool that can import and export different models (i.e., *Application Mapping* category) as well as analyze them (i.e., *Evaluation & Verification* category). Furthermore, we note that the number of tools for subcategories do not necessarily add up to the number of the parent category. On the one hand, we only present subcategories with at least 3 tools (i.e. there were more subcategories with only 1 or 2 tools). On the other hand, tools may serve more than one purpose, which also affects subcategories. For example, SPIN is a verification tool with model checking and simulation capabilities, thus, counting for two subcategories. In the following we provide a brief description and the purpose of some relevant tools/languages, which we

Table 6. Summary of identified tools.

Purpose	Number of tools
Design flow	12
IDE	6
RTP	6
Specification	15
Notation/specification language	*12*
Programming language	*3*
Application mapping	35
Cad	*14*
Model transformation	*5*
Evaluation & validation	32
Simulation	*9*
Model checking	*9*
Optimization	1
Testing	2

identified based on the number of studies referring to the tool/language, as well as on the amount of citations these studies have. Due to space limitations a detailed discussion of tools and languages is omitted from this manuscript, but discussed in detail, in the supplementary material [24].

Summary of Languages. In Table 7, we list the top five recurrent languages within the primary studies, i.e., those discussed by three or more papers. We consider these languages relevant also due to the amount of citations obtained by the studies that refer to them. We observed that most languages are mentioned indirectly, i.e. not being the focus of the paper. For example, the Promela language is recurrent because researchers are interested in the SPIN verification tool, which defines models in Promela. In addition, most languages are also not specific to CES, although they are heavily used for this class of systems. Languages (e.g., Z) were created to enable representation of formal/mathematical constraints, which are common to CES.

Table 7. Highlighted languages.

Language	Number of studies	Number of citations	CES specific
AADL	20	294	Yes
Promela	7	162	No
SystemC	7	51	No
Z	5	153	No
EAST-ADL	3	19	Yes

Summary of Tools. The top five tools according to the number of studies and citations are presented in Table 8. We observe that most tools are not specific to designing CES. We believe this is related to the fact that most tools in this list have Evaluation & Validation purposes. Tools from this category, are mainly focused on ensuring the hard constrains imposed w.r.t. meeting critical quality attributes; such CQAs are not particular to CES only. Finally, we notice that the tools focused on CES are mostly (a) from the Application Mapping category (e.g., modelling tools and schedulers), which are specialized for one or a group of application domains; and (b) RTPs and IDEs, which are tailored for this class of systems, and normally include some tools that are not specific to CES (e.g., verification tools).

Table 8. Highlighted tools.

Tool	Number of studies	Number of citations	CES specific
Simulink	15	132	No
UPPAAL	8	79	No
DECOS	7	164	Yes
SPIN	7	162	No
NuSMV	4	112	No

4.6 Evidence Type

To investigate the maturity of the primary studies, we considered the type of evidence they provide. For that, we use the classification proposed by Alves et al. [23], as mentioned in Sect. 3.5. At the lowest level, the primary study does not provide any evidence, whereas at the highest level, the study provides evidence from actual use of the approach within an industrial application. In Fig. 9, we present the distribution of the primary studies, per year, according to the evidence type. By observing Fig. 9, one can notice that the amount of studies that provide evidence from academic studies has been growing considerably, exhibiting the highest growth among the six types of evidence. This also reflects the fact that most primary studies (approx. 55%) are supported by such type of evidence. This result is understandable, as studies performed in academic settings usually have a lower threshold to conduct than those performed in industrial settings. In addition, considering the hard constraints of CES, multiple studies may need to take place before a mature technology emerges and industrial studies can be performed. Interestingly, the second most common type of evidence is industrial studies (approx. 20%), which is one step further according to the classification of Alves et al. [23], and may suggest successful transition of a fair number of technologies to industrial maturity level.

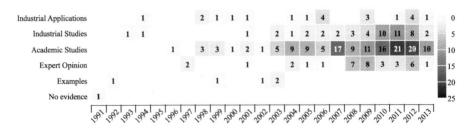

Fig. 9. Number of studies per type of evidence, per year.

Another interesting observation is that most studies are distributed among higher levels of evidence (academic studies, industrial studies and industrial applications). This may be, again, a consequence of the hard constraints imposed to CES, as tackling them would require stronger evidence to support the reported results. Another complimentary reason may be that embedded systems have been extensively investigated already, and management of hard constraints is not a new research topic for this class of system. Therefore, much of the exploratory research that has been done for embedded systems is now reused to investigate CES. To further investigate the evidence type, we classified the studies according to the purpose that their approaches serve, as well as the application domain. Similar to Figs. 8, Fig. 10 depicts the distribution of the studies, based on evidence type (Y axis), with respect to the purpose (X axis—left side) and the application domain (X axis—right side).

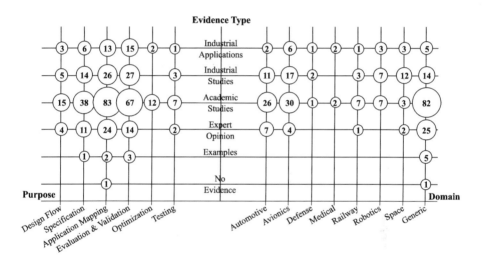

Fig. 10. Classification of studies based on evidence type, purpose, and application domain.

When verifying the distribution according to purpose, we observe that it follows a similar trend to that of the general data (presented in Sect. 4.2). We checked this hypothesis by calculating the correlation between each pair of evidence type, which showed a minimum correlation coefficient of 0.900. Conversely, while a visual inspection of the distribution according to domain suggests similarities between evidence types, the statistical correlation reveals minor differences between types of evidence, with coefficients varying from 0.500 to 0.927. These minor differences suggest that the application domain may affect what kind of research is performed.

5 Discussion

5.1 Relationship Between Quality Attributes

The approaches investigated in this mapping study tackle various CQAs, as presented in Sect. 4.4. While investigating this research question (RQ$_3$), we recorded the CQAs as used by the authors, i.e., we neither grouped nor merged any quality attributes, based on the definition used or implied in the primary studies. However, it is undeniable that some CQAs are related and, therefore, the identified quality attributes should be further investigated/synthesized. In this subsection, we group CQAs that have a similar or related meaning and map them to a quality model. For this purpose, we consider: (a) the SQuaRE quality model [31] which is a well-known quality model adopted by both researchers and practitioners; and (b) the ISO/IEC/IEEE vocabulary for system and software engineering [32], which is used within SQuaRE and provides additional definitions. We note that other quality models could be used to map the CQAs and that we do not assume that SQuaRE is the best model. We selected this model due to our experience with it and the possibility to fit all our recorded CQAs and observed terminologies. In Table 9 we present the CQAs identified in this study (presented in Sect. 4.4) on the right, and the characteristic (i.e., quality attribute) from SQuaRE to which they are mapped on the left. We note that SQuaRE presents a set of characteristics (left column of Table 9) and sub-characteristics (e.g. sub-characteristics of Performance Efficiency are Time Behavior, Resource Utilization and Capacity), which were both used to map CQAs. In addition, a CQA can be directly related if the terms are equivalent (e.g., *safety* maps to *freedom from risk*), or indirectly related if it is one of the aspects of the main quality attribute (e.g., *correctness* is a sub-characteristic of Functional suitability) or if it is related to one of them (e.g., *energy efficiency* regards Resource utilization, i.e., sub-characteristic of performance).

Table 9. Grouping and mapping of critical quality attributes.

CQA from SQuaRE	Identified CQA
Functional suitability	Correctness
Security	Security
Performance efficiency	Performance Energy efficiency Timeliness
Reliability	Reliability Fault tolerance Dependability
Freedom from risk	Safety

Correctness and *security* are directly mapped, since they similarly referred in the primary studies. However, the grouping of the remainder CQAs is not as straightforward. Performance efficiency is defined as the degree to which functionalities are delivered within given constraints [31], i.e., how well the system uses its resources to accomplish the designed functions. This definition encompasses the interpretations of *performance, energy efficiency,* and *timeliness* among the primary studies. *Fault tolerance* is a well-known aspect of reliability and the interpretations of the authors meet the definition of the sub-characteristic in SQuaRE (also named Fault tolerance). Although dependability is commonly addressed as a separate quality attribute, we decided to map it to Reliability. Dependability is not part of SQuaRE but it is explained within the description of reliability. It comprises a more subjective definition, which is not easily quantifiable, and reflects whether or not a system can be trusted [32]. Due to its subjective definition, dependability is commonly improved through addressing other, more objective, quality attributes that can contribute to the trustworthiness of the system, in particular, reliability, maintainability, and availability. By observing the primary studies of our mapping, it is also clear that dependability is commonly used as proxy to other quality attributes, in particular, aspects of reliability, such as fault tolerance. Therefore, since the primary studies exploit dependability mostly as a proxy to reliability, we decided to group them together. *Safety* is another subjective CQAs, which is mentioned within SQuaRE's model for quality in use, i.e., how well the product can be used by specific users [31]. Similar to dependability, safety is commonly used as a proxy to other quality attributes, although not always the same ones. Particularly, safety is related to the avoidance of hazardous situations (i.e., that lead to endangerment of humans, environment or properties), which can originate from various sources, depending on the system. In our study, we identified connections between safety and various aspects: security [S215], performance, correctness [S50, S198] and fault-tolerance [S50, S84]. For example, when using a Time-Triggered Architecture (TTA) for communication (instead of an event-triggered one), timeliness become a safety threat.

In summary, CQAs as defined in primary studies are uniformly understood (i.e. their definitions are the same or similar across the studies) and that some can be grouped based on similarity. This culminated into the identification of five attributes: Functional Suitability, Security, Performance efficiency, Reliability, and Safety (Freedom from risk). We acknowledge that other CQAs may exist in individual cases depending on application-specific constraints. However, these five QA are by far the most recurrent ones. We also noticed that Safety is more abstract, since it depends on other CQAs. Therefore, is achieved by meeting requirements related to other CQAs. Furthermore, we note that identifying these CQAs is not always a trivial task as different components in the same systems may pose different constraints, i.e., may be subject to different kinds of hazards. A common approach to handle this mixed criticality is the use of integrity levels [33], which reflect the degree of compliance within a certain characteristic. Components with different integrity levels will be subject to different safety checks, which may also reflect the different concerns of that level. For example, the drive-by-wire feature is subject to hard reliability checks, while GPS navigation should only be assured to not interfere with the critical components. Therefore, it is important to identify and monitor the CQAs that are tightly related to safety.

5.2   Domain-Specific Research for CES

In Sect. 4.3 through Sect. 4.6, we presented an overview of the primary studies with respect to application domains, as well as how other facets (e.g., evidence type) related to domains. In summary, we did not notice major differences across application domains regarding which CQAs are the most relevant. This observation might be an indication that CQA-related challenges in CES are common to all application domains and have similar relevance. The only difference we observed was that studies focused on the automotive domain seem more concerned about dependability rather than reliability. However, these two fall under the umbrella quality of reliability in the SQuaRE model (see Sect. 5.1). Furthermore, we also notice that domains may influence the kind of research that is performed; for example, most studies on medical and defense domains focused on approaches for evaluation & validation rather than application mapping (as the general trend).

The difference between domains becomes clearer when looking at the type of evidence that studies provide (see Sect. 4.6). We separated the studies into three groups and verified their distribution among the different types of evidence (see Fig. 11). The three groups consist of studies that: (a) focus on a specific domain; (b) do not focus on any domain but present an example of application on a specific domain; and (c) neither focus nor present an example on specific domains. We notice that application domains become more relevant when a technology is being transferred to industry, as the two rightmost types of evidence (Industrial Study and Industrial Application) account mostly for studies that focus on application domains.

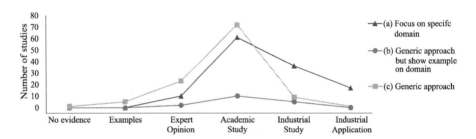

Fig. 11.   Distribution of studies according to type of evidence and application domain.

It is understandable that studies conducted with industrial partners or in an industrial setting are focused on specific domains, as companies are by and large interested into applying approaches on certain products, which in turn fall under specific domains. As expected, generic approaches that solve domain-independent problems are first validated in academic settings, and subsequently find applications in industry that in turn customize and validate them in specific application domains. The opposite is also possible: there are also technologies that initially emerge as domain-specific solutions and are later applied to other domains. For example, the Architecture

Analysis and Design Language (AADL) was standardized by the Society of Automotive Engineers (SAE) with focus on the avionics domain[3] and is currently being applied in other CES domains.

5.3   Relationships Among Approaches, Tools, and Languages

The data analysis in this SMS resulted in the identification of many concepts related to the research questions, namely approaches, tools, languages, critical quality attributes, and application domains, as well as relationships between them. While we were able to present and discuss all CQAs and application domains found in the primary studies (see Sects. 4.3, 4.4, 5.1 and 5.2), the amounts of approaches, tools and languages was too large to present and discuss all concepts and relationships. To tackle this issue, we created a concept map to help us visualize these approaches, tools, and languages and identify relevant findings.

The concept map was created as a webpage that features an interactive interface, which is available[4]. To avoid loss of information, we also created a text version of the concept map. The text version and source code of the web version are available within the supplementary material [24]. In Fig. 12, we show a screenshot of the concept map and its interface. The concept map consists of a network in which nodes represent concepts and edges relationships. Each type of concept (i.e., approach, tool or language) is represented by an icon for easy identification. Upon clicking on a concept, an information panel is prompted on the right side, showing: (a) name of the concept, which is a link if a URL (Uniform Resource Locator) is available (shown by the chain icon next to the name); (b) a brief description of the concept; (c) the list of purposes, according to our classification scheme; and (d) a list of relationships (i.e., links) attributed to the concept. The relationship between concepts can be of two types:

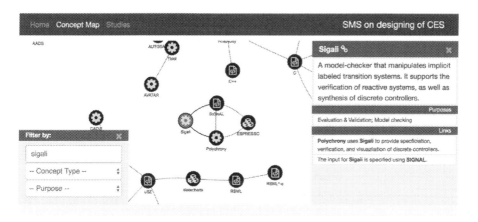

Fig. 12. Screenshot of the concept map interactive interface. (Color figure online)

---

[3] Note that SAE does not limit itself to the automotive domain.

[4] http://feitosa-daniel.github.io/sms-ces-design.

"use/is used" (e.g., "Polychrony uses Sigale to provide specification ... of discrete controllers"), or "is kind of" (e.g., "SystemC is a subset of C++").

The interface also provides a feature to filter concepts based on name, type of concepts, or purpose. Upon typing on the name field or selecting type of concept or purpose, the filtered items are highlighted in red (see Fig. 12). For example, in the screenshot we typed "sigali" and the tool "Sigali" was automatically highlighted (the search looks for partial matches and is not case sensitive). After that, we clicked on the node, which prompted the information panel on the right. Finally, the interface is responsive, i.e., it adapts to different screen sizes (e.g., smartphones), which improves the usability of the concepts map.

Based on the concept map, we can make several observations. However, due to space limitations, we provide only one of them, also explaining how we identified it. We note that the main purpose of the concept map is to support the investigation of its concepts by third-parties and, therefore, we encourage the reader to further analyze it. The Architecture Analysis and Design Language (AADL) appears to be a rather mature technology. The results of the study showed that AADL is cited in multiple papers (see Sect. 4.5). In addition, by looking at the concept map we notice a fair number of related concepts (see Fig. 13) when compared against the average of 2.13 edges per node, and we notice that there are related concepts that serve different purposes: (a) specification, (b) application mapping, and (c) evaluation & validation. In particular, there is a toolset that is able to read AADL models, tools to evaluate AADL models and a language (EAST-ADL) that is partially derived from AADL.

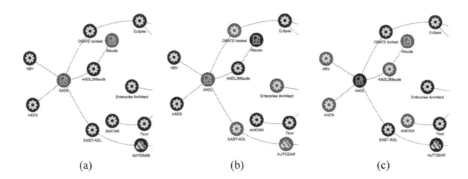

Fig. 13. Part of the concept map surrounding AADL.

5.4   Implications to Researchers and Practitioners

The results and discussion presented in this SMS have potential value for both researchers and practitioners. The information compiled in this study may support readers that want to get acquainted with the design process of CES or may be interested in specific outcomes, e.g., identified CQAs and how they are tackled by primary studies. Researchers can use the information in this SMS to identify work that is related or that can contribute to theirs, as well as identify opportunities for future work. For example, researchers interested in a specific application domain have access pointers to the existing literature, as well as how studies are distributed within the domain. We envisage similar learning opportunities to practitioners, through a more practical perspective. For example, practitioners can investigate a tool that is being considered for the designing of a new system or investigate the ecosystem around an approach, i.e., tools and related approaches.

In addition, we specifically aimed at the reuse of the information collected during our SMS when we created the concept map, which contains the complete set of approaches, tools and languages. Based on the information and features provided by the user interface, we believe that the concept map is valuable to both practitioners and researchers. Regarding practitioners, it can be used to support the exploration of problem and solution spaces while designing CESs. For example, using filters, one is able to search for approaches and or tools that fit the requirements of the systems (e.g., model-checking of models specified in SIGNAL). Also, if one has decided for a specific approach or tool, she can also explore related concepts and identify alternatives or tools that support the approach (e.g., tools that evaluate Binary Decision Diagrams). Regarding researchers, the concept map helps identifying potential links between different research results. For example, researchers interested into investigating a certain approach can use the concept map to easily visualize some of the involved approaches and tools that support it. We note that despite our great effort on collecting and analyzing the selected studies, the concepts and relationships presented in this map do not present the entire set of approaches, tools and languages available to design CES. Therefore, we hope that by providing access to the concept map, we can support others on developing it even further.

6   Threats to Validity

Concerning studies identification, the main threat is that the automatic search may not have been able to collect all relevant primary studies, i.e., the search string was not as inclusive as necessary or the considered digital libraries did not include all relevant venues. To mitigate this risk, we defined a gold standard and ensured that the automatic search returned all papers in the gold standard. In addition, we included digital libraries of the main publishers in the topic, and Scopus, which indexes papers from additional venues. Another potential threat is that the inclusion and exclusion criteria may have left relevant studies out of the final set of primary studies. This was mitigated not only by the usage of the gold standard but also by having key points of our protocol (e.g., inclusion and exclusion criteria) inspected by other external researchers with experience in CES. To mitigate risks related to data collection and analysis, we considered several strategies. The filtering of papers and data extraction involved at least two researchers on every step, while there were extensive discussions on topics such as selection criteria and understanding of CES terminology. In addition, the alignment of researchers involved in these steps where verified by calculating the Cohen's kappa coefficient between them. For data analysis, we applied frequency analysis, cross-tabulation and statistical tests, which are less prone to researcher bias. However, we acknowledge that our results are limited to the set of design approaches, CQAs, and application domains that were discussed in the collected primary studies. Although considering non-peer-reviewed literature was out of the scope of our SMS, we argue that the digital libraries we considered, do catalog most of the work relevant to the research of CES design.

Finally, to mitigate replicability threats, the steps of our study were clearly stated in our protocol and can be reproduced by other researchers. However, we acknowledge that the reproduction of the SMS by other researchers may lead to slight different sets of primary studies due to biases, e.g., when applying the inclusion and exclusion criteria. We mitigated this threat to some extent by comprehensively documenting faced challenges and decisions made upon them. Thus, despite some potential minor differences, we believe that the results and observations would be predominantly similar in replication studies.

7 Conclusions

In this paper, we presented a Systematic Mapping Study (SMS) on designing Critical Embedded Systems (CES) that investigated five facets: (a) approaches for designing CES; (b) application domains for which these approaches are developed; (c) Critical Quality Attributes (CQAs) considered on these approaches; (d) tools used for designing CES; and (e) type of evidence provided by these approaches. We considered five digital libraries and collected an initial amount of 1673 primary studies, which were then filtered, resulting in 269 selected primary studies. Subsequently, we extracted and analyzed all data necessary to answer our research questions.

The results of our SMS show that the body of knowledge on designing CES is vast, and this is partially due to the overlap of knowledge with other classes of systems such as hard real-time systems. Results also suggest that the CQAs that are relevant to the design of CES, are common for this whole class of systems, i.e. they are mostly independent of application domain. The main contributions of our work are the classification scheme for approaches and tooling, the provided collection of CQAs and approaches (with associated tools), as well as the webpage that supports exploring this information. We believe that both researchers and practitioners can benefit from these contributions, taking advantage of our provided overview of this vast body of knowledge; they can thus focus on more relevant tasks such as identification of related and future work, and exploration of problem and solution spaces. Based on our results and observations we envisage several opportunities for future work. Among them, we highlight the possibility of investigating approaches that might be potentially beneficial to CES and have not being thoroughly explored yet, like using design patterns to improve levels of CQAs. The body of knowledge presented in this SMS has considerable overlap with other classes of system, thus we find it relevant to continue exploring such related classes (e.g., hard-real time systems) and seek approaches that can be applied to the designing of CES.

Acknowledgements. The authors would like to thank the financial support from the Brazilian and Dutch agencies CAPES/Nuffic (Grant N.: 034/12), CNPq (Grant N.: 204607/2013-2), as well as the INCT-SEC (Grant N.: 573963/2008-8 and 2008/57870-9).

References

1. Marwedel, P.: Embedded System Design: Embedded Systems Foundations of Cyber-Physical Systems. Springer, Dordrecht (2010). https://doi.org/10.1007/978-94-007-0257-8
2. Bate, I.: Systematic approaches to understanding and evaluating design trade-offs. J. Syst. Softw. **81**, 1253–1271 (2008)
3. Medikonda, B.S., Panchumarthy, S.R.: A framework for software safety in safety-critical systems. ACM SIGSOFT Softw. Eng. Notes. **34**, 1 (2009)
4. Aguiar, A., Filho, S.J., Magalhães, F.G., Casagrande, T.D., Hessel, F.: Hellfire: a design framework for critical embedded systems' applications. In: 11th International Symposium on Quality Electronic Design, pp. 730–737 (2010)
5. Ampatzoglou, A., Gkortzis, A., Charalampidou, S., Avgeriou, P.: An embedded multiple-case study on OSS design quality assessment across domains. In: Seventh ACM/IEEE International Symposium on Empirical Software Engineering and Measurement, pp. 255–258. IEEE (2013)
6. Linares-Vásquez, M., Klock, S., McMillan, C., Sabané, A., Poshyvanyk, D., Guéhéneuc, Y.-G.: Domain matters: bringing further evidence of the relationships among anti-patterns, application domains, and quality-related metrics in Java mobile apps. In: 22nd International Conference on Program Comprehension, pp. 232–243. ACM Press (2014)
7. Cawley, O., Wang, X., Richardson, I.: Lean/agile software development methodologies in regulated environments – state of the art. In: Abrahamsson, P., Oza, N. (eds.) LESS 2010. LNBIP, vol. 65, pp. 31–36. Springer, Heidelberg (2010). https://doi.org/10.1007/978-3-642-16416-3_4
8. Eklund, U., Bosch, J.: Archetypical approaches of fast software development and slow embedded projects. In: 39th Euromicro Conference Series on Software Engineering and Advanced Applications, pp. 276–283 (2013)
9. Kitchenham, B., Charters, S.: Guidelines for performing systematic literature reviews in software engineering. Engineering **2**, 1051 (2007)
10. Karlström, D., Runeson, P.: Integrating agile software development into stage-gate managed product development. Empir. Softw. Eng. **11**, 203–225 (2006)
11. Selim, G.M.K., Wang, S., Cordy, James R., Dingel, J.: Model transformations for migrating legacy models: an industrial case study. In: Vallecillo, A., Tolvanen, J.-P., Kindler, E., Störrle, H., Kolovos, D. (eds.) ECMFA 2012. LNCS, vol. 7349, pp. 90–101. Springer, Heidelberg (2012). https://doi.org/10.1007/978-3-642-31491-9_9
12. Barbosa, J.R., Delamaro, M.E., Maldonado, J.C., Vincenzi, A.M.R.: Software testing in critical embedded systems: a systematic review of adherence to the DO-178B standard. In: Third International Conference on Advances in System Testing and Validation Lifecycle, pp. 126–130 (2011)
13. Elberzhager, F., Rosbach, A., Bauer, T.: Analysis and testing of matlab simulink models: a systematic mapping study. In: 2013 International Workshop on Joining AcadeMiA and Industry Contributions to testing Automation, pp. 29–34 (2013)
14. Dybå, T., Dingsøyr, T.: Empirical studies of agile software development: a systematic review. Inf. Softw. Technol. **50**, 833–859 (2008)
15. Petersen, K., Feldt, R., Mujtaba, S., Mattsson, M.: Systematic mapping studies in software engineering. In: 12th international conference on Evaluation and Assessment in Software Engineering, pp. 68–77 (2008)
16. Antonio, E.A., Ferrari, F.C., Ferraz Fabbri, S.C.P.: A systematic mapping of architectures for embedded software. In: Second Brazilian Conference on Critical Embedded Systems, pp. 18–23 (2012)

17. Guessi, M., Nakagawa, E.Y., Oquendo, F., Maldonado, J.C.: Architectural description of embedded systems: a systematic review. In: Third International ACM SIGSOFT Symposium on Architecting Critical Systems, pp. 31–40. ACM (2012)

18. Nakagawa, E.Y., Gonçalves, M., Guessi, M., Oliveira, L.B.R., Oquendo, F.: The state of the art and future perspectives in systems of systems software architectures. In: 1st International Workshop on Software Engineering for Systems-of-Systems, pp. 13–20 (2013)

19. Basili, V.R., Caldiera, G., Rombach, H.D.: Goal question metric paradigm. In: Marciniak, J. J. (ed.) Encyclopedia of Software Engineering, pp. 528–532. Wiley, New York (1994)

20. Dieste, O., Grimán, A., Juristo, N.: Developing search strategies for detecting relevant experiments. Empir. Softw. Eng. **14**, 513–539 (2009)

21. Dybå, T., Dingsøyr, T., Hanssen, G.K.: Applying systematic reviews to diverse study types: an experience report. In: First International Symposium on Empirical Software Engineering and Measurement, pp. 225–234 (2007)

22. Zhang, H., Babar, M.A.: On searching relevant studies in software engineering. In: 14th International Conference on Evaluation and Assessment in Software Engineering, pp. 111–120. British Computer Society, Keele (2010)

23. Alves, V., Niu, N., Alves, C., Valença, G.: Requirements engineering for software product lines: a systematic literature review. Inf. Softw. Technol. **52**, 806–820 (2010)

24. Feitosa, D., Ampatzoglou, A., Avgeriou, P., Affonso, F.J., Andrade, H., Felizardo, K.R., Nakagawa, E.Y.: Supplementary Material: "Design Approaches for Critical Embedded System: A Systematic Mapping Study". https://doi.org/10.5281/zenodo.996480

25. Bass, L., Clements, P., Kazman, R.: Software Architecture in Practice. Addison-Wesley Professional, Upper Saddle River (2012)

26. Sommerville, I.: Software Engineering. Addison Wesley, Boston (2000)

27. Hofmeister, C., Kruchten, P., Nord, R.L., Obbink, H., Ran, A., America, P.: A general model of software architecture design derived from five industrial approaches. J. Syst. Softw. **80**, 106–126 (2007)

28. Bartelt, C., Bauer, O., Beneken, G., Bergner, K., Birowicz, U., Bliß, T., Cordes, N., Cruz, D., Dohrmann, P., Friedrich, J., Gnatz, M., Hammerschall, U., Hidvegi-Barstorfer, I., Hummel, H., Israel, D., Klingenberg, T., Klugseder, K., Küffer, I., Kuhrmann, M., Kranz, M., Kranz, W., Meinhardt, H.-J., Meisinger, M., Mittrach, S., Neußer, H.-J., Niebuhr, D., Plögert, K., Rauh, D., Rausch, A., Rittel, T., Rösch, W., Saas, E., Schramm, J., Sihling, M., Ternité, T., Vogel, S., Wittmann, M.: V-Modell XT Gesamt 1.3 (2010)

29. Gajski, D.D., Zhu, J., Dömer, R., Gerstlauer, A., Zhao, S.: SPECC: Specification Language and Methodology. Springer, New York (2000). https://doi.org/10.1007/978-1-4615-4515-6

30. Kacimi, O., Ellen, C., Oertel, M., Sojka, D.: Creating a reference technology platform - performing model-based safety analysis in a heterogeneous development environment. In: Second International Conference on Model-Driven Engineering and Software Development, pp. 645–652 (2014)

31. ISO/IEC: ISO/IEC 25010:2011 - Systems and software engineering – Systems and software Quality Requirements and Evaluation (SQuaRE) – System and software quality models (2011)

32. ISO/IEC/IEEE: ISO/IEC/IEEE 24765-2010 - Systems and software engineering – Vocabulary (2010)

33. ISO/IEC: ISO/IEC 15026-3:2015 Systems and software engineering – Systems and software assurance – Part 3: System integrity levels (2015)

Author Index

Affonso, Frank J.   243
Alfonso Hoyos, Jean Pierre   183
Ampatzoglou, Apostolos   243
Andrade, Hugo   243
Attiogbé, J. Christian   158
Avgeriou, Paris   243

Blech, Jan Olaf   141
Bocicor, Maria Iuliana   70
Bsaies, Khaled   158

Carbonnel, Jessie   116

Dascălu, Maria   70
Dhaou, Fatma   158

Feitosa, Daniel   243
Felizardo, Katia R.   243
Foster, Keith   141

Gaczowska, Agnieszka   70
García S., Alberto   3

Hamza, Haitham   23
Hassan, Hoda   23
Hosny, Hoda M.   93
Hostiuc, Sorin   70
Huchard, Marianne   116

Iñiguez-Jarrín, Carlos   3, 48

Jamaluddin, Tashreen Shaikh   23

Khaled, Osama M.   93

Lagartos, Ignacio   224

Miralles, André   116
Moldoveanu, Alin   70
Molina, Antonio   70
Molnar, Arthur-Jozsef   70
Mouakher, Ines   158

Nakagawa, Elisa Y.   243
Nebut, Clémentine   116
Negoi, Ionuţ   70

Ortin, Francisco   224

Pastor López, Óscar   3
Pastor, Óscar   48
Prévost, Guillaume   141

Racoviţă, Vlad   70
Redondo, Jose Manuel   224
Restrepo-Calle, Felipe   183
Reyes Román, José F.   3, 48

Schmidt, Heinrich W.   141
Shalan, Mohamed   93
Spichkova, Maria   208

Printed in the United States
By Bookmasters